The Philosopher's English King

Also by Leon Harold Craig

The War Lover: A Study of Plato's 'Republic'

Of Philosophers and Kings:
Political Philosophy in Shakespeare's 'Macbeth' and 'King Lear'

The Platonian Leviathan

Philosophy and the Puzzles of 'Hamlet': A Study of Shakespeare's Method

LEON HAROLD CRAIG

The Philosopher's English King

Shakespeare's *Henriad* as Political Philosophy

UNIVERSITY OF ROCHESTER PRESS

Copyright © 2015 by Leon Harold Craig

All Rights Reserved. Except as permitted under current legislation, no part of this work may be photocopied, stored in a retrieval system, published, performed in public, adapted, broadcast, transmitted, recorded, or reproduced in any form or by any means, without the prior permission of the copyright owner.

First published 2015
Transferred to digital printing and reprinted in paperback 2018

University of Rochester Press
668 Mt. Hope Avenue, Rochester, NY 14620, USA
www.urpress.com
and Boydell & Brewer Limited
PO Box 9, Woodbridge, Suffolk IP12 3DF, UK
www.boydellandbrewer.com

hardcover ISBN: 978-1-58046-531-1
paperback ISBN: 978-1-58046-925-8

Library of Congress Cataloging-in-Publication Data

Names: Craig, Leon Harold.
Title: The philosopher's English king : Shakespeare's Henriad as political philosophy / Leon Harold Craig.
Description: Rochester, NY : University of Rochester Press, 2015. | Includes bibliographical references and index.
Identifiers: LCCN 2015028443 | ISBN 9781580465311 (hardcover : acid-free paper)
Subjects: LCSH: Shakespeare, William, 1564–1616—Histories. | Shakespeare, William, 1564–1616—Political and social views. | Historical drama, English—History and criticism. | Kings and rulers in literature. Politics and literature—Great Britain—History—16th century. | Politics and literature—Great Britain—History—17th century.
Classification: LCC PR2982 .C73 2015 | DDC 822.3/3—dc23 LC record available at http://lccn.loc.gov/2015028443

A catalogue record for this title is available from the British Library.

This publication is printed on acid-free paper.
Printed in the United States of America

Cover design: Susan Colberg

To my grandchildren: may they each someday find communing with Shakespeare as enjoyable as I do.

So that in the first place, I put for a generall inclination of all mankind, a perpetuall and restlesse desire of Power after power, that ceaseth only in Death. And the cause of this, is not alwayes that a man hopes for a more intensive delight, than he has already attained to; or that he cannot be content with a moderate power: but because he cannot assure the power and means to live well, which he hath present, without the acquisition of more. And hence it is, that Kings, whose power is greatest, turn their endeavours to the assuring it at home by Lawes, or abroad by Wars.

—Hobbes, *Leviathan*, chap. 11, para. 2

Contents

Acknowledgements		ix
Prologue		xi
1	Begins the Woefullest Division: The Tragic Reign of King Richard II	1
2	A Punishing of Mistreadings: The Turbulent Reign of King Henry IV Proceeds	46
3	The Noble Change Long Purposed: The Turbulent Reign of King Henry IV Concludes	95
4	A Curious Mirror of Christian Kings: The Brief Glorious Reign of King Henry V	129
An Alternative Epilogue: Imagining What Might Have Been		181
Notes		195
Bibliography		265
Index of Names		269

Acknowledgements

The study of Shakespeare these past forty years has been among my most enriching and enjoyable experiences, not least because it was shared with so many congenial students and colleagues. This book reflects, as do my others on the plays, the contributions such friends have made to my understanding of mankind's premier philosopher-poet. I have more specific debts that deserve mention, however. A portion of the book (mainly chapter 1) was presented to a faculty seminar at the University of Calgary, generating a lively discussion from which I benefitted. Similarly, the two anonymous assessors of the manuscript made several helpful suggestions; I am especially grateful for their strong endorsement of its publication. Both Kent Cochrane and Heidi Studer critiqued portions of the text in the course of its being written, and proofed the final version; Kent also helped with the Hobbes annotations, and Heidi with the index. Sue Colberg, my favourite book designer, provided (as usual) a beautifully fitting cover. The editorial and production staff of the University of Rochester Press did all one might wish to improve the readability of the book. My principal editor, Ryan Peterson, deserves special credit for the patience with which he dealt with my requests, and for the labour he invested in seeing the project through to a successful conclusion.

Speaking of patience, my greatest debt, in this and all respects, is to my wife and life-long partner, Judith Ann.

Prologue

> In a good Poem, whether it be *Epique*, or *Dramatique*, as also in *Sonnets*, *Epigrams*, and other Pieces, both Judgement and Fancy are required: But the Fancy must be more eminent; because they please for the Extravagancy; but ought not to displease by Indiscretion.
> In a good History, the Judgement must be eminent; because the goodnesse consisteth, in the Method, in the Truth, and in the Choyse of the actions that are most profitable to be known. Fancy has no place, but onely in adorning the stile.
> —Hobbes, *Leviathan*, chap. 8, paras. 4–5

The plays of Shakespeare's so-called second tetralogy, unlike those of the first, constitute a coherent whole in more than an historical sense. For despite their respective titles, they are unified by their underlying focus on a single individual of unique historical stature, whose entire political career is shaped by a problem fundamental to both politics and philosophy. The man and his problem is the spine supporting the limbs upon which the flesh of these four dramas is overlain. All the machinations, the battles, all the interwoven actions and reactions of all the actors, both high and low, derive a special significance from how they bear on the life story of England's most famous warrior king.

Each play does have its own integrity, of course, lent by its own set of themes and issues, and they are treated as such in the chapters which follow. Still, the fact remains that the tetralogy as a whole is mainly about the making of this almost legendary figure, as acknowledged in the coining of *Henriad* to identify collectively this quartet of dramas. Accordingly, how each play contributes to that end is my primary focus. As Shakespeare tells it, the life story of Henry V is shaped by the problem which from early youth haunted him: that of establishing his own *legitimacy* as King of England—a challenge which points beyond itself to the problem of political legitimacy per se. It arises in the context of a regime riddled with corruption, and ruled by a monarch who displays tyrannical inclinations, partly if not wholly because he presumes to rule by 'divine right'. As his reign devolves, however, it results in a situation primed for rebellion and usurpation, given the presence of a bold, ambitious, popular pretender willing and able to exploit the opportunity that any egregious abuse of power would provide—especially one aimed at him. Not surprisingly, this is what occurs: an inept and reckless king is supplanted by a man who would seem eminently qualified to rule with fairness, efficiency, and appropriate firmness, whose advent is thus welcomed by nobles and commons alike.

The usurpation is not entirely successful, however, inasmuch as the new King's rule is soon plagued by major civil unrest and resistance, not least because his kingship remains open to challenge on the same grounds and by the same means as it was itself established. The story of his tumultuous reign is told in two parts. The first part features a challenger who lives for *honour*—a problematic good of potent appeal, as the play provides occasion to learn. But it also depicts the degeneracy of civil life at 'street level', so to speak, mainly through the amusing hijinks of a crew of ne'er-do-wells led by a fat old fraudster with whom the King's own son, Crown Prince and central figure of the entire tetralogy, chooses to spend his free time—surprisingly, and to the dismay of his father and the worry of all decent citizens (not surprisingly).

The disorder that was introduced into the kingdom by the usurpation, along with the increasing toll it takes upon the King's health, continues to be portrayed in the second part, but with small-scale crime and corruption given still more prominence, along with indications of the danger it poses to political stability and civic decency. This part is dominated, however, by the conclusion towards which it inexorably builds: the Prince of Wales, becoming Henry V upon inheriting a Crown compromised by the usurpation of his father, stuns the populace—including members of his own family—by totally, and quite publicly, repudiating his former low-life associates, and promising to prove an exemplary ruler dedicated to the eradication of the sort of misconduct with which he had previously been associated. His astonishing about-face retroactively casts his previous behaviour in a radically different light. The culmination of the tetralogy depicts the glorious first half of the reign of this, England's most illustrious king.

Carefully considered, however, this final chapter of Henry's story raises questions that threaten to undermine his claim to historical preeminence. Indeed, probably no play in the canon has had such a polarizing effect on audiences and readers, and especially on scholar-critics, as has Shakespeare's *Henry V*. In the past century, that is.[1] Whereas for the first three hundred years of its existence, it was generally accepted for what it seemed on its surface to be: an epic-scale memorial to Britain's warrior king and the doughty band of brothers who achieved a near-miraculous victory at Agincourt, prelude to the conquest of nearly the whole of France. As such, the play excited little passion apart from patriotic pride, at least among the vast majority of English-speaking peoples.² No doubt there were always some who regarded the play as merely an entertaining piece of jingoistic propaganda—skilfully wrought, to be sure (after all, Shakespeare wrote it)³—but little more than a celebratory retelling of an episode which any nation with a comparable achievement to boast of would enjoy, repeatedly, with smug pleasure. So, whether assessed approvingly or otherwise, the long prevailing view among serious students of Shakespeare's canon was that, with respect to intellectual interest, the play is of minor consequence compared to any of his great tragedies, and not a few of his comedies.

Moreover, while most scholars are cognisant of the fact that *Henry V* concludes a story that begins with the downfall of Richard II and continues in a pair of plays bearing the name of Henry's father, very few discussions of these dramas attribute any significance beyond the biohistorical to that fact. Given the reasonable presumption that in his so-called history plays, Shakespeare is more or less confined to the basic script established by England's known past (a veritable gold mine of ready-made plots), relatively little consideration has been given to the possibility that he contrived to adapt this raw material to some additional purpose, or purposes, of his own. Much less are the plays of this second tetralogy generally regarded as having been conceived from the outset as the means whereby to convey some larger political truth that only a coherent *sequence* of dramas could depict.⁴

As for the two parts of *Henry IV*, they have long been relished, not primarily for their depiction of a turbulent portion of English history and the actions of the eponymous king then ruling, but for their portrayal of his heir and namesake's early days as the rapscallion Prince Hal. Or rather, for the lad's relationship with an endearing rogue named Sir John Falstaff. Legend has it that this fat poseur and congenital liar proved so popular (with no less a theatre-lover than the Queen herself) that Shakespeare was obliged to create *The Merry Wives of Windsor* as a vehicle in which to showcase Sir John's irrepressible wit and abortive machinations. In any event, neither of the two *Henry IV* plays have ever been the subject of especial controversy. Considered in themselves, that is.

In recent times, however, they have been subjected to fresh scrutiny, and as a consequence have provided fodder for some debate, due mainly to a spillover from the controversies that have arisen regarding the concluding chapter of the tetralogy. For, as noted, *Henry V* has become the subject of heated disputes: about the historical person, his virtues and vices and motivations, the significance of his achievements, and the propriety whereby they were accomplished; about the character of the man as the play portrays him, and the philosopher-poet's own judgment regarding that portrayed character (as distinct, perhaps, from that regarding the historical Henry); and about the larger issues raised by the career of this famous monarch, such as the nature of war, the legitimacy (or otherwise) of conquest, the propriety of deceit, and Shakespeare's own views about such matters.[5] While these sets of issues are in principle analytically discrete, in critical discussions they frequently become intertwined—not always wittingly, it would seem—often with results more confusing than illuminating. Suffice it to say, a play that was once regarded as almost too straightforward to be worthy of intelligent attention has become a matter of impassioned, even bitter dissension.[6]

As the preceding remarks indicate, I treat the four plays of the *Henriad* as so many chapters of a single continuous story which concludes with *Henry V*, though it begins with a play in which the Prince destined to become a glorious king does not actually appear, but is merely spoken of—disparagingly, one must add, while nonetheless attesting to his importance. His royal father is expressing exasperation with the heir designate:

> Can no man tell me of my unthrifty son?
> 'Tis full three months since I did see him last.
> If any plague hang over us, 'tis he.
> I would to God, my lords, he might be found.
> Enquire at London, 'mongst the taverns there,
> For there, they say, he daily doth frequent,
> With unrestrained loose companions.
> (*Richard II*, 5.3.1–7)

The King's question does not elicit a reassuring response. Accordingly, we also are left in the dark regarding the occupations and whereabouts of this allegedly unthrifty, pub-crawling heir to the throne. But the problem that will dominate his political life as both prince and king arises as a result of the events depicted in this first play of the sequence.

With respect to the series of dramas thus initiated, I shall focus special attention on what I find most perplexing about each, and about the tetralogy as a whole. In my experience, by concentrating on what is puzzling in a Shakespeare play, thus studying it with an eye towards solving those puzzles, one not only discovers its deeper coherence as a work of dramatic art, but one is also more apt to learn whatever its author therein attempts to teach.[7]

The tetralogy presents puzzles at three different levels—that is, of three different scales of extent, or degrees of comprehension. The most basic and delimited are puzzling features woven into the plots of each play. With respect to *Richard II*, for example, there is the tightly circumscribed puzzle of why the Welsh army mistakenly believed King Richard to have died, and so disperse the day before he returns from Ireland, thereby dooming any chance of his suppressing Henry Bolingbroke's rebellion and subsequent usurpation. Shakespeare's sources provided him no explanation for this strange happening. Thus he devised his own plausible account, which readers may piece together out of his story of this fatally flawed King. As for *Henry V*, perhaps the most significant puzzle concerns the bizarre conspiracy of Scroop, Cambridge, and Grey, allegedly in the pay of France, to kill the King. But even more perplexing is how Henry learned of it. As the Duke of Bedford tells us, "The King hath note of all they intend, / By interception, which they dream not of" (2.2.6–7). And while Shakespeare's sources do offer an alternative account of the conspiracy, which he chose to leave implicit, they provided him no explanation whatsoever for Henry's learning of the traitors' scheme. In both cases, then, history itself tempted Shakespeare with teasing conundrums too good not to exploit by way of adding some intellectual challenge to his dramas.

Of broader reach, however, is the puzzle that extends through all four plays of the sequence, though it is concentrated mainly in the two parts of *Henry IV*. It concerns Shakespeare's using these two plays to create the impression that Prince Hal prior to his succession was little better than an idling juvenile delinquent. Why this massive departure from the historical record? Most historians, including those available to Shakespeare, essentially agree that few princes since Alexander the Great came to their throne better prepared in terms of military and political experience. To be sure, replacing fact with fiction in this case provided a splendid opportunity for entertaining theatre: the psychic metamorphosis of a low-living, law-breaking, convention-flaunting, devil-may-care prince into a sober, responsible, chaste, scrupulously just king—famously fastidious about propriety and virtuous appearance—has all the dramatic appeal of the supernatural. And depicting the amusing hijinks of a rebellious Crown Prince warrants the invention of various scruffy companions for him to cavort with, most notably the immortal Falstaff, universally acknowledged one of Shakespeare's most brilliant creations. Still, the popularity of this outsized irreverent jester—his existence vaguely foreshadowed in *Richard II*, a dominating personality throughout both parts of *Henry IV*, pathetically dying offstage at the outset of *Henry V*—coupled with the manner in which the Prince-become-King dispenses with his services, presents its own set of puzzles.

Whereas the puzzle of the *Henriad* as a whole is that of Shakespeare's own view of the Henry whose kingship he depicts as he chooses. The once popular assumption that he simply celebrates Henry V as more or less a paragon—which might seem implied by denominating him 'the mirror of all Christian kings'—is easily shown to be problematic. There are many considerations that are at odds with this simplistic assessment, if not point in another direction entirely, but let three suffice initially. First, the author has relegated the task of eulogizing Henry almost entirely to the Chorus, which prefaces each act with what purports to be explanatory comment on the action it anticipates. But as often as not, something in the scenes that immediately follow such pronouncements contradict what the Chorus has just claimed, thereby undermining its general credibility. Second, with respect to Henry's most controversial action—ordering the killing of the French prisoners taken in the initial stage of the Battle of Agincourt—Shakespeare seems to have departed ever so slightly from the event as recounted in his principal historical source (Holinshed's *Chronicles*). The effect of his doing so is to render the King's decision more morally questionable than would be the case were the source scrupulously followed. Third, anyone sufficiently familiar with Machiavelli's teachings cannot fail to be struck by the extent to which Shakespeare's Henry appears to be an exemplary practitioner of that notorious Florentine's advice to princes. This seems an unlikely way to recommend the protagonist as a suitable model for all Christian kings.

And yet, there is reason to believe that our philosopher-poet judged Henry V to have been greater in reality than is acknowledged in his reputation even amongst his most ardent admirers. Or so I conclude, for reasons laid out in an epilogue of my own imagining.

CHAPTER ONE

BEGINS THE WOEFULLEST DIVISION

The Tragic Reign of King Richard II

> There is no action of man in this life, that is not the beginning of so long a chayn of Consequences, as no humane Providence, is high enough, to give a man a prospect to the end. And in this Chayn, there are linked together both pleasing and unpleasing events; . . . he that will do any thing for his pleasure, must engage himselfe to suffer all the pains annexed to it; and these pains, are the Naturall Punishments of those actions, which are the beginning of more Harme than Good. And hereby it comes to passe, that Intemperance, is naturally punished with Diseases; Rashnesse, with Mischances; Injustice, with the Violence of Enemies; Pride, with Ruine; Cowardise, with Oppression; Negligent government of Princes, with Rebellion; and Rebellion, with Slaughter.
>
> —Hobbes, *Leviathan*, chap. 31, para. 40

The historian G. M. Trevelyan observed that 'the reign of Richard II has interested people more, perhaps, than any other equally brief period of English medieval history', because (he explains) in the 'long-drawn-out process' whereby the so-called Middle Ages came to an end, the events of Richard's reign hold 'a peculiarly important place'.[1] From Shakespeare's depiction of the final year of that unhappy reign, seen in the context of the historical sequence of plays his *Richard II* initiates, one may surmise that he held a similar view—indeed, suspect that Shakespeare's portrayal has substantially contributed to the peculiar interest Trevelyan notes.

Doubtless much of that interest, whatever its source, derives from an awareness that the deposing of Richard precipitated a century of civil strife in England, leading to the Wars of the Roses, which in turn resulted in the termination of some three and a half centuries of unbroken

Norman-Plantagenet rule and the ascension of the House of Tudor (whose early years continued to be troubled by disturbances in favour of rival claimants). By the time Shakespeare wrote his dramatic accounts of English history, the de facto basis of royal authority in England, of its 'legitimacy', had been radically transformed. For though lip service continued to be paid to its de jure basis of 'divine right', that principle was increasingly viewed as moribund even as it was first being declaimed as absolute. Indeed, Shakespeare's *Richard III* shows how little supposed 'divine right' really mattered already a century prior. As for the chivalric code of honour (epitomized by the knight's right of 'trial by combat'), which along with custom and tradition was practically more important in Great Edward's day than the rule of law for ordering relations within the ruling class, this code—like jousting—had long been confined to the realm of pantomime. Moreover, the relation of the English Church to the English State, and the character of the Church itself, had similarly undergone a radical change.

Seen in retrospect, this profound alteration in the ordering of England's political life is set in motion by the usurpation of its throne by Henry Bolingbroke. The How and Why of this pivotal event is ostensibly what is being depicted in *The Tragedie of King Richard the second*.[2] Whether the fall of this particular English king does amount to a tragedy, or even 'a second fall of cursed man' (as one distraught victim characterizes it), is a significant question in its own right. If it is, why so?

The play certainly has a markedly English flavour, a feature I shall expand upon in the commentary that follows. But despite its emphatic Englishness, its structuring problem is not at all parochial, being nothing less than the question of what 'legitimates', not just political authority in England, but political authority as such: what set of rational criteria (such as would satisfy a political philosopher) does, or should, constitute an *objective* basis of a *right* to rule; and what readily recognisable indicators would, or might, instill in the minds of the Ruled a *subjective recognition* of a Ruler's said right; and what is the practical relationship between these two facets of the problem. The general problem comes to sight, however, as do all such problems of politics, in the guise of the particular. In this case, through the portrayal of the conflicts, both personal and political, that arose in a particular instance within a particular polity ostensibly governed according to a particular conception of legitimacy, that of so-called divine right. It is a case ideally suited to reveal the danger implicit in any conception of a ruler's right to rule that does not somehow offer assurance of at least minimal competence and inclination to rule *well*.

The play's first puzzle arises out of the action portrayed in its first scene. King Richard has assembled his Court for the purpose of formally hearing, purportedly with intent of adjudicating, an allegation of treason brought by Henry Bolingbroke, Duke of Hereford, against Thomas Mowbray, Duke of Norfolk. The King orders the two principals to be ushered into his presence, where 'frowning brow to brow, ourselves will hear / The accuser and the accused freely speak'.[3] Thus is introduced a theme threaded throughout the play: 'free speech', one dimension of the peculiar importance of language, and of peculiar language, in the conduct of political life.[4]

Mowbray, however, professes a reluctance to comply with Richard's admonition to speak freely. Citing Bolingbroke's blood relationship to the King, he responds, 'the fair reverence of your highness curbs me / From giving reins and spurs to my free speech' (1.1.54–55). The King, in a response coloured with more irony than he intends, reassures him on that point:

> Mowbray, impartial are our eyes and ears.
> Were he my brother, nay, my kingdom's heir,
> As he is but my father's brother's son,
> Now, by my sceptre's awe, I make a vow
> Such neighbour nearness to our sacred blood
> Should nothing privilege him nor partialize
> The unstooping firmness of my upright soul.
> He is our subject, Mowbray; so art thou.
> Free speech and fearless I to thee allow.
> (Ibid., 115–23)

Doubtless, the depreciative manner in which Richard refers to his relationship to cousin Bolingbroke is not lost on the man himself. One suspects that he already contemplates a day Richard's fragile soul will stoop sure enough.

Although in his earlier exchange with Henry's father (John of Gaunt, Duke of Lancaster), the King spoke as if Henry alone was an appellant, having accused Mowbray of treason (ibid., 4, 9, 17), it comes out differently when he addresses the two men directly: 'Yet one but flatters us, / As well appeareth by the cause you come, / Namely, to appeal *each other* of high treason' (ibid., 27). Puzzling. For in the passionate exchanges of charges and insults which follow—all made in open court—it is indeed only Bolingbroke who accuses his adversary of offences against the Crown; Mowbray, for his part, simply rebuts Henry's charges.[5] In the course of their ranting, however, each man pledges his sacred honour as a knight for the truthfulness of his words, while accusing the other of being a 'false traitor', or a 'foul liar'—charges that prompt each to throw down his gage, challenging the other to prove his honesty in mortal combat. We are several times reminded over the course of the play of the practical relationship between truthfulness, on the one hand, and honour, probity, and fidelity, on the other. And because it often requires *courage* to speak the truth 'freely', to give one's 'honest opinion', to stand by one's words, by oaths and vows and sworn testimony, truthfulness is a sine qua non of knighthood and its chivalric code. To be sure, there are situations in which lying also requires courage—and this first scene may portray an instance if one of these knights is lying, as would seem necessarily to be the case.

The King obviously does not take seriously Bolingbroke's charge that Mowbray, Richard's right-hand man, is guilty of treason, or that he poses any threat to the throne. Consequently, despite uncle Gaunt's prior assurance to the contrary, he chooses to treat Henry's appeal as if motivated simply by personal animosity ('ancient malice') towards the Duke of Norfolk (1.1.13–14). We must suppose Henry knows full well that his allegation will not be credited, but is nonetheless determined to force this charade on the King. Moreover, by goading Mowbray into insisting on a trial by combat, he preempts the possibility of Richard's pretending to judge the case and find it without merit. Thus Richard—perhaps sensing danger, not from Mowbray but from whatever Bolingbroke is up to—would prefer to disregard the whole matter, and so urges the two protagonists to kiss and make up:

> Wrath-kindled gentlemen, be ruled by me:
> Let's purge this choler without letting blood.
> This we prescribe, though no physician;
> Deep malice makes too deep incision.
> Forget, forgive, conclude and be agreed;
> Our doctors say this is no month to bleed.
> (Ibid., 152–57)

He then turns to Gaunt, 'Good uncle, let this end where it begun; / We'll calm the Duke of Norfolk, you your son'. The two men's efforts at peacemaking, however, do not avail. Both disputants are eloquent in insisting that they cannot allow this defiling of their honour to go unchallenged. Mowbray is especially emphatic regarding the disgrace attached to Bolingbroke's 'slander' of him, should he tolerate it:

> The purest treasure mortal times afford
> Is spotless reputation; that away,
> Men are but gilded loam or painted clay.
> A jewel in a ten-times-barred-up chest
> Is a bold spirit in a loyal breast.
> Mine honour is my life; both grow in one.
> Take honour from me, and my life is done.
> Then, dear my liege, mine honour let me try;
> In that I live, and for that will I die.
> (Ibid., 176–85)

Having failed to placate Mowbray, the King tries to do so with Bolingbroke, but is met with an equal intransigence: 'O, God defend my soul from such deep sin! / Shall I seem crest-fallen in my father's sight?' Finally, Richard concedes: 'We were not born to sue but to command; / Which since we cannot do to make you friends, / Be ready as your lives shall answer it / At Coventry upon Saint Lambert's Day'.

In allowing 'swords and lances [to] arbitrate' the conflict between Henry Bolingbroke and Thomas Mowbray, it would seem that the King thereby confirmed his own faith in, and allegiance to, the chivalric code: 'we shall see / Justice design the victor's chivalry' (1.1.200–203)—*divine* justice, presumably, according to the will and judgment of God. So the Lord Marshal officiating at the scheduled trial by combat warns the combatants, first Thomas Mowbray, Duke of Norfolk: 'Speak truly, on thy knighthood and thy oath, / As so defend thee heaven and thy valour'; then Harry of Hereford, Lancaster, and Derby: 'Speak like a true knight, so defend thee heaven!' (1.3.14–15, 34). For this is the premise of their duel, to be conducted according to a 'chivalrous design of knightly trial' (1.1.81): that victory will indicate who *speaks* truly and who lies—this, on the further premise that the victor was favoured by God.

On the day of the mortal contest, however, Richard abruptly halts the proceeding—indeed, halts the protagonists literally in their tracks, for the Lord Marshal had already given the command, 'Sound trumpets, and set forward, combatants' (1.3.117). The disputants are then countermanded to 'lay by their helmets and their spears' and return to their chairs, whereupon Richard withdraws with his councillors. When he returns, he cancels the contest outright on the grounds, first, 'that our kingdom's earth should not be soiled / With that dear blood which it hath fostered'; and, second, lest this quarrel, which he now ascribes to 'eagle-winged pride / Of sky-aspiring and ambitious thoughts / With rival-hating envy' (descriptors that could apply with plausibility only to Bolingbroke), somehow precipitate a broader conflict—that it 'Might from our quiet confines fright fair peace, / And make us wade even in our kindred's blood'. Why might a fight to the death between these two willing antagonists so threaten domestic peace? Or would this depend on who was victorious? Whatever the supposed rationale behind this supposed worry, on this basis the King banishes not only the 'envious rival' who fomented the quarrel with accusations Richard must know are false and actually aimed at him, but also one of his staunchest, most loyal, and able adherents[6]—sacrificed in a show of impartiality that is more apt to be seen for what it is: royal ingratitude and rank injustice.

Nor does the King offer any explanation for the perplexing inequity of the royal judgment. Why does Mowbray, the accused, receive the 'heavier doom' of permanent exile, whereas the accuser and instigator Bolingbroke is initially sentenced to only ten years banishment (which is promptly reduced to six)?[7] Was Mowbray's lifetime expulsion 'imposed' on the King by his councillors in camera as the price of their being publicly implicated in the double-banishment alternative? ('Draw near, / And list what *with our council* we have done'.) In particular, was Richard's permanently divesting himself of his trusted lieutenant the quid pro quo for Bolingbroke's father, 'old time-honoured Lancaster', agreeing to the temporary banishment of his own son (cf. 1.3.233–46)? We know that Gaunt holds the King responsible for Gloucester's death, for he privately acknowledged as much to Woodstock's widow, while nonetheless refusing to act directly against him:

> God's is the quarrel, for God's substitute,
> His deputy anointed in His sight,
> Hath caused his death, the which if wrongfully,
> Let heaven revenge, for I may never lift
> An angry arm against His minister.
> (1.2.37–41)

Gaunt would have no such reservations, however, about going after one of the King's agents who, he believed, actually had a hand in the bloody deed: 'butcher Mowbray' (as the Duchess of Gloucester characterizes him; 1.2.48; cf. 1.3.80–82).

That Richard professes 'some unwillingness' to pronounce the more onerous verdict on Norfolk would be cold comfort to the knight in whom he had earlier claimed to see 'Virtue with Valour couched in [his] eye' (1.3.97–98). Well might Mowbray protest:

> A heavy sentence, my most sovereign liege,
> And all unlooked for from your highness' mouth.
> A dearer merit, not so deep a maim
> As to be cast forth in the common air,
> Have I deserved at your highness' hands.
> (Ibid., 154–58)

A neutral familiar with Mowbray's service would sympathize. True, Richard may intend to recall his erstwhile factotum from exile after a 'decent interval'. But the banished knight gives no hint that he harbours any such expectation or has received any such assurance, which he could well have been provided had Richard actually planned in advance to substitute the double-banishment.

Thus, the primary puzzle: *why* has Richard waited until almost the final second to call off this deadly duel, leaving the principals to be dealt with in the manner he has? It is baffling, and pondering the matter only deepens one's perplexity. Even were one to credit the rationale he provides, it obviously has been operative from the moment he first authorized trial by combat. Thus, it provides no justification for his waiting until the very last instant to deny the two knights the right to settle their quarrel in the manner they both insist they prefer? Moreover, the right they invoke is woven into the fabric of the social order that it is the King's foremost duty to uphold. Did he when initially granting his permission presume that one or the other protagonist would eventually back out of a commitment of honour which each had in the heat of the moment so strenuously insisted upon (perhaps expecting, or hoping, to be approached privately to find some pretext to cancel the contest)? If so, he misjudged these two men—with whom he is thoroughly familiar—to an extent hardly credible.[8]

To repeat, thus the puzzle. Having acknowledged and acceded to the two knights' right to settle the dispute on the field of honour, and having accordingly ordered the Lord Marshal to make all preparations for the event—elaborate and expensive preparations that involve, either directly or indirectly, thousands of people, including all the notables of the realm as well as foreign dignitaries (after all, it is a ceremony-hedged fight to the death between two *dukes*, one of whom is royal)—why call it off? Why not let it proceed as arranged, rather than invite the awkward questions any cancellation would elicit? True, Richard is regarded as he regards himself: as King by divine right, entitled to having his every ruling obeyed. But he is aware that, in practice, no English king can rule in the capricious manner of an Asian despot, with no need to justify his actions—a fact he tacitly acknowledges by his subsequent attempt to explain his curious interruption of the trial. The explanation he provides, however, does not address what virtually everyone present would find bewildering at the time, and deeply suspicious thereafter: his cancelling the contest *so belatedly*—for *this* is what makes the King's behaviour so especially puzzling: the timing. Can he be wholly unaware of this? And that people will be left wondering how, then, is judgment to be rendered regarding what has become a more complicated issue? For what is now at stake is *not* simply, or even *primarily*, Hereford's original allegations against Norfolk, but both men's very *knighthood*, and all that implies (cf. 1.1.74–83, 167–73, 187–90).

It is hardly conceivable that only at the last moment did Richard realize the implications of a Bolingbroke victory: that it will validate his charge against the Duke of Norfolk regarding the murder of Woodstock (with everyone who counts believing that Mowbray does only what the King bids), while adding further lustre to Hereford's name and increasing his popularity among the people, both lesser nobility and commoners. Does Richard not truly believe that *God* determines who will emerge victorious according to the justice of his cause? Or is this precisely what he fears?

Placing the King in this quandary was, presumably, Henry's purpose in appealing Mowbray in the first place. We can be pretty sure it was not for the reason he claims, 'Tend'ring the precious safety of my prince' (1.1.32), in the genuine belief that it was *Norfolk*, of all people, who was conspiring against Richard's Crown. So, what else *could* be Bolingbroke's motive in bringing these specious charges against Mowbray—especially 'That he did plot the Duke of Gloucester's death'—to be judged by the very man whom the whole Lancaster clan holds responsible for that death? What might Henry be hoping to accomplish if not to discomfit Richard in some such way as he has? For once the King has agreed to hear the 'boist'rous late appeal', as he must (though apparently he had delayed doing so; cf. 1.1.5), Henry can by accusations and scurrilities practically force Sir Thomas to insist on defending his innocence on the field of honour. And so long as both appellant and defendant stand firm in their declared determination of settling the dispute in the manner of true knights—as they must, given what each has said of the other in the presence of the entire Court—the King has little choice but to grant this 'knightly trial', to be conducted according to a strictly prescribed 'chivalrous design'.

Thus Richard was maneuvered into a situation he cannot be happy with. Yet, what alternative is there now that the trial has been royally authorized, and all the elaborate arrangements for it set in motion? He could banish both men. This would avoid England's ground being 'soiled / With that dear blood which it hath fostered' (if one credits his caring about that). Moreover, with both principals exiled, supposedly leaving their respective partisans leaderless (as per Richard's public pretence that each is the head of a rival faction threatening open hostilities), domestic peace can be maintained. And while this would have the superficial appearance of impartiality, there is little else that could be alleged as to its *justness*, since without addressing the merits of Hereford's allegation against Norfolk—and what might come out in the course of evidence being presented and witnesses heard?—neither man's honour is cleared.

A double-banishment is doubtless attractive to Richard in that, at the price of one loyal adherent, it would rid his realm of an especially dangerous rival (presuming the popular duke would go peacefully, despite the dismay of his many partisans).[9] Yet for that very reason it is apt to be regarded as a confession of weakness, as well as an abnegation of his royal responsibility to oversee justice (in effect, sweeping a mess under the carpet). And needless to add, this solution ill-requites Mowbray for his loyal service—a lesson not apt to be lost on the King's other adherents—though his permanent absence might also have a silver lining: riddance of a confederate who perhaps knows too much for the King's own good. But supposing Richard had steeled himself to live with the risks and other political liabilities of this 'banishment solution', he could have enacted it well before the promulgated date of the trial, thereby obviating the (predictable) embarrassment and consternation that his apparently spontaneous abrogation later caused. So, the *basic* problem remains: why at the very last instant did he annul the permission freely granted to settle a dispute between two knights according to their traditional right of trial by combat, as both insist is their fervent desire.

One may reasonably suppose that Richard has been stewing over the matter ever since he first authorized the trial, lacking any plausible grounds then, and still, for denying the venue for justice both men passionately professed to seek. Having weighed, over and again, the pros and cons of each course of action—allowing the trial to proceed versus the only alternative he can think of: banishment—he has concluded that he must adhere to his original decision; that whatever the consequences of a possible Bolingbroke victory, it is preferable to face them rather than those of the alternative.

Yet, on the combatants' Day of Decision, he decides to call it off and to banish instead both challengers. Why? And in any case, what could explain his waiting until trumpets sound the charge to put a stop to it? For as everyone would recognise, he will thus have subjected each of the principals, *gratuitously*, not only to the necessity of raising his spirit to the pitch required for mortal combat, but also to the high anxiety of confronting his immediate death! Bolingbroke calls attention to the stakes: 'For Mowbray and myself are like two men / That vow a long and weary pilgrimage; / Then let us take a ceremonious leave / And loving farewell of our several friends' (1.3.48–51). Richard's own response to Henry's request to kiss and kneel before him by way of leave-taking suggests that even at this point, Richard himself remains settled, however uneasily, upon the trial proceeding as planned:

> We will descend and fold him in our arms.
> Cousin of Hereford, as thy cause is right,
> So be thy fortune in this royal fight.
> Farewell, my blood, which if today thou shed,
> Lament we may, but not revenge thee dead.
> (Ibid., 54–58)

It is *very* difficult to believe, given the circumstances, that this is a purposely deceptive charade, with Richard intending all along to cancel the contest at the last instant. Performed with the appropriate aplomb, this would be an almost unimaginable show of scorn for the social order of which he stands at the apex. Chivalric behaviour may have decayed, but the code itself had not at this point sunk to the status of a toy.

Presuming Richard had at some *earlier* juncture decided on cancelling the trial, one could perhaps accept his delay in *announcing* his decision until the appointed day—though just barely, given the resulting chagrin of the thousands of people, both noble and common, who will have gathered to witness this extraordinary event, many having travelled days for the opportunity.[10] But at least there could be a tactical advantage in this course of action, since it would preclude any sort of protest to be organized or counterpressure applied—an arrangement the more effective if Richard had also earlier decided on banishing the two men forthwith.[11] But this could not explain his halting the trial only upon its having actually begun. One must consider further possibilities.

Did Richard hold out hope to the very end that when confronted with the immediate prospect of entering into mortal combat, then—and only then—would the courage of one or the other of the contestants fail, and he then give way, perhaps finessing his withdrawal with some sort of exculpatory rationale?[12] An unlikely prospect, to say the least: that either of these two fully mature professional warriors would, in the presence of his country's assembled nobility, and hedged by the pomp and circumstance of punctilious ceremony, subject himself to the utter humiliation of declining the very trial by arms upon which he had so boldly and emphatically insisted. Moreover, it would be tantamount to declaring oneself guilty of perjury, hence subject to being punished accordingly (in the case of a knight, most likely by a disgraceful death).

Is it not far more likely that it was *Richard's* courage that failed? That for all his sangfroid when acceding to this event and assigning the time and place, and for all his efforts to fortify himself to accept the outcome of the trial as preferable to cancelling it—and after all, Mowbray *might win*—when it came to the crunch his resolve simply melted, and he fell back on the discarded alternative. Richard's behaviour is, quite simply, *bizarre*, and surely would astonish and bewilder everyone present.[13] Its aberrant character is somewhat masked, however, by his immediately withdrawing with his councillors. Doubtless, all those who witnessed the King's puzzling action would be speculating regarding its cause. Had something of consequence come to light only at the last minute? Did the King spot some impropriety on the part of one or the other of the combatants? As for how he might explain himself in private to those with whom he is supposedly taking counsel, God only knows. But when he returns, he is able to announce the banishment of both parties, along with its dubious rationale, as a *collective* decision: 'list what with our council we have done' (1.3.123–24).[14] Whereupon attention becomes occupied with what each man voices are the consequences of banishment for him. Hence, many people may at the moment overlook the impertinence of the King's rationale for so belatedly aborting the trial, as well as its puzzling implications with respect to the status of the original allegation and its implications for each man's knightly honour. But it is sure to be a subject of discussion, not to say invidious speculation, thereafter.

Richard's announcement of the curiously unequal banishments is followed, however, by an action that should be seen as equally curious. The King summons the two disputants, and obliges them, 'Lay on our royal sword your banished hands' and swear by God 'to keep the oath that we administer':

> You never shall, so help you truth and God,
> Embrace each other's love in banishment;
> Nor never look upon each other's face;
> Nor never write, regreet, nor reconcile
> This louring tempest of your home-bred hate;

Has there ever, anywhere, been proposed such a strange, not to say perverse, oath—much less by a supposedly Christian prince? Then Richard adds,

> Nor never by advised purpose meet
> To plot, contrive or complot any ill
> 'Gainst us, our state, our subjects or our land.
>   (1.3.179–80)

One could view extracting a promise to continue to hate one's enemy, rather than forgive and love him, as downright diabolical on the part of God's anointed deputy.[15] Moreover, it directly contrasts with the King's apparent effort to do the Christian thing when their dispute was first brought before him: 'Wrath-kindled gentlemen, be ruled by me: . . . Forget, *forgive*, conclude and be agreed'. But *then* he had (as noted) chosen to regard Hereford's appeal of Mowbray as if it were something strictly personal between the two men—not, that is, as actually posing any threat to him as King. *Now*, however, both men having been denied the satisfaction each had sought, and been instead de facto punished—thus each having ample reason to regard himself as aggrieved, especially Mowbray—one can readily understand the prudence of obliging the two not to plot any ill against king or country. Strangely, however, the oath Richard administers does not actually do that; it merely forbids the two men's *collaborating* in any such plot, hence that they ever be reconciled, ever so much as meet or communicate. We can only presume the King is unaware that he has not in fact secured from either man the promise he surely intended—another indication, perhaps, that his cancelling of the trial was not premeditated. Of course, the two disputants would not have had a common grievance to complain of had they not been banished in lieu of the trial rightfully their due. Nor, consequently, any reason for them to meet in exile and compare notes.

The resolution of everything that is puzzling about this whole episode depends on conjecturing why, so strangely and at the very last instant, King Richard felt compelled to halt the trial, then cancel it and substitute banishment.[16] And it would seem that the only plausible explanation for doing so is a failure of nerve on Richard's part, indicative of the same weakness of soul that has allowed his kingdom to be bled of resources by flattering 'caterpillars', and which will contribute to his precipitous undoing when confronting the Bolingbroke-led rebellion.

The 'Englishness' of *Richard II* is conspicuous. Indeed, despite the universality of the problem it illustrates, it is the most overtly English play in the Shakespearean canon. Appropriately so, it should be said, inasmuch as it anchors what is in effect a national epic extending over seven more 'chapters'.[17] By its Englishness, I have in mind more than the play's many explicit references to England and things English, though this in itself is evocative. As if to drive home the point, some allusions to England seem conspicuously laboured—Bolingbroke's in particular, such as his avowed willingness to battle Mowbray anywhere 'That ever was survey'd by English eye' (1.1.94), and his elliptical reference to his exile as the time when he 'sighed [his] English breath in foreign clouds' (3.1.20). His final words on banishment sound this national theme: 'Then England's ground, farewell! Sweet soil, adieu— / My mother and my nurse that bears me yet! / Where'er I wander, boast of this I can, / Though banished, yet a true-born Englishman (1.3.306–9).

To be sure, there are other of Shakespeare's history plays that have even more mentions of England. However, in *Richard II* there are speeches regarding the philosopher-poet's native land that truly stand out. One is among the most famous of the many famous addresses he crafted, and is surely the most oft-quoted encomium of England anyone ever penned: that which he supplies Henry's father, 'Old John of Gaunt, time-honoured Lancaster'.

> This royal throne of kings, this sceptred isle,
> This earth of majesty, this seat of Mars,
> This other Eden, demi-paradise,
> This fortress built by Nature for herself
> Against infection and the hand of war,
> This happy breed of men, this little world,
> This precious stone set in the silver sea [etc.].
> (2.1.40–46)

Bolingbroke would seem to have acquired at the least the rhetoric of his father's patriotism, whether or not he inherited his sentiments as well.[18] However, there is another speech that is hardly famous at all, though it points directly to one especially important theme of the play: the eloquent lament of Thomas Mowbray upon learning that he is banished for life. He focuses on the overwhelming practical consequence of his exile: his being thereby linguistically isolated, and to that extent cut off from the community of men.

> The language I have learnt these forty years,
> My native English, now I must forego,
> And now my tongue's use is to me no more
> Than an unstringed viol or a harp,
> Or like a cunning instrument cased up— . . .
> Within my mouth you have engaoled my tongue,
> Doubly porticullised with my teeth and lips,
> And dull unfeeling barren Ignorance
> Is made my gaoler to attend on me.
> I am too old to fawn upon a nurse,
> Too far in years to be a pupil now.
> What is thy sentence then but speechless death,
> Which robs my tongue from breathing native breath.
> (1.3.159–73)

Whatever else, Mowbray's plaint directs the reader's attention to the peculiar role of language in this play. It is generally acknowledged that linguistic patterns and images—such as the plenitude of references to Nature in *King Lear*, or to Fortune in *The Merchant of Venice*—afford helpful clues to the interpretation of Shakespeare's dramas. Once recognised, however, the challenge such patterns present is that of seeing their peculiar appropriateness, not only to a play's plot, but also to whatever theoretical problem lies at its heart.

Why, then, is there in *Richard II*—one of four Shakespearean plays written entirely in verse—this conspicuous density of language referring to language itself. Why this emphasis, first of all, on speaking, saying, telling, with characters unnecessarily saying that they say what they say, rather than merely saying it: 'Look what I speak. . . .', 'Besides I say . . .', 'Further I say . . .' (1.1.87, 93, 98; cf. 4.1.127, 76; 5.3.43). And on the physical *means* of speech: on mouths, lips, and especially tongues—the organ so essential to articulate speech that it serves as a synonym for speech itself, or for a particular dialect. Gaunt avows he counseled the banishment of his son with an 'unwilling tongue' (1.3.245); and later, anticipating a final opportunity to admonish Richard, invokes the opinion that 'the tongues of dying men / Enforce attention like deep harmony' (2.1.5–6);

Ross fears indulging 'a liberal tongue' (2.1.229); Scroop regrets his 'care-tuned tongue' (3.2.92); the Queen berates the gardener for his 'harsh rude tongue' (3.4.74); Aumerle is credited with a 'daring tongue' that 'Scorns to unsay what once it hath delivered' (4.1.8–9). And invoking an image that recalls Mowbray's lament, Northumberland informs Richard of uncle Gaunt's death: 'His tongue is now a stringless instrument; / Words, life, and all old Lancaster hath spent' (2.1.149–50).

Moreover, there are some two dozen references in the play to the physical *medium* of speech, that is, breath—another word often used as a stand-in for speech itself. Thus, for example, the King banishes Mowbray: 'The hopeless word of "never to return" / Breathe I against thee' (1.3.152–53). And when Richard reduces Bolingbroke's exile by four years, the Duke observes, 'Four lagging winters and four wanton springs / End in a word; such is the breath of kings' (ibid., 214–15). York counsels Gaunt, 'Vex not yourself, nor strive not with your breath, / For all in vain comes counsel to his ear'. Whereas Gaunt would prefer to believe that the fact he is dying can make the profligate King listen to reason: 'Where words are scarce (2.1.3-4, 7–8) they are seldom spent in vain, / For they breathe truth that breathe their words in pain' (2.1.7–8). The gardener ruefully assures the Queen, 'Little joy have I / To breathe this news; yet what I say is true' (3.4.81–82). And King Richard, facing rebellion, vainly assures himself that 'the breath of worldly men cannot depose / The deputy elected by the Lord' (3.2.56–57; cf. 1.1.170–73, 1.3.255–57, 4.1.126–30, 5.3.45–46).

In the course of the play we are reminded of some of the many things that are *done* through speech—not merely talking, telling, saying, and speaking, but greeting, describing, reporting, impugning, cursing, vowing, demanding, pleading, slandering, placating, thanking, arguing, taunting, urging, blaspheming, denying, lying, scolding, damning, swearing, foreswearing, proclaiming, complaining, counseling, wooing, informing, recounting, apologizing, lamenting, begging, prophesying (inter alia). Noticeable by their absence are virtually all those lighthearted 'speech acts' so common in most of Shakespeare's plays (e.g., bantering, joking, teasing, kidding). But of the practically countless things *done* simply through distinctive forms of speech, there are several that have a special pertinence to this play, as to political life generally: for example, denouncing, accusing, banishing, confessing, pardoning, sentencing, and not least of all, *flattering*.

King Richard—who is the first to mention the subject (1.1.25)—is depicted as a fool for flattery, that his ear is deaf to wise counsel because 'stopped with other, flatt'ring sounds' (2.1.16–17; cf. 93–103, 241–42, 2.2.85). His subsequent depreciation of flattery's value bespeaks hard-won wisdom: 'O flatt'ring glass, / Like to my followers in prosperity, / Thou dost beguile me' (4.1.279–81; cf. 3.2.216, 4.1.305–9). Whereas, both friends and enemies attest from the outset that Bolingbroke is adept at flattering *others*, especially the commoners (1.4.24–36, 5.2.18–21); and we are allowed to see for ourselves his graceful flattering of his uncle (2.3.114–17), his father (1.3.67–72), and even cornered Richard (3.3.187–99). All of this might imply not only a superior understanding of the political efficacy of flattery, but also an indifference to flattery himself. This suspicion is not necessarily contradicted by the fact that he is the recipient of the play's most fulsome *display* of flattery, that of Northumberland as together they traipse across the Cotswolds towards Berkeley Castle:

> These high wild hills and rough uneven ways
> Draws out our miles and makes them wearisome.
> And yet your fair discourse hath been as sugar,
> Making the hard way sweet and delectable.
> But I bethink me what a weary way
> From Ravenspurgh to Cotshall will be found
> In Ross and Willoughby, wanting your company,
> Which I protest hath very much beguiled
> The tediousness and process of my travel.
> But theirs is sweetened with the hope to have
> The present benefit which I possess . . .[19]
> (2.3.4–14)

Notice how modestly Bolingbroke reciprocates: 'Of much less value is my company / Than your good words'. Did he not seem such a blunt, unsubtle, direct-action sort of fellow, one might suspect the man of irony.

There is more to language than names, but personal names are more than just words, as they can be indicative of reputation, status, relations, and power. The play includes almost three dozen mentions of the term and its cognates, beginning with Bolingbroke's challenge to Mowbray, 'With a foul traitor's name stuff I thy throat' (1.1.44). In anticipation of killing Mowbray, Henry intends thereby to 'furbish new the name of John o'Gaunt' (1.3.76). For his part, Mowbray declares, 'If ever I were traitor, / My name be blotted from the book of life' (1.3.201–2). The formalities of the trial by combat begin with each principal being required to identify himself by name (ostensibly because he is concealed within his armour): 'In God's name and the King's, say who thou art' (1.3.11). In meeting with Richard for a final time, Gaunt chides his nephew with a laboured play on his own name: 'O, how that name befits my composition! / Old Gaunt indeed, and gaunt in being old'—to which the King rejoins, 'Can sick men play so nicely with their names?' Gaunt replies, 'No, misery makes sport to mock itself. / Since thou dost seek to kill my name in me, / I mock my name, great King, to flatter thee' (2.1.73–87). When addressed as 'My Lord of Hereford' by Lord Berkeley before his castle, Henry makes an issue of his name: 'My lord, my answer is—to "Lancaster", / And I am come to seek that name in England; / And I must find that title in your tongue / Before I make reply to aught you say' (2.3.69–73). More questionable, not to say sophistical, is his justification to York for his 'repealing' his own exile: 'As I was banished, I was banished Hereford; / But as I come, I come for Lancaster' (ibid., 113–14).

In feudal society, where chivalry had its home, one's titled status was integral to one's name. Indeed, that the two are practically interchangeable is several times emphasized. So young Percy's report on the manning of Berkeley Castle: 'in it are the Lords of York, Berkeley, and Seymour— / None else of name and noble estimate' (ibid., 55–56). One's name and the title attached to it typically stands for the quantum of power at one's command. Upon arriving back from Ireland and learning that there is no Welsh army to meet him, Richard momentarily rallies from his despondency with the thought, 'Is not the King's name twenty thousand names? / Arm, arm, my name!' (3.2.85–86). Traditionalist York, resolutely refusing to face facts, chides Northumberland for referring to King Richard merely by his Christian name (3.3.7–14). In making his point, however, York tacitly confirms the relation between name, status, and power. So too does Richard when brought before those assembled to witness his coerced abdication. Addressed by Northumberland as 'My lord', he interrupts:

> No lord of thine, thou haught insulting man,
> Nor no man's lord! I have no name, no title—
> No, not that name was given me at the font—
> But 'tis usurped. Alack the heavy day,
> That I have worn so many winters out
> And know not now what name to call myself.
> (4.1.254–59)

What's in a name, a naive young girl once asked. Plenty, apparently, when it betokens more than merely a pleasant aroma, but calls to mind character, status, familial relations, influence—even, perhaps, a divine connection. Thus in uttering his formulaic 'In God's name I'll ascend the regal throne' (ibid., 114), Bolingbroke hopes that being thus *named* 'King', he, like Richard and the seven Plantagenets before him, will be recognised as God's vicar and so be supported as a matter of piety, whatever else. But he soon finds that his manner of acquiring the name has undermined the power of the name.

One further point worth noting is the play's especially piquant example of that peculiar exploitation of ambiguity in language called 'insinuating', and of the misunderstandings—whether real or merely professed—to which it may give rise:

> Exton: Didst thou not mark the King, what words he spake:
> Have I no friend will rid me of this living fear?'
> Was it not so?
> 1 Servant: These were his very words.
> Exton: 'Have I no friend?' quoth he. He spake it twice,
> And urged it twice together, did he not?
> 2 Servant: He did.
> Exton: And speaking it, he wishtly looked on me,
> As who should say, 'I would thou wert the man
> That would divorce this terror from my heart',
> Meaning the King at Pomfret.
> (5.4.1–10)

By definition, insinuation allows some indeterminate latitude of interpretation. Hence, acting on the basis of what someone merely insinuates he wishes done risks one's deed being disavowed by the insinuator, as Exton learns to his regret. A cautionary tale about the hazards of sycophancy, it would seem.[20]

The most important 'deed of speech' in this story is, of course, that of Richard's *abdicating*. Inasmuch as the scene depicting his doing so in the presence of the Parliament—arguably the dramatic zenith of the play—is entirely Shakespeare's invention (for according to Holinshed, Richard abdicated while imprisoned in the Tower, and Parliament was simply notified of the fact the following day, whereupon both Lords and Commons approved Henry's claiming the throne), we may presume this major departure from the historical record has some special significance, and accordingly wonder about it. I shall return to this question 'anon'.

In Shakespeare's version of this event, Bolingbroke and his supporters wish their *de facto* deposing of Richard to be seen *de jure* as a voluntary abdication, and publicly witnessed as such in Parliament: that 'plume-plucked Richard ... with *willing* soul / Adopts thee [Henry] heir' (as pliant York blithely announces; 4.1.109–10).[21] Better still for this purpose were such a declaration accompanied by another deed of speech: Richard's *confession* of the 'grievous crimes / Committed by [his] person and [his] followers / Against the state and profit of this land'—crimes that would justify his being deposed, hence would more than justify his being pressed to abdicate (ibid., 223–25). However, there is only one way Richard can abdicate, much less confess: by his own words, freely spoken before credible witnesses. The bishop of Carlisle's eloquent protest that even thieves caught red-handed 'are not judged but they are by to hear' (hence, are able to respond) makes this requirement practically impossible to ignore. Accordingly, Henry orders, 'Fetch hither Richard, that in common view / He may surrender. So we shall proceed / Without suspicion' (4.1.156–58).[22]

Thus the doomed King is brought into the assembled presence, whereupon he asks, 'To do what service am I sent for hither?' Old York replies, 'To do that office of thine own good will / Which tired majesty did make thee offer— / The resignation of thy state and crown / To Henry Bolingbroke'. In responding, Richard shows qualities of spirit and mind not previously so evident: first, in the poignancy with which he replies to Henry prior to abdicating; then, in the deftness with which he parries Northumberland's insistence that he confess to grievous crimes. Though apparently resigned to his fate, and for the most part outwardly compliant with what his enemies require of him, he uses the remarkable power of language, of wit and irony as well as pathos, to turn what was intended to be Bolingbroke's triumph into his own finest hour.

> Now mark me how I will undo myself:
> I give this heavy weight from off my head,
> And this unwieldy sceptre from my hand,
> The pride of kingly sway from out my heart;
> With mine own tears I wash away my balm,
> With mine own hands I give away my crown,
> With mine own tongue deny my sacred state,
> With mine own breath release all duteous oaths.
> All pomp and majesty I do foreswear;
> My manors, rents, revenues I forgo;
> My acts, decrees and statutes I deny.[23]

As Richard continues, however, a tone of subtle irony becomes increasingly evident:

> God pardon all oaths that are broke to me;
> God keep all vows unbroke are made to thee.
> Make me, that nothing have, with nothing grieved,
> And thou with all pleased that hast all achieved.
> Long mayst thou live in Richard's seat to sit,
> And soon lie Richard in an earthly pit!
> 'God save King Henry', unkinged Richard says,
> 'And send him many years of sunshine days!'
>   (4.1.203–21)

Shakespeare portrays 'unkinged Richard' as a maestro of theatrics, of drama, of using a mock-ceremony to make a spectacle of himself, even directing the parts played by his enemies ('Here, cousin, seize the crown. Here, cousin, / On this side, my hand, on that side thine. / Now is this golden crown like a deep well'; 4.1.182–84). Thus is Henry upstaged at every turn in the scene, his succession rendered an anticlimax.

Bearing in mind that there is no such confrontation in the historical record, we may well wonder why Shakespeare has orchestrated Richard's abdication in the manner he has. Of course, this concoction serves Shakespeare's own *theatrical* purpose exceedingly well; the scene he created from whole cloth is, as noted, one of the dramatic high points of *Richard II*. And, admittedly, there may be no more to the puzzle than that. But there are other possibilities worth considering. For one, Shakespeare's version raises, be it ever so slightly, the importance of Parliament, as if to suggest that it would be the appropriate setting of such a momentous event, its members the fitting witnesses thereof.

However, there is a possibility more significant for the whole tetralogy of which this play is the first chapter. The scene displays a different kind of *power* than that wielded by a king as the dispenser of honours and offices, penalties and punishments, and not least as commander of a regime's physical force. Might Shakespeare mean to suggest that only through wedding the power of the dramatic arts with the power that comes with exercising sovereignty can one rectify the damage done to the very basis of political legitimacy which we see depicted in this scene? That is, the scene portrays the origin of the problem that will dominate the political career of King Henry V, while hinting at the political strategy whereby he will attempt to solve it.

Whatever the explanation for Shakespeare's relocating the coerced abdication from the Tower to the Parliament, Richard's cooperation in his 'unkinging' ceremony is so noticeably lacking in enthusiasm that Henry pretends to be puzzled: 'I thought you had been willing to resign'. Richard explains his equivocal affirmation: 'My Crown I am, but still my griefs are mine. / You may my glories and my state depose, / But not my griefs; still am I king of those' (ibid., 190–93).

Speaking of grief, the play is fairly steeped in it. It is professed at one time or another by almost every character of importance. The Duchess of Gloucester, murdered Woodstock's widow, is the first to mention this debilitating passion, alluding to its oppressive power as she bids a final farewell to Gaunt: 'Thy sometimes brother's wife, / With her companion, Grief, must end her life' (1.2.54–55). Banished Bolingbroke, responding to his father's 'What is six winters? They are quickly gone' also attests to the domineering effect of this passion: 'To men in joy; but grief makes one hour ten' (1.3.260–61). When the King visits his dying uncle, already determined to expropriate his estate, Lancaster explains why he is 'Old Gaunt indeed': 'Within me Grief hath kept a tedious fast' as a result of contemplating an England subjected to Richard's wasteful rule (2.1.73–78).

The language of despondency is particularly dense in the two scenes featuring Isabel, Richard's Queen.[24] In the first, with Bushy and Bagot, she complains of a sadness she cannot account for, a premonition that 'Some unborn sorrow, ripe in Fortune's womb, / Is coming towards me'. Bushy tries to reassure her, 'Each substance of a grief hath twenty shadows, / Which shows like grief itself, but is not so; / For sorrow's eyes, glazed with blinding tears, / Divides one thing entire to many objects' (2.2.10–17). All too soon, however, Green arrives with sobering news: 'The banished Bolingbroke repeals himself'. The Queen fully understands the dire implications: 'Now hath my soul brought forth her prodigy, / And I, a gasping new-delivered mother, / Have woe to woe, sorrow to sorrow joined' (ibid., 64–66). Her second scene is set in a garden, where she declines to be cheered by anything her ladies suggest. Dancing? 'My legs can keep no measure in delight / When my poor heart no measure keeps in grief'. Tales? 'Of sorrow or joy?' Neither would lighten her burden (3.4.7–16). Instead, she wishes to eavesdrop upon a gardener and his assistants: 'They will talk of state, for everyone doth so / Against a change; woe is forerun with woe' (ibid., 27–28).

Not surprisingly, it is Richard who is most unremitting in voicing his grief, and is at his most eloquent in doing so, commencing the moment on the Welsh coast when he realizes he has lost his kingdom, and so proposes to 'sit upon the ground / And tell sad stories of the death of kings'.[25] Shortly thereafter he decides he will proceed 'to Flint Castle. There I'll pine away. / A king, woe's slave, shall kingly woe obey' (3.2.155–56, 209–10). Upon finding himself trapped at Flint, Richard laments to Aumerle, 'O, that I were as great / As is my grief, or lesser than my name!' (3.3.136–37). His forced abdication, as already noted, is laced with repeated references to griefs, tears, woes, and sorrows. Richard's story ends with King Henry professing sorrow that it should end as it has: 'Lords, I protest, my soul is full of woe / That blood should sprinkle me to make me grow. / Come, mourn with me for what I do lament' (5.6.45–7). Perhaps Henry is sincere. But Aumerle reminds us early on that grief, like most human emotions, can be feigned when doing so serves a purpose, as it did him in responding to banished Bolingbroke's 'Farewell': 'And, for my heart disdained that my tongue / Should so profane the word, that taught me craft / To counterfeit oppression of such grief / That words seemed buried in my sorrow's grave' (1.4.11–15).

'Grief' and its cognates occur no less than forty times in this play, far more often than in any other of Shakespeare's works. The frequent mentions of the term, along with comparable frequencies of 'sorrow', 'woe', 'sadness', and 'tears' (altogether, these five terms occur some 130 times in the text), impart a decidedly somber mood to this tale of Richard's downfall. Why is this? Simply because the play is, as originally advertised, a 'Tragedy'? But none of the other tragedies—not even the truly heart-rending *King Lear*—share anything like this linguistic feature. And few would argue that, by comparison, the qualities of Richard the man make his precipitous descent from grace and power to ignominy and death *especially* pitiable. Is the deeper tragedy, then, the loss of whatever falls with him? Or rather, perhaps, the inevitability of both that fall, and of its results?[26]

Whatever the case, the bishop of Carlisle proves only too prescient regarding the consequences for England precipitated by Bolingbroke's usurping 'the regal throne':

> The blood of English shall manure the ground,
> And future ages groan for this foul act.
> Peace shall go sleep with Turks and infidels,
> And in this seat of peace tumultuous wars
> Shall kin with kin and kind with kind confound. . . .
> O, if you raise this house against this house,
> It will the woefullest division prove
> That ever fell upon this cursed earth.
> (4.1.138–48)[27]

We might suppose the good Bishop to have in mind the years immediately ahead, which were, as he predicted, marked by a succession of bloody conflicts that paused only in the time of Henry V. From Shakespeare's historical vantage point, however, he knew that the respite of that celebrated King's reign proved all too temporary. And that due to the loss of a clear, universally respected principle of political legitimacy, England's destructive civil wars would soon resume—that what were in Richard's day still 'future ages' would pay a heavy price indeed for Bolingbroke's successful usurpation. This might seem strange, given that at the time he was so broadly popular with both the nobility and the common people, and that his seizing of power met with widespread celebration (cf. 1.4.24–36; 3.2.109–20; 5.2.7–21).[28] Even so, however, his success was far from certain. How did he manage it?

One pivotal event ensured Bolingbroke an almost bloodless victory in what might well have been a vicious civil war. To wit, the desertion of the Welsh army that Richard expects to meet him at Harlech, the army in which 'The King reposeth all his confidence' (2.4.6). And rightly so, for it is—or rather, *was*—a force substantially greater than that which accompanied Bolingbroke, and as such a superior nucleus bound to attract the majority of political pragmatists (cf. 2.1.285–88). Richard learns of this catastrophe in the central scene of the play (3.2). The Earl of Salisbury enters bearing the fatal news at the exact midpoint of the play.[29] Richard greets him with, 'Welcome, my lord. How far off lies your power?' Salisbury replies:

> Nor near nor farther off, my gracious lord,
> Than this weak arm. Discomfort guides my tongue
> And bids me speak of nothing but despair.
> One day too late, I fear me, noble lord,
> Hath clouded all thy happy days on earth.
> O, call back yesterday, bid Time return,
> And thou shalt have twelve thousand fighting men!
> To-day, to-day, unhappy day too late,
> O'erthrows thy joys, friends, fortune and thy state.
> (3.2.64–72)

Aumerle's comment indicates the effect this news has on the King: 'Comfort, my liege. Why looks your grace so pale?' The shaken Richard explains:

> But now the blood of twenty thousand men[30]
> Did triumph in my face, and they are fled;
> And till so much blood thither come again,
> Have I not reason to look pale and dead?
> (Ibid., 76–79)

But *why*, after waiting ten days, did the Welshmen decide to disperse? Superficially, the answer is simple. As we learned in an earlier scene, when Salisbury begged the Welsh captain to remain but one more day, he replied, ''Tis thought the King is dead. We will not stay'. The captain is even more emphatic upon parting: 'Farewell. Our countrymen are gone and fled, / As well assured Richard their king is dead' (2.4.7, 16–17). And so Salisbury reports when Richard arrives the following day: 'For all the Welshmen, hearing thou wert dead, / Are gone to Bolingbroke, dispersed and fled' (Ibid., 73–74).

Here, then, is the *key puzzle* of the play: why did the Welsh soldiers bivouacked in the vicinity of Barkloughly Castle (i.e., Harlech) come to believe that Richard is dead? No one else does.[31] Yet these Welshmen had been 'well assured' of it. By whom? It must have been by someone whose veracity they would have reason to trust, which means someone known to be an intimate of Richard's inner circle. So, who is the source of this false, but all too plausible rumour—for over the centuries Englishmen by the hundreds sickened and died in Ireland—a rumour that doubtless spread through the Welsh ranks like wildfire?

Thanks to a genius for crafting not only memorable characters but memorable *sets* of characters, 'Bushy, Bagot, & Green' are as inseparably associated in the minds of Shakespeare's admirers as are Salerio and Solanio, or Rosencrantz and Guildenstern. Mentioning by name any one of these individuals immediately calls forth the other(s) with whom he is associated. So it is with this trio of parasitic sycophants so favoured by King Richard. Seemingly indistinguishable, hence interchangeable, these three 'caterpillars of the commonwealth' (2.3.165–66; cf. 3.4.47–53) may be taken to represent the hundreds of fashion-aping hedonists with whom Richard filled his court, exhausting the resources of his realm to support a liberality towards those who least deserved it (cf. 2.1.21–26, 246–55).[32] Each member of this notorious trio appears in a total of five scenes, although not the same five scenes.

We first set eyes on the threesome at Coventry when King Richard enters to supervise the trial by combat of Bolingbroke and Mowbray.[33] We first hear any of them *speak*, however, in the following scene. Richard is privately discussing 'high Hereford's' public behaviour with what are obviously three of his intimates: his royal cousin, the Duke of Aumerle (York's son), who openly shares Richard's animosity towards their other royal cousin; Green, who urges the King to turn his thoughts to the rebellion in Ireland, for which 'Expedient manage must be made' (1.4.39); and Bagot, who is a silent observer. Richard has just expressed his intention to go 'in person to this war' and indicated the extraordinary measures he has set in motion to finance it ('for our coffers with too great a court / And liberal largess are grown somewhat light'),[34] when Bushy enters with the news that 'Old John of Gaunt is grievous sick', and is asking that the King come to him at Ely house (ibid., 54–58). In response, Richard, along with praying God arrange that his uncle die immediately, elliptically alludes to an intention thereupon to appropriate the contents of Gaunt's coffers to pay for equipping soldiers for the Irish wars.

Bushy, Bagot, and Green (among others) accompany the King and Queen on their visit to the dying Lancaster, and thus overhear themselves castigated in Gaunt's final admonition to his profligate nephew:

> Thy death-bed is no lesser than thy land,
> Wherein thou liest in reputation sick;
> And thou, too careless patient as thou art,
> Committ'st thy anointed body to the cure
> Of those physicians that first wounded thee.

> A thousand flatterers sit within thy crown,
> Whose compass is no bigger than thy head;
> And yet, encaged in so small a verge,
> The waste is no whit lesser than thy land.
> (2.1.95–103)

They also witness Richard's angry, threatening response, which elicits Gaunt's scarcely veiled accusation of Richard as the murderer of his uncle Woodstock (ibid., 124–31). And upon the subsequent announcement of Gaunt's death, they see the callous manner in which Richard receives it, immediately proclaiming the seizure of all the Lancastrian property. They hear the extended remonstrance and warning this provokes from his uncle York ('You pluck a thousand dangers on your head, / You lose a thousand well-disposed hearts'), and they observe the King's casual dismissal of this warning (ibid., 205–10). Having registered his futile protest, York leaves, whereupon Richard orders Bushy to bid the Earl of Wiltshire come to Ely house to oversee the expropriation of the Lancaster estate. He then declares his intention to appoint his sole surviving uncle, this same feckless York, Lord Governor of England during the King's own absence in Ireland ('For he is just and always loved us well'). Bushy, Bagot, and Green leave with the King and Queen, not having spoken a word.

The following scene (the first part of which has already been examined, but to a different purpose) features their most substantial contribution to both the speech and the action of the play; it is also the last time they appear together. It opens with Bushy attempting to cheer the Queen, who is saddened by Richard's having departed for Ireland, but also by some vague anxiety she 'cannot name' (2.2.40). A silent Bagot looks on. Green arrives, obviously in something of a lather, for after only a perfunctory salutation he exclaims, 'I hope the King is not yet shipped for Ireland'. The Queen querying 'why so', Green explains that 'an enemy' has landed in England: 'The banished Bolingbroke repeals himself, / And with uplifted arms is safe arrived / At Ravenspurgh' (ibid., 49–51). The Queen, aghast at this news, can now put a name to her previously 'nameless woe': Bolingbroke.

Shortly thereafter, York arrives 'with signs of war about his aged neck' and a worried look on his face. The Queen nonetheless hopes he may 'speak comfortable words'. He declines, warning, 'Comfort's in heaven, and we are on the earth, / Where nothing lives but crosses, cares and grief' (ibid., 78–79). And though he is attempting to take some measures to defend the realm for Richard, he openly admits that he 'knows not what to do'. Beyond his practical ineptitude, however, he confesses having a divided soul, which manifests in personal terms a shadow of the larger philosophical problem that Richard's irresponsible, self-indulgent reign presents:

> If I know how or which way to order these affairs
> Thus disorderly thrust into my hands,
> Never believe me. Both are my kinsmen.
> Th'one is my sovereign, whom both my oath
> And duty bids defend; th'other again
> Is my kinsman, whom the King hath wronged,
> Whom conscience and my kindred bids to right.
> (Ibid., 109–15)

Taking the Queen into his personal care, he leaves with her, having ordered Bushy, Bagot, and Green to muster their men and meet him at Berkeley Castle.

The trio of caterpillars now left alone, the following uneasy conversation takes place (with Bagot speaking for the first time in the play):

Bushy:	The wind sits fair for news to go for Ireland,
	But none returns. For *us* to levy power
	Proportionable to the enemy is all unpossible.
Green:	Besides, our nearness to the King in love
	Is near the hate of those that love not the King.
Bagot:	And that's the wavering commons, for their love
	Lies in their purses; and whoso empties them,
	By so much fills their hearts with deadly hate.
Bushy:	Wherein the King stands generally condemned.
Bagot:	If judgement lie in them, then so do we,
	Because we ever have been near the King.
Green:	Well, I will for refuge straight to Bristol Castle.
	The Earl of Wiltshire is already there.
Bushy:	Thither will I with you, for little office
	Will the hateful commons perform for us
	Except like curs to tear us all to pieces.
	Will you go along with us?
Bagot:	No, I will to Ireland to his majesty.
	Farewell. If heart's presages be not vain,
	We three here part that ne'er shall meet again.
Bushy:	That's as York thrives to beat back Bolingbroke.
Green:	Alas, poor Duke! The task he undertakes
	Is numbering sands and drinking oceans dry.
	Where one on his side fights, thousands will fly.
	Farewell at once—for once, for all, and ever.[35]
Bushy:	Well, we may meet again.
Bagot:	I fear me, never.
	(Ibid., 123–48)

Whereupon the 'three here part that ne'er shall meet again', Bushy and Green for Bristol, Bagot presumably for Ireland. We know the former pair go to Bristol Castle just as they proposed (*not* to Berkeley, notice, as York had commanded), for there they are captured by Bolingbroke, who—acting every inch the King—orders them summarily executed after a farce of a hearing (3.1.29–30).

But what about Bagot? Did he, as he indicated, take advantage of the wind sitting fair for Ireland to convey to Richard the news of Bolingbroke's having raised the standard of revolt? Or did he get only as far as the northwest coast of Wales, perhaps with a detour along the way? We know that Richard somehow got the news, for he arrives at Harlech fully aware of the task awaiting him—suppression of the Henry-led rebellion—and expecting to find there ample means of doing so: the Welsh army. So it might seem that Bagot carried out his announced mission. But by the time Richard returns to England—and sufficient time has passed to summon soldiers scattered throughout Wales, for them to assemble, and then cool their heels for ten days—any number of Richard's endangered supporters may have done as did Aumerle, who availed himself of that fair wind for Ireland to warn the King of the emergency back home (2.2.86–88). Was Bagot among their number?

Apparently not, for he is not accompanying the King upon his return, as one would then expect. Indeed, Richard seems to have no reason to believe that Bagot is anywhere but in England, and so rails against him along with the other 'Judases' who he presumes have allowed Henry to proceed without opposition:

> Where is the Earl of Wiltshire? Where is Bagot?
> What is become of Bushy? Where is Green?—
> That they have let the dangerous enemy
> Measure our confines with such peaceful steps?
> If we prevail, their heads shall pay for it!
> I warrant they have made peace with Bolingbroke.[36]
> (3.2.122–27)

After some initial confusion, Richard learns that he's at least three-quarters wrong: Wiltshire, Bushy, and Green are no Judases, having paid the ultimate price for their affiliation with him. But what about Bagot? Did he, shrewd realist, see which way the *political* winds were blowing—especially with Richard's interests left in the hands of hapless old York—and so opportunely 'make peace with Bolingbroke' (an intention perhaps forming, if not already formed, prior to his confident prediction that these three 'ne'er shall meet again')? And to establish his bona fides with Henry, did he undertake a mission for which he was perfectly suited because well known to 'ever have been near the King'? Namely, to subvert the Welsh army by 'confidentially' revealing to a few supposedly special friends that King Richard has perished in Ireland, knowing full well that this false report would rapidly spread throughout the Welsh ranks?[37] Moreover, what Bagot knew, and thus could testify, concerning 'noble Gloucester's death / Who wrought it with the King, and who performed / The bloody office of his timeless end' (4.1.3–5), would be a valuable bargaining chip. Indeed, might he have entered into collusion with banished Bolingbroke even earlier? For *someone* privy to royal intentions is supplying Henry with accurate intelligence about Richard's movements (cf. 2.1.289–90).[38]

Be that as it may have been, we know that Bagot survives to serve Henry in this other capacity, that of implicating both his royal cousin Aumerle and King Richard himself ('Who wrought it *with the King*') in the death of their uncle Woodstock, Duke of Gloucester (4.1.2–13).[39] Bagot also accuses Aumerle of opposing Bolingbroke's ever returning to England, and even of favouring his death; that this squares with what we earlier witnessed, and with Aumerle's later conspiring, lends credence to Bagot's claims concerning Gloucester (cf. 1.4.6–19). However, for Bagot's accusations to register their full effect, this erstwhile 'caterpillar' must still be seen as one of Richard's men, not as complicit with Henry. And so Henry sustains the appearance of having no earlier connection with Bagot, hence no knowledge of his true whereabouts during the rebellion (note, for example, his reference to 'Bristol Castle, which, *they say*, is held by Bushy, Bagot, and their complices'; 2.3.164–65). As for Henry's declared intention at Bristol next to fight the Welshmen, led by Richard's supporter Owen Glendower (3.1.42–43),[40] this is subsequently vacated by his announcing, 'So that by this intelligence we learn / The Welshmen are dispers'd' (3.3.1–2). Who are we to suppose supplied 'this intelligence' of the Welsh dispersal, a momentous development for which Henry offers no explanation?

The puzzle of the Welsh army's desertion is philosophically important for at least three reasons. First, its solution is essential for a deeper understanding of the *plot* of *Richard II*. As was touched upon in the preface, the challenge of achieving a full understanding of Shakespeare's plots, which are seldom as simple and straightforward as they first seem, is one of the ways he promotes philosophical activity in those readers for whom gaining a clear understanding of things is a priority. Just as the actual workings of political life, however transparent they may initially appear, upon closer examination are often found to be murky and puzzling, so too are the carefully crafted plots of Shakespeare's plays. That is, gaining intellectual clarity in either case requires the exercise of all one's rational powers: of observation, of memory and imagination, of analysis and synthesis. As such, interpreting his plays—determining what is really happening, how, and why—provides practice in that multifaceted activity whereby one may make sense of the world, while simultaneously strengthening through activity those aforementioned rational powers.

Second, and closely related, this puzzle of why the Welshmen think Richard is dead, and thus desert his cause, provides a particularly effective illustration of the general pedagogical principle that Shakespeare shares with Plato. Namely, that the most effective stimulus to philosophic *activity* in people with an aptitude for it is *not* simply curiosity, but *perplexity*, puzzlement, paradoxicality—the famous aporia of Sokrates.[41] Thus, the incorporation of some feature of speech or action, itself more or less unobtrusive, but which once noticed and wondered about is *puzzling*, activates a fresh-eyed reexamination of the entire text in search of clues to its resolution. In the course of such a scrutiny, one will notice things overlooked before or whose significance was unrecognised. For these puzzles—frequently involving some minor character, such as a Bushy, a Bagot, or a Green—may well hold the key to the deeper teaching of the play in which they occur.

Third, the puzzle concerning the abused Welshmen demonstrates an important aspect of Shakespeare's own view of war and politics, namely, his agreement with Machiavelli as to what is required to succeed as a prince, especially as a new prince. One must combine in one's nature the qualities of the lion and the fox, for 'one needs to be a fox to recognise snares and a lion to frighten the wolves. Those who stay simply with the lion do not understand this'. Indeed, 'the one who has known best how to use the fox has come out best. But it is necessary to know well how to color this nature, and to be a great pretender and dissembler'.[42] While basking in the status and privileges of his inherited kingship, Richard speaks as if he were a lion (1.1.174), but is hardly credible in the role. His spiritual frailty in adversity is pitiful, being so wholly reliant upon his followers, and even upon his wife, to stiffen his moral spine (3.2.82–89, 144–60, 186–93, 203–18; 5.1.26–34). Moreover, his spiritual weakness is in no way compensated for by foxlike cunning. For instance, he makes no effort—because he sees no need—to colour with a cosmetic legitimacy his most politically damaging crime (confiscating the Lancastrian estates),[43] and his one attempt at political cleverness (banishing both dangerous Bolingbroke and loyal Mowbray) is peculiarly inept.[44]

Henry is a far more plausible lion. But in order to understand how he manages his almost bloodless usurpation—despite Richard's dire warning that Henry's action will 'open / The purple testament of bleeding war', resulting in 'Ten thousand bloody crowns' bedewing England's pastures 'with faithful English blood' (3.3.94–100)[45]—one must appreciate the vulpine side of his nature, manifested foremost (I suggest) in his using Bagot to engineer the subversion of Richard's Welsh army by a masterly exploitation of the power of words. More precisely, of the power of *false* words, *lies*.[46]

However, as one reviews Bolingbroke's rise from Duke of Hereford to Duke of Lancaster to King Henry IV, one sees that he relied on the skilful use of language all along the way, and *especially* on false or misleading language. There are his punctiliously correct, but questionably sincere, addresses to King Richard, such as preface his rhetorical attack on Mowbray: 'First—heaven be the record to my speech!— / In the devotion of a subject's love, / Tend'ring the precious safety of my prince' (and so on), ending with 'What my tongue speaks my right-drawn sword may prove' (1.1.30–32, 46; cf. 1.3.46–47). And there is the equanimity with which he accepts Richard's exiling him (in marked contrast to Mowbray's protest), delivering a brief speech that—viewed in retrospect—is suffused with irony:

> Your will be done. This must my comfort be:
> That sun that warms you here shall shine on me,
> And those his golden beams to you here lent
> Shall point on me and gild my banishment.
> (1.3.144–47)

And, as noted before, there is the patriotic flavour of the speech with which he takes his public leave from the 'sweet soil' of England, 'My mother and my nurse' (ibid., 306–9).

Especially important is the sustained pretence, repeatedly voiced to friend and foe alike, that the sole reason he returns to England is to claim his rightful inheritance (2.3.112–36; 3.3.31–41, 103–20, 196–99)—a rationale that appeals to a principle which everyone with anything to bequeath or inherit has a personal stake in (cf. 1.3.20; 2.1.189–206, 238–45). As Northumberland puts it, albeit with dubious innocence: 'The noble Duke has sworn his coming is / But for his own; and for the right of that / We all have strongly sworn to give him aid' (2.3.148–50). Whereas we know, because we are privy to Northumberland's telling his confederates, that Henry was already at sea with certain noble friends and 'three thousand men of war' *before* his father had died, hence before there was any Lancastrian inheritance to claim—indeed, that his landing on England's north coast was merely awaiting 'The first departing of the King for Ireland' (2.1.277–90). Subsequently, someone in the know informed Henry of that precipitating event.

As the capstone of Henry's usurpation, there is his wishing aloud that some 'friend' would rid him of his dangerous captive, the deposed Richard, only to publicly repudiate the murderer afterwards (5.6.41–42). For his own part, he expresses in suitably pious terms his deep repentance for the deed, and a resulting intention to undertake a pilgrimage in penitence. Throughout the story, Henry is at pains to practice what Machiavelli emphatically advises: 'A prince should thus take great care that nothing escape his mouth that is not full of . . . five [esteemed] qualities and that, to see him and hear him, he should appear all mercy, all faith, all honesty, all humanity, all religion. And nothing is more necessary to appear to have than this last quality'.[47] From the play's first scene, however, we are provided grounds for suspecting the sincerity of Henry's piety, since he repeatedly invokes divine ratification for the truthfulness of claims we can be sure are false (1.1.30, 38, 187; cf. 1.3.37–41).

In short, throughout the course of his rise and Richard's fall, Henry shows himself to be every bit the accomplished 'pretender and dissembler' that Machiavelli would recommend he be, exploiting for the purpose all the means that language provides. From the time he so graciously accepts his banishment—an appearance easily explicable in retrospect—he in effect enacts the prescription Aumerle recommends to Richard: 'Let's fight with gentle words / Till time lend friends, and friends their helpful swords' (3.3.131–32). Whereupon, Henry's claims and pleas, married with demands and threats—indeed, all of his 'acts of speech'—are effective because backed by the credible force of his friends and their helpful swords.

Given the peculiar emphasis on language and related themes woven into the text of *Richard II* (e.g., names, rhetoric, flattery, honesty, vows), the challenge presented to the reader is not merely that of seeing their special bearing on the plot, but also on what is presumably the primary philosophical problem that the play explores: what we moderns are accustomed to call 'political legitimacy'.[48] Within the drama, this is the question that divides the various critics of Richard's reign.

There are those who, like the old dukes Lancaster and York, are prepared to endure it regardless, sharing in Richard's own belief that he rules as 'God's substitute, / His deputy anointed in His sight' (1.2.37–43; cf. 2.3.96; 3.2.27–62, 98–101; 3.3.9, 74–81; 4.1.126–28), and who are accordingly fearful of the turmoil that will be unleashed, whether by God or man, should any radical action be taken against him. Shakespeare's readers' awareness that these fears are only too justified—that Richard's deposition begins a century of civil strife, culminating in the Wars of the Roses and their troubled aftermath—lends special poignancy to the various characters' jeremiads (2.2.98–99; 2.3.140–45; 3.3.85–100; 4.1.137–50).

But there are also those, such as Bolingbroke and Northumberland, who are prepared to take matters into their own hands regardless. Whether so fearful of the existing or threatening evils implicit in continued submission to Richard's government (2.1.241–45, 263–69), or so tantalized by the personal opportunities offered through active resistance to it (2.3.45–50, 65–67; 5.6.11–18; cf. 5.1.55–68), or—as is most likely—some combination thereof, they are prepared to risk the adverse, even possibly calamitous consequences of undermining irremediably this vital prerequisite of their polity's health: its solidly established standard of legitimacy.

The idea of political legitimacy, however, is inherently problematic due to its comprising two distinguishable components which are only tenuously related, rendering it not simply, nor even primarily, a rational matter—as Shakespeare makes clear in *Richard II*. We can call one component *subjective*, since it consists of the *recognition* in the minds of the Ruled that their Rulers have a *right* to rule, whether or not one approves of how they govern. The other, then, is *objective*, being whatever qualities rational analysis discloses are required for a ruler to rule *well*, to be a *good* ruler. Viewed rationally, only a ruler who manifested these qualities to a sufficient degree would be objectively legitimate, and so (in turn) *ought* to be recognised as having a right to rule.

These objective criteria that would subjectively satisfy a rational person—including the rational man par excellence: the philosopher—are derivable from the ruling task itself. The most *truly* legitimate rulers are those possessing the qualities requisite to best fulfilling the responsibilities of political rule, namely, to administer justice, to make and enforce laws and policies that serve the common good, and to protect the polity from both internal and external threats. Hence they must be the strongest, most prudent, and most patriotic citizens, not distinguishing their own good from the common good, thus willing as well as able to rule.[49] But the philosopher's criteria, derived strictly from what ruling *well* requires, will not suffice for people in general. For these criteria in effect treat the question of *legitimacy* as answered upon first answering the practically most important question of political justice: *who ought to rule*, and thereby impart a specific character to a polity's whole way of life. These questions are *not* equivalent, but it takes some pondering to grasp why so, and (consequently) to consider the diverse implications of that fact.

To begin with, there is a profound difference between the philosopher's perspective on the question of who ought to rule and that of almost everyone else, and this difference clearly shows itself in the diverse way this 'ought' is interpreted. Most people treat the 'ought' as if it meant who *deserves* the *privilege* of ruling—as if ruling were on balance a *reward*, something good or beneficial for whoever rules, hence personally desirable. Such people, the vast majority, presume that this is simply obvious, given their view of human nature: that practically everyone is practically always motivated primarily by selfish desires, which are better served by being a ruler than by being among the ruled. Whereas the philosopher treats that same 'ought' as meaning who should be *obliged* to rule, as if ruling were a burden that one would personally prefer to avoid, given the existence of others that could and would do the job as well.[50]

Thus, for the philosopher the question of *desert* is 'in principle' irrelevant, since ruling a polity in accordance with natural standards of *just* rule is *not* personally rewarding (except, perhaps, insofar as it strengthens through exercise a ruler's own virtue). Consequently, the various alleged grounds of desert that have some natural appeal—such as the diverse kinds of service or material contributions to the polity, or exemplary personal qualities such as honesty or courage or piety, as well as lesser claims grounded in desire or fear or sheer popularity—are similarly irrelevant.[51] In deference to practicalities, one might add that positions of political rule are typically attended by honour; and without question, most people value honour (status, respect, admiration), even if it comes mingled with envy or resentment. But the very best people do not accord much *intrinsic* value to public honouring given the qualities of the judgments of those who bestow it, though being admired or revered has some instrumental value for the tasks of ruling itself.[52]

However, these radically divergent assessments as to the personal desirability of exercising political rule are not the main problem with the philosopher's objective criteria of legitimacy. Even more important is the fact that they require some considerable philosophical understanding to *accept* them (i.e., subjectively) as definitive, and a trained prudential judgment to *apply* them in particular cases. Whereas, practically speaking, a ruler's legitimacy requires that the criteria indicating it, if not actually conferring it, be quite broadly accepted, subjectively, by those they rule. But for such 'acceptance' to matter, it is imperative that these criteria be easily *recognised* and *applied* by the many ruled. For this is the practical significance of political legitimacy: it facilitates civil peace and stability by obviating the most dangerous *threat* to civil peace, namely, quarrels over who ought to rule.[53]

As a practical matter, then, the subjective recognition of legitimacy in the minds of the ruled must be conceded priority over whatever objective criteria might be disclosed by a strictly rational analysis of what ruling *well* requires.[54] And insofar as these rational criteria do not of themselves generate the necessary subjective consensus (though a shadow or reflection of them is formally present in virtually everyone's own conception of a *good* ruler), some other criterion of legitimacy—something credible as conveying a right to rule, yet readily recognisable by all who are expected to acknowledge and respect it—must serve instead. This need raise no difficulties provided there is some simple criterion that reliably correlates, at least approximately and usually, with the philosopher's objective criteria. But apparently there is not. Herein, then, lies the problem intrinsic to the very idea of political legitimacy: in the interests of civil peace and stability, the *right* to rule, legitimacy, is necessarily treated as separate from *good* rule, and moreover granted absolute priority—justifiably so, inasmuch as the breakdown of civil order threatens everyone with regressing to an existence that is solitary, poor, nasty, brutish, and short.[55]

But though subordinated, the concern for good rule, for rule that is both competent and just (however controversial the judging of such qualities may be), never goes away. Thus, the *tension* between these two claims on subjects' allegiance—the *right* to rule versus *good* rule—remains a potential source of civil discord (implicit in old York's plaintive, 'How long shall I be patient? Ah, how long / Shall tender duty make me suffer wrong?' 2.1.163–64). Consequently, should the discrepancy between people's conception of good governance and their perception of their ruler's actual governance become great enough, some people (often including, importantly, men motivated more by public spiritedness than by personal gain) are apt to challenge that ruler's continuing 'right' to rule, regardless of his admitted legitimacy. They will be opposed, however, not only by that ruler's supporters but also by those who remain steadfast in respecting the claims of legitimacy ahead of all other considerations.

The problem comes more clearly into focus when one considers a *change* in rulers. The concern is that whoever succeeds a legitimate ruler be himself regarded as legitimate 'from day one', as it were, thereby ensuring a *peaceful transition* through what is inherently a politically hazardous period—and one which periodically must recur, men being mortal. Again deferring to practicalities, the legitimate successor will necessarily be he who succeeds to power in accordance with whatever criteria, that is, whatever principles and procedures, are generally recognised within a given polity as the prerequisites, if not the very source, of subjective legitimacy.

Whatever the legitimating principles and procedures may be, they in turn tend to gain in credence, in 'legitimacy' themselves, with use; the longer they are in place and serve their purpose, the more solidly they become established in people's minds as 'the right way'. And, correspondingly, the more suspect will alternative claims be regarded. Hence the great importance of *Time* in 'legitimating' a polity's established principle(s)—and, accordingly, the significance of the word's prominence in this play (forty-five occurrences), a point I shall expand upon presently. And thus the role of tradition in bestowing legitimacy, strengthened by the psychical effects of legal forms (cf. 3.3.74; 4.1.223–24, 273), ceremonies (such as coronations and jubilees; 4.1.319–20), manners (such as bowing or kneeling before the sovereign; 1.3.46–47; 3.3.35–41, 72–76, 187–93; 4.1.165–66), engagements of personal honour (pledges of allegiance, vows of obedience; 1.3.19–20, 178–92; 5.2.39–40), symbols (such as crown and sceptre; 1.1.118, 3.3.80, 4.1.181–83), modes of respectful address (such as titles; 3.3.7–9; cf. 5.2.41–43)—none of which work on a strictly rational basis, yet nonetheless serve the purpose, perhaps all the better for their being somehow endowed with an inexplicable mystique.

Many of these formalities, notice, rely crucially on *linguistic formulae*, which, along with names and titles, may become invested with almost totemic powers. We are reminded of both their importance and their insubstantial, not to say ephemeral, nature by Richard's eloquent expression of despair when he returns from Ireland and learns that all is lost:

> For within the hollow crown
> That rounds the mortal temples of a king
> Keeps Death his court; and there the antic sits,
> Scoffing his state and grinning at his pomp,
> Allowing him a breath, a little scene,
> To monarchize, be feared and kill with looks,
> Infusing him with self and vain conceit,
> As if this flesh which walls about our life
> Were brass impregnable; and humoured thus,
> Comes at last and with a little pin
> Bores through his castle wall, and farewell, king!
> Cover your heads, and mock not flesh and blood
> With solemn reverence. Throw away respect,
> Tradition, form and ceremonious duty,
> For you have mistook me all this while.
> I live with bread like you, feel want,
> Taste grief, need friends. Subjected thus,
> How can you say to me I am a king?
> (3.2.160–77)

We here witness Richard's dawning realization that however effective various 'time-honoured' conventions and devices may be in instilling, sustaining, and reinforcing people's subjective sense of legitimacy, the danger lurking in the very idea of 'legitimate rule' remains: its practical and conceptual separation from—hence possible conflict with—altogether competent, *good* rule.

This much and more is borne out by the particular case of King Richard's reign and deposition as Shakespeare depicts it. Judging the evidence by the philosopher's rational criteria, Henry Bolingbroke would make a far more suitable ruler than does Richard, and as such is objectively more legitimate. And this assessment is in no way refuted by the fact that Henry's subsequent reign is a tumultuous one (again, as Shakespeare presents it, more or less accurately, in this and the following two plays of the tetralogy). For Henry's problems stem in large part from his being widely *regarded*—i.e., subjectively—as *illegitimate*; hence, he is castigated as a usurper of sovereign power. Seen as having displaced its rightful possessor and seized the throne simply by force, running roughshod over the established principle of legitimacy, he is the more vulnerable to challenge by ambitious rivals who, regardless of what they themselves believe, are free to cloak their actions in the rhetoric of opposition to his usurpation.[56]

Thus, *Richard II* implicitly teaches, and the balance of the *Henriad* confirms, that as a matter of practicality, subjective legitimacy—whatever its arational, irrational, subrational, or allegedly suprarational basis—necessarily has priority over rational, objective requisites of superior rulership. And that, as a consequence, political life is fundamentally flawed by the permanent tension between political legitimacy and political excellence, between what is conventionally right and what is naturally good. Moreover, whatever is gained by strengthening one desideratum is necessarily at the expense of the other. Taken together, these facts amount to an incorrigible limitation on the justness and rational coherence of political life: every conceivable arrangement is a compromise.[57]

In particular, the support imparted to legitimacy (and through it civil peace and stability) by the doctrine of divine right comes at a heavy price, since, strictly interpreted, it exposes the polity to the worst excesses of tyrannical rule without allowing for any forms of justifiable resistance, much less of changing rulers be they ever so inept, weak, corrupt, or cruel.[58] For according to this view, to subject God's choice of ruler to merely human judgment implicitly impugns both God's omniscience and omnipotence, as if God makes mistakes, or lacks the power to remove an earthly deputy who displeases *Him*; after all, He may confer a bad ruler upon a people as punishment for their sins (cf. 1.2.4–8, 4.1.118–34). Treating legitimacy as practically absolute, such a doctrine (presuming it is sincerely believed by a sufficiently numerous portion of the ruled) permits no actions that challenge a legitimate ruler directly. Hence the standard tactic of blaming malfeasance, not on the ruler, but on those underlings upon whom he relies. As Northumberland expresses it, 'The King is not himself, but basely led / By flatterers' (2.1.241–42). Bolingbroke similarly pretends that his actions aim only at 'the caterpillars of the commonwealth', which he has 'sworn to weed and pluck away' (2.3.166–67). Still, it must be conceded that God Himself does sometimes withdraw the 'Mandate of Heaven' from His duly anointed deputy, but there is no way for people to determine whether this has occurred other than ex post facto: when the rare rebellions even more rarely succeed. It is out of some such belief that the pious old Duke of York pragmatically interprets Henry's easy victory over Richard: 'But heaven hath a hand in these events, / To whose high will we bound our calm contents. / To Bolingbroke are we sworn subjects now, / Whose state and honour I for aye allow' (5.2.37–40).

Rebellion, then, is in effect an unauthorized trial by combat on a grand scale, but based on the same presumption: that God determines the outcome (as the Marshal proclaims prior to the aborted showdown between Henry and Mowbray: 'and God defend the right!'; 1.3.101). However, open rebellion risks not merely the lives of a pair of combatants who willingly engage in a mortal contest that is both brief and decisive, but the lives and property of virtually everyone in the polity (the vast majority of whom would prefer to be left to live in peace), and does so in a struggle of uncertain scale, duration, and finality. Whereas this is precisely what firmly established principles of legitimacy are meant to avoid.[59]

Probing beneath the doctrine of divine right,[60] as surely Shakespeare invites us to do, it is hard to avoid suspecting that, as a practical matter, its acceptance has little to do with divine revelations. True, one can argue that the political form implicitly endorsed throughout Scripture is that of kingship—or more generally, monarchy, bearing in mind the importance of patriarchy in the Old Testament, and that the political context of the New is the regime of the Caesars. Moreover, whatever biblical precedent one might defer to, genealogy matters. But the belief that *Christian* kings rule as God's deputy by virtue of a divine appointment owes more to the post-Constantine development of Church dogma than it does to Scripture. In any event, this doctrine of legitimacy by divine right is more complex than merely prescribing monarchy, as it must be in order to specify, clearly and immediately, a particular individual as the rightful ruler or successor. Thus the importance, first, not simply of genealogy, but of a genealogy divinely blessed: it is by virtue of descent from a supposedly *sacred bloodline* that particular individuals are eligible to assume the mantle of legitimacy. Both King Richard (quite explicitly) and his usurper (a bit less so, but unmistakably) invoke their lineage in justifying a right to sovereignty.

Mowbray is the first to mention this material medium whereby legal supremacy is conveyed, referring to Bolingbroke's 'high blood's royalty' (hence kinship to the King) as the reason he feels obliged to temper his response to the Royal Duke's accusation. Henry's rejoinder affirms his special status, even as he purports to 'lay aside [his] high blood's royalty' for the purpose of challenging Mowbray. Richard, however, subtly puts some distance between him and his cousin, speaking of merely a 'neighbour *nearness* to our sacred blood' (1.1.58–59, 70–71, 119)—though later, embracing Bolingbroke prior to the trial by combat, he affirms the normal view: 'Farewell my blood, which if today thou shed [etc.]' (1.3.57). When Woodstock's widow seeks to move old John of Gaunt to avenge her husband's murder, the *divinity* of their common lineage figures prominently: 'Edward's seven sons, whereof thyself art one, / Were as seven vials of his sacred blood': 'But Thomas, . . . / One vial full of Edward's sacred blood, / . . . / Is cracked, and all the precious liquor spilt' (1.2.11–19).[61]

In his embassage from Duke Henry to King Richard ensconced at Flint Castle, Northumberland is careful to emphasize the common descent of the two cousins:

> Thy thrice-noble cousin,
> Harry Bolingbroke, doth humbly kiss thy hand;
> And by the honourable tomb he swears
> That stands upon your royal grandsire's bones,
> And by the royalties of both your bloods—
> Currents that spring from one most gracious head— [etc.]
> (3.3.103–8)

Having assassinated a surprisingly vigorous Richard, Exton attests to how strong can be the hold on men's minds of a common belief in the unique status of a certain bloodline, worrying aloud, 'As full of valour as of royal blood! / Both have I spilled. O, would the deed were good! / For now the devil that told me I did well / Says that this deed is chronicled in hell' (5.5.113–16).

However, as noted before, being graced with sacred royal blood is but a necessary condition of inheriting the sovereignty according to divine right doctrine; it is not in itself sufficient, as it does not designate who in particular of those who share this 'precious liquor' is the chosen one. Thus the blood requirement must be supplemented by a second principle, such as primogeniture, which synthesizes two important principles of natural justice, each having some broad appeal, hence regularly invoked in everyday life: 'the right of first-comer',[62] and 'the right to bequeath and inherit'. As applied to political succession, the principle of primogeniture is (usually) unproblematic,[63] not least because it operates—for better or worse—without regard for the designated individual's personal qualities, much less any actual performance in office. In addition to its natural appeal, primogeniture has the practical advantage that the legitimate heir is known from the moment the first viable child/son is born, who can then be treated and trained accordingly.

But the rightness of primogeniture is not so self-evident as to preclude alternative arrangements, whereas its liabilities are sufficiently self-evident to enhance the attractiveness of those alternatives. First and foremost, it makes no allowance for the actual fitness of the designated heir, who may be sickly of body (as was Edward VI, the short-lived son of Henry VIII), of weak mind (as was Henry VI, the rather simple and later deranged son of Henry V), or of weak spirit (as was Richard, though also born of a great warrior prince). A second problem is the frequency with which the Crown may descend upon a child (as it did upon the ten-year-old Richard), even upon an infant (as in the case of Henry VI), requiring that a regency be established. And lacking a clear rule determining who shall be Regent, the competition among rivals exposes the polity to the very power struggle that a settled principle of legitimacy is supposed to avoid (as was the situation in England throughout much of the reign of Henry VI, culminating in the infamous Wars of the Roses). Equally worrisome is the possibility that a regent might exploit his prerogatives to somehow usurp the sovereignty for himself (as did Richard III).[64] For these and other such reasons, even in monarchies where the heir must be of a certain bloodline, primogeniture is not universal.

As for polities in which primogeniture does operate in conjunction with genealogy, one may doubt that its broad acceptance is due to divine sanction so much as to time. Not for nothing are the first words of the play, '*Old John of Gaunt, time-honoured Lancaster*'. Indeed, it is reasonable to suspect that not only a popular belief in divine right—but equally in any alternative authorization of a right to rule that continues to command people's allegiance—owes more to its being 'time-honoured' than it does to a faith in revelation, reason, or any other ostensible authority. Or at least one might suspect this to be Shakespeare's view, given the prominence of various characters' reflections on time, as well as the crucial role of 'timing' in determining the course of the plot.

The practical importance of time shows itself most obviously—and often more or less immediately, and crucially—in the consequences of the temporal relationships among events. With that in mind, it is worth noting how many examples of timing, and mistiming, bear significantly on King Richard's story. First, there is his bizarre halting of Henry and Mowbray's long-scheduled trial by combat at the very instant it commences, substituting in its place unequal periods of banishment for the principals. Then there is the indecent haste with which Richard moves to confiscate the vast Lancastrian estate, aggravating the offensiveness of the expropriation itself. The body of the old duke is not even cold before Richard, citing as justification the anticipated expense of his Irish campaign—though no doubt welcoming the opportunity to emasculate the power of England's richest family—announces the seizure of all Lancaster property (2.1.160–62). This outrage, which Richard's impious manner only amplifies, overcomes the patience of even pliant old York, whose rebuke and warning point directly to the practical basis of the king's legitimacy:

> Take Hereford's rights away, and take from Time
> His charters and his customary rights;
> Let not tomorrow then ensue today;
> Be not thyself, for how art thou a king
> But by fair sequence and succession?
> (Ibid., 195–99)

The old Duke of York may be no bright light, but he speaks the practical truth: 'how art thou a king' other than by the time-honoured custom of 'fair sequence and succession'?

Of special significance is the urgency of the Irish expedition, which Green impresses upon Richard: 'Now for the rebels which stand out in Ireland, / Expedient manage must be made, my liege, / Ere further leisure yield them further means / For their advantage and your highness' loss' (1.4.38–41). Richard accedes to the need for haste (cf. 2.2.43–45). However, his forces no sooner sail for Ireland than Bolingbroke returns to England. According to the suspiciously well-informed Northumberland—and why *is* he already at ailing Gaunt's residence when the King and his retinue arrive? (2.1.147)—this was no coincidence, as Harry and several noble friends, along with a small army, were already at sea, awaiting only the King's departure for Ireland to land in England (ibid., 288–91).[65]

The most critical event bearing upon Richard's fate, however, is that which has already been discussed: his tardy *return* from Ireland. As the dispirited Salisbury reports, 'One day too late, I fear me, noble lord, / Hath clouded all thy happy days on earth. / O, call back yesterday, bid Time return' (3.2.67–69). Salisbury's pessimism infects Richard, who immediately despairs, 'All souls that will be safe, fly from my side, / For Time hath set a blot upon my pride'. But as 'Old time-honoured Lancaster' had earlier reminded Richard, a king can no more 'call back yesterday' than can anyone else, nor retard time's determined consequences for mortal beings:

> I thank my liege that in regard of me
> He shortens four years of my son's exile.
> But little vantage shall I reap thereby,
> Fore ere the six years that he hath to spend
> Can change their moons and bring their times about,
> My oil-dried lamp and time-bewasted light
> Shall be extinct with age and endless night.

Richard politely protests, 'Why uncle, thou hast many years to live'. To which Gaunt drily replies:

> But not a minute, King, that thou canst give.
> Shorten my days thou canst with sullen sorrow,
> And pluck nights from me, but not lend a morrow.
> Thou canst help Time to furrow me with age,
> But stop no wrinkle in his pilgrimage.
>
> (1.3.216–30)

Of course, it is only because human beings are self-conscious of their mortality that time acquires the significance that it has, aware as we are from childhood that we are fated to age and eventually die within a matter of decades. We're apt to chafe at our time being 'wasted'. Were men immortal, or even just blessed—or cursed—with Old Testament life-spans, the burden of Bolingbroke's and Mowbray's respective banishments would change profoundly. It would lighten Henry's, whereas Mowbray would likely find the 'speechless death' of his lifetime ban only that much more oppressive. As it is, Bolingbroke's lamenting that 'grief makes one hour ten' reminds us of the *subjective* aspect of time: how the sensation of its passing is *felt* differently according to one's circumstances. There are some situations in which time seems to drag 'insufferably', others in which it passes all too quickly.

But time works less conscious effects on the human soul, notably that which is most pertinent to the philosophical problem at the heart of this play: it tends to endow long-established practices and arrangements with a status akin to whatever is *natural*. And insofar as Nature is regarded as God's handiwork, time can even impart a sense of divine approval to such things. Rationally considered, of course, 'old, time-honoured' is analytically distinct from 'divinely sanctioned'. But in practice these two run together well enough to be conflated, given the belief that God could readily change whatever does not suit Him. And if He has not done so over hundreds of years, it is not unreasonable to conclude He is well enough pleased. Thus, it is not merely the fact that Richard himself has been 'Anointed, crowned, planted many years' (as Bishop Carlisle reminds those assembled to witness his deposition; 4.1.128), but that he can trace his 'legitimacy' over the course of three and a half centuries, as the undisputed heir of William I via the intervening ten kings—the last, as it turns out, who can do so. Any reservation on his claim derived from the fact that it *originates* with a man known to history as William *the Conqueror* has long since been occulted by the passage of time.

In light of the manifold ways that time has had a bearing on Richard's reign, it is hardly surprising that it figures prominently in the melancholic reflections that Shakespeare provides him as captive at Pomfret Castle.

> Music do I hear?
> Ha, ha, keep time! How sour sweet music is
> When time is broke and no proportion kept!
> So is it in the music of men's lives.
> And here have I the daintiness of ear
> To check time broke in a disordered string,
> But for the concord of my state and time
> Had not an ear to hear my true time broke.

I wasted time, and now doth Time waste me;
For now hath Time made me his numb'ring clock.
(5.5.41–50)

As the fate of Shakespeare's Richard attests, time's power over people's souls is not to be slighted. Sad for him, he recognises only belatedly that, as a practical matter, there is indeed 'an appointed time . . . to every purpose under the heaven', and that (accordingly) success in this world often depends on being 'in tune with Time'.[66] For the basic fact remains: however firmly time would seem to have ratified the legitimacy of an institutional arrangement, it may not be sufficient to save the throne of an utterly inept ruler, nor to preserve a profoundly defective institution. Still, it surely works against prospective usurpers, and is an obstacle for whoever would introduce 'new modes and orders'.

What alternative doctrines are there that might provide a credible basis for a *right* to rule? The most obvious candidate is what in practice so often determines the matter: natural force, strength—or as it came to be called, the Right of Conquest. Richard himself points to this basis with his sardonic rejoinder to Henry's professed offer of such service as will deserve the doomed King's love: 'Well you deserve. They well deserve to have / That know the strong'st and surest way to get! / . . . / What you will have, I'll give, and willing too; / For do we must what force will have us do' (3.3.200–207). It bears emphasizing, however, that on this view the *fact* of conquest—not as a divine judgment, but in itself—carries a *moral* implication: the conqueror has the *right* to rule the conquered, who *ought* to concede that right, and so *willingly* obey in return for their lives being spared.[67]

Moreover, the justification for this view is also obvious: Nature. The whole natural order apart from man attests to the fact that the strong prevail and the weak submit, suggesting that such an arrangement is *naturally right*. And is not man, for all of his rational powers, nonetheless also a natural being? To be sure, those who wish can construe this doctrine as 'divinely ordained' insofar as Nature is understood more or less as Hobbes and his ilk would have us understand it, namely, as 'the Art whereby God hath made and governes the World'.[68] But there is a radical difference in the two doctrines' respective authorities: revelation in the case of divine right; natural reason brought to bear on the observable facts of nature (i.e., 'science') in the case of what might be called the 'Natural Right of Might'.[69]

The problem with this doctrine is equally obvious: it cannot guarantee the longed-for civil peace and stability, since the supposed legitimacy of an established sovereign is perpetually open to challenge by whoever can claim to be stronger still, and is willing to put his claim to the test. Shakespeare has his Richard point to this implication as well.

> Northumberland, thou ladder wherewithal
> The mounting Bolingbroke ascends my throne,
> The time shall not be many hours of age
> More than it is ere foul sin, gathering head,
> Shall break into corruption. Thou shalt think
> Though he divide the realm and give thee half
> It is too little, helping him to all.
> He shall think that thou, which knowst the way
> To plant unrightful kings, wilt know again,
> Being ne'er so little urged, another way
> To pluck him headlong from the usurped throne.
> (5.1.55–65)

There is, however, a further alternative to both divine right and the Right of Conquest/might, albeit barely hinted at in the play: that legitimacy could be bestowed upon rulers by the *will* of those they rule. Although Henry attempts to legitimate his ascension by posing as Richard's designated heir, and so preserve the appearance that the established mode and order remain unchanged (thus his 'In God's name I'll ascend the regal throne'; 4.1.114; cf. 109–10), he as well as Northumberland would prefer that 'The commons ... be satisfied' (ibid., 272)—that his ascension be, in effect, *ratified* by Parliament.[70]

The anabasis of Richard is manifested in his changing view of his own kingship. He comes to power believing in what will subsequently be termed 'divine right'. Provided the belief that he rules as 'God's substitute' (1.2.37) is widely shared, and universally acknowledged—that he is indeed 'the deputy elected by the Lord' (3.2.57), the very 'figure of God's majesty, / His captain, steward, deputy elect' (4.1.126–27)—this may well be the strongest source of subjective legitimacy conceivable. For what is ordered or offered in a king's name is, accordingly, understood as being so in God's as well, their divine relationship being verbally reaffirmed every time any variation on the formula 'In the name of God and the King' is invoked (1.3.11, 20, 24, 40, 105, 108, 114; cf. 4.1.112–13). Seeing himself as the choice of God by virtue of his genealogy, Richard is sure 'Not all the water in the rough rude sea / Can wash the balm off from an anointed king', nor 'the breath of worldly men' depose him (3.2.54–57). Moreover, as God's agent, he presumes he enjoys some divine protection, that 'God omnipotent' will protect His own, as the bishop of Carlisle reminds him at Harlech: 'That Power that made you king / Hath power to keep you king in spite of all' (3.2.27–28; cf. 60–62; 3.3.85–90, 101). That this is an arrangement devoutly to be wished by one and all is attested by the standard verbal formula Richard has doubtless heard ten thousand times: 'God save the King' (cf. 4.1.173, 175, 220). On this view, then, rebellion is not merely a crime backed by awful punishment in this world, but a *mortal sin* that endangers one's immortal soul for all eternity, being a breach of faith with God (3.2.51–53, 100–101; 3.3.16–19). This is to endow legitimacy with, arguably, the most potent sanction imaginable.[71]

In the course of the play, however, Richard's understanding of himself, and of the basis on which a king rules, undergoes a profound change, indicative of his ascent from conventional opinions to something more akin to philosophical insight. It would be much too much to say that he is transformed from a mere king into a philosopher, but he does reveal—alas, belatedly—a reflective capacity that, had it been activated earlier, would have served him well as both king and man. For he comes to have thoughts worthy of the magnificent poetic talent Shakespeare has bestowed upon him, unmatched by anything the philosopher-poet provides Bolingbroke. This, it would seem, is the real tragedy of Richard the man: that it took a fall from the highest heights to the lowest depths to awaken what was best in himself. But in this respect, his is an all-too-human story: that so often it takes profound suffering to make one 'philosophical'.

Richard's enlightenment seems to grow as his resignation deepens. In the wake of the first untoward news (the Welsh desertions), he expresses a patient acceptance of whatever may come—almost surely more than he actually feels—while still holding to his orthodox view of legitimate kingship: 'Mine ear is open and my heart prepared. / The worst is worldly loss thou canst unfold. / Say, is my kingdom lost? Why, 'twas my care; / And what loss is it to be rid of care?" (3.2.93–96). But his recovery of spirit is short-lived. The next jolt of bad news precipitates an open meditation on graves, worms, epitaphs, wills, and 'sad stories of the death of kings'. Whether this reflects the dawning of a new suspicion, or the surfacing of doubts secretly brooded on before, Richard now reveals a surprising realism about monarchy: his crown is 'hollow'; death awaits him just as it does every other mortal; pomp and ceremony merely infuse a 'vain conceit'. Thus he bids those with him at Harlech: 'Cover your heads, and mock not flesh and blood / With solemn reverence; throw away respect [etc.]' (ibid., 171–72). Conspicuous by its absence now is any reference to God, or to the sanctity of kingship. And supplanting his presumption that royalty elevated him far above the rest of humanity is an emphasis on his sharing mankind's common limitations ('I live with bread like you, feel want, / Taste grief, need friends [etc.]').

When finally brought face to face with Henry, 'In the base court . . . where kings grow base' (3.3.180), Richard's melancholic irony expresses a larger political truth than perhaps he realizes: kingship per se has been diminished, debased. Yet he steadfastly refuses to play his part in sustaining Bolingbroke's pretence that he seeks only his rightful Lancastrian inheritance ('My gracious lord, I come but for mine own'). Instead, Richard insists upon speaking the truth openly: 'Your own is yours, and I am yours and all'. Shrewd Henry, better appreciating the political importance of appearances, nonetheless plays on, modestly insisting, 'So far be mine, my most redoubted lord, / As my true service shall deserve your love'. Richard responds with the Florentine realism previously quoted ('Well you deserve. They well deserve to have / That know the strong'st and surest way to get').[72]

To the extent that one accords any sincerity to Richard's words, one must conclude that his view of legitimacy—of who rightly *deserves* to rule—has undergone a profound transformation. That right is grounded ultimately, not in conventional indications and fanciful attributions of divine will, but in real power.[73] Customs and other trappings can augment and amplify the political efficacy of superior power, but they are not an adequate substitute for it, nor (consequently) can they compensate for continuing gross deficiencies in the quality of government. Regardless of their analytical distinctiveness, one's *right* to rule cannot in practice be utterly divorced from one's *ability* to rule, which is necessarily made manifest in the course of actually ruling.

Facing the truth about political legitimacy is but one indication of Richard's anabasis. The other is his coming to terms with the truth about himself.[74] This is revealed mainly in the play's only soliloquy, that of Richard during his final hour in prison. It is a meditation redolent of the most fundamental text in all of philosophic literature, Plato's inexhaustible *Republic*. Shakespeare's Richard begins with an allusion to the most renowned image of that dialogue, indeed in all of philosophy, Sokrates' Allegory of the Cave: 'I have been studying how I may compare / This prison where I live unto the world' (5.5.1–2; cf. Plato, *Republic*, 514b, 517b, 529c–d). His effort to become androgynous—'My brain I'll prove the female to my soul, / My soul the father'—exemplifies the essential teaching of the 'first wave' of Sokrates's 'feminine drama' of book 5 as applied to the individual soul: that the philosopher must synthesize within himself the psychic powers of both male and female natures (ibid., 451c, 457b). And Richard's intention to produce thereby fertile thoughts, viable 'brain-children' to populate his mental world—'and these two beget / A generation of still-breeding thoughts, / And these same thoughts people this little world'—similarly exemplifies the psychic implications of the second wave.[75] Like Plato in order to compose his dialogues and Shakespeare his dramas, so Richard proposes, 'Thus play I in one person many people', adding according to his own observation, 'And none contented': neither the sincerely Pious, troubled by the inconsistencies of supposed revelations; nor the Ambitious, animated by aspirations doomed to be frustrated; nor the indifferent

Many, who seek comfort from their sheer ordinariness. Something like this dialectical comparing of a variety of archetypal partial perspectives is the prerequisite of synthesizing an adequate synoptic view of the world—a seasoned capacity for which practically defines a political philosopher (cf. ibid., 534b, 537c, 398a–b).

What is perhaps most significant about Richard's prison soliloquy is his observing, 'how sour sweet music is / When time is broke and no proportion kept! / So it is in the music of men's lives' (5.5.42–44).[76] For Shakespeare thereby points more or less directly to the *Republic*'s teaching about justice, that its natural ground is the harmonious soul, with its three major parts, 'just like three notes in an harmonic scale', working well together, such that a person becomes 'entirely one from a plurality, moderate and harmonized' (443d–e).[77]

Chapter Two

A Punishing of Mistreadings

The Turbulent Reign of King Henry IV Proceeds

> The Kingdome of God is gotten by violence: but what if it could be gotten by unjust violence? were it against Reason so to get it, when it is impossible to receive hurt by it? and if it be not against Reason, it is not against Justice: or else Justice is not to be approved for good. From such reasoning as this, Successfull wickednesse hath attained the name of Vertue: and some that in all other things have disallowed the violation of Faith; yet have allowed it, when it is for the getting of a Kingdome. . . . This specious reasoning is nevertheless false.
> —Hobbes, *Leviathan*, chap. 15, para. 4

The eponym of the two plays bearing the title *King Henry IV* is not in fact the principal focus of these dramas. This is a bit puzzling. After all, it is not as if Henry IV was merely a cipher in the turbulent events of his reign, or the pawn of more powerful and active men (as one might reasonably say about his grandson, Henry VI). Rather, as Shakespeare showed in *Richard II*, Henry Bolingbroke was a strong, popular, ambitious, talented, and vastly experienced nobleman capable of seizing for himself the Crown of England. Nor was the period of his rule one in which nothing of consequence happened. Had our philosopher-poet wished to, he could have woven an entertaining and instructive tapestry in which this Henry was the central commanding figure. He declined to do so. Instead, he used the father's reign as mainly the backdrop for a largely mythic portrayal of the son who will succeed him, and thereafter become England's most glorious warrior king, Henry V. 'Mythic', in that Shakespeare's portrayal of Prince Hal prior to his succession as a profligate young 'wanton' whose preferred associates are a motley collection of London's lowlife is pure invention. One companion in particular would seem scarcely credible as the crony of a Crown Prince: the immortal Falstaff, universally acknowledged to be a preeminent example of Shakespeare's creative genius.[1]

The resulting entertainment value of the fictitious relationship between lithe young Prince Hal and fat old Sir John, which practically dominates the two *Henry IV* plays, might seem to justify quite amply whatever poetic license Shakespeare took with the historical record regarding the early life of England's most celebrated warlord. Still, the *scale* of the liberties he took in this case is so extensive, and make the man's subsequent success as king so perplexing, as to raise the suspicion of some ulterior purpose being served. But to appreciate fully the puzzle posed by Shakespeare's portrayal requires a summary review of modern historians' accounts of the younger Henry's life prior to his acceding to the kingship.

The Man who would be King Henry V was born at Monmouth Castle in either August or September of either 1386 or 1387; historians have not been able to agree.[2] The year matters to some extent: just how prodigious was this youth who on the Ides of October 1399 was declared Prince of Wales, Duke of Cornwall, and Earl of Chester? For in his case, the responsibility for ruling Wales was neither nominal nor uneventful. Throughout the opening decade of the fifteenth century, this ancient Celtic nation— supposedly pacified by the great castle-builder King Edward I, the first to bestow the title Prince of Wales on his heir apparent—was almost continuously in revolt, led by a shrewd and charismatic Welsh nobleman, Owen Glendower (*Owain Glyn Dŵr*). And Prince Hal, consequently, was almost continuously occupied with military operations, of which by his teenage years he was in overall charge, as well as being himself thoroughly blooded in combat.

Henry of Monmouth was not, in fact, his parents' first son. Henry of Bolingbroke was but fourteen years old in 1380 when it was arranged that he marry the heiress Mary Bohun, age twelve (or less).[3] Two years later they had a son who died soon after birth. Then between 1386 (or 1387) and 1394, they had in quick succession four sons—Henry, Thomas, John, and Humphrey—followed by two daughters, Philippa and Blanche. Given her relentless child-bearing, it is hardly surprising that their mother, though but twenty-four years old, died giving birth to the last. Thus at the age of seven or eight, Hal along with his brothers and sisters was left motherless. Though his father was still a young man, he did not remarry for almost another decade, and then only for the usual political reasons that kings found it useful to make some woman their queen. But he had been largely absent throughout much of Hal's childhood in any case (on crusade, travelling to the Holy Land and on the Continent, attending his scattered estates, and involving himself in Crown business). During this time the boy resided with his mother, and after her death mainly with his maternal grandmother (Joan, dowager Countess of Hereford), but also partly with his paternal grandfather, John of Gaunt, Duke of Lancaster. Upon their mother's demise, the children's household was broken up, and they were dispersed to live with various other relatives or retainers. They did, however, all receive a good basic education according to the standards of the day; and with the exception of Thomas, the sons continued in maturity to show a special regard for music, books, and scholars.[4] Later as king, Henry V patronized writers, as had his father; and his two youngest brothers, John and Humphrey, were in their day among the foremost royal patrons of the arts.[5]

In the autumn of 1398, events transpired which would result in young Henry's life taking a wholly unforeseen, and radically consequential, turn. For it was then that his father and Thomas Mowbray met at Coventry for their widely publicized trial by combat ('the social event of the year'),[6] but which King Richard aborted, banishing both men instead. Thus, on the thirteenth of October, Henry Bolingbroke left England for exile, and his eldest son was taken into the King's household, apparently as surety for his father's good behaviour. Less than four months later, Bolingbroke's own father, 'Old John of Gaunt, time-honoured Lancaster', died; whereupon the King seized all the ducal property—violating not only common law and ancient tradition but his own prior authorizations as well. In May of 1399, the King left for Ireland to suppress a rebellion that had begun the previous year with the killing of Roger Mortimer, Earl of March and designated successor of childless Richard. Along with the bulk of his army, the King took with him young Henry and several other sons of nobility.

Richard treated Henry Jr. well, and may have knighted the boy while in Ireland.[7] When he learned of Bolingbroke's rebellion, however, he had Hal and the son of the late Thomas of Woodstock imprisoned in Trim Castle near Dublin. But as soon as Bolingbroke captured Richard, he sent for his son, and the three met in Chester under curious circumstances. According to a source partial to Richard, when young Henry returned from Ireland, he straightaway resumed his attendance on the King, who had gained the boy's affectionate loyalty while his father was in exile. There Bolingbroke found him when he called upon his royal captive.[8] According to the scholar who recounts this episode, 'at the back of the new Prince of Wales' growing estrangement from his father was a boy's ardent loyalty for the King his father deposed and murdered'.[9]

Be that however it may have been, with Henry's seizure of the English Crown, the status of his eldest son changed accordingly. Almost immediately made Prince of Wales[10]—as well as Duke of Lancaster and of Cornwall, Earl of Chester, then shortly thereafter also Duke of Aquitaine (all of which lordships were intended to provide the Prince with the resources needed to fulfill his duties, as well as to live in a manner befitting the heir apparent)—he was soon set to acquiring the practical experience that would prepare him for his future royal responsibilities. His first exposure to military activity came soon enough. In August of 1400, he and a battalion of his Cheshire archers accompanied his father on a punitive expedition into southern Scotland. In the course of returning, the King learned of an uprising in northeastern Wales, led by the English-educated Welsh nobleman Owen Glendower, who had just claimed the title 'Prince of Wales' for himself.

Thus began a decade of Welsh troubles, which occupied the Prince almost continuously until 1408. During that time, young Henry was to see a lot more of Chester, Shrewsbury, Ludlow, Hereford, Leominster, and other border towns than he was of London. At first, he was but nominally in charge of efforts to quell the recurrent outbreaks of rebellion, while being in fact the understudy of experienced military men—Hugh de Despenser, Henry Percy ('Hotspur', more than twenty years Hal's senior), Richard Beauchamp (Earl of Warwick), Sir Thomas Erpingham, Sir John Oldcastle, Thomas Percy (Earl of Worcester), Lord Powys, inter alia. Even so, he took an active part from the first. So, for instance, when rebels captured Conwy Castle in the spring of 1401, the prince participated in Hotspur's successful siege to recapture it. Henry was to learn much about siege warfare from his Welsh experiences. Soon after the Conwy action, King Henry officially indicated that although he had placed more experienced men in charge of controlling particular sectors of Wales and the marches, they nonetheless were subordinate to the Crown Prince, who was ultimately responsible for achieving military success. This was made further evident on April 1, 1403, when he was appointed royal lieutenant for the whole of Wales.[11] He was then not quite sixteen, or not quite seventeen—roughly the same age at which Alexander, commanding one wing of his father's army, personally led the charge that overcame the previously undefeated Theban Sacred Band at the decisive battle of Chaeronea (the engagement which established King Philip's hegemony over all of Greece; 338 BC).[12]

Later in the summer of 1403, the political situation in Britain took a still more ominous turn. The Percys switched sides, and made common cause with Glendower. But before the forces of Hotspur and his uncle, the Earl of Worcester, could be joined by those of Hotspur's father (Henry Percy Sr., Earl of Northumberland) or by Glendower's Welshmen from the West, King Henry forced them into battle at Shrewsbury. As a consequence, the Percy army was almost surely outnumbered. But it included a strong contingent of Cheshire archers (provocatively displaying the White Hart badge of the late King Richard);[13] and in the early stages of the battle the Prince—who was in command of the right wing of the King's army—suffered a serious arrow wound in the face.[14] He nonetheless refused to leave the field, lest doing so dispirit his troops. And on the plus side, he acquired an enhanced respect for the tactical use of archers; in the aftermath of the battle, he intervened in favour of pardoning the surviving Cheshire men on payment by the county of a substantial fine. And though at most but seventeen, it is possible that he did kill the older, battle-hardened Hotspur (someone did), but there is no reliable source for the claim; likewise for his saving his father's life.[15]

Recovering from the wound suffered at Shrewsbury kept the Prince out of action against Welsh rebels for several months, during which time he undertook a pilgrimage to Canterbury.[16] Later historians, especially among the French, have hypothesized that Henry's piety was largely, if not entirely, a pretence, but there seems no direct evidence for this, and a fair bit to the contrary, that can be gleaned from the fifteenth-century sources of whatever nationality.

The Welsh troubles continued, and in July 1404 the prince was assigned general oversight of a war that was not going well for the English, the military situation being aggravated by the King's straited financial situation. Wales itself was providing virtually no revenue, and Parliament—unsympathetic to continuing expenditures on an effort whose importance to the stability of the realm many members failed to appreciate—balked at voting funds.[17] For much of 1404–5, the Prince was obliged to pay his soldiers out of his own household accounts (supplied mainly by the duchy of Cornwall), supplemented by loans. Possibly this was instrumental in his cultivating the personal loyalty so evident among those serving with him. He spent the winter on the southern marches, concerned especially with a threatened rebel attack on Hereford. In March of 1405, upon learning that an eight-thousand-man Welsh army was menacing Grosmont southwest of Hereford, he sent a small force under Lord Gilbert Talbot to engage it; Talbot was victorious, slaying some thousand Welshmen and dispersing the rest. Two months later, Prince Henry's forces engaged the Welsh at Pwll Melyn, killing another fifteen hundred (including Glendower's brother, Tudor), and capturing many prisoners (including Glendower's eldest son, Gruffydd).

Meanwhile, the situation was deteriorating in northern Wales, and so the Prince once more made Chester his base. Also, Northumberland was again intriguing with Glendower, joined now by the Earl Marshal (Thomas Mowbray, son of the man King Richard banished along with Bolingbroke at Coventry) and the Archbishop of York (Richard Scroop, cousin of the Earl of Wiltshire, William Scroop, whom Henry summarily executed at Bristol six years previous). Various other disaffected magnates in the north of England joined the rebellion, most notably the young Earl of Nottingham, Thomas Bardolf. The Prince took an active part in suppressing the revolt, first at Newcastle in June, then at Berwick in June and July. Possibly through a cynical ruse, Mowbray and the Archbishop were captured by forces nominally under the command of Hal's younger brother, Prince John, (though in fact led by Westmorland) and were shortly thereafter executed[18]—to the profound shock of most people in the region, who held the Archbishop in high regard. The impolitic severity of this reprisal on a respected churchman redounded to the lasting scandal of King Henry, whose health at this time began to fail. Not surprisingly, this was popularly seen as divine punishment for his blasphemous act.[19] Northumberland escaped into Scotland, and so once again dodged punishment. Meanwhile, Glendower had persuaded the French to lend military assistance, who about this time landed a contingent in south Wales. The joint Welsh-French army penetrated to within eight miles of Worcester, but by then the King had occupied the town with such a strong force that the invaders were obliged to withdraw.

The year 1405 was a period of crisis for the House of Lancaster. It was a close-run thing, but the regime of Henry IV survived, and this proved to be the turning point.[20] In 1406, the Welsh revolt stalled and then gradually diminished. Accordingly, the Prince was freed to take a more active part in the government of the whole realm, becoming a member of the King's royal Council (to the considerable relief of Parliament, worried about the King's failing health). In May of 1407, however, Hal was back in Wales along with several senior military men (including York, Warwick, Talbot, Carew, and Sir John Oldcastle) to undertake the siege of Aberystwyth Castle; the effort failed, as a force led by Glendower came timely to its relief. Accordingly, the Prince's household remained based along the Welsh border through 1408. That year Aberystwyth Castle was again besieged, this time successfully, as was Harlech by 1409. This finally put paid to Glendower's cause. All of his family except one son were captured, though the man himself never was.[21]

After nearly a decade of managing the English effort to retain rule over Wales—hence distributing offices and military commands, dispensing annuities and fees, directing and coordinating the services of those whose estates were threatened by Welsh depredations—the Prince had acquired a coterie of fellows, both noble and common, with whom he enjoyed personal relationships.[22] Consequently, he was well prepared in terms of both personal experience and political support to play a more active role in governing the realm.[23] In 1406, Parliament had demanded a reform of the King's Council as the price of voting Henry his requested subsidy. Specifically, he was obliged to agree to be advised by men of more competence and political standing ('and not by a clique of *familiares*').[24] In Parliament's view, it was of greatest importance that the Council include the Crown Prince, given the perilous condition of the King's health.

In January of 1407, Thomas Arundel, Archbishop of Canterbury, was appointed Chancellor, and from that point it seems that he, and increasingly the Prince (when affairs in Wales permitted his attendance), were the dominant members of the Council, Arundel managing mainly financial affairs and young Henry military matters. As the Prince gained in influence, he promoted the standing of close allies and kin, especially his own brothers and his Beaufort uncles (sons of Gaunt and Katherine Swynford,[25] thus half brothers of the King). Meanwhile, Henry's health continued to deteriorate, leaving him ever less able to take a personal hand in ruling. When at the end of 1409 Arundel, ostensibly having lost the King's confidence, was replaced as chancellor by Thomas Beaufort, the Prince and his allies became the effective rulers of England, and remained so for the next two years.

During this period troubles in and with France were an increasing concern, offering both opportunities to exploit and threats to English holdings on the Continent. In November of 1407, a bitter, long-simmering feud led to civil war in France, sparked by the murder of the Duke of Orleans by his cousin, John the Fearless, Duke of Burgundy. For years both men had been maneuvering to fill the chronic power vacuum that resulted from King Charles VI's periodic bouts of mental illness. After Orleans's assassination, the rivalry became an open conflict between the Burgundians and their allies and the Orleanists supported by their Armagnac allies. 'Their hatred of each other was so great that in their search for allies, both sides were prepared to overlook their shared dislike of the English. They were even prepared to buy the support of the king of England at the price of recognising his "just rights and inheritances", including, eventually, his title to the throne of France'.[26] Thus, which side England should support became a bone of contention between the King, who favoured siding with the Orleans-Armagnac faction, and the Crown Prince, who preferred its Burgundian opponents, whose Flemish weavers were the principal customers for English wool.[27]

It was in this context that King Henry, increasingly resentful of being shouldered aside, made an effort to regain control over England's affairs despite his failing health. The Beauforts had expressly advocated his abdicating in favour of his heir—an idea which, not surprisingly, offended Henry. Moreover, the Prince had enemies at Court who did what they could to blacken his reputation and heighten his father's suspicions of him.[28] In November of 1411, the King publicly reasserted his authority in Parliament. The Prince and several of his allies were replaced on the Council—but not without the Commons voting them a special thanks for their service.[29] From that point until the end of his father's reign less than eighteen months later, the Prince and most of his associates were excluded from power.

Archbishop Arundel was brought back as chancellor, and Henry's second son, Thomas—apparently his favourite, and always an envious rival of Hal[30]—was elevated to something like the position previously enjoyed by the Crown Prince. He, meanwhile, retired to the country where, as an energetic young man in his mid-twenties, presumably he enjoyed himself in ways for which soldierly types have long had a reputation. However that may have been and with whom, in the summer of 1412 he issued a letter from Coventry in which he defended himself against various accusations that had been circulating, including of financial malfeasance, and professed his continued loyalty to his father. After this, he staged a reentry into London at the head of a great throng 'of lords and gentles', which attested to his standing with the English elite. He eventually brought things to a head by demanding a personal interview with the King, who lay ill at Westminster. Admitted to the royal presence, he pled his case; 'he then offered the King a dagger, and asked that he should kill him. The King, unable to do this, burst into tears, threw away the dagger, and forgave his son'.[31]

Thus, when on March 20, 1413, Henry IV, but forty-six years old, died in the Jerusalem Chamber of Westminster Abbey, he was reconciled with the son and namesake who would succeed him as Henry V. And far from the young man's ascension being met with widespread anxiety, much less foreboding, Shakespeare would have read in Holinshed, 'Such great hope, and good expectation was had of this mans fortunate success to follow, that within three daies after his fathers decease, diverse noble men and honorable personages did him homage, and sware to him due obedience, which had not beene seene doone to any of his predecessors kings of this realme, till they had beene possessed of the crowne'.[32]

I presume my point in summarizing the life of Prince Henry as our modern historians reconstruct it is sufficiently obvious: it bears scant similarity to the Prince Hal we meet in the two parts of Shakespeare's *Henry IV*.[33] Why is that? Is it because Shakespeare's historical sources, mainly but not exclusively Holinshed, provided a radically different portrait of the Prince? They do not. Nor is this surprising, since they are also among the primary sources for the views of modern historians.

That said, the accounts upon which Shakespeare was dependent, all written some century and a half after the already famous King's premature death, include allusions to various pranks reputed to have been committed in his supposedly dissolute younger days. References to these episodes, however, do not bulk large in any of the accounts available to Shakespeare, much less to the exclusion of his extensive service in Wales and later as the dominant figure of the King's Council; rather, they figure almost as addenda.[34] But, as one of Henry's modern biographers concedes, 'Too many chroniclers speak of his dissipation for the traditional stories of a wild youth to be dismissed out of hand'.[35] Accordingly, most modern accounts include some reference to them, though usually tempered by an awareness that 'Henry was one of those men about whom legend gathers. As the art of biography revived in the generation after his early death, memories of his wild youth came to replace the full story of his devotion to duty and hard work. It was on these memories that Shakespeare built'.[36] Perhaps 'memories' is not the best term for the status of stories that are more aptly characterized as romantic legends which may, or may not, have some substantial historical basis. But whatever their status, they certainly provided raw material for entertaining theatre.[37] Shakespeare, however, chose to feature them to the exclusion of the prince's long and admirable record of actions and achievements, thereby distorting the historical record—both that of his time and ours—almost beyond recognition.[38]

Why has he done this? Why has he so radically fictionalized the younger years of England's most famous warrior-king? With regard to no other important historical character has he chosen to fashion anything remotely comparable.[39] Thus, as I suggested at the outset, a serious reader familiar with Shakespeare's other plays must suspect an ulterior purpose behind the comic facade.[40]

Prince Hal's first 'appearance' is rather like Mistress Shore's in *Richard III*: offstage, spoken of, but not seen. However, the existence of that lady and the effects of her charms are germane to the plot of her play, whereas the brief discussion about the Crown Prince in *Richard II* is altogether extraneous. Apparently its sole purpose is to anticipate the character whose seemingly scandalous behaviour and dissolute associates will dominate the following two plays, preparatory to his emerging in glory thereafter. King Henry, attended by several lords—among whom is young Harry Percy—is expressing his exasperation:

> Can no man tell me of my unthrifty son?
> 'Tis full three months since I did see him last.
> If any plague hang over us, 'tis he.
> I would to God, my lords, he might be found.
> Enquire at London, 'mongst the taverns there,
> For there, they say, he daily doth frequent,
> With unrestrained loose companions,
> Even such, they say, as stand in narrow lanes
> And beat our watch and rob our passengers,
> While he, young wanton and effeminate boy,
> Takes on the point of honour to support
> So dissolute a crew.
> (5.3.1–12)

Who are 'they' that say such things, one might wonder. Young Percy—who as Prince Hal's chosen rival will become immortalized by the fitting name 'Hotspur'[41]—volunteers more recent intelligence: 'My lord, some two days since I saw the Prince, / And told him of those triumphs held at Oxford'. A perhaps wishful Henry inquires further, 'And what said the gallant?' Percy's reply offers little comfort: 'His answer was he would unto the stews, / And from the common'st creature pluck a glove / And wear it as a favour, and with that / He would unhorse the lustiest challenger'. This report of the lad's impudent boast draws from his father, 'As dissolute as desp'rate! Yet through both / I see some sparks of better hope, which elder years / May happily bring forth'.

This exchange between the King and Harry Percy introduces most of the elements of Prince Hal's reputed character and way of life that will be fleshed out in the two succeeding plays: he is a prodigal son, estranged from a father who has suffered repeated disappointments in him, and so thinks of him only with worry and chagrin; London's taverns are his favourite haunts, where he consorts mainly with the city's lowlife, to whose material support he contributes; he is reputed to be involved with ruffians who rob honest travellers, and even assault civic officers; he is undisciplined, self-indulgent, licentious, insolent, altogether a 'young wanton'. There is a slight hint, however, that there may be persons who make a point of maligning the lad. Percy doesn't indicate where he encountered the Prince, nor do we know how seriously to take his reported intention. But presuming he did say what is claimed, did he do so only to annoy Hotspur by expressing contempt for those contests of manly honour-seeking that he knows his rival—and his own father—so value? In which case, Henry's describing him as an 'effeminate boy' is understandable. Or did he truly plan to participate in the tournament (however suitably, or unsuitably, accoutred), and even to emerge victorious over all comers? If so, his father's discerning some 'sparks' of a better nature may not be just so much wishful thinking. And surely the King must have some awareness of his son's athletic prowess.

We first meet Prince Hal in the flesh, as we imagine, in part 1 of *Henry IV*. Indeed, he overshadows the play, literally from beginning to end. For although he is not actually present in its first scene, which opens on a dejected King Henry admitting that the incessant political 'broils' have taken a toll on his health, leaving him 'wan with care', the scene ends with him lamenting that it is Harry Monmouth who is his son and Crown Prince, not Harry Percy.

From the very onset of his reign, Henry has had his hands full managing the consequences of his usurpation of Richard's throne. The realm has known almost no peace; nor, he now learns, is it likely to any time soon. For the King's cousin-by-marriage, the Earl of Westmorland, reports that the previous night a post arrived with bad news from Wales: royal forces led by Edmund Mortimer were defeated by the Welsh irregulars of the 'wild Glendower'; a thousand Herefordshire men were killed, their bodies profanely mutilated by the Welsh women, and Mortimer himself was captured. But that is not all. Even more disturbing news has come from the North: an army of Scots led by a battle-tested warrior, the Earl of Douglas, have invaded. They were met at Humbleton with English opposition led by 'gallant Hotspur', but so far as Westmorland knows, the outcome was uncertain.

Henry, however, has just received a welcome report from this front, brought by his friend Sir Walter Blount: Douglas has been defeated, some ten thousand Scotsmen slain, and a number of noblemen made prisoner. But these glad tidings are muted, for victorious young Hotspur has added to the King's aggravation by refusing to surrender up the valuable prisoners his forces captured—a challenge to royal authority that Henry cannot allow to go unchecked. He asks Westmorland, half rhetorically, 'What think you, coz, / Of this young Percy's pride?' Westmorland attributes it to the malevolent influence of Hotspur's Percy uncle, the Earl of Worcester, that it is he who encourages Hotspur to so preen himself, 'and bristle up / The crest of youth against your dignity'. No doubt agreeing, Henry responds, 'I have sent for him to answer this', then adds:

> Cousin, on Wednesday next our Council we
> Will hold at Windsor. So inform the lords,
> But come yourself with speed to us again,
> For more is to be said and to be done
> Than out of anger can be uttered.
> (1.1.90–106)

We do not know precisely what the King wishes to consult privately with Westmorland about, but since he is concerned that it be considered in cold blood, it must have something to do with how best to deal with Hotspur—or perhaps the whole Percy clan. Nor do we know the results of their consultation, other than whatever can be surmised from the King's behaviour when next he confronts the young victor.

These high matters of State provide an unflattering contrast to the circumstances in which we first set eyes on the Prince. We come upon him in the midst of his bestowing some comic abuse upon his 'fat-witted' companion, Sir John Falstaff, who deftly parries the attack with embellished allusions to his nocturnal thievery. In the course of their ensuing conversation, however, a certain topic does recur which foreshadows the disquieting conclusion of their relationship: when Hal ascends the throne, what will be his policy towards the likes of Falstaff. Will he be sympathetic to such 'gentlemen of the shade, minions of the moon'? (1.2.25). The Prince's response is in keeping with this lunar image, noting that the fortune of such 'moon's men doth ebb and flow like the sea', their high tide being 'the ridge of the gallows'. Shortly thereafter, Falstaff pointedly asks, 'I prithee, sweet wag, shall there be gallows standing in England when thou art king? . . . Do not thou, when thou art king, hang a thief' (1.2.55–59). Again, Hal uses a jest to deflect attention from the issue: 'No, thou shalt'. Falstaff exults in the mistaken assumption that this means he will be appointed a judge. Hal claims he meant instead that the old profligate will be appointed the hangman. But a far more ominous interpretation of Hal's 'No, thou shalt' is left reverberating in the air: that Falstaff himself shall 'hang [as] a thief'.

Most consequential, however, is the conclusion of this, the Prince's first scene. It consists of a soliloquy in which he professes to be engaged in a deep deception of indefinite duration. He begins by addressing rhetorically his now departed companions:

> I know you all, and will awhile uphold
> The unyoked humour of your idleness.
> Yet herein will I imitate the sun,
> Who doth permit the base contagious clouds
> To smother up his beauty from the world,
> That, when he please again to be himself,
> Being wanted, he may be more wondered at
> By breaking through the foul and ugly mists
> Of vapours that did seem to strangle him.
> If all the year were playing holidays,
> To sport would be as tedious as to work;
> But when they seldom come, they wished-for come,
> And nothing pleaseth but rare accidents.
> So when this loose behaviour I throw off
> And pay the debt I never promised,
> By how much better than my word I am,
> By so much shall I falsify men's hopes;
> And, like bright metal on a sullen ground,
> My reformation, glittering o'er my fault,
> Shall show more goodly and attract more eyes
> Than that which hath no foil to set it off.
> I'll so offend to make offence a skill,
> Redeeming time when men think least I will.
> (1.2.185–207)

If we may take him at his word, the Prince here reveals that his unseemly behaviour, played out in the company of base companions, is actually a carefully plotted strategy, one which exploits a shrewd psychology and presumes cultivating an unusual skill.

Evidently he needed no help from Machiavelli to learn a basic truth of human nature, nor to work out for himself uses to which it might be put: people better appreciate an occasional goodness that relieves some prolonged distress, or that brightens gloom, or that pleasantly surprises, than do they value a consistent goodness which they soon take for granted. Their assessments are always relative to the given context. Hal sees this as the principle common to the striking effect of various phenomena, each of which also manifests something distinctive: the relief from the tedium of workaday life that the occasional holiday brings; the pleasant surprise that would attend a written-off debt being unexpectedly repaid; and the enhanced brightness of some glittering thing if set against a sombre background. He likewise intends, he claims, to foster low expectations, to encourage a pessimistic forecast, a gloomy background against which he can shine the brighter 'when he please again to be himself'.

There is nary a hint in any of the sources that the historical Prince Hal pursued such a strategy. Nor would his doing so make sense in the context of history's very different story of how from an early age the young man spent his time. Nor is there anything comparable in the earlier *Famous Victories*, nor in any other precursor of which we are aware. This scheme, which evinces a canny single-mindedness in young Henry's character—*Shakespeare's* young Henry, that is—colours the entirety of his association with Falstaff and the rest of the Eastcheap crew.[42] But since 'Hal's' plan is entirely an invention of the philosopher-poet, should we not presume that it is pertinent to whatever political lesson(s) he has embedded in this four-part depiction of the rise to power and glory of England's most storied warrior king? More precisely, that it is integral to his hero's strategy for addressing the problem he inherited: that of establishing his own legitimacy as king?

Shakespeare's Crown Prince plans to imitate the *sun*—*not*, that is, the celestial body of which Falstaff professes himself a devotee. Or rather, the sun as people experience it in the British Isles, where it is so frequently obscured by clouds, rain, mists, and fogs which attenuate its warmth and mask its beauty. Analogously, then, if he is to enjoy the special welcome with which people greet the sun after an extended period of dreary, overcast skies, he must somehow keep his own brilliance shrouded, saving it for a situation in which he may reveal it to maximum effect. He does not specify when that might be, but we are left with the anticipation that it will be upon his acceding to the kingship, that he intends to make the occasion one of delightful surprise and welcome relief, and cause for joyful celebration. Having witnessed his father's rise and his godfather's fall, apparently Prince Hal has surmised that the political world is to a considerable extent 'theatrical', and that successfully ruling one's portion requires not merely the talents of an actor, able to play a variety of roles, but the skills of a stage-master as well.[43]

What is equally noteworthy about his revelation, however, is what the Prince does *not* say. For example, there is no indication here that he consorts with the denizens of Eastcheap in order to familiarize himself with the ways of 'the common man'. Or that it is his means of escaping the oppressive and corrupting atmosphere of life at Court, with its false courtesy and preponderance of polished schemers and flatterers, of sycophants and gossipmongers. Nor is there any suggestion that he prefers the company of Falstaff for the worldly wisdom he might gain therefrom. Or that he finds the fat old knight a more genial 'father' than he does the King—whom he does not mention, notice, much less express any concern that his 'shrouded-sun' strategy is causing his father chronic distress.

Attributing to Hal a disposition not unlike that of other young men, one may suppose that pursuing the strategy he has laid out is not exactly a chore. That quite to the contrary, he finds the devil-may-care way of life of Falstaff and the other Boar's Head scallywags congenial for the time being. This is not to dismiss his professed rationale as mere rationalization—for events bear out its singular effectiveness. Nor is it to deny that it may provide him other benefits than that which he expressly anticipates. Rather, it is to credit him with having devised a strategy whereby to minimize the burdensomeness of being a crown prince, while maximizing the public's satisfaction upon his ascending the throne: he gets to enjoy a more carefree life, while incidentally expanding his understanding of the commoners he will rule, confident that he will pleasantly astonish the worried nobility and ecclesiarchs upon his inheriting the Crown. That the father suffer heartburn in the meantime is a price the son is willing to pay.

Still, Hal's scheme would seem to carry a certain risk. Is not one's soul shaped by one's practices—that a given person's individual nature, his 'individuality', is at least partially a consequence of his nurture, including self-nurture? Could a young man, having led a life of self-indulgence and irresponsibility, nonetheless acquire the psychic strength—the self-control, the self-mastery—to suppress tastes and habits thereby formed, and to summon instead qualities normally cultivated in the course of living quite differently? Can moderation, courage, justice, and prudence be wished into existence simply upon recognising their utility? The qualities of God's sun are entirely due to nature, not to nurture; hence, the sun is *always* 'pleased to be himself', whether seen as such or obscured by clouds—indeed, whether it be day or night. But might the natural constancy of God's sun somehow be the secret of King Henry's son as well: that, appearances to the contrary notwithstanding, he too is always nurturing the self he intends to become, striving to establish a kingship over his own soul before ascending to the kingship of England,[44] indulging only such passions and desires on only such occasions as his reason approves—that is, such as are compatible with his strategic goal? If we may credit what he privately professes, his intentional 'offending' of the norms of conduct expected of an heir apparent, far from being evidence of wayward self-indulgence, is actually in accord with a developing *skill*. And everything done by skill presumes self-control.

It is Prince Hal's perverse employment of this skill that is the subject of a private confrontation with his father in a scene set near the centre of the play. In the course of the King's splenetic upbraiding of his heir for the sorts of dissolute behaviour that have become a subject of public scandal, he compares it with his own conduct prior to acquiring the Crown. The contrast is diametrical, or so it would seem. But one should not overlook the important respect in which they agree, namely, that political effectiveness requires recognition that one's public life amounts to a continuous theatrical performance, and that (consequently) one must not only 'act the part', but be ever careful how one stages oneself. There are also other, perhaps more surprising, points of agreement, however.

The King begins with a particularly bitter speculation regarding the Prince: his reported behaviour is so reprehensible that Henry fears his son has been visited upon him as a divine punishment (apparently, the usurpation of Richard's Crown is never far from Henry's mind):

> I know not whether God will have it so
> For some displeasing service I have done [!],
> That, in His secret doom, out of my blood
> He'll breed revengement and a scourge for me;
> But thou dost in thy passages of life
> Make me believe that thou art only marked
> For the hot vengeance and the rod of heaven
> To punish my mistreadings.
>   (3.2.4–11)

How else to account for a prince of the blood being given over to 'such inordinate and low desires, / Such poor, such bare, such lewd, such mean attempts, / Such barren pleasures, rude society'? Apparently Hal's 'shrouded sun' strategy has been only too successful. And doubtless the notoriety of his conduct has lost nothing in the reporting. Moreover, it has provided credibility for 'many tales devised / . . . / By smiling pickthanks and base newsmongers' that are simply false. So, while Hal must ask pardon 'for some things true, wherein [his] youth / Hath faulty wandered', he seeks exoneration for the rest. Henry leaves the pardoning to God, and continues to catalogue Hal's sins, the kinds of wanton behaviour which have resulted in his replacement on the King's Council by his younger brother Thomas,[45] and his alienation from his princely siblings and all the Court, spoiling his prospects in the views of nearly everyone: 'The hope and expectation of thy time / Is ruined, and the soul of every man / Prophetically do forethink thy fall' (3.2.36–38). It seems the prince's efforts to craft a 'sullen ground' against which his true 'metal' will someday shine the brighter has been all he might wish.

Reflecting on Hal's delinquency leads Henry to discourse upon the radically different manner in which he cultivated acceptance for his assuming the Crown:

> Had I so lavish of my presence been,
> So common-hackneyed in the eyes of men,
> So stale and cheap to vulgar company,
> Opinion, that did help me to the crown,
> Had still kept loyal to possession
> And left me in reputeless banishment,
> A fellow of no mark nor likelihood.

This is a curious claim, as if Bolingbroke means to imply that he was somehow brought back from exile 'by popular demand', rather than returning as a matter of his own deliberate plotting—for which he solicited foreign assistance and thus was 'well furnished by the Duke of Brittany / With eight tall ships, three thousand men of war' (*Richard II*, 2.1.285–86). Has Hal never been apprised of the fact that his father schemed for the throne well *before* he could return under the pretence of merely claiming his Lancastrian inheritance? Does Henry hint the truth to his son only when on his deathbed (*2 Henry IV*, 4.5.181–85, 189–94)? Here, the king expands on the rationale behind his fastidious public behaviour:

> By being seldom seen, I could not stir
> But, like a comet, I was wondered at. . . .
> And then I stole all courtesy from heaven
> And dressed myself in such humility
> That I did pluck allegiance from men's hearts,
> Loud shouts and salutations from their mouths,
> Even in the presence of the crowned King.
> Thus did I keep my person fresh and new,
> My presence like a robe pontifical,
> Ne'er seen but wondered at; and so my state,
> Seldom but sumptuous, showed like a feast
> And won by rareness such solemnity.
> (3.2.39–59)

Henry contrasts this economical management of his own carefully staged appearances with the conduct of the man he replaced, a 'skipping King' who publicly frequented the company of 'shallow jesters', mingling 'his royalty with cap'ring fools'. He thereby allowed his name to become the subject of mockery, and even 'Grew a companion to the common streets'. As a result, the late King simply confirmed an age-old truth: familiarity breeds contempt.

Having raised the possibility that 'mistreadings' might draw down divine punishment, there is surely some irony in Henry's recommending to his son the very behaviour whereby he alienated people's allegiance from the King whose Crown he planned to usurp. Moreover, the irony is compounded by the illustration Henry uses to make his point: that which are common sights to men 'Afford no extraordinary gaze / Such as is bent on sun-like majesty / When it shines seldom in admiring eyes' (3.2.78–80)—the very same image illustrating the very same principle as Hal invoked in his soliloquy: the sun's grandeur enhanced by virtue of being seen only occasionally. However, Hal's 'shrouded sun' strategy applies this principle, not in his being seldom seen—quite the contrary: it requires his being seen a lot—but by crafting a *persona* that conceals his true self, which therefore remains seldom seen,[46] and has the added advantage of serving as a dark background against which to emerge with enhanced brilliance whensoever it pleases him to reveal his true self.

Meanwhile, it is precisely this persona that is causing his father such distress. The Prince, he believes—or has been led to believe—is behaving in a manner much like that of the late King. Consequently, Henry warns, 'thou hast lost thy princely privilege / With vile participation. Not an eye / But is a-weary of thy common sight, / Save mine, which hath desired to see thee more' (3.2.86–89). Since Hal's response does not sound like a promise to reform—'I shall hereafter, my thrice-gracious lord, / Be more myself'—it does nothing to mollify his father, who turns to praising young Harry Percy. By virtue of his accomplishments, this other Harry has acquired a standing in the realm that threatens an all-too-vulnerable Lancastrian dynasty. Indeed, if the Crown went by merit, 'He hath more worthy interest to the state / Than thou, the shadow of succession' (ibid., 98–99). Henry speaks at length about the gathering threat posed by 'this Hotspur, Mars in swaddling-clothes', and of the potential allies he has attracted, which Henry fears may even include his 'nearest and dearest enemy': the Crown Prince himself.

If the King intended by this outrageous accusation to elicit a strong denial, he succeeds in spades. For it provokes the Prince to reveal for the first time a power of eloquence for which he will become famous—the eloquence, that is, with which Shakespeare has endowed him. Given its effect upon his father, one must imagine for oneself the calm, cold-blooded, steely resolution with which Hal utters these lines, contrasting so markedly with the light-hearted bantering that has beguiled us previously.

> Do not think so. You shall not find it so;
> And God forgive them that so much have swayed
> Your majesty's good thoughts away from me.
> I will redeem all this on Percy's head
> And in the closing of some glorious day,
> Be bold to tell you that I am your son,
> When I will wear a garment all of blood
> And stain my favours in a bloody mask,
> Which washed away shall scour my shame with it.
> And that shall be the day, whene'er it lights,
> That this same child of honour and renown,
> This gallant Hotspur, this all-praised knight,
> And your unthought-of Harry chance to meet.
> For every honour sitting on his helm,
> Would they were multitudes, and on my head
> My shames redoubled, for the time will come
> That I shall make this northern youth exchange
> His glorious deeds for my indignities.
> Percy is but my factor, good my lord,
> To engross up glorious deeds on my behalf;
> And I will call him to so strict an account,
> That he shall render every glory up,
> Yea, even the slightest worship of his time,
> Or I will tear the reckoning from his heart.
> This, in the name of God, I promise here....
> And I will die a hundred thousand deaths
> Ere break the smallest parcel of this vow.
> (3.2.129–59)

Hal's words reverberate with a tone of such sobriety and resolve as immediately persuades his father: 'A hundred thousand rebels die in this'. Thus does Hal lift a corner of his veil, anticipating an occasion when his 'shrouded sun' strategy will pay its first dividends. It will be at Hotspur's expense.

The political significance of honour and dishonour, of fame and shame, for the larger story being dramatized—concretely represented by Hotspur's 'glorious deeds' versus Hal's 'indignities'—is implicit in both the King's taunting accusation and the Prince's emphatic response. Indeed, that larger story virtually begins with a clash over honour, one which sets the trajectory for all that follows. Learning that the Hotspur-led English forces have met and defeated a Scottish invasion at Humbleton, killing some 'ten thousand bold Scots' and taking prisoner a number of Scottish nobles in the process, the King enthuses to Westmorland, 'And is not this an honourable spoil, / A gallant prize? Ha, cousin, is it not?' Westmorland agrees, 'it is: a conquest for a prince to boast of'. An unfortunate choice of words, for it reminds Henry that he can boast of no such prince himself.

> Yea, there thou mak'st me sad and mak'st me sin
> In envy that my lord Northumberland
> Should be the father to so blest a son,
> A son who is the theme of honour's tongue,
> Amongst a grove the very straightest plant,
> Who is sweet Fortune's minion and her pride;
> Whilst I, by looking on the praise of him,
> See riot and dishonour stain the brow
> Of my young Harry.
>   (1.1.77–85)

Having registered this personal disappointment, Henry now professes to dismiss it, being confronted by a serious matter needing his immediate attention. But his dissatisfaction with the character and conduct of his Crown Prince resurfaces often enough in the course of the King's story to suggest it is a worry never far from his mind. As for this more serious matter, it has to do with those prisoners Hotspur took, but with one exception has refused to pass on to the King despite their being demanded of him—an act of lese-majesty that Henry is not inclined to let pass. Having consulted privately with Westmorland, Henry is determined to put the headstrong young man in his place. Perhaps on the advice if not the urging of his confidant—the principal rival of the Northumberland Percys for supremacy in northern England—he may have more in mind than that, however. Whatever the case, he has ordered Hotspur to appear personally at Windsor to answer for his open defiance of royal authority, dishonouring the man who wears the crown.

Young Percy, accompanied by both his father and his uncle (as Henry may well have expected), does obey the royal summons to Windsor. The scene of their meeting begins with the King seeming to admit a lapse on his part: 'My blood hath been too cold and temperate, / Unapt to stir at these indignities, / ... / And therefore lost that title of respect / Which the proud soul ne'er pays but to the proud'. When Worcester protests that the House of Percy 'little deserves / The scourge of greatness to be used on it', bearing in mind their part in making that greatness, Henry brusquely orders him from the royal presence, interrupting Northumberland to do so:

Worcester, get thee gone, for I do see
Danger and disobedience in thine eye.
O sir, your presence is too bold and peremptory,
And majesty might never yet endure
The moody frontier of a servant brow.
You have good leave to leave us. When we need
Your use and counsel we shall send for you.
                    (1.3.15–21)

'*Servant*'! Henry clearly has no intention of smoothing relations with *this* Percy. Stifling his indignation, Worcester leaves without responding. But his oily brother Northumberland attempts to sooth the King's roiled spirit by suggesting there's been something of a misunderstanding, that those prisoners demanded in the King's name were not 'with such strength denied' as Henry has been misled to believe. Now the junior Percy himself speaks, claiming that he never actually refused to submit the prisoners. By way of explaining, he launches into a lengthy sarcasm about the fastidious 'popinjay' who conveyed the King's demand, and whose manner so infuriated him in his battle-tired condition that he's not sure what response he made. In any case, Hotspur entreats Henry not to let that coxcomb's report 'Come current for an accusation / Betwixt my love and your high majesty'. An equivocal profession, one might notice. Are we to credit this blunt-speaking young war lover with subtlety?

At this point, Sir Walter Blount intervenes, suggesting that whatever was said then may be overlooked, provided 'he unsay it now'. But Henry refuses to be so easily placated. Moreover, he now reveals that the matter is not that simple. Apparently Hotspur had indicated a willingness to surrender his prisoners, but only upon the condition that the King first ransom the captured Earl of March, Edmund Mortimer, who happens to be Hotspur's brother-in-law. Needless to say, that anyone subject to the King should presume to make his obedience to a royal command *conditional* is an insult not to be borne. Moreover, Henry expresses a very different view of the man in question from that of young Percy. Henry treats Mortimer as a traitor, claiming that he 'wilfully betrayed' the men he led against 'that great magician, damned Glendower'. Why might Henry, or anyone, think so? Because, though supposedly 'captured' in battle, *Mortimer married Glendower's daughter*! Surely this is a plausible ground for suspecting some sort of connivance. And given his new matrimonial status, why should Mortimer either want or need to be *ransomed from his own father-in-law*? Not only does Henry profess to regard Mortimer as having 'forfeited' himself, hence can be left to starve on a mountainside for all he cares, he provocatively adds, 'I shall never hold that man my friend / Whose tongue shall ask me for one

66   CHAPTER TWO

penny cost / To ransom home revolted Mortimer' (1.3.90–92). Why this apparently extreme reaction? Does it reflect passion? . . . or policy?

Although having just been warned off—most emphatically—Hotspur immediately challenges the King's characterization of the captured brother-in-law, denying that he openly 'revolted', claiming that he changed allegiance only under duress. Percy then provides a glowing description of how long and hard 'noble Mortimer' battled 'hand to hand . . . with great Glendower', receiving multiple grievous wounds in the process, and so insists he not be 'slandered with revolt'. In response, Henry as much as calls Hotspur a liar, that he ought to be ashamed of himself for trying to foist off such an improbable story, whereas the truth is Mortimer never actually battled Glendower at all. In brief, Henry wants to hear no more about Mortimer, and young Percy had best send on his prisoners by 'the speediest means' or he'll be hearing from the King in such a manner as he will not find pleasant. Without allowing for any further protest, Henry and his entourage depart. Had it been his settled intention to provoke a rupture with his erstwhile allies, he could hardly have improved on this performance.

One would not have to be the honour-sensitive soul Hotspur notoriously is to be offended by how the King has treated him. We have no way of knowing who, if either, is speaking the truth about the alleged confrontation between Mortimer and Glendower. Neither man was present at the battle; each would (at best) be relying on the report of someone who was. Henry may be sufficiently acquainted with Mortimer's personal fighting skills to discount Hotspur's flowery portrayal of the supposed hour-long, man-on-man battle. Or he may not. For as it soon becomes clear, he would not be eager to retrieve the Earl of March from Wales, whatever the truth.

The two Percys, father and son, are left alone to digest the results of their visit to the throne; they are joined almost immediately by Uncle Thomas, the Earl of Worcester. Hotspur, who not surprisingly is now hot indeed, threatens to chase down the King and defy him to his face about sending the prisoners. As for the ban on speaking about Mortimer, Hotspur vows not only to speak of him but to join with him, and fight to the last drop of blood to restore the good name and station of 'down-trod Mortimer'. When Worcester inquires of his brother the cause of his nephew's being so inflamed, the junior Percy tells of Henry's latest demand for the prisoners, and how he—though fresh from a victory in the service of the Crown—was rebuffed when he urged the ransoming of his wife's brother: 'then [Henry's] cheek looked pale / And on my face he turned an eye of death, / Trembling even at the name of "Mortimer"' (1.3.141–43). Whereupon Hotspur learns for the first time that the Earl of March, Edmund Mortimer, had been proclaimed by the late King Richard II his 'heir to the crown'—that the kingship Henry usurped rightfully belongs to Hotspur's brother-in-law.[47]

It is a bit strange that Hotspur was not previously aware of this fact. But then again, perhaps not so strange, given that the elder Percys were themselves up to their necks in fostering Henry's usurpation. Young Percy is well aware of the part they played, and now jettisons all restraint, not to mention filial piety, in berating them for it, repeatedly emphasizing the shame and dishonour they have brought upon themselves.

> Nay, then I cannot blame his cousin King
> That wished him on the barren mountains starve.
> But shall it be that you that set the crown
> Upon the head of this forgetful man
> And for his sake wear the detested *blot*
> Of murderous subornation—shall it be
> That you a world of *curses* undergo,
> Being the agents or *base* second means,
> The cords, the ladder, or the hangman rather? . . .
> Shall it for *shame* be spoken in these days,
> Or fill up chronicles in time to come,
> That men of your *nobility* and power
> Did gage them both in an unjust behalf
> (As both of you, God pardon it, have done)
> To put down Richard, that sweet lovely rose,
> And plant this thorn, this canker, Bolingbroke?
> And shall it in *more shame* be further spoken
> That you are fooled, discarded and shook off
> By him for whom these *shames* ye underwent?
> No! Yet time serves wherein you may redeem
> Your banished *honours* and restore yourselves
> Into the *good thoughts* of the world again,
> *Revenge* the jeering and *disdained contempt*
> Of this proud King.
>   (1.3.157–83)

Worcester interrupts this harangue to inform his overheated nephew that secret plans are already being laid to undo what they have imprudently done. And doubtless the two elder Percys are motivated by more material considerations than their standing in 'the thoughts of the world'. But for Hotspur—who emerges as clearly the leader of this first Northern rebellion—it is all about honour versus shame, about how one is regarded not only in one's own time, but in times to come. Ironically, it is a preoccupation with honour that may well have scuttled any chance of that rebellion succeeding.

Whither the Archbishop? As originally conceived, the rebellion presumed a conjunction of several forces: there were to be those commanded by the elder Percy, the Earl of Northumberland; and those led by Hotspur and his uncle, the Earl of Worcester; also a contingent from Scotland, led by Archibald, Earl of Douglas; and the wild Welshmen of Owen Glendower, with whom Mortimer now served. But when Worcester first revealed to Hotspur the existence of a conspiracy to unseat Henry, he included as a party to it the Archbishop of York, Richard Scroop. And he assigned his brother Northumberland the task of recruiting the 'noble prelate well beloved', who (he claims) 'bears hard / His brother's death at Bristol' (1.3.264–66). Worcester here refers to William Scroop, Earl of Wiltshire, whom Bolingbroke captured at Bristol Castle and executed along with the 'caterpillars' Bushy and Green. Worcester assures his two kinfolk,

> I speak not this in estimation
> As what I think might be, but what I know
> Is ruminated, plotted and set down,
> And only stays but to behold the face
> Of that occasion that shall bring it on.
> (1.3.267–71)

Hotspur is all enthusiasm, especially with Archbishop York being involved: 'I smell it. Upon my life, it will do well'. His father chides him for his typical impulsiveness: 'Before the game is afoot thou still let'st slip'. A prophetic observation, which Hotspur deflects: 'Why, it cannot choose but be a noble plot— / And then the power of Scotland and of York / To join with Mortimer, ha?' Worcester seconds him: 'And so they shall'. Hotspur doubles down: 'In faith, it is exceedingly well aimed'.

The next we hear of the Archbishop's participation comes in the course of Hotspur's sarcastic rejoinders to a reply he is reading from some possible ally whom he has solicited to join their effort, but who declines, giving his reasons: '*The purpose you undertake is dangerous, the friends you have named uncertain, the time itself unsorted, and your whole plot too light for the counterpoise of so great an opposition*'. Hotspur is indignant:

> Say you so; say you so? I say unto you again you are a shallow, cowardly hind, and you lie. What a lack-brain is this! By the Lord, our plot is a good plot as ever was laid, our friends true and constant; a good plot, good friends, and full of expectation; an excellent plot, very good friends. What a frosty-spirited rogue is this! Why, my lord of York commends the plot and the general course of the action. . . . Is there not my father, my uncle and myself, Lord Edmund Mortimer, my lord of York and Owen Glendower? Is there not, besides, the Douglas? Have I not all

their letters to meet me in arms by the ninth of the next month, and are they not some of them set forward already? (2.3.9–27)

Hotspur berates himself for having approached 'such a dish of skim-milk with so honourable an action', and supposes the knave will now reveal the plot to the King. Not to worry: 'We are prepared; I will set forward tonight'. For as Worcester had earlier warned, ''tis no little reason bids us speed' (1.3.278).

There is reason to suspect, however, that in railing against the 'pagan rascal' who declined to participate, Hotspur is labouring, at least in part, to persuade *himself* of both the excellence of 'the plot' and the certainty of 'the friends'—that in truth, he's not as confident of either as he would prefer to believe. The source of this suspicion is none other than Hotspur's domestic partner, his beloved Kate, who queries him prior to his departure as to why he has denied her his bed. Why has he lost his appetite for her and other pleasures? Why is he so pale? Why spend so much time alone, staring at the ground, jumpy and melancholy? When he does sleep, it's shallow and disturbed by nightmares of battles: 'Thy spirit within thee hath been so at war, / And thus hath so bestirred thee in thy sleep, / That beads of sweat have stood upon thy brow . . . , / And in thy face strange motions have appeared' (2.3.55–59). These are 'portents' of some 'heavy business', and Lady Percy insists on knowing what it is. Hotspur replies with a barrage of clever teasing that softens his refusal to confide in her: 'for I well believe / Thou wilt not utter what thou dost not know' (ibid., 106–7). To be sure, this is sound military practice: revealing one's plans only on a strictly 'need to know' basis. But is it not rather strangely invoked here, given Percy's presumption about the 'pagan rascal' whose letter indicated he is privy to 'the whole plot'?.

If one may rely on Hotspur's claim to have written confirmation from all those he names, the Archbishop is not merely in favour of a rebellion against Henry, but committed to actively participate. It seems clear that Hotspur regards this as especially significant. Thus York's absence from the subsequent action is puzzling. For whereas certain others named were also absent (Northumberland, Mortimer, Glendower), in their cases various excuses were offered—which simply highlights the curious silence about the Archbishop. Perhaps in his eagerness young Percy read more in the prelate's reply than was promised. However, his surmise about Sir Milque-Toast seems to have been valid, for when Henry has his biting confrontation with the wayward Crown Prince, he is well aware of Hotspur's leading role in a conspiracy to 'shake the peace and safety of our throne'. Henry likens the status of young Percy to that of himself upon returning from exile: 'And even as I was then is Percy now'.

> For, of no right, nor colour like to right,
> He doth fill fields with harness in the realm,
> Turns head against the lion's armed jaws,
> And, being no more in debt to years than thou,
> Leads ancient lords and reverend bishops on
> To bloody battles and to bruising arms.
>
> (3.2.96–105)

The King's cold tirade becomes more specific about the immediate danger: 'And what say you to this? Percy, Northumberland, / The Archbishop's grace of York, Douglas, Mortimer, / Capitulate against us and are up' (3.2.118–20). He finishes his rebuke with that scandalous suspicion he couldn't possibly believe: that Prince Hal himself is likely to be making common cause with Percy. But the King apparently does believe that this is so of Archbishop Scroop of York.

As for the Archbishop himself, he appears in just one scene. What he says therein, however, does little to dissipate one's puzzlement concerning his involvement in the Hotspur-led rebellion. The scene opens with him instructing a Sir Michael to deliver various letters to various addressees: 'If you knew / How much they do import, you would make haste'. The messenger is pretty sure that he can guess (4.4.4–6). We do not know the identities of all the intended recipients, but one of the two named—the Lord Marshal, eldest son and namesake of Thomas Mowbray, whose trial by combat versus Bolingbroke was aborted at Coventry—is implicated in a second rebellion against the King (this being the principal political action of *2 Henry IV*). We may presume that the other recipients are likewise parties to some sort of 'confederacy' hostile to Henry's reign.

The Archbishop is keenly aware of the showdown building at Shrewsbury, that there 'The King with mighty and quick-raised power / Meets with Lord Harry'. He knows as well that the rebel forces are not all that were originally supposed to assemble; but he does not include himself among the absentees:

> I fear, Sir Michael,
> What with the sickness of Northumberland,
> Whose power was in the first proportion,
> And what with Owen Glendower's absence thence,
> Who with them was a rated sinew too,
> And comes not in, o'erruled by prophecies,
> I fear the power of Percy is too weak
> To wage an instant trial with the King.
>
> (4.4.12–19)

The Archbishop gives no indication that he ever intended to join his forces with those of the rebel leaders who have gathered north of the town, nor that he ever committed himself to doing so—indeed, that he was *ever invited* to collaborate with them. But he is active in marshaling sufficient strength to provide security should 'Lord Percy thrive not', for in that case he is sure 'the King ... means to visit us, / For he hath heard of our confederacy' (4.4.35–37). Again urging his message bearer to make haste, he returns to penning solicitations to still more political friends. On the eve of the battle, Hotspur receives a letter which he declines to read (5.2.80). Are we not meant to assume that it is from the Archbishop? If so, to what point?

Whatever the answer, it would necessarily be subordinate to the basic puzzle here: what explains the conflicting expectations regarding the Archbishop's contribution to the rebellion gathering head at Shrewsbury? Given anything like the 'five and twenty thousand men of choice' he and his allies muster to confront the King's forces after Hotspur's defeat (cf. *2 Henry IV*, 1.3.11, 16; 3.1.95–98), their presence at the battle—which despite the rebels being outnumbered seems to have been a near-run thing (4.3.28; cf. 4.2.55, 5.3.40–44, 56, 5.4.4–13, 43–45)—would likely have reversed the outcome.[48] By the Archbishop's troops *not* being conjoined with those of Hotspur, those favouring rebellion violated one of the most basic principles of military strategy and tactics: 'Concentration of Forces'. That is, given the option, one should attempt to bring together assets sufficient to overwhelm one's enemy with manifestly superior strength. Whereas divided forces can be confronted and defeated, one division at a time, by a larger unified corps, more or less as happens in this pair of plays depicting Henry IV's reign.[49]

For when the King learns that 'Douglas and the English rebels' have met at Shrewsbury, and that a 'mighty and a fearful head they are, / If promises be kept on every hand'—which fortunately for Henry, they were not—he immediately sets in motion efforts to marshal and concentrate all the power he can in the shortest possible time. Three columns are to gather numbers as they move through the east, the centre, and the west of England, and then all come together at Bridgnorth, some short distance from Shrewsbury.[50] And the King is no sooner victorious there than he dispatches thirty thousand men under Prince John and Westmorland towards York 'at dearest speed / To meet Northumberland and the prelate Scrope', while he and the Crown Prince lead a contingent into Wales to deal with the truants Glendower and Mortimer (5.5.35–40; cf. *2 Henry IV*, 4.1.21–24).

Hence, the play's primary puzzle: why did the Archbishop remain at York, rather than muster forces in time to join those with Hotspur at Shrewsbury?

A meeting of the conspirators occupies the very centre of the play. Or rather, of some of the conspirators, for Douglas, understandably, has not ventured down from Scotland. But neither is Northumberland present, which is a bit curious, given his importance to their enterprise succeeding. Perhaps he regards his son and heir as an adequate representative of his earldom's interests. What is more than just a bit curious, however, is not merely the absence of any representative of the Archbishop, but equally the resounding silence about him. Might this be a consequence of what those present are scheming, something which they know this much-respected prelate would not support—indeed, would emphatically condemn (as would any other responsible subject of the kingdom)? For their ambition entails nothing less than the dismemberment of the realm forged by Edward I, and brought to such power and prominence under the glorious reign of Henry's grandfather, great Edward III. And the main business of the conspirators' gathering is to ratify the distribution of the fragments that they anticipate upon the overthrow of Henry.

As they await the map on which is indicated each party's share, we witness some banter between Glendower and Hotspur consisting mainly of the former's claims of magical powers and signs, and the latter's scoffing responses, which become so acerbic that Mortimer, worried about their offensiveness, attempts to restrain his brother-in-law: 'Peace, cousin Percy; you'll make him mad' (3.1.51). But neither contestant is to be reined in. Glendower continues to boast ('I can call spirits from the vasty deep'), and Percy to lampoon his claims ('Why, so can I, or so can any man, / But will they come when you do call for them?').

This testy colloquy illustrates an important, and puzzling, difference among honour-loving men, and even of whole honour-based societies—puzzling, insofar as there is no obvious explanation of *why* what would seem the same 'cause' should manifest itself in such radically diverse ways. For there are honour-lovers who enjoy boasting about their feats and qualities, and whose societies not merely accept the propriety of their doing so, but actively encourage it. This is not necessarily to the discredit of those they brag of having bested—quite the contrary. The martial prowess of Hector is tacitly extolled in the honour Achilles claims for having defeated him.[51]

However, there is another kind of honour-lover, one who regards such self-glorifying as vulgar, as fostering vanity and undermining truthfulness by encouraging exaggeration (not to say, balderdash), and who consequently prefers to let his deeds speak for themselves—which *in practice* means leaving it to *others* to praise them. Doing so falls especially to the poets. Strange, then, that Hotspur should profess to despise 'mincing poetry', though he may say this simply to further annoy his boastful ally, who, among his many other accomplishments, claims to be musical (ibid., 120–31). For Glendower exemplifies the former kind of honour-lover; Hotspur the latter. Not surprisingly, then, they clash, repeatedly. So, upon the Welshman's alleging, 'I can teach you, cousin, to command the devil', Hotspur, seemingly indifferent to the respect due his host, comes perilously close to calling him a liar: 'And I can teach thee, coz, to shame the devil: / By telling truth. "Tell truth and shame the devil"' (3.1.55–57). In the nick of time, the arrival of the map puts an end to this 'unprofitable chat'.

But it does not put an end to honour-chafing disputes. With respect to the country they hope to seize, Mortimer announces, 'The Archdeacon hath divided it / Into three limits very equally'. All of Wales east of the Severn goes to Glendower, all of England north of the Trent to Hotspur (presumably representing the Northumberland estate), with remainder of the country south of the Trent to Mortimer. The basic division must have been previously agreed upon, for the 'indentures tripartite' have been drawn up, and the closing of the deal awaits only the interchange of the properly signed and sealed copies (ibid., 70–80). It is of some interest that Mortimer, supposedly legitimate heir to the throne of the entirety of England and Wales, submits so tamely to this dismemberment of his kingdom. Admittedly, his position is weak, for he commands no independent forces, and a third of a pie is better than none. However, it is not he who protests the proposed division, but rather Hotspur.

Contemplating the River Trent on the map, he now professes to discover his share is not truly equal in that a loop in the river's course leaves a 'huge half-moon' of rich bottom land on the 'wrong' side for his purpose. Rather than suggest they rectify the alleged discrepancy by redrawing the articles, he proposes to *change the course of the river* by digging a new channel straight across the loop! Moreover, his uncle Worcester, usually so practical, *seconds* the idea (3.1.109–11)! Not surprisingly, Glendower demurs; and Mortimer uses the map to point out another bend in the river that favours the Percy interest an equal amount. Hotspur nonetheless insists, 'I'll have it so; a little change will do it'. Glendower is equally insistent: 'I'll not have it altered'. The Welshman's adamancy is the more curious, since the dispute in no way affects his portion. Is he endeavouring to protect the interests of his new son-in-law? Or is he now simply not in a cooperative mood? The wrangling continues until Glendower finally concedes (perhaps wryly, confident that no such channel will ever be cut), 'Come, you shall have Trent turned'. Whereupon Hotspur, mollified by being granted his way, withdraws his objection: 'I do not care. I'll give thrice so much land / To any well-deserving friend'; but when it comes to bargaining— when, that is, he regards his honour engaged—'I'll cavil on the ninth part of a hair' (3.1.133–36).

Given the prickliness of the several parties, of Hotspur and Glendower in particular, one wonders whether they could have sustained their amicable arrangement had their rebellion been successful. The petty quarrel between these two serves to illustrate the likely consequence of a tripartite division of the kingdom among ambitious, war-hardened men—warlords—who regard the ready resort to violence for political ends as only natural. Would there not be increasingly frequent border disputes, and clashes over coveted properties, steadily escalating in the scale of forces involved, eventually resulting in outright war, with perhaps first one pairing, then another allying themselves against the third, with no prospect of enduring peace in sight unless and until there emerged at last another Edward I—that is, a lord strong enough to subdue the others, and so once again unify the parts under a single sovereignty? And judging from past experience, this might not happen for generations, if not centuries.

The rebellion is not successful, however—pretty much for the reasons Sir Milque-Toast foresaw. At the time the conspirators met to finalize their division of the prize, Mortimer indicated that he, Percy, and Worcester would be proceeding to Shrewsbury, where they expected to link up with Northumberland and the Scottish power. Meanwhile, Glendower was to assemble his followers and join them within a fortnight. In the event, however, not all of these engagements are kept. First, Northumberland fails to show, sending a messenger to inform his son that he is 'grievous sick'. Perhaps because he knows his brother, Worcester queries the messenger, 'I prithee, tell me: doth he keep his bed?' The dutiful servant confirms that the Earl has been bedridden for at least four days, and 'was much feared by his physicians'.[52] So, 'Who leads his power?' Hotspur wonders. No one, he is dismayed to learn, for his father writes that 'his friends by deputation could not / Be so soon drawn; nor did he think it meet / To lay so dangerous and dear a trust / On any soul removed but his own' (4.1.16–24, 32–35). Ah, yes—so *dangerous* and *dear* a *trust!* One suspects young Percy would have crawled to Shrewsbury on his hands and knees rather than renege on his commitment, leaving his allies in the lurch. The elder Percy, however, is not so fastidious about his honour. Moreover, his failure either to bring or to send his forces does not merely diminish the numbers of the rebels' army ('a very limb lopped off'). But also, as both Hotspur and Worcester realize—and surely Northumberland must have, too—his absence undermines the credibility of the enterprise in the eyes of the soldiers already present.

So, does the good Earl accordingly recommend that his son and brother immediately withdraw their forces and seek safety, whether with him in the North, or in Scotland or in Wales? Not a bit. Instead, he gives them 'bold advertisement' that with their admittedly '*small* conjunction' of power they should try their luck! 'For, as he writes, "there is no quailing now, / Because the King is certainly possessed / Of all our purposes"' (ibid., 36–41). Might this fact have something to do with his illness? Hotspur and Douglas strain to find some silver lining in this nimbus of disappointment. Could it actually be a good thing that they not risk 'the exact wealth of all our states / All at one cast' of the die? For now they may fight the more boldly, knowing there will be retained some power to which they can retire should things begin badly for them: 'A rendezvous, a home to fly unto, / If that the devil and mischance look big / Upon the maidenhead of our affairs' (4.1.56–58). Worcester is not so sanguine; he knows full well that the nature of their attempt 'brooks no division'; and there is that additional consideration: 'It will be thought / By some that know not why he is away / That wisdom, loyalty and mere dislike / Of our proceedings kept the Earl from hence'. But Hotspur is determined; trading military logic for psychological speculation, he argues that 'his [father's] absence . . . lends a lustre and more great opinion, / A larger dare to our enterprise', which men will interpret as bespeaking confidence of success.

Moreover, they yet have 'the hope of what is to come in'—presumably Douglas is referring to the anticipated reinforcements being brought by Glendower and Mortimer (though why the latter is not already present is puzzling, given that he was to accompany Percy and Worcester to Shrewsbury to meet Northumberland and the Scots; 3.1.81–84). But now Sir Richard Vernon arrives with two more kinds of bad news. First, he reports that three large contingents of royal forces are hurrying to meet up and confront the rebels where they stand, including one being led by a brilliantly accoutred and sprightly Crown Prince. On hearing this, Hotspur rhetorically summons the horse that will bear him 'like a thunderbolt / Against the bosom of the Prince of Wales. / Harry to Harry shall, hot horse to horse, / Meet and ne'er part till one drop down a corpse' (4.1.118–22). And though he denies being nonplussed by the news of the King's advancing battalions, he nonetheless wishes aloud, 'O, that Glendower were come'. This prompts Vernon to report his second item of unhappy news: that as he passed through Worcester he learned that Glendower 'cannot draw his power this fourteen days'. Douglas admits, 'That's the worst tidings that I hear of yet'. Worcester agrees: 'Ay, by my faith, that bears a frosty sound'.

And it is rather strange. For when the conspirators last met and allotted Glendower those fourteen days to draw together his 'tenants, friends and neighbouring gentlemen', the Welsh chieftain assured his fellows, 'A shorter time shall send me to you, lords' (3.1.85–89). And we know that when he wished to muster his forces to confront the invading royal army of Herefordshire men led by Mortimer, he apparently had no difficulty doing so (1.1.38–42). Indeed, he boasts, 'Three times hath Henry Bolingbroke made head / Against my power; thrice from the banks of Wye / And sandy-bottomed Severn have I sent him / Bootless home and weather-beaten back' (a claim which Hotspur openly satirized; 3.1.62–67). Why, then, can he not manage to assemble a force in time to assist those being led by Hotspur? The Archbishop of York somehow learned that Glendower, 'a rated sinew' of the rebellion, had not in fact joined with those at Shrewsbury. York's sources, however, did not attribute this to inadequate time to muster his men; rather, to his being 'o'erruled by prophecies' (4.4.15–17). But whether 'that great magician' (1.3.83) would have his tardiness be attributed to insufficient time or to inauspicious divinations, one suspects he would have tried harder, or had the auguries reread, had young Percy treated him and his claims with the respect he felt he deserved.

Speaking of the Archbishop, the rebels—faced with an advancing royal army thirty-thousand strong (4.1.129)—would certainly have welcomed any part of the twenty-five thousand Scroop and his allies muster to confront the column Henry dispatches *after* Shrewsbury. So, once again, why did the prelate, though favouring this first rebellion (cf. 4.4.33), and himself a leader of the second, not throw in his lot with that of the Percys, the Scots, and the Welsh? Could it be he was never so much as invited to do so? Recall, Worcester delegated to brother Northumberland the task of communicating with the disaffected Archbishop: 'You, my lord, / . . . / Shall secretly into the bosom creep / Of that same noble prelate well beloved, / The Archbishop'. Worcester claims to know that Scroop is already involved in plotting against the King, is already primed to act, 'And only stays but to behold the face / Of that occasion that shall bring it on' (1.3.261–71). Thus, it should not have taken much arm-twisting to draw him into acting jointly with the Percy-Glendower-Douglas alliance, especially given its inclusion of Edmund Mortimer, Richard II's legitimate heir to the usurped throne (supposedly). But, as noted before, the Archbishop gives no indication that his participation was ever solicited. Did the Earl of Northumberland never make it to York? If not, why not?

Certainly the careful Earl's failure to recruit the Archbishop would be of a piece with the rest of his role in the rebellion, for he did absolutely nothing to further its success, and much to undermine it. First and foremost, of course, is his failure to provide the contingent of troops upon which his confederates are counting, amounting to a crippling loss of strength. For even if he were as seriously ill as he professes, which may be doubted (and perhaps is by Worcester), he should have sent them under some lieutenant, who could then have placed them under the command of the other two Percys. His excuse for not doing so is virtually self-contradictory, invoking the dangerousness of the project to justify doing nothing, making it more dangerous still for those already exposed. Add to this the demoralizing effect of his absence on those who remain. As Hotspur exclaims, 'Sick now? Droop now? This sickness doth infect / The very lifeblood of our enterprise. / 'Tis catching hither, even to our camp' (4.1.28–30).

Then, rather than recommend that his son withdraw the remaining 'small conjunction' of forces while there is still time—thus saving them for a later opportunity—he instead 'boldly' urges Hotspur, 'To see how fortune is disposed to us'! What's with the 'us'? And if we may presume that rumours of Northumberland's paralyzing 'illness' could have reached Glendower, that would be one more reason for his also staying away from an enterprise which now has such a diminished prospect of success. Were Northumberland in the pay of Henry, he could hardly have done more to cripple the rebellion. Well might Shakespeare have Percy's widow later chide her father-in-law: 'The time was, father, that you broke your word / When you were more endear'd to it than now; / . . . / Who then persuaded you to stay at home? / There were two honours lost, yours and your son's' (*2 Henry IV*, 2.3.10–16). Two honours lost, but only one lost honourably.

Hotspur, 'child of Honour'—or veritable '*king* of honour', according to the redoubtable Douglas (4.1.10)—is a lens whereby to study honour-loving per se. Moreover, his commitment to pursuing this adornment of life as its be-all and end-all throws into relief the very different posture of the Crown Prince, who mentions honour but four times, three being in descriptions of his rival. Whereas upon his first appearance in the play, Percy practically preaches a sermon on the surpassing importance of 'honour'. It comes in the course of that blunt chiding of his father and his uncle for their part is making 'this thorn, this canker, Bolingbroke', the king of England: 'Yet time serves wherein you may redeem / Your banished honours and restore yourselves / Into the good thoughts of the world again' (1.3.179–81). Hotspur treats as self-evident that one's standing in 'the world'—which, practically speaking, necessarily means one's more or less limited corner of it—is a matter of first importance. Assured by Uncle Worcester that his elders are hatching a scheme whereby to rectify their mistake, though it is a matter 'deep and dangerous, . . . full of peril', Hotspur immediately rises to the bait: 'Send danger from the east unto the west, / So honour cross it from the north to south [etc.]' (ibid., 189–95).

Amused by his son's enthusiasm regardless of what be the particulars, Northumberland comments to Worcester, 'Imagination of some great exploit / Drives him beyond the bounds of patience'—incidentally alluding to a flaw characteristic of high-spirited men: an overeagerness to act, and proportional impatience of delay. It will prove fatal to young Hotspur. But just the mention of a 'great exploit' is enough to prompt him to a paean about the pursuit of honour:

> By heaven, methinks it were an easy leap
> To pluck bright honour from the pale-faced moon,
> Or dive into the bottom of the deep,
> Where fathom-line could never touch the ground,
> And pluck up drowned honour by the locks,

> So he that doth redeem her thence might wear,
> Without corrival, all her dignities.
> (Ibid., 200–206)

This extravagance moves Worcester to observe, 'He apprehends a world of figures here / But not the form of what he should attend'. By his own admission, Hotspur's lust for honour is insatiable, as if increase of appetite grew by what it fed upon.

But notice his 'without corrival'. For he sees exclusivity as of the essence of honour: ideally, he would have it *all*, 'all her dignities' for himself. Unlike lovers of wisdom (a good that is shareable without loss), lovers of honour, like those of wealth, are inherently competitors. For the extent one must *share* honour with others, the value of one's own portion is diminished. So in another place and time young Henry, become king, will exhort his depleted 'band of brothers' prior to battle with a far more numerous French host, 'The fewer men, the greater share of honour', and 'God's peace, I would not lose so great an honour / As one man more, methinks, would share from me' (*Henry V*, 4.3.22, 31–32).[53] Hotspur would not share *any*, if that were possible, as it virtually never is in battles between armies such as meet at Shrewsbury. And yet, ironically, *that* is the one occasion it *would* have been possible, had Worcester faithfully delivered Prince Hal's challenge, 'to save the blood on either side, / Try fortune with [Hotspur] in a single fight' (5.1.99–100)—a challenge Percy professes he would willingly have accepted had he learned of it prior to the opposing forces being set in motion (5.2.47–49).

Hotspur, however, is more than just an aspiring *lover* of honour; he is a premier achiever of it—indeed, thus far practically 'without corrival'. Or so attests King Henry, envious 'that my lord Northumberland / Should be the father to so blest a son, / A son who is the theme of honour's tongue', whereas he sees only 'riot and *dis*honor stain the brow' of his own young Harry' (1.1.78–85). Later, the King elaborates the same comparison in berating the Prince for his dissolute ways, and makes explicit the political implication: 'What never-dying honour hath he got / Against renowned Douglas, whose high deeds' are famous throughout Christendom. Yet, 'Thrice hath this Hotspur . . . / Discomfited great Douglas' (3.2.106–14; cf. 4.1.1–5). No surprise, then, that Douglas would pronounce young Percy 'the king of honour'; nor that 'ancient lords and reverend bishops' should submit to his leadership. So high has Hotspur's standing mounted that Henry claims to suspect that his own son and heir might be base enough to throw in his lot with Percy. It is this hyperbole that draws from the Prince that eloquent denial quoted earlier, in which he declares his intention to defeat 'this gallant Hotspur' and thereby harvest for himself all the glories presently 'sitting on his helm'.

When at last the two men do meet on the battlefield, Hotspur speaks first: 'If I mistake not, thou art Harry Monmouth'. There must be something in his voice that implies the disdain with which he has always referred to the Prince (cf. 1.3.228–31, 4.1.93–96), for Hal replies, 'Thou speak'st as if I would deny my name'. Hotspur then, like a participant in a formal tournament, identifies himself: 'My name is Harry Percy'. Whereupon the Prince rejoins:

> Why then, I see
> A very valiant rebel of the name.
> I am the Prince of Wales, and think not, Percy,
> To share with me in glory any more.
> Two stars keep not their motion in one sphere,
> Nor can one England brook a double reign
> Of Harry Percy and the Prince of Wales.
> (5.4.60–66)

How Hotspur must resent Hal's presumption! That a notorious delinquent who has not a single martial achievement to embellish his name should nonetheless claim to have hitherto *shared* the glory that Percy alone has garnered, and have the further audacity to insist on having it all!

Duly considered, the prince's audacity is more than a little puzzling, since what he says seems absurd on the face of it. After all, Hal has himself on several occasions conceded Hotspur's preeminence in fame, indeed insisted on it, while admitting that he—far from gathering glories—has so far accumulated only 'shames' and 'indignities' to his discredit; that compared to the renown of 'gallant Hotspur', he is 'unthought-of' (cf. 3.2.137, 140–46). In the presence of all who witness Worcester's embassy prior to the battle, the Prince freely admits having 'a truant been to chivalry' (5.1.94). Even so, might he sometimes be given to vainglorious boasting? Recall our first hearing of him: this same Hotspur reported that upon telling him of the upcoming tournament at Oxford, Hal indicated he would deck himself in the favours of some trollop and 'unhorse the lustiest challenger' among the participants. Was he merely teasing—needling, rather—this fervent honour-lover about the martial games of bygone chivalry that he takes so seriously? We do not know whether Hal made good his boast, or even cared to show up for the tournament. It would seem not, given his admitting to be bereft of accolades won, that he is a virtual unknown so far as any honorable exploits are concerned. Whatever the truth regarding that ceremonial occasion, Hal's apparent presumption upon confronting his adversary when the stakes are mortal may actually be quite calculated, an intentional provocation meant to anger a man well known to act impulsively—not to say, recklessly—when his blood is up.

We certainly have ample evidence of Hotspur's short fuse, including the testimony of those who know him well. The man himself admits acting in anger by way of explaining how arose that 'misunderstanding' regarding the prisoners captured at Humbleton. He had been provoked beyond courtesy by the effete, finicky manner of the King's envoy: 'To be so pestered with a popinjay, / Out of my grief and my impatience / Answered neglectingly, I know not what— / He should or he should not—for he made me mad' (1.3.50–53). And after Henry upbraids him for not having turned over the prisoners, but also about his intervention in favour of ransoming Mortimer, the young man erupts when the King leaves, vowing disobedience: 'An if the devil come and roar for them / I will not send them. I will after straight / And tell him so, for I will ease my heart, / Albeit I make a hazard of my head'. His father urges restraint—'What, drunk with choler? Stay and pause awhile'—but the young man continues to rant, eventually provoking his father to exclaim, 'Why, what a wasp-stung and impatient fool' (ibid., 124–37, 234). We have his wife's testimony that he is 'altogether governed by humours' (3.1.230). And when Mortimer rebuked him for the derisive manner in which he treated Glendower, Percy's excuse is perfectly in character: 'I cannot choose. Sometime he angers me' (3.1.144). Worcester also warns his nephew about so readily indulging his spirit:

> You must needs learn, lord, to amend this fault.
> Though sometimes it show greatness, courage, blood
> (And that's the dearest grace it renders you),
> Yet oftentimes it doth present harsh rage,
> Defect of manners, want of government,
> Pride, haughtiness, opinion and disdain. . . .
> (Ibid., 176–81)

Does the Prince aim to exploit his opponent's 'want of government' when angered, intending to 'madden' him by the apparently absurd claim that Hal presently shares preeminence in glory with Hotspur, but that England will 'brook a double reign' no more?

Whatever the case, Percy replies, 'Nor shall it, Harry, for the hour is come / To end the one of us, and would to God / Thy name in arms were now as great as mine'. Chided thus, Hal proclaims his intention to redeem his promise to his father: 'I'll make it greater ere I part from thee, / And all the budding honours on thy crest / I'll crop to make a garland for my head'. Only further offended by the effrontery of this threat, Percy rejoins, 'I can no longer brook thy vanities', and attacks. Both men having acknowledged that this will be a duel to the death, they set to it without interruption. However long they fought (cf. 1.3.98–107), it is the cool Prince, not the hot Percy, who emerges victorious.

Hotspur falls with a plaintive, 'O Harry, thou hast robbed me of my youth'. His dying words prove him an honour-lover to the bitter end:

> I better brook the loss of brittle life
> Than those proud titles thou hast won of me.
> They wound my thoughts worse than thy sword my flesh.
> But thoughts, the slaves of life, and life, time's fool,
> And time, that takes survey of all the world,
> Must have a stop....
>   ... No, Percy, thou art dust
> And food for—

He expires, leaving his vanquisher to finish the melancholy thought: 'For worms, brave Percy' (5.4.77–86). Because Hal assumes the eulogy he then pronounces over his fallen rival is heard by no ears but his own, we may assume it reflects his genuine respect for the man.

>   Fare thee well, great heart.
> Ill-weaved ambition, how much art thou shrunk!
> When that this body did contain a spirit
> A kingdom for it was too small a bound,
> But now two paces of the vilest earth
> Is room enough. This earth that bears thee dead
> Bears not alive so stout a gentleman.
> If thou wert sensible of courtesy
> I should not make so dear a show of zeal.
> But let my favours hide thy mangled face ...
> Adieu, and take thy praise with thee to heaven.
> Thy ignominy sleep with thee in the grave
> But not remembered in thy epitaph.
>   (Ibid., 86–100)

Clearly, Hal ranks highly the kind of man Hotspur represents, one who is ruled by his love of honour—rather than ruled, as are the vast multitudes of men, by love of wealth for all the pleasures and comforts it can buy. This is not to say, however, that he regards him as of the very *highest* rank. For he surely does not rank Percy higher than the kind of man the Prince himself represents, whatever that might be. That the earth now bears 'not alive so *stout* a gentleman' is to credit love of honour with imparting adamant fortitude to a man thus constituted, such that he may willingly fight to the death, whether or not reason would approve the cause and circumstance in which he did so. This is a strength of soul not to be despised, but neither can a rational person endorse it unqualifiedly.

Having delivered his generous benediction over his fallen foe, the Prince then spots nearby the gross body of Hotspur's antistrophe, Falstaff, who (Poins assured Hal) will fight no longer 'than he sees reason' (1.2.175). Judging by all the evidence we are provided, that means 'practically never'. In the present instance, accordingly, he has been feigning death—and continues to feign as he hears Hal speak of him. Why does he do so? And what must he think about what he hears? For the memorial tribute Hal addresses to this 'old acquaintance'—*acquaintance!*—contrasts markedly with that which he spoke over the 'noble Percy':

> Poor Jack, farewell.
> I could have better spared a better man.
> O, I should have a heavy miss of thee
> If I were much in love with vanity.
> Death hath not struck so fat a deer today,
> Though many dearer in this bloody fray.[54]
> (5.4.102–7)

What a pregnant 'If'! And it hardly matters that those 'many dearer' remain nameless—if anything, this simply heightens the disparity in regard.

When left once more alone, Falstaff resurrects himself, and seems grandly indifferent to his having overheard the invidious comparison the Prince had drawn. Instead, true to form, he launches into a sophistical rationalization for having 'counterfeited' death. Embedded in his specious reasoning is the famous maxim, 'The better part of valour is discretion' (ibid., 118–19). Of course, this is an exceedingly flexible principle, of a piece with his fighting no longer than he 'sees reason': one man's discretion is another's desertion.

The value of honour is never questioned by the Prince, much less repudiated. Shakespeare has relegated the disparagement of honour to his funny fat man, who expresses it privately just prior to the battle. The old faker, who in a time long past somehow managed to get himself dubbed a knight, had proposed to Hal, 'if thou see me down in the battle and bestride me, so; 'tis a point of friendship'. Hal's response is noncommittal, not to say evasive: 'Nothing but a colossus can do thee that friendship. Say thy prayers, and farewell'—adding as he leaves, 'Why, thou owest God a death' (5.1.121–26). As do we all, of course. The best that may remain to any of us is to choose the manner. Left thus alone, Falstaff soliloquizes:

> 'Tis not due yet. I would be loath to pay him before his day. What need
> I be so forward with him that calls not on me? Well, 'tis no matter;

honour pricks me on. Yea, but how if honour prick me off when I come on? How then? Can honour set to a leg? No. Or an arm? No. Or take away the grief of a wound? No. Honour hath no skill in surgery, then? No. What is honour? A word. What is in that word 'honour'? What is that 'honour'? Air. A trim reckoning. Who hath it? He that died o'Wednesday. Doth he feel it? No. Doth he hear it? No. 'Tis insensible then? Yea, to the dead. But will it not live with the living? No. Why? Detraction will not suffer it. Therefore I'll none of it. Honour is a mere scutcheon. And so ends my catechism. (5.1.127–40)

There are some who publicly applaud Falstaff's 'realism' here, and doubtless many more (given the fatness of these pursy times) who do so in the privacy of their hearts.[55] That Falstaff's view is transparently self-serving is not an argument against its validity, of course. But it is reason enough to examine it more closely.

Consider, for example, his rather lame rebuttal of the view that the honour accorded he who has died in the course of earning it lives on in the living. He alleges that this is not so because 'detraction will not suffer it'. Whereas Hal later proves the contrary in his eulogy of the departed Hotspur. His generous benediction is enough to remind us that whatever the limited validity of Falstaff's claim, it is more applicable to the living than to the dead. That is, honour-lovers are more apt to 'detract' from the honour accorded their living rivals than those with whom they are no longer competing. Perhaps this partly explains Hal's parenthesis in the eulogy he addresses to Hotspur, 'If thou wert sensible of courtesy / I should not make so dear a show of zeal'.[56]

Falstaff's common presumption that the dead are insensible to whatever respect they are paid by the living does, however, raise a perplexing question. For it is obvious that, generally speaking, the living pay a *lot* of respect to the dead, albeit quite how and how much varies with place and time. Why do we? Are not the tombs of various prehistoric peoples, often laboriously and artfully constructed, evidence of an inclination deeply grounded in human nature? Why the more or less elaborate funeral rites—'more' in the case of those who have gained special distinction, 'honour', in their lives; 'less' in the case of ordinary people, but still far from none. Why the ceremony that attends burials, why the prayers, why the eulogies, why the flowers, why the solemn requiems, why the customary periods of mourning, why the permanent grave-markers (to say nothing of grand statuary and lavish sepulchres), each dedicated to the memory of whosoever's grave they mark? These markers, not incidentally, provide a location where those who care to may periodically pay tribute, keeping alive a memory of the deceased. Why all of this, the various means various peoples use to indicate respect and concern for the person who has died? Doubtless many of those who participate presume (like Falstaff), or at least suspect, that the one who has died is 'insensible' to his being so 'honoured'. Why, then—to repeat—are these things done? Must it not be for the sake of the living?

Difficult as it is to account for in strictly rational terms, virtually everyone would prefer to be remembered after he dies. More precisely, be remembered fondly, gratefully, better yet, admiringly: *honoured*—preferably by more people than by less, and for a longer than a shorter time, and thought of more highly than others with whom one might be compared—but in any event, *not* immediately forgotten. For the thought that one might depart this world and be neither missed nor remembered reduces the felt significance of one's present life, along with one's achievements and labours, sufferings and sacrifices. It is at least partly to counteract the notion that human lives have no more intrinsic importance than those of beasts—indeed, of insects—that peoples virtually everywhere have instituted funeral ceremonies and rites of mourning (to say nothing of the mourning, the grieving itself).

These practices express some sort of *care*, that whenever a person of even minor consequence dies, that his having existed be acknowledged and suitably remembered, memorialized. For a person to receive no recognition at all upon his *death* is to imply that his *life* was of negligible importance. Perhaps, objectively considered, that was so; and perhaps many of those who thus 'pay their respects' upon his passing would privately admit to sharing such a view. But that is not really the point. Whatever else, funeral rites and markers serve people as wardings against the spectre of their *own* possible meaninglessness. Hence, the scanting of such ceremonies erodes the significance people are apt to feel regarding their own lives. Moreover, the customary prohibition against speaking ill of the dead provides the living some security with respect to how they will be spoken of when they can no longer speak for themselves—tacit confirmation that people naturally do care about how they will be regarded once they are beyond all caring. Similarly, the dead are eulogized by the living, not least in the hope of being praised in their turn.

Whereas beasts exist in a timeless 'present', preoccupied with the bodily requirements of mere life—and upon dying are as if they never were—man is aware that he 'lives in Time', but only 'for a time'. By virtue of his rational imagination, he entertains speculations about what may lie 'before' him, possible futures, including the certainty of a Future in which he is no longer present. And by virtue of a rational memory, he has a continuing awareness of what not only he has left 'after' him, but what countless others have as well: an incorrigible Past, largely inconsequential, but occasionally illuminated by deeds of either glory or shame. Though he may experience episodic stints of forgetfulness in moments of high passion or excitement—in the midst of a battle, say—he cannot ultimately suppress his temporal awareness. Nor what is implicit in it: awareness of a rational capability whereby, day in and day out, he *decides* what to do, how to act—such as whether to stand and fight, or turn and run—while knowing that whatever he does, or fails to do, is not isolated in the moment but has consequences for an uncertain future that will afterwards become a past, to be remembered with pride or shame, gratitude or regret.

Any person worth considering has enough reason to understand that this *is* the human condition: neither that of an oblivious beast nor that of an omniscient god, but a mortal being denied eternity in the only world he can be sure of, yet capable of actions and achievements for both good and ill that will 'live after him' in people's memories, to his honour or his disgrace. And his spirit cares which it will be. Now, suppose you are the 'he'. The question is: *can* you *entirely* eradicate that care with (supposedly) rational assurances that you will be oblivious to whatever is said and thought about you once you are dead, especially by friends and family, but to some extent by all who have known you? If you suspect you cannot, you have thereby an inkling of your political nature. The imagination of being honoured in death (as others have been), rather than dismissed as of no account—much less despised or reviled—encourages the living to undertake honourable actions and practices, and to avoid dishonourable ones, to the benefit of all whom such behaviour serves. In this respect, the real value of honour accrues not to he who receives it, but rather to they who pay it.

His 'catechism' recited and the bloody battle under way, the false knight comes upon the body of a true knight, Sir Walter Blount, who, while bravely serving as one of the King's decoys had been killed by the mighty Douglas, as had Lords Stafford and Shirley before him (5.3.1–13). Falstaff sees in Blount's fate only a confirmation of his own doctrine: 'There's honour for you', shortly thereafter adding, 'I like not such grinning honour as Sir Walter hath. Give me life, which if I can save, so. If not, honour comes unlooked for, and there's an end' (ibid., 32–33, 59–62). No honour attended the miserable 'end' Shakespeare crafts for Falstaff in *Henry V*, that of a frightened old shell of himself playing with his fingers like a child while damning women and babbling about God and green fields (2.3.13–30). Nor did honour come 'unlooked for' in Blount's case. When confronting Douglas, he expressly challenges him: 'What is thy name that in battle thus thou crossest me? / What honour dost thou seek upon my head?' Douglas identifies himself, and adds, 'I do haunt thee in the battle thus / Because some tell me thou art a king'. Blount lies, 'They tell thee true'. Douglas then commands him to yield or die. Sir Walter replies, 'I was not born a yielder', and so fights to his death (ibid., 6–13).

Douglas subsequently engages the King himself and has him in some danger when, fortunately for Henry, his heir arrives, warning the redoubtable Scot, 'It is the Prince of Wales that threatens thee, / Who never promiseth but he means to pay' (5.4.41–42)—a claim whose significance, we may assume, is not limited to contexts like that in which it is spoken. Moreover, it would seem to imply some collateral claims. For example, that the Prince may feel no obligation to pay what he did *not* expressly promise, though he may nonetheless choose to do so out of magnanimity, or for reasons of his own (cf. 1.2.198–99). The vigour of Hal's defence of his father causes Douglas to break off and flee in search of easier game. The Prince then indicates an eagerness to set off in aid of others hard-pressed, but the King bids him pause in order that he may acknowledge a further significance to his son's action than simply Henry's own survival. It marks a turning point in their relationship: 'Thou hast redeemed thy lost opinion / And showed thou mak'st some tender of my life / In this fair rescue' (ibid., 47–49). This is not to say that their common future is all sweetness and light, however.

Some indefinite time and who knows how many victims later, the bold Scot comes upon Falstaff cheering on Prince Hal as he duels with Hotspur. Douglas assaults the old fraudster, 'who falls down as if he were dead' (more or less immediately, we may assume), and thereafter is apparently left alone (ibid., 75). How does he get away with this? Does he feign a heart attack? Or did he actually faint in fright? And does Douglas desist simply out of contempt? For we would suppose that were a swordsman to go down in the midst of an assault, whether or not conscious, normally his attacker would make assurance double sure and so deliver a mortal stroke—rather as Falstaff claims to worry that Percy may be 'counterfeiting', and so to ensure he is truly dead stabs his corpse *in the thigh*! Is he so genuinely fearful that Hotspur may still be alive that he dare not approach closer than required to prick him in the leg? Whatever the case, when he meets Prince Hal and Prince John after the battle, he dumps Hotspur's body at their feet, and—ever shameless—announces, 'There is Percy. If your father will do me any honour, so; if not, let him kill the next Percy himself. I look to be either earl or duke, I can assure you' (ibid., 140–43).[57]

Falstaff's preposterous claim does, however, indicate one respect in which the pursuit of honour as a good, much less as life's greatest good, is problematic (to say the least). Honour is subject to being awarded, and enjoyed, under false pretences—though, strictly speaking, the satisfaction that comes purely from being *honoured* presumes one's awareness that one is *deserving*: that the external recognition is roughly proportionate to one's awareness of actual achievement. To the extent this is *not* the case, the pleasure brought by the recognition is apt to be attenuated, or even cancelled entirely by the pain of shame, at least in souls graced with some natural nobility, hence probity. Honour that has been undeservedly bestowed may stimulate other pleasant feelings, such as that of being envied, or famous, or even admired (which is not always the same thing as being honoured), as well as bring various external benefits—perhaps an exalted title and attendant revenue, as Falstaff (facetiously?) claims to deserve.

Moreover, being honoured, whether deservedly or not, may be politically useful in various ways. To mention only the most obvious: acquiring military distinction often leads to 'popularity', thereby enhancing one's personal power with respect to political achievements in which popular support is a factor. Thus, one may adjudge honour (however gained, and whether deserved or not) as an *instrumental* good, even should one agree with Falstaff's catechism that so-called 'honour' is practically worthless in and of itself, being but a verbal embellishment. In light of such considerations, among others, Shakespeare invites a serious reader to address in all seriousness the question Falstaff poses, then answers so flippantly: 'what *is* honour', and what is its real value, if any? *Is* it merely a flattering word, and as such, little more than so much air? Or does the word refer to something more substantial?

First of all, as the above discussion implied, ordinary usage can be ambiguous because the term is used in two distinct, albeit related, ways. In some contexts, it refers to public recognition, whether bestowed by someone in some sort of official capacity, or as a spontaneous reaction of people to qualities or accomplishments that command their respect. But the word is also used in referring to one's internal standards of fitting behaviour. There are certain things a 'man of honour' will not do, regardless the incentive, provocation, or threat; and other things he will not fail to do if he possibly can, regardless of the risk to body or soul.[58] This personal internal sense of honour is reflective of what one regards as base or despicable, as well as of what natural duties and obligations one recognises and what qualities, actions, and achievements one takes pride in oneself, hence respects in others.

Now, can this be just *anything*? Could anyone be honoured, or truly 'honour' himself (as opposed to construct rationalizations whereby to excuse himself), for being fat, lazy, cowardly, and dishonest? Or is it not the case that certain qualities *naturally* command admiration?[59] The most obvious is courage, the most visible of the virtues, and it is not difficult to explain why this is so. Virtually everyone is aware of his own fears, especially of injury and death, and of how difficult it can be to exert control over these fears in the face of danger, however much one might wish to. Consequently, people naturally admire as well as envy the person who proves by his actions that he is not ruled by his fears—that he has the self-mastery they would prefer to have themselves—hence is free to attempt 'heroic' deeds despite the risk, should he so choose.

Similar observations pertain to moderation, or temperance (what the Greeks called *sophrosunë*, 'sensibleness'), being the self-discipline required to rule one's appetites and desires, indulging them only when and as much as one's reason approves. Most people would recognise the value of such self-mastery, that it is the foundation of most achievements requiring dedication and skill, hence manifests itself in a range of excellences deserving of honour, from the scientific to the artistic to the athletic. But even so, their recognition of the desirability of moderation may be tinged with regret inasmuch as it precludes the way of life to which the bestial residue in human nature naturally inclines: that of just 'letting go', surrendering to the body's desire for pleasure and sloth. This perhaps explains the lingering envy of Falstaff that doubtless many people feel.

Wisdom likewise would be honoured by most people—in principle, that is—but as the least visible of the virtues (for it requires a certain degree of wisdom to recognise genuine wisdom), there is not apt to be broad agreement on *who* truly deserves to be so honoured. For example, there are some who profess to regard Falstaff as wise, and even cite his view of honour as evidence (though, to be sure, no one in the play endorses his view).

But granted the intrinsic value of certain personal qualities and achievements, the essential question remains: what is the value of the *honour* people pay to the person who deserves it on these bases, as distinct from the value of what they are honoured *for*? Or to put the question in a slightly different way, does being honoured *add* anything of intrinsic value, as distinct from whatever instrumental value it may have? And does it matter *who* does the honouring? Perhaps the answer—or at least Shakespeare's answer—is implicit in how the future King Henry V treats the value of honour.

Prince Hal's view of honour is nuanced. He first mentions it in a jest. He and Poins having arrived at the tavern where they await Falstaff and the other cowards that they robbed at Gad's Hill, Hal had gone down into the tavern's buttery with a few of the drawers. As a result of the time spent with them, he learned to speak their idiom, and so claims to have proven a general capacity: 'I am so good a proficient in one quarter of an hour that I can drink with any tinker in his own language during my life. I tell thee, Ned, thou has lost much honour that thou wert not with me in this action' (2.4.16–20). Obviously Hal is joking; one cannot imagine *any* honour accruing from such an 'action', much less 'much'. Still, it is a curious thing to say. Is it an oblique way of acknowledging that what is truly honourable is not just any sort of 'distinction' one might claim, hence is not simply 'relative', much less purely subjective? *Why* can't one imagine Hal's achieving 'much honour' from quickly learning to speak like a tinker?

The one venue Shakespeare provides that would seem to offer some clear insight regarding the Prince's stance towards honour and honour-seeking is the obvious one: the battlefield at Shrewsbury. For thereupon occurs the 'glorious day' Hal promised his father would come, namely, when he 'redeemed' all his shames and delinquencies on Percy's head, the day 'That this child of honour and renown, / This gallant Hotspur, this all-praised knight. / And your unthought-of Harry chance to meet'. The Prince, however, is not content to leave their meeting altogether to chance, possibly letting slip the perfect opportunity Shrewsbury affords him to shine forth—briefly—like the sun breaking through on a mainly cloudy day. Thus when Worcester comes to the King's camp, ostensibly in a last-ditch attempt to negotiate a settlement of his side's grievances, Hal offers to confront Hotspur directly, and 'Try fortune with him in a single fight'. Since this proposal comes to naught, it is left to the Prince to seek out his rival on the battlefield (cf. 5.4.30–31). Eventually they do meet, allowing Hal in one fell swoop to seize for himself all the 'glorious deeds' that currently grace Hotspur's name, all the honours painfully accumulated in the numerous hardships and battles of previous campaigns (cf. 1.3.30–32, 43–51).

How does Hal accomplish this? In the same way that Percy garnered each and every accolade, defeating whoever opposed him, thereby proving his superiority not only to all who faced him directly, but also to those whom these challengers had themselves bested. For this is the 'logic' of honours gained by feats of martial prowess: it is, in principle, transitive. If warrior B has proven himself superior to warrior C by defeating him, then should warrior A defeat B, he must be conceded superior to *both* B and C (and however many Ds, Es, Fs, and Gs these latter two will have defeated).

Or ought one not say, 'superior *on that day*; on another day, perhaps B would defeat A'? For this is surely true of other physical contests in which the prize is honour: foot-races, weight-lifting, boxing, . . . tennis. And similarly of mental contests, from spelling bees to chess. In a rematch, today's winner may be tomorrow's loser. But this presumes that a rematch is a possibility. Admittedly, even in the case of battlefield 'contests', that can sometimes be so. For given the conventions of chivalry, one may allow one's opponent an alternative to death: to yield, surrendering oneself a prisoner in return for one's life being spared—as Douglas threatens Blount with death, 'Unless thou yield thee as my prisoner' (5.3.10). For a prisoner may somehow regain his freedom, perhaps to fight another day; for example, were his captor to accept a ransom payment for his release, as Hotspur insists the King ransom Mortimer, who was captured battling the forces of Glendower (1.3.77–118). Or he may simply be set free gratis. Apparently Douglas himself was captured on one of the three times his forces were 'discomfited' by those of Hotspur, who chose to release him without charge for the sake of establishing a friendship that might pay off at some later time—as it has (3.2.112–15). Prince Hal persuades the King to do likewise when the famous Scot is made a prisoner at Shrewsbury—whether to any future effect is left unclear (5.5.17–31; cf. *2 Henry IV*, 4.4.97–99).

But these are mere secondary complications that do not significantly alter the implications of the logic of honour, and are of no consequence at all with respect to the contest between Henry Monmouth and Henry Percy, in which no quarter will be sought or given. With them, there will be no rematch, no 'best two out of three'; the outcome of their one contest will be final. As Hotspur vows prior to the battle: 'Harry to Harry shall, hot horse to horse, / Meet and ne'er part till one drop down a corpse' (4.1.121–22). Accordingly, when at last they do meet, Percy declares, 'the hour is come / To end the one of us'. Which is as happens, with the result that Hal makes good his apparently impudent boast: 'And all the budding honours on thy crest / I'll crop to make a garland for my head'. Hotspur's dying words concede this to be the result: 'those proud titles thou hast won of me / . . . wound my thoughts worse than thy sword my flesh'. Now, how should we suppose the Prince regards the honour-loving ethos Percy has lived by?

Some indication of his own view of the pursuit of battlefield glory is provided by how he treats the honour he has just 'cropped' from Hotspur. Not only does he decline to exult publicly in his glorious victory over this famous king of honour-lovers, he seems prepared to let another take the credit (5.4.156–58). Of course, this may be only a 'seeming', for the false claimant is hardly credible. Moreover, the truth is sure to become known since Hal's brother John is not only privy to who in fact did what, but also witnesses the prince's apparently cavalier attitude regarding the truth of the matter—that he seems careless about the public recognition of his triumph, treating the victory itself as if it were all that really counts for him. The result in this instance will likely be a double benefit to Hal: honour not only for the valiant deed but also for his magnanimity. What, then, can one conclude from this as to his view of the *intrinsic* value of such bestowed honour? Nothing certain, it would seem. To be sure, the latter source of honour, insofar as it is contrived, could not yield the same sort of personal satisfaction as would doing something honourable for its own sake (versus doing something clever); hence, its value could only be instrumental—which, of course, is still a good, and so not to be despised. Shortly thereafter, Prince John himself will be the beneficiary of Hal's generosity with respect to honour. Having received the King's permission to dispose of the captured Douglas, Hal passes the privilege on to his younger sibling: 'Then, brother John of Lancaster, to you / This honourable bounty shall belong', namely that of releasing the noble Scot 'ransomless and free' out of respect for his 'high deeds' of valour (5.5.25–31).

Reflecting on the Prince's words and actions, one notes that he is ever careful to show respect for the fact that most men do regard being honoured, especially for distinction won on the battlefield, with intrinsic value. Moreover, he is well aware that words alone cannot prove one's own high regard for such honour. One's actions must confirm it. Thus, though bleeding profusely from a grievous wound, and urged by both the King and Westmorland to retire from the action, Hal adamantly refuses: 'God forbid a shallow scratch should drive / The Prince of Wales from such a field as this' (5.4.1–11). His courageous resolve in the perilous circumstance, so inspiring to others, will naturally be interpreted as confirmation of the value he places upon honour. For even though not yet himself a king, Hal acts in anticipation of the day he will be. He appreciates that 'the economy of honour' can be a ruler's most precious resource, a disposable good to be carefully husbanded, and dispensed with discretion so as to encourage and reward behaviour that serves his interests, while also cultivating gratitude and affection.[60]

So much for appearances. But what might we suppose is *truly* the Prince's own valuation of the honour he has gained at Hotspur's expense? The first words of his eulogy perhaps offer a hint: 'Fare thee well, great heart. / Ill-weaved ambition, how much art thou *shrunk*!' '*Ill-weaved ambition*'! All that Hotspur has lived for, striven for in how many desperate encounters, glory acquired in how many mortal actions, all taken from him within an hour, diminishing his significance to that of second-best—which is not to say that of merely an also-ran (after all, that it took an Achilles to defeat a Hector leaves the latter some renown). However, according to the same ruthless logic of honour—as Hal, no fool, doubtless realizes—the same could happen to him, and sooner or later surely *will* happen to him as his physical powers decline (much as have those of his once formidable father).[61] Given Hal to be an acute observer and unsentimental analyst of his world and its ways—the reflective sort of man who could conceive and execute the 'shrouded sun' strategy he vouchsafes us in his first scene—he can hardly put much stock in the intrinsic value of battlefield honour: so vulnerable a good, so impermanent a possession, so subject to misappropriation, and to chance, to say nothing of the fickle public who bestow it according to powers of judgment one can hardly esteem.

Thus, with respect to the problem he must eventually face and solve: that of establishing, once and for all posterity, his legitimacy as King of England, it will have to be on some basis more substantial than the sort of honour Hotspur so craved, some distinction *not* subject to transitivity. If there is recognition worthy of pursuit by a superior man—a '*well*-weaved ambition'—it must be for some accomplishment offering the prospect of a fame that is *truly* 'never-dying' (cf. 3.2.106). Now, what might that be?

Prince Hal's reconciliation with his father begins with his eloquent denial of the outrageous accusation that possibly he is so 'degenerate' as to consider collaborating with the enemy. It will be sealed with Hal's vigorous defence of the endangered King on the battlefield at Shrewsbury (5.4.38–56). But in defending himself from Henry's allegation, notice, Hal never admits that all this time he had been but playing a part. Rather, he promises his father in the name of God to make good his boast to vanquish Percy, or die trying, and hopes his so vowing 'may salve / The long-grown wounds of [his] intemperance' (3.2.153–59). That resolution, so forcefully expressed, not only rehabilitates him in the eyes of the King; it also persuades him that his prodigal son, of whose physical capabilities he is aware—being, as he elsewhere acknowledges, 'the noble image of [his] own youth' (*2 Henry IV*, 4.4.55)—poses a mortal threat to those contemplating rebellion. Accordingly, he now assures the Prince with respect to the coming action, 'Thou shall have charge and sovereign trust herein' (3.2.161).

These words are no sooner spoken than Sir Walter Blount arrives with confirmation of a conspiracy amongst rebellious nobles, such that if all 'promises are kept', their combined numbers will amount to as 'mighty and fearful head . . . as ever offered foul play in a state'. The Prince, accordingly, is given his marching orders; he's to lead a force that he will augment as he travels through Gloucestershire, and link up at Bridgnorth near Shrewsbury with an army led by the King. So the stage is set for the climax of this first part of *King Henry IV*.

Reviewing the action to this point, one notices a curious thing. In Shakespeare's actual *portrayal* of Prince Hal (as distinct from how others *speak about* him, and from his own sometimes coarse, even ribald repartee), he *does* very little to live up to—or down to, rather—his scandalous reputation. We never see him drunk, or hung over, or sleeping off a hard night's partying. He's never shown wenching, or drabbing; indeed, so far as the sampling of female charms go, he never so much as fondles a barmaid. He doesn't gamble, or brawl, or gourmandise (cf. *Hamlet* 2.1.18–27). He apparently maintains himself in excellent physical condition (cf. 4.1.103–9). In all this he presents a studied contrast to his sybaritic companion, the famously obese and self-indulgent Falstaff (cf., e.g., 3.3.13–20). The one piece of 'lawlessness' with which Hal associates himself, the robbery of the Travellers, he had initially refused to participate in: 'Who? I rob? I a thief? Not I, by my faith' (1.2.131). He subsequently agrees to partake, but only for the sake of frustrating the enterprise so as afterwards to enjoy 'the virtue of this jest' (as Poins characterizes it in recruiting Hal), meaning 'the incomprehensible lies that this same fat rogue will tell us when we meet at supper' (1.2.176–78). And Hal is careful to ensure that the stolen money is paid back, 'with advantage' (compensating its rightful possessors for the trouble this escapade causes them; 2.4.533–34; cf. 3.3.174–77). So, with respect to the one instance we're shown of the sort of mischief his father referred to, we see it in a radically different light.

As for the Prince's deeds subsequent to his confrontation with his father—having vowed to live up to his lineage and then some—his actions leading to, during, and after the Battle of Shrewsbury mostly reflect only credit upon him. The one blemish on Hal's conduct in this latter half of the play is his persistent indulgence of Falstaff. Despite knowing full well the beefy pretender's cupidity and cowardice, he nonetheless had procured him royal authorization to raise and lead a company of soldiers (albeit with a barb in the tail: 'I'll procure this fat rogue a charge of foot, and I know his death will be a march of twelvescore'; 2.4.531–33; cf. 3.3.185–86).

Falstaff exploits to the full the opportunity which the prince has arranged for him, shamelessly soliloquizing:

> If I be not ashamed of my soldiers, I am a soused gurnet. I have misused the King's press damnably. I have got, in exchange of a hundred and fifty soldiers, three hundred and odd pounds. I press me none but good householders, yeomen's sons [etc.].... none but such toasts-and-butter, with hearts in their bellies no bigger than pins' heads, and they have bought out their services; and now my whole charge consists of ... the cankers of a calm world and a long peace, ten times more dishonourable-ragged than an old feazed ensign.... You would think I had a hundred and fifty tattered prodigals lately come from swine keeping.... No eye hath seen such scarecrows. I'll not march through Coventry with them, that's flat. Nay, and the villains march wide betwixt the legs as if they had gyves on, for indeed I had the most of them out of prison. (4.2.11–41)[62]

While passing through Warwickshire, Falstaff and his unfortunate draftees encounter the Prince and Westmorland hurrying on to Shrewsbury. The Earl emphasizes the potential importance of every man to the anticipated battle: 'The King, I can tell you, looks for us all'. However, noting the quality of Falstaff's company, Hal observes, 'I did never see such pitiful rascals'. Indifferent to what may be at stake in the looming engagement, and how a full company of able-bodied men might affect its outcome, the bogus knight blithely admits that his contribution to the affair is mere cannon-fodder: 'Tut, tut, good enough to toss; food for powder, food for powder. They'll fill a pit as well as better. Tush, man, mortal men, mortal men' (ibid., 63–66).[63]

Such proves to be these poor men's fate once the battle is joined, as Falstaff admits in a second soliloquy: 'I have led my ragamuffins where they are peppered; there's not three of my hundred and fifty left alive, and they are for the town's end to beg during life' (5.3.35–38). We are left to wonder how the grosser target managed to remain unpeppered. Hal, who comes on scene immediately thereafter, would seem at last to be fed up with his fat pub-mate's shirking: 'What, stands thou idle here? Lend me thy sword'—since you're not using it, he implies—'Many a noble man lies stark and stiff / Under the hoofs of vaunting enemies, / Whose deaths are yet unrevenged'. But Falstaff, learning that Hotspur still haunts the battlefield—and, as Hal facetiously taunts, 'living to kill thee'—refuses to give up his sword, offering his pistol instead, which Hal discovers to be a bottle of sack. He throws the bottle at the old fraud, chiding as he rushes off, 'What, is it a time to jest and dally now?' (ibid., 49–56).

Later, however—the King's forces victorious and the Prince having killed Hotspur—Hal would appear to have recovered his unseemly tolerance of this shameless imposter. Traipsing with brother John through the area where before he had bid such a tepid and equivocal farewell to what he presumed to be Falstaff's corpse, Hal learns that the old tosspot was merely feigning death, and that he now claims to have killed Hotspur. The Prince protests, 'Why, Percy I killed myself, and saw thee dead'. Falstaff blusters on, and Hal, clearly amused, offers to lend him credibility: 'For my part, if a lie may do thee grace / I'll gild it with the happiest terms I have' (5.4.157–58). True, as noted previously, this is inexpensive generosity on his part since with his brother privy to the truth of the matter, there would seem no real chance in the long run of the credit for Hotspur's death being misplaced.[64] Still, Hal's permissive attitude towards such an irresponsible rascal is disquieting.

Suppose, however, the Prince is fully aware that the unfit knight is not as harmless as he seems—that however amusing his schemes and escapades may seem to those in no way affected by their consequences, those who are would regard the man quite differently. That, objectively considered, he is a menace and a disgrace.[65] But might this be his peculiar utility to the success of Hal's 'shrouded sun' strategy? Were Falstaff merely the incorrigible buffoon he is meant to seem to most audiences and readers, his public rejection could hardly generate the dramatic effect *among his citizen-subjects* that Hal intends upon his ascension to the throne. Nor would that rejection seem so wholly justified by those who witness or learn of it. Yet if such is the case—that the Prince has condoned Falstaff's pernicious activities, and tacitly encouraged his presumption that he enjoys a privileged relationship with the future king (which further emboldens his amoral ambition), and done so for the very purpose of cultivating a figure who can represent everything that, as King Henry V, he will publicly disavow—should this be so, we must allow Hal a capacity for cold-blooded theatrics not unlike that with which Machiavelli credits Cesare Borgia in his infamous dealings with Messer Remirro de Orco.[66]

Chapter Three

The Noble Change Long Purposed

The Turbulent Reign of King Henry IV Concludes

> *Sudden Glory*, is the passion which maketh those *Grimaces* called LAUGHTER; and is caused either by some sudden act of their own, that pleaseth them; or by the apprehension of some deformed thing in another, by comparison thereof they suddenly applaud themselves. And it is incident most to them, that are conscious of the fewest abilities in themselves; who are forced to keep themselves in their own favour, by observing the imperfections of other men.
>
> —Hobbes, *Leviathan*, chap. 6, para. 42

Prince Hal's story continues in the second part of *Henry IV*, but in a different key, as it were—indeed, the play as a whole has a different tonal colour. The sense of urgency that pervaded part 1 is noticeably muted, when not simply absent. To be sure, there are still threats to Henry's reign, but they are neither as dramatically dominant as was that of Hotspur and his co-conspirators, nor are they dealt with in such a violent and exciting manner. The rebellion led by Archbishop Scroop, Mowbray, and Hastings never comes to an open battle at Gaultree, as did the near-run thing at Shrewsbury, but is instead defeated by trickery. There is a second challenge that does come to blows, but we no sooner learn of its existence than of its defeat: 'The Earl of Northumberland, and the Lord Bardolph, / With a great power of English and of Scots, / Are by the shrieve of Yorkshire overthrown' (4.4.97–99). Moreover, with the exception of the spectacle that Prince Hal has crafted for his ascending the throne as King Henry the Fifth, there is not much of either political or philosophical substance being dramatized in this play. But what an exception that is! For the lesson conveyed by a proper understanding of this sensational *coup de théâtre* is one of comprehensive importance, though doubtless many find it not to their taste. Perhaps it is meant to test the depth of a person's 'love of truth'. Since preparing for this spectacular finale is apparently the philosopher-poet's underlying intention guiding almost everything portrayed in the action which precedes it, that intention serves to focus my interpretive comments on the events leading up to this contentious conclusion.

Prior to this transformative event, Hal's relationship with Falstaff continues, but with a marked difference. In part 1, the Prince is physically present almost half the time, appearing in ten of its nineteen scenes. Whereas in part 2, that presence is greatly reduced, confined to less than a fifth of the play and to five of its nineteen scenes. By contrast, Falstaff is present almost half of the time, featuring in eight scenes. One consequence of this difference is a shifting of the balance between Comedy and History, the former gaining prominence at the expense of the latter. This partially accounts for the diminution of material having obvious political or philosophical significance. Moreover, in part 1 both men are seen *together* for fully a quarter of the play, Hal appearing in all of Falstaff's scenes. But in part 2, they are together less than a twentieth of the time, Hal featuring in only two scenes with Falstaff, including that in which he repudiates the man.

This quantitative disparity is somewhat misleading, however, insofar as the existence of the Prince and his notorious relationship with Falstaff is implicit in so much of what the fat rascal does, and often enough explicit in what he says. Thus, while lithe young Hal recedes into the background and gross Sir John's shenanigans dominate one's attention, Shakespeare sets the stage for the dramatic climax of the play: the seemingly brutal manner in which the Prince, now His Majesty the King, severs all association with the old grifter and his disreputable crew. But Hal's action raises, retrospectively, a puzzle that embraces both parts of *Henry IV*: why did that relationship, which when thoroughly examined is not merely strange but troubling, ever exist? Whatever the explanation, it is the shocking termination of that relationship, so abrupt and violent (which many people find wrenching, not to say painful and repulsive), that Shakespeare chose as a fitting conclusion for his portrayal of young Henry V in the context of his father's reign. It therefore presents an invitation—or, rather, a provocation—to reflect on the political lesson embedded in that termination, apt as it is to be obscured by sentiment. And this subjective reaction, so common in political life, is a fact which in itself is instructive about both politics and political analysis. These matters will be addressed in due course.[1]

There are, however, a couple of curious features of part 2 worth noting at the outset. Although seemingly minor, they are nonetheless puzzling enough to warrant comment. One pertains to the role of the strangely well-informed Earl of Warwick. Are we to suspect a 'hidden side' to his participation in this story? The other is the strange way the play begins: with an 'Induction' spoken by personified *Rumour*, suitably bedecked with a multiplicity of painted tongues. The substance of its declamation is divided into two roughly equal parts by the question it poses in the centre, and then proceeds to answer: 'Why is Rumour here?' The explanation which follows, while superficially pertinent, actually leaves its presence quite superfluous, being simply a description of what is so clearly portrayed in the first scene as hardly to need a prolepsis: that though the King's forces were in fact victorious at Shrewsbury and Hotspur killed, the Earl of Northumberland (who 'Lies crafty-sick' at home awaiting news) first receives cheering reports to the contrary—'that Harry Monmouth fell / Under the wrath of noble Hotspur's sword', and that likewise the King was subdued by Douglas. Yet almost immediately the Earl learns the sad truth. Rumour takes responsibility for both sets of reports: 'The posts come tiring on, / And not a man of them brings other news / Than they have learnt of me. From Rumour's tongues / They bring smooth comforts false, worse than true wrongs'.

Perhaps rumours of all sorts especially abound amidst 'the fog of war'. But still, Rumour's explanation of 'why it is here' contributes nothing of importance to one's understanding of the action it introduces. So might the real significance of this 'Induction' be found in its first half? The points made there are about rumour-mongering in general—which, it is reasonable to presume, would have a special relevance to the story played out in what follows. We are reminded that whatever their native language, almost everyone readily attends to rumours. And that slanderous rumours in particular are continually in circulation, and get about quickly, 'Stuffing the ears of men with false reports'. Speaking summarily,

> Rumour is a pipe
> Blown by surmises, jealousies, conjectures,
> And of so easy and so plain a stop
> That the blunt monster with uncounted heads,
> The still-discordant wav'ring multitude,
> Can play upon it.

Suffice it to observe, Rumour's advertisement of its existence is flattering neither to its own nature nor to the countless many who, as a consequence of their excessive susceptibility to its influence, are seldom in agreement with each other, or with themselves for any extended duration. Doubtless King Henry IV's heir, who has relied upon the 'base contagious clouds' of rumour to smother up his beauty from the world, would add his silent 'amen'.

Prince Hal is absent from the entire first act of the play, but we are reminded of him from the very outset by Morton's reporting to Northumberland the sorry fate of his honour-loving son at Shrewsbury: 'Rend'ring faint quittance . . . / To Harry Monmouth, whose swift wrath beat down / The never-daunted Percy to the earth' (1.1.108–10). This scene is followed by one in which Falstaff meets the Lord Chief Justice, 'the nobleman that committed the Prince for striking him about Bardolph'. Or so the Lord Justice is identified by the diminutive pageboy we learn Hal has supplied Falstaff, who grudgingly complains that he did so simply to enjoy the amusing spectacle of their contrasting size ('like a sow that hath overwhelmed all her litter but one'; 1.2.10–13, 55–56). The Lord Justice upbraids Falstaff at some length about his various offences—for 'the truth is, Sir John, you live in great infamy'—and reprimands him especially for his having 'misled the youthful Prince', following him about 'like his ill angel'. Falstaff pretends the contrary: that it is the young Prince that has misled the old knight, who for his part has endeavoured to amend the young man's misbehavior. Thus: 'For the box of the ear that the Prince gave you, he gave it like a rude prince, and you took it like a sensible lord. I have checked him for it, and the young lion repents'. This barely disguised taunt draws from his lordship, 'Well, God send the Prince a better companion!'—to which Falstaff rejoins, 'God send the companion a better prince! I cannot rid my hands of him' (1.2.135–36, 143, 162–63, 193–201).

This scene sets the pattern for Falstaff's part throughout the balance of the play: his association with the Crown Prince, which he would have known as one of intimate friendship, is a tacit premise of almost his every word and deed. Even the scene wherein Hostess Quickly is pursuing legal remedy against Falstaff for 'breach of promise', Hal's curious—very curious—relationship with the old cadger features in her recounting the occasion of the promise: 'upon Wednesday in Wheeson week, when the Prince broke thy head for lik[en]ing his father to a singing-man of Windsor[2]—thou didst swear to me then, as I was washing thy wound, to marry me, and make me my lady thy wife' (2.1.86–90). So, apparently at this stage of their association, Hal's retorts to Falstaff's wit are not exclusively verbal, but literally 'draw blood'. The Lord Chief Justice, siding with Dame Quickly, addresses Falstaff: 'You have, as it appears to me, practised upon the easy-yielding spirit of this woman, and made her serve your uses both in purse and in person'. But Falstaff manages to placate the poor besotted creature with more lies, and even has the effrontery to con her out of still more money in doing so. The Chief Justice departs, pronouncing the plausible knave 'a great fool'—to no good effect, of course, since Falstaff positively enjoys scandalizing his lordship.

Not incidentally, this second scene includes indications of the civil disorder which characterized Henry IV's reign, suiting well the criminal class, which the historical Henry V moved quickly to remedy. As the Lord Justice admits to Falstaff, 'You may thank th'unquiet time for your quiet o'er-posting' (i.e., offences 'quietly overlooked'; 1.2.148–49). The fat knight himself refers to 'the malice of this age' (171–72), which, we may recall, he invoked before in exoneration of one of his many lies: 'Thou knowest in the state of innocency Adam fell, and what should poor Jack Falstaff do in the days of villainy?' (*1 Henry IV*, 3.3.163–65).

The play is fully a quarter way through before we first meet again with the Prince. He is in a melancholy mood, but apparently also a confessional one, regretting that his exalted status precludes ordinary sources of comfort, and vaguely hinting that soon it will also preclude acknowledging the very existence of his erstwhile companions. One such is his present company, Poins. But this anticipated estrangement, it turns out, is *not* what primarily is bothering Hal. Rather, it is that his 'shrouded sun' strategy has a consequence he never anticipated:

Prince: Marry, I tell thee it is not meet that I should be sad now my father is sick; albeit I could tell to thee, as to one it pleases me for fault of a better to call my friend, I could be sad, and sad indeed too.
Poins: Very hardly, upon such a subject.
Prince: By this hand, thou thinkest me as far in the devil's book as thou and Falstaff, for obduracy and persistency. Let the end try the man.

Given the context, this invocation of what is apparently a bit of proverbial wisdom is rather puzzling. Might Hal mean it ironically, having in mind the planned 'end' of his association with Falstaff and others of his ilk, proving ('trying') his character as king? Whatever the case, the Prince continues:

But I tell thee, my heart bleeds inwardly that my father is so sick; and keeping such vile company as thou art hath in reason taken from me all ostentation of sorrow.
Poins: The reason?
Prince: What wouldst thou think of me if I should weep?
Poins: I would think thee a most princely hypocrite.
Prince: It would be every man's thought; and thou art a blessed fellow, to think as every man thinks. Never a man's thought in the world keeps the roadway better than thine: every man would think me a hypocrite indeed. And what accites your most worshipful thought to think so?
Poins: Why, because you have been so lewd, and so much engraffed to Falstaff.
Prince: And to thee.

(2.2.38–60)

100 CHAPTER THREE

This confession, its pertinence apparently lost on Poins—or perhaps he simply discounts the possibility of its being seriously meant—is interrupted by the arrival of Bardolph and the page the Prince supplied Falstaff, who has clothed the boy in such extravagant garb that Hal observes, 'a had him from me a Christian, and look if the fat villain have not transformed him ape' (cf. 1.2.16–18).

Bardolph has brought a letter from his master. Given Hal's mood at the time—which seems, whatever else, rueful that his choice of companions has so misled people about his feelings for his father—the sending of it just then was unfortunate from the bogus knight's perspective. For as he reads the letter, Hal is reminded of what he regrets, musing sardonically, 'I do allow this wen' (that is, this swollen tumour of a man) 'to be as familiar with me as my dog' (2.2.101–2; cf. 1.2.144–45).[3] The missive is a case in point, for in it Falstaff presumes the same presumptive privilege towards the Prince that he trades on in his dealings with others. Moreover, he has the cheek to accuse Poins of this very thing: 'Be not too familiar with Poins, for he misuses thy favours so much that he swears thou art to marry his sister Nell'—as if such a ludicrous claim might be credited! Why did the old sponger bother to send such an absurd letter? Is he concerned that Hal has taken to spending more time with Poins than with him? Apprised that Falstaff will be supping at his favourite pub in the company of Hostess Quickly and Doll Tearsheet, Hal and Poins concoct a scheme whereby they may 'see Falstaff bestow himself tonight in his true colours, and not [themselves] be seen': they will be disguised as waiters in order to overhear how the impudent pretender presents himself when not in the Prince's company.

And so they do. The evening's festivities are well under way by the time the disguised pair arrive and ensconce themselves inconspicuously, but within earshot of Falstaff and Doll, who is perched on the old man's knee while he entertains her with his boasting. So situated, Hal and Poins overhear the following conversation:

Doll: Sirrah, what humour's the Prince of?
Falstaff: A good shallow young fellow; a would have made a good pantler, a would ha' chipped bread well.
Doll: They say Poins has a good wit.
Falstaff: He a good wit? Hang him, baboon! His wit's as thick as Tewkesbury mustard; there's no more conceit in him than is in a mallet.
Doll: Why does the Prince love him so, then?
Falstaff: Because their legs are both of a bigness, and plays at quoits well, and . . . such other gambol faculties a has that show a

weak mind and an able body, for which the Prince admits him: for the Prince himself is such another, the weight of a hair will turn the scales between their avoirdupois.

(2.4.233–52)

Having heard just this much, the prince mutters, 'Would not this nave of a wheel have his ears cut off?' (i.e., as punishment for defaming royalty). Poins whispers, 'Let's beat him before his whore'. Instead, they continue to eavesdrop on Falstaff's lovemaking until he calls for more sack, whereupon they come forth and so are shortly recognised—apparently first by Hostess Quickly: 'O the Lord preserve thy good Grace! By my troth, welcome to London! . . . O Jesu, are you come from Wales?' (2.4.290). This, it is worth noting, is one of only two acknowledgements in the whole *Henry IV* sequence that Prince Hal ever set foot in Wales (cf. *1 Henry IV*, 5.5.39–40). Alerted by Madam Quickly's greeting, Falstaff adds his own irreverent salutation, 'Thou whoreson mad compound of majesty, by this light flesh and corrupt blood [apparently meaning the trollop on his lap], thou art welcome'.

Poins, already chagrined by the accusation in Falstaff's letter, has now had his spirit raised to a still higher pitch by hearing himself described as a weak-witted baboon. And Poins is wise to Falstaff's favourite tactic: using humour to squelch anger and deflect attention from the consequences of his transgressions. Thus he warns the Prince, 'My lord, he will drive you out of your revenge and turn all to merriment, if you take not the heat' (2.4.295–96). However, the funny fat man's tactic of evasion would appear to have worked again, for Hal's verbal chastisement hardly seems serious: 'You whoreson candle-mine you, how vilely did you speak of me even now, before this honest, virtuous, civil gentlewoman' (i.e., Doll!). Their exchange continues in like vein until interrupted by Peto informing the Prince that the King is in receipt of bad news from the North. Hal is immediately sobered by it, as the sudden formality of his language emphasizes: 'By heaven, Poins, I feel me much to blame, / So idly to profane the precious time. / . . . / Give me my sword and cloak. Falstaff, good night' (2.4.358–63).[4]

This is the last occasion we see the Prince on familiar terms with Falstaff, and these are the last genial words he bestows upon him. If Hal was ever under the illusion that Falstaff's 'friendship' was other than mercenary—which seems most unlikely—he would be finally disabused by having here seen Sir Paunch 'bestow himself tonight in his true colours'. But then and there is not the time, and certainly not the place, to stage a public rupture of their relationship. That event is to be saved for circumstances in which it will create a sensation savoured and celebrated by many more people of much more consequence than the patrons of some Eastcheap tavern.[5]

Since the Prince plays no part in suppressing the rebellion led by Mowbray and the Archbishop of York, he is absent from the end of act 2 until the final scene of act 4—in body, that is, not in effect. Recalling the conclusion of the first part of *Henry IV*, the King had divided his forces after his victory at Shrewsbury, dispatching Prince John of Lancaster and the Earl of Westmorland to deal with a second rebellion led by Northumberland (supposedly) and the Archbishop of York, while he and the Prince Hal headed towards Wales to deal with Glendower and the Earl of March.[6] It turns out that the leaders of the Northern rebellion, rather than engage in battle straightaway, agree to a parley with the royal commanders, who have expressed a willingness to hear and rectify all legitimate complaints. The proceedings include one curious sidelight. Brought face to face with the Archbishop, Prince John chides him at some length: 'But you misuse the reverence of your place, / Employ the countenance and grace of heav'n / As a false favourite doth his prince's name, / In deeds dishonourable' (4.2.23–26). Must not the inspiration for this simile surely be John's awareness of how Falstaff exploits his apparently privileged standing with the Crown Prince?

Supposedly in an effort to defuse the military confrontation, Prince John pledges his soul to redress speedily all the rebels' grievances (ibid., 52–60), professes 'restored love and amity' with the rebel leaders, and proposes that both sides immediately discharge their powers. This the rebel leaders agree to, and Hastings orders it done with respect to their troops, while the Archbishop toasts the royal commander: 'To you, my noble Lord of Westmorland'. The noble Lord responds with words that, viewed in retrospect, are maliciously ironic:

> I pledge your Grace; and if you knew what pains
> I have bestow'd to breed this present peace
> You would drink freely; but my love to ye
> Shall show itself more openly hereafter.
Arch: I do not doubt you.
West: I am glad of it.
> (Ibid., 73–77)

For the royal leaders do not reciprocally dismiss their power; nor had they expressly granted amnesty for those participating in the rebellion. Admittedly, if one carefully parses Lancaster's words—attending to what he has 'sworn by the honour of his blood' and has taken 'upon his soul', as distinct from what he has merely implied (ibid., 55–65)—his actions do not transgress honesty, most strictly interpreted. And by his clever, not to say cynical, use of ambiguity and insinuation, the harm to the forces in his charge is minimized, which we would normally regard as to the credit of a commander. But no one for whom the word 'honour' names anything real could argue that the rebel leaders are dealt with honourably. Once their forces have been released and begun to disperse, Scroop, Mowbray, Hastings, and others are promptly arrested on the charge of high treason (4.2.106–15)—but not Northumberland, who yet again failed to arrive with the anticipated support (cf. 1.3.12–28; 2.3.46–68). Meanwhile, the rebels' now disorganized soldiers are pursued by those of Lancaster and Westmorland.

One of the fleeing rebel knights encounters the just-arrived Falstaff, to whom he surrenders. Shortly thereafter, the victorious commanders happen upon the pair, whereupon Lancaster addresses his brother's questionable associate, 'Now Falstaff, where have you been all this while? / When everything is ended, then you come. / These tardy tricks of yours will, on my life, / One time or other break some gallows' back' (4.3.24–29). As we were shown, Falstaff had been chided to hasten on his way by no less than the Lord Chief Justice (2.1.63–65, 181–82). But dilatory on principle whenever and wherever fighting is involved,[7] the old humbug is expert in concocting excuses—as he does here with a cloud of bluster about having worn out 'nine score and odd' horses with his hurrying (!), while claiming credit for having frightened his prisoner into surrendering. Lancaster is skeptical, but as he leaves he nonetheless assures Falstaff that he will report of him better than he deserves. That's not promising much, but any garnishing of his performance that Prince John might provide would likely be in deference to his brother rather than out of regard for the obese imposter.

The disdain is mutual. Left to soliloquize, Falstaff compares John unfavourably with Hal: 'Good faith, this same young sober-blooded boy doth not love me, nor a man cannot make him laugh'—thus Prince John is impervious to old Sir John's special charm—'but that's no marvel, he drinks no wine'. Such men, he claims, 'are generally fools and cowards' (4.3.84–93)—which is patently false about young Lancaster (cf. *1 Henry IV*, 5.4.16–23). Falstaff then proceeds to eulogize sack at some length for its wondrous effects on both mind and spirit, claiming 'valour comes of sherris'—which were that true, this insatiable indulger would be as brave as he pretends. It is on this suspect basis, however, that he professes to believe, 'Hereof comes it that Prince Harry is valiant; for the cold blood he did naturally inherit of his father he hath like lean, sterile, and bare land manured, husbanded, and tilled, with excellent endeavour of drinking good and good store of fertile sherris, that he is become very hot and valiant' (4.3.115–21). Prince Harry is indeed valiant, but there is no reason to trust this explanation of why so. Indeed, that Hal inherited his father's cold-bloodedness may be the only truth Falstaff has here uttered.

Relieved of his prisoner by the officers attending Prince John—who having heard that 'the King [his] father is sore sick' hurries away to the

Court—Falstaff indicates to Bardolph that he intends a return to London via Gloucestershire in order to work a scam on his old friend, the well-named Justice Shallow. Thus Falstaff is being regaled at the good Justice's expense when Pistol arrives with the news of King Henry IV's demise, which he prefaces by announcing, 'Sweet knight, thou art now one the greatest men in this realm' (5.3.84–86). Allowing for an exaggeration reflective of his limited perspective, Pistol's anticipation of the consequence of Prince Hal's ascension would seem to be widely shared.

Shared . . . and **feared**—especially by the ailing king, for it represents the worry that most troubles his final hours. Attended by the Earl of Warwick and two of his sons, Thomas Duke of Clarence and Humphrey Duke of Gloucester, Henry asks young Humphrey the whereabouts of his eldest brother. Told that he is believed to be off hunting near Windsor, the King asks whether Thomas is with him. Somehow Henry is unaware of his second son's presence in the chamber. Upon the young man's stepping forward, his father directs towards him an extended exhortation, expressly on the supposition that Thomas 'hast a better place in [Hal's] affection' than do his other brothers. This is a claim for which there is no evidence whatsoever in the entire *Henriad*, and subtle indications to the contrary.[8]

On this suspect basis, likely more wish than reality, Henry urges Thomas to cultivate the closest possible friendship with his elder brother for reasons that reflect the dying King's foremost concern: the questionable suitability of Prince Hal to succeed him. But this is not explicit in the rationale Henry first offers, stressing rather that were Thomas solidly established in good stead with the future king, he could more effectively mediate between Hal and his other brothers. Henry seems concerned that the Prince, once become king, may treat his brothers as rivals rather than as junior partners, which could threaten domestic tranquility. We are shown no grounds for this suspicion. But the King's worry may nonetheless be shared, for when Hal first meets his brothers after having donned the title 'Majesty', he apparently detects some apprehension on their part, and so immediately seeks to reassure them that they stand in no danger from him: 'Brothers, you mix your sadness with some fear. / This is the English, not the Turkish court' (5.2.46–47).[9]

It would seem that the King does not know his eldest son and heir at all well; this is not surprising in light of his complaint that he hardly ever sees him (*Richard II*, 5.3.1–2; *1 Henry IV*, 3.2.87–89). Henry believes what may actually be farthest from the truth: that Hal's temper is mercurial, that he is ruled by his spirit, his passions, not his reason. Thus Henry further advises Thomas to heed Hal's humours: 'His temper therefore must be well observ'd. / Chide him for faults, and do it reverently, / When you perceive his blood inclin'd to mirth; / But being moody, give him time and scope' (4.4.36–39). On that basis, the dying King suggests that Thomas may the better 'prove a shelter' to his friends and bind all four brothers together. When, however, Thomas assures his father, 'I shall observe him with all care and love', and Henry asks why then is he not hunting with him at Windsor, Thomas informs his father that Hal is actually not off hunting, but is in London dining 'With Poins, and other his continual followers'.[10]

This news provokes the King to express more openly his abiding concern, reflective of his mistaken view of Prince Hal's character:

> Most subject is the fattest soil to weeds,
> And he, the noble image of my youth,
> Is overspread with them; therefore my grief
> Stretches itself beyond the hour of death.
> The blood weeps from my heart when I do shape
> In forms imaginary th'unguided days
> And rotten times that you shall look upon
> When I am sleeping with my ancestors.
> For when his headstrong riot hath no curb,
> When rage and hot blood are his counsellors,
> When means and lavish manners meet together,
> O, with what wings shall his affections fly
> Towards fronting peril and oppos'd decay!
> (4.4.54–66)

Henry's pessimism does not go entirely unchallenged, however. Although neither of Hal's brothers takes issue with their father's forecast—a point of some interest, to say the least—the Earl of Warwick offers an altogether different explanation for Hal's conduct, one which largely exonerates him.

> My gracious lord, you look beyond him quite.
> The Prince but studies his companions
> Like a strange tongue, wherein, to gain the language,
> 'Tis needful that the most immodest word
> Be look'd upon and learnt; which once attain'd,
> Your Highness knows, comes to no further use
> But to be known and hated. So, like gross terms,
> The Prince will, in the perfectness of time,
> Cast off his followers, and their memory
> Shall as a pattern or a measure live
> By which his Grace must mete the lives of other,
> Turning past evils to advantages.
> (Ibid., 67–78)

As this would seem a rather implausible account of the Prince's conduct, it is no wonder Henry expresses some skepticism. Nonetheless, he seems inclined here, as elsewhere, to respect Warwick's judgment, for he lets the matter drop. But we might wonder about it. For the good Earl is never portrayed in company with the Prince, much less in conversation with him. And yet Shakespeare has chosen him to be the one character who expresses valid insight with respect to Hal's true character and motives. Strange.

Warwick's intervention on behalf of the Prince presents the puzzle referred to earlier. First of all, who is he? Historically, he is Richard de Beauchamp, thirteenth Earl of Warwick and father-in-law of the famous 'kingmaker' earl, Richard Neville of the powerful Neville clan, who inherited Beauchamp's title by marrying his heiress daughter, Anne.[11] Beauchamp gained a considerable military reputation serving with the Prince in the long campaign to suppress the Welsh rebellion.[12] Later, during Hal's reign as Henry V, he was a prominent member of the King's Council, entrusted with various embassies and governorships. As a further indication of the respect in which he was held, when Henry died Warwick was chosen to oversee the education of the deceased King's infant son, the future Henry VI, during whose reign he again served on the royal council.

Within the confines of the second tetralogy, however, Warwick is a rather shadowy figure.[13] Perhaps this is partly a consequence of Shakespeare's near suppression of the whole Wales portion of Prince Hal's life; but given the two teasers of his possibly having access to knowledge 'behind the scenes', we are entitled to speculate that there may be more to his role than his scant appearances would seem to imply. Warwick does not appear at all in either *Richard II* or part 1 of *Henry IV*. He is a silent member of the council that witnesses the arrival of the infamous tennis balls in *Henry V*, but he is not mentioned as present at the exposure of Cambridge's conspiracy, nor at Harfleur. He is at Agincourt, a silent presence in one late scene (4.7), and speaks a total of seven words in the following scene; also, he is part of the English entourage, again silent, in the scene set at the French Court (5.2).

In part 2 of *Henry IV*, Warwick appears in only one scene prior to his astute intervention here in 4.4. Late one night, the King sends for him and the Earl of Surrey, but with the instruction that both men first read over certain letters whose contents he wishes to discuss with them. While he awaits their coming, he laments his inability to sleep, and thus to enjoy the 'forgetfulness' that 'gentle sleep, / Nature's soft nurse' brings to even the rudest peasant, but not to a king: 'Uneasy lies the head that wears a crown' (3.1.5–8, 31).[14] It is fair to rejoin, however, that the primary source of *this* king's sleep-disturbing uneasiness is traceable to how he came by his crown. So in the present case: for when the two earls arrive, Warwick—the only one who speaks—affirms that they have read the letters informing the King of various disturbances threatening his reign. Warwick expresses confidence, however, that the 'diseases' the body politic suffers from are amenable to cure, 'With good advice and little medicine'. In particular, the fever caused by 'Northumberland will soon be cool'd' (3.1.43–44).

The mention of Northumberland prompts Henry to muse at length about the man and his altering relationships—first with King Richard, then with Henry himself—and how Richard prophesied the time would come when this Percy turned against Henry, just as he did Richard. Because the King seems profoundly unsettled by the fulfillment of Richard's prophecy—as if it attested to some supernatural insight or power at work, and carried the further implication that Northumberland would help engineer Henry's overthrow as he did Richard's—Warwick attempts to demystify that late King's 'guess': 'There is a history in all men's lives', he reasons, thus anyone familiar with Northumberland's record of falseness could predict that he would eventually prove false to Henry; no prophetic power was required (3.1.80–92).

Warwick's 'naturalist' analysis seems to comfort Henry, who then voices a more material worry: 'They say that the Bishop and Northumberland / Are fifty thousand strong'. Again, Warwick offers reassurance: 'It cannot be, my lord. / Rumour doth double, like the voice and echo, / The numbers of the feared. Please it your Grace / To go to bed: upon my soul, my lord, / The powers that you have already sent forth'—i.e., those led by Prince John and Westmorland—'Shall bring this prize in very easily' (ibid., 96–101). Henry agrees to abide by Warwick's counsel. We do not know whether the Earl's confidence as to the actual size of the rebel army (cf. 1.3.10–17), or in the outcome of the rebellion, was merely feigned in order to ease the soul of the ailing King, or genuine, based on a shrewd suspicion—or perhaps even on reliable intelligence—that 'false Northumberland' would again desert his allies. But we do know that events bear out Warwick's assessment.

Here too, then, Warwick seems curiously well informed with regard to this quite different matter: what Prince Hal is up to. Or rather, at least half-informed; for he shows no awareness of the Prince's intention to stage a brilliant spectacle at some chosen time in the future, which will glitter all the more brightly against the dark record of his reputedly dissolute behaviour. Of course, if Warwick is fully in Hal's confidence, he could not so much as hint at that intention without spoiling its effect. Whatever the case, one cannot simply dismiss Warwick's intervention on the Prince's behalf as no more than an impromptu rationalization intended to comfort the dying King, since it jibes with what Hal had revealed in private by way of concluding his initial appearance in the *Henriad*: to be following a plan wherein his spending time among London's lowlife was merely temporary: 'I know you all, and will awhile uphold / The unyoked humour of your idleness'. Later, he made a point of professing to value Poins precisely because he served as a practical stand-in for 'everyman' ('to think as every man thinks'). In observing his career as the Crown Prince, one must bear in mind that every step is governed by a strategic plan, one partially inspired—as he implied and I have emphasized—by a godlike sun who passively 'permits' his beauty to be obscured by clouds in order that he might be the more appreciated, not to say worshipped, when that beauty is revealed. Only partially so inspired, since unlike the sun, Hal must himself intentionally, that is, *actively*, cloud over his own beauty by plebian behaviour with base companions, skilfully, thus carefully and selectively, offending the established proprieties of princely conduct.

Moreover, he can be confident that the exaggerations characteristic of rumour-mongering will greatly amplify the offensiveness of his lifestyle. As Warwick warned Henry, 'Rumour doth double, like the voice and echo'. And as personified Rumour itself reminds us: 'Upon my tongues continual slanders ride, / ... / Stuffing the ears of men with false reports'. Then it asks, 'Why is Rumour here?' Why indeed? To explain how might initially arise the immediately refuted rumour that Hal was killed by Hotspur at Shrewsbury? As suggested earlier, this seems utterly superfluous to an adequate understanding of the play. Is not the reason, rather, to hint at the part it plays in Hal's scheme? For the prince well understands the workings of rumour and gossip in the formation of so-called public opinion, his 'shrouded sun' strategy relies crucially upon it. Given his status, he can be sure that his every escapade, especially anything rambunctious or 'wicked', will be amplified and retailed far and wide.

But the rumour mill can be exploited in other advantageous ways as well. For example, the truth of who killed Hotspur will eventually percolate through the populace, and reflect all the more to Hal's advantage for his seeming content to allow Falstaff to take the credit for the feat (improbable as the fat braggart's claim might be regarded). And will there be anyone in London who has not within twenty-four hours heard of the new King's magnanimous treatment of the Lord Chief Justice?[15] Likewise his other demonstrations of prudence, justice, temperance, and (most important of all) of *piety*. The effects of such actions will be magnified by his having previously *crafted*, literally, such pessimistic expectations, that his 'reformation, glittering o'er [his] fault], / Shall show more goodly and attract more eyes'—though it will only *seem* a near-miraculous 'reformation', since like the sun he will have no need to change his true self, but merely to reveal it.

Yet there is more to Hal's purpose in consorting 'With Poins, and his other continual followers'—including most notably, and scandalously, Sir John Falstaff—than simply using them to mislead the world about his own tastes and principles. Warwick alleges that 'The Prince but studies his companions / Like a strange tongue, wherein, to gain the language'—with the intent, however, of subsequently discarding both the companions and their vulgar speech. Again, the prescient Earl is right. But as he must surely realize, there has to be some further purpose guiding such a 'study'. We know that Hal tacitly indicates as much in private, boasting of his conversancy with some lowly tavern personnel when Poins asks where he has been:

> With three or four loggerheads, amongst three or four score of hogsheads. I have sounded the very base string of humility. Sirrah, I am sworn brother to a leash of drawers and can call them all by their Christian names, as Tom, Dick and Francis. They take it already, upon their salvation, that, though I be but Prince of Wales, yet I am the king of courtesy, and tell me flatly I am no proud jack, like Falstaff, but a Corinthian, a lad of mettle, a good boy—by the Lord, so they call me—and when I am King of England I shall command all the good lads in Eastcheap.

Furthermore (he claims), 'I am so good a proficient in one quarter of an hour that I can drink with any tinker in his own language during my life' (*1 Henry IV*, 2.4.7–19). Taking such a claim seriously entitles one to suspect that this is not the only occasion in which he has honed this skill, becoming so adept at picking up dialects and vernaculars that within short order he can converse socially with any tinker, tailor, soldier, sailor, tradesman, or farmer he might come across, whether English or Welsh, Irish or Scottish. So, for example, he could converse with soldiers in the dark of night, assessing their morale, with neither his accent nor his vocabulary compromising his anonymity. Moreover, he can adapt to their manners whenever it suits him, ease whatever discomfort inferiors might feel in his presence, even for the moment seem almost like a 'sworn brother' ('We few, we happy few, we band of brothers'). The Prince has been studying the common folk such as will compose the bulk of the army he takes to France, hence has come to know their cares and desires, their pleasures and fears, how they think and what they think about, their perspective on those placed above them—all the better to lead and rule them.[16] In short, Hal has been learning 'the common touch' in the only way it can be learned: by extensive companionship with common people—the touch that will prove so valuable at Agincourt, that 'little touch of Harry in the night'.

For Shakespeare's Prince Henry is every bit as aware as is his father that, practically speaking, the *legitimacy* of his future hold on the Crown hangs precariously in the balance. He will not be able to rely on a widespread belief that he rules as God's 'chosen' simply by virtue of his *lineage*; his father's manner of gaining the Crown, and the chronic instability of his reign, have compromised beyond remedy the credibility of that view. If Hal

110   CHAPTER THREE

is to be accepted as the legitimate king in the eyes of God—hence, able to command the willing obedience of the vast preponderance of his subjects (as he here claims regarding 'all the good lads in Eastcheap')—it will have to be on some basis other than simply grace (*charisma*) supposedly conveyed by blood. He will have to *prove* that he enjoys divine approval and protection by *deeds* that can be plausibly interpreted as primarily God's doing. In the meantime, he has good reason to court 'popularity'. And it bears repeating, the practical problem the future Henry V is facing within this story of his life is the theoretical problem Shakespeare is himself explicating in the whole of the second tetralogy.

The King's anxiety regarding the Crown Prince may not have been entirely assuaged by Warwick's explanation of Hal's choice of associates, but for the moment his attention is diverted by the arrival of Westmorland reporting that the northern rebels led by Mowbray, Scroop, and Hastings have been defeated by Prince John's royal army. Almost immediately thereafter come more good tidings: the forces of Northumberland and Lord Bardolph have also been defeated. Warwick's optimism has been vindicated. However, the ailing King can only regret that he is in no condition to enjoy the happy news, and momentarily lapses into unconsciousness. Clarence ventures that his father's life cannot last much longer, and both he and Gloucester recall that various unnatural happenings have been reported among the populace—the sorts of phenomena that presage momentous events, such as the passing of a king. Henry shortly regains consciousness, and asks to be moved to some chamber where he can rest, comforted by soft music, and for his crown to be set beside him on his pillow.

At this point, Hal enters the chamber in high spirits, and inquires whether anyone has seen the Duke of Clarence. Why does he ask? Were they supposed to have met? Strangely, he also does not notice that Thomas is actually in the room. What accounts for this? Does Thomas have a preference for the shadows? Apparently Hal was not sent for, as then he would be aware of his father's grave condition. Rather, having heard of the recent victories, he has rushed to Henry's side simply in order to share in the rejoicing. Told that the King is 'exceeding ill', but that he too has heard the good news, Hal ventures, 'If he be sick with joy, he'll recover without physic'—speaking rather boisterously, it would seem, as the ever-solicitous Warwick warns, 'Not so much noise, my lords. Sweet Prince, speak low; / The King your father is dispos'd to sleep' (4.5.15–16).

Taking the cue, Clarence proposes they all withdraw into an adjacent room. Hal, however, chooses to stay and watch over the sleeping King. The sight of the crown resting on the pillow moves him to muse on its irony, given the sleep-disturbing cares that go with that crown. But then he observes that his father seems not to breathe. Concluding that he has expired, the Prince exclaims aloud, 'My gracious lord! My father! / This sleep is sound indeed; this is a sleep / That from this golden rigol hath divorc'd / So many English kings'. Promising to pay most plenteously and sincerely the sorrow due his 'dear father', Hal takes up the crown that is now due him and places it on his head. As he does so, he vows that nothing shall force 'this lineal honour' from him—that just as it was passed to him, he will pass it on to his own son. With that he leaves the room. The King is dead; long live the King.

But the King is not dead. He awakens and calls out, first for Warwick, then for Gloucester and Clarence. When they return, he asks them why they left him alone. Clarence replies, 'We left the Prince my brother here, my liege, / Who undertook to sit and watch by you'. Whereupon Henry asks after him, since he is not in the room. He then notices the crown is missing from his pillow. When Warwick assures him it was there when the rest of them withdrew, the King concludes, 'The Prince has ta'en it hence', and—perhaps luckily for Hal—orders Warwick to find him, and 'chide him hither'. Meanwhile, Henry waxes sadly indignant on the selfless labours of fathers and the ingratitude of sons. Upon Warwick's return, Henry enquires, 'Now where is he that will not stay so long / Till his friend sickness have determin'd me?' Hal could not have hoped for a report better suited to mollify his father's distress than that which Warwick delivers.

> My lord, I found the Prince in the next room,
> Washing with kindly tears his gentle cheeks,
> With such a deep demeanour in great sorrow,
> That tyranny, which never quaff'd but blood,
> Would, by beholding him, have wash'd his knife
> With gentle eye-drops. He is coming hither.
> (4.5.82–87)

Apparently Warwick means that were anyone, even a bloodthirsty tyrant, to witness such a scene of abject sorrow as the Prince presents, he would perforce weep in sympathy. But it seems a rather strained rhetorical figure whereby to emphasize the depth of Hal's grief—and curiously theatrical. Did Warwick weep to behold him? In any event, his report seems to have little of its intended effect—but one cannot be sure.

Seeing the Prince approach, the King calls him hither, and orders the others to depart the chamber. Hal greets his father with 'I never thought to hear you speak again', who responds with 'Thy wish was father, Harry, to that thought', followed by a litany of complaints and accusations against his heir. It seems that nothing so stirs Henry to flights of eloquence as do the perceived sins of the Crown Prince. Fully half of his diatribe describes what he imagines is in store for England once 'Harry the fifth is crown'd! Up, Vanity! / Down royal state! [etc.]'. Hal manages an equally eloquent reply, insisting that but for his tears he would have 'forestall'd this dear and deep rebuke', and saved them both the grief of it.

> God witness with me, when I here came in
> And found no course of breath within your Majesty,
> How cold it struck my heart! If I do feign,
> O, let me in my present wildness die,
> And never live to show th'incredulous world
> The noble change that I have purposed!
> (Ibid., 149–54)

Purposed. Hal's elliptical allusion to his dissolute behaviour having been strategic is unlikely to register with his dying father, preoccupied as he is with the Prince's most recent transgression, which Hal proceeds to explain. He avows that he handled the ornament merely as a means of galvanizing his resentment of what it symbolized: 'Accusing it, I put it on my head, / To try with it, as with an enemy / That had before my face murder'd my father'. Suffice it to observe, this does not quite square with what we heard him speak when, presuming his father dead, he left the chamber wearing the crown (ibid., 165–67; cf. 40–46).

Whether in this case, too, 'the wish was father to the thought', Henry professes himself persuaded by Hal's fervent apology—having been primed to do so, perhaps, by Warwick?—even seeing the Hand of God in his son's premature appropriation of the crown: 'God put it in thy mind to take it hence, / That thou mightst win the more thy father's love / Pleading so wisely in excuse of it!' Not for having pled so convincingly, but for having pled so *wisely*! The King may not be as naive about the Prince as he sometimes seems. And no question, Hal is a clever sophist as well as a gifted rhetorician, powers he will use time and again as king. Henry, now reconciled with his 'wise' son and heir, has some last counsel for him. Though he has at other times insisted that necessity forced the Crown upon him (e.g., 3.1.72–74), he here admits what God knows, namely, 'By what by-paths and indirect crook'd ways / I met this crown, and I myself know well / How troublesome it sat upon my head'. But his namesake will be able to wear it 'with better quiet, / Better opinion, better confirmation', since whatever dirty dealings were entailed in its acquisition will be buried with Henry Sr. (4.5.183–90).

The son may not be blamed for what comes to him simply by time-honoured rules of inheritance, but he should not assume his reign will be smooth sailing: 'Yet though thou stand'st more sure than I could do, / Thou art not firm enough, since griefs are green; / And all my friends, which thou must make thy friends, / Have but their stings and teeth newly ta'en out'. Whereas those false friends who subsequently had proven a danger to Henry's hold on the Crown have been eliminated. And to preclude new threats arising, he 'had a purpose now / To lead out many to the Holy Land, / Lest rest and lying still might make them look / Too near unto [his] state'. Here, then, the truth comes out: his repeated references to undertaking a crusade to liberate the Holy Land (e.g., *Richard II*, 5.6.48–50; *1 Henry IV*, 1.1.18–26, 47–48, 100–101; *2 Henry IV*, 3.1.107–8) was all along a stratagem, the more effective for its being cloaked in piety. Machiavelli would approve. And it is this same stratagem that is the father's 'last counsel' to his son: 'Be it thy course to busy giddy minds / With foreign quarrels, that action hence borne out / May waste the memory of the former days' (4.5.202–215). Needless to say, Hal takes this last counsel and runs with it.

The King's interview with the Prince concludes with one final lament about the sin of his usurpation: 'How I came by the crown, O God forgive, / And grant it may with thee in true peace live!' Hal's response offers the comfort of political realism, and the assurance that his father's strivings and sufferings will not have been in vain:

> My gracious liege,
> You won it, wore it, kept it, gave it me;
> Then plain and right must my possession be,
> Which I with more than with a common pain
> 'Gainst all the world will rightfully maintain.
> (4.5.220–24)

At this point, Prince John—apparently just returned from the successful repression of Archbishop Scroop's rebellion—enters with the Earl of Warwick. He wishes his father 'Health, peace, and happiness', who in turn acknowledges that his son has brought the latter two, but that health is now quite beyond him. Anticipating his death, Henry calls for Warwick; and learning that the chamber in which he first swooned is called 'Jerusalem', he asks to be moved back there so that upon his dying, a long-standing prophecy might be ironically fulfilled.

Prince Hal's transformation into King Henry V is marked by two dramatic events, both staged so as to leave 'the people at once satisfied and stupefied'.[17] The first, his surprising confirmation that the Lord Chief Justice will continue to officiate in his high office—not merely despite, but precisely because of his earlier chastisement of Hal in his guise as the wayward Crown Prince—would be universally applauded by people of whatever century. Whereas the second, Hal's public repudiation and disavowal of Falstaff

('I know thee not, old man'), strikes many modern viewers and readers as a callous act of betrayal. They see it as revealing an unattractive, not to say repellent side of the new King: scheming, heartless, disloyal, ungrateful, and opportunistic.[18] Indeed, some find his action unforgivable, and of a piece with his (allegedly) 'criminal' command to kill the French prisoners in the midst of the Battle of Agincourt.

The episode with the Lord Chief Justice begins with his meeting the Earl of Warwick, presumably by chance. He asks after the King, only to learn that the cares of Henry IV are over, once and for all. This news moves the good Justice to wish likewise for himself, since the service he provided the late King has left him open to persecution by his successor. Warwick agrees he has reason to worry: 'Indeed I think the young King loves you not'—to which the Justice replies, 'I *know* he doth not', adding that he has armed his soul by imagining the worst (5.2.9–13). Warwick's apparently mistaken view on this particular matter might seem to indicate that his astute understanding of Prince Hal's conduct was not based on a confidential relationship with the Prince himself.

More curious, however, is Warwick's musing as the two men are approached by Hal's brothers: 'O that the living Harry had the temper / Of he, the worst of these three gentlemen! / How many nobles then should hold their places / That must strike sail to spirits of vile sort!' What then of Warwick's having earlier assured Henry Sr. that 'The Prince but studies his companions / Like a strange tongue, wherein, to gain the language', but that he will 'in the perfectness of time, / Cast off his followers'? Was this implausible but strangely accurate explanation contrived solely to provide the ailing King a spurious comfort, and its validity simply a coincidence? Whereas all the while Warwick himself believed, along with everyone else, that worthy nobles would be displaced from office and favour by the likes of Falstaff and other of Hal's dissolute companions? Perhaps so. But then again, perhaps not. For if he *is* privy to the Prince's stratagem, we may further presume he would not wish anything he said to compromise its effect at the moment of payoff, or at any time thereafter. If anything, he would seek to reinforce that effect by publicly pretending to share the general anxiety.

Be this as it may, these five having met together now proceed to discuss the future, commiserating with the Lord Chief Justice in particular, who assures the others that he has no intention of begging a pardon for simply doing his duty as honour required: 'If truth and upright innocency fail me, / I'll to the King my master that is dead, / And tell him who hath sent me after him' (ibid., 39–41). Thus the stage is set for the new King Henry to enter a scene tense with anxiety, not to say foreboding, which he will exploit to maximum advantage.

Greeted with the traditional formula of 'God save your Majesty', Hal admits he is not yet comfortable with his new title 'majesty'. He then proceeds to reassure his brothers that they have no need to fear his ascension: 'I'll be your father and your brother too; / Let me but bear your love, I'll bear your cares'. They all claim never to have expected otherwise, but something in their countenances must suggest less than complete confidence, for Henry observes, 'You all look strangely on me'—then turning to his father's Chief Justice, he continues—'and you most; / You are, I think, assur'd I love you not'. The man replies, 'I am assur'd, if I be measured rightly, / Your majesty hath no just cause to hate me'. This manly response allows Henry to amplify the display of magnanimity he has planned. For we may assume that it was always his intention to confirm the Lord Justice in his position, knowing the quality of the man. Thus he can 'taunt' him ('How might a prince of my great hopes forget / So great indignities [etc.]'), confident that his lordship will neither apologize nor beg a pardon, much less grovel, which would detract from Henry's intended effect of reappointing him. Rather, that he will instead give a spirited defence of his conduct, thus enhancing this effect. For upon that basis, the new King can then make it seem as if he were in fairness and largeness of spirit acceding to the merit of his lordship's argument.

The Chief Justice's defence of his conduct with respect to Hal as Prince is all that now as King he could wish for, and then some. The judge reminds his new sovereign that in every action he took then, he was simply and properly impersonating their previous sovereign. And that it was in the course of his conducting the business of the commonwealth that 'Your Highness pleased to forget my place', and dared to physically assault 'The majesty and power of law and justice'. As this was an offence against the sitting King, he sentenced the offender, even though he was then the Crown Prince, to an appropriate punishment. Would Henry, now having become King, have it be otherwise? Thus, turning from respondent to interrogator, the Lord Justice asks, 'Be you contented, wearing now the garland / To have a son set your decrees at naught?'

> To pluck down justice from your aweful bench?
> To trip the course of law, and blunt the sword
> That guards the peace and safety of your person?
> Nay more, to spurn at your most royal image,
> And mock your workings in a second body?
> Question your royal thoughts, make the case yours,
> Be now the father, and propose a son,
> Hear your own dignity so much profan'd,
> See your most dreadful laws so loosely slighted,
> Behold yourself so by a son disdain'd:
> And then imagine me taking your part.
>   (5.2.84–96)

That the Prince did strike the Lord Chief Justice for some cause having to do with Bardolph is one offence that cannot be written off as just hearsay (cf. 1.2.55–56, 193–96). But as for the rest of the judge's litany of Hal's misbehavior—bearing in mind how Shakespeare has actually portrayed the young man's conduct—it may less reflect reality than rumour and reputation. A skilfully cultivated reputation, one hastens to add, as his 'shrouded sun' strategy required, exploiting the notoriety of his chosen associates.

In responding, the new King disputes not a word the old lord has spoken: 'You are right, Justice, and you weigh this well. / Therefore still bear the balance and the sword'. Then he neatly, subtly, turns the catalogue of his past delinquencies to his own present advantage.

> And I do wish your honours may increase
> Till you do live to see a son of mine
> Offend you and *obey* you, *as I did.*
> So shall I live to speak my father's words:
> 'Happy am I, that have a man so bold
> That he dares do justice on my proper son;
> And not less happy, *having such a son
> That would deliver up his greatness so
> Into the hands of justice.*
>   (Ibid., 104–12)

However, Henry not only affirms his desire that the 'balance and the sword' of justice remain in these experienced hands, insisting that its bearer use it 'With the like bold, just, and impartial spirit' as he did against the offending Prince Hal. But also, in a gesture of singular modesty and graciousness, he now offers the Lord Chief Justice his own hand by way of pledging to regard him as a surrogate parent:

> You shall be as a father to my youth,
> My voice shall sound as you do prompt mine ear,
> And I will stoop and humble my intents
> To your well-practis'd wise directions.
> And Princes all, believe me, I beseech you,
> My father has gone wild into his grave,
> For in his tomb lie my affections;
> And with his spirits sadly I survive
> To mock the expectation of the world,
> To frustrate prophecies, and to raze out
> Rotten opinion, who hath writ me down
> After my seeming.
>   (Ibid., 118–29)

'My *seeming*'! This faint echo of his first soliloquy is as close as the new King ever comes to admitting to anyone—at least in our hearing—that as Prince Hal he followed a strategy of pretence whereby he might set the stage for the moment in which he would 'mock the expectation of the world', renounce 'vanity', and come forth in 'formal majesty'.[19] What might be called the positive aspect of that moment is this embracing of his father's chief legal officer, accompanied by his proclaiming an intention to summon Parliament after his coronation so that, in consultation with that gathering of the country's notables, he might 'choose such limbs of noble counsel / That the great body of our state may go / In equal rank with the best-govern'd nations' (5.2.135–37; cf. *Henry V*, 2.4.33).

But Hal always intended to 'mock the expectation of the world' with a negating action as well, something even more surprising—and incomparably more gratifying and reassuring. Or so at least we must imagine it would be regarded by every English subject of the new King, whether noble or common, who was sick of the civil disorder that plagued the father's reign, and who had worried that it would continue if not intensify during the reign of his son.

The public rejection of Falstaff immediately follows the coronation of Hal as King Henry the Fifth. The portly knight, bullishly expectant and accompanied by his latest gull, Justice Shallow, along with Pistol, Bardolph, and the pageboy—but notably, not Poins—stand in wait along the route the King and the coronation train will follow. Falstaff had earlier assured his simpleton friend, 'Master Robert Shallow, choose what office thou wilt in the land, 'tis thine' (this, in return for a hefty 'loan', we soon learn). He then boasted, 'I am Fortune's steward! Get on thy boots, we'll ride all night. . . . I know the young King is sick for me. Let us take any man's horses [!]—the laws of England are at my commandment. Blessed are they that have been my friends, and woe to my Lord Chief Justice!' (5.3.118–20, 126–34).

Now as the buoyant crew wait for the procession to come into view, Falstaff promises Shallow, 'I will make the King do you grace'—though as a fashion-conscious courtier-to-be (cf. 1.2.28–44), he regrets that his party is still attired as when they hurried from Shallow's Gloucestershire residence: 'O, if I had had time to have made new liveries, I would have bestowed the thousand pound I borrowed of you. But 'tis no matter, this poor show doth better, this doth infer the zeal I had to see him'. (Shallow agrees.) 'It shows my earnestness of affection—' (Shallow agrees.) 'My devotion—' (Shallow emphatically agrees). The old pretender nonetheless continues to elaborate upon what he wishes his presumed protégé to believe is shown by waiting for him in clothing still 'stained with travel'.

His self-deluding fantasy is briefly interrupted by Pistol's florid report of what he is sure will infuriate the 'good knight': 'Thy Doll, and Helen of thy noble thoughts', has been dragged off to prison (5.5.31–34). He is silent as to the reason. Whereas we learned in the preceding scene that she is accused of complicity in *manslaughter*, as is Pistol himself; for so the arresting beadle had informed her and Hostess Quickly, 'the man is dead that you and Pistol beat amongst you' (5.4.17–18). Doll Tearsheet and Pistol, two of Falstaff's habitués, have *beaten a man to death*! Were they—are they all—infected with the hubris of the rogue they follow, fancying themselves immune to 'the rusty curb of old Father Antic the law'? Without any knowledge of the case, Sir John blithely assures his newly dubbed lieutenant, 'I will deliver her'. Such is the influence he anticipates.

Just then the coronation procession approaches. Conspicuous by Henry's side is the Lord Chief Justice. The implication of their conjoined presence is lost on Falstaff, however, who with his usual impertinent familiarity confidently calls out, 'God save thy Grace, King Hal, my royal Hal!' Apparently receiving no acknowledgement, he again calls out, 'God save thee, my sweet boy!' This draws from the King, 'My Lord Chief Justice, speak to that vain man'. His lordship does as he is bid: 'Have you your wits? Know you what 'tis you speak?' Ignoring the rebuke, Falstaff foolishly persists, 'My King! My Jove! I speak to thee, my heart!' But the King has had enough of his obtuse presumption:

> I know thee not, old man. Fall to thy prayers.
> How ill white hairs become a fool and jester!
> I have long dreamt of such a kind of man,
> So surfeit-swell'd, so old, and so profane;
> But being awak'd I do despise my dream. . . .
> Reply not to me with a fool-born jest;
> Presume not that I am the thing I was;
> For God doth know, so shall the world perceive,
> That I have turn'd away my former self;
> So will I those that kept me company.
> When thou dost hear I am as I have been,
> Approach me, and thou shall be as thou wast,
> The tutor and feeder of my riots.
> Till then I banish thee, on pain of death,
> As I have done the rest of my misleaders,
> Not to come near our person by ten mile.
> For competence of life I will allow you,
> That lack of means enforce you not to evils;
> And as we hear you do reform yourselves,
> We will, according to your strengths and qualities,
> Give you advancement.
>
> (5.5.47–69)

Banished from the royal presence! on pain of *death!* With that, the King turns to the Lord Chief Justice, 'Be it your charge, my lord, / To see perform'd the tenor of my word', and moves on. Not to be overlooked is Henry's maintaining the pretence both that he did indeed behave riotously as a youth and that he did so mainly because, being an impressionable youth, he was grossly misled by base companions, especially old Falstaff. Now, however, he's a changed man, having 'turn'd away from his former self'. Henry never admits—never *can* admit—that this was all a carefully crafted charade on his part, for to do so would ruin the political effect it was designed to cause, and compromise his ability to cause like effects in the future. For the first rule of a successful dissembler is never to betray the slightest hint that one is a dissembler.

The false knight is at first abashed: 'Master Shallow, I owe you a thousand pound'. He could immediately return the money, as poor Justice Shallow begs (ibid., 74–75, 82–84), since he's had no time to spend it on new liveries or anything else. But the fat con assures him, 'That can hardly be' (leaving the poor Justice to imagine why not), and instead offers more vain hope: 'Do not you grieve at this; I shall be sent for in private to him. Look you, he must seem thus to the world. Fear not your advancements; I will be the man yet that shall make you great'. What optimism he has left is soon squelched, however, for his nemesis returns along with Prince John and a squad of constables. The Lord Justice orders the officers to escort Falstaff and his companions to prison; and when the old man attempts to plead his case, the Justice cuts him off with, 'I will hear you soon'—after, that is, a spell of confinement will have convinced the habitual fantasist of his altered reality (ibid., 91–95). Sober Prince John is rightly pleased:

> I like this fair proceeding of the King's.
> He hath intent his wonted followers
> Shall all be very well provided for,
> But all are banish'd till their conversations
> Appear more wise and modest to the world.
> (5.5.97–101)

Henry has severed relations with this crew of ne'er-do-wells, but has not cut them utterly adrift; moreover, he has provided them incentive to reform (unlikely as such a prospect might be).

This fair proceeding should please us even more than it does Prince John, for unlike him we know that Prince Hal had given Falstaff, along with whoever else was present, sufficient notice of his intention. And, what is equally important, he gave no indication, much less made any promises, to the

120 CHAPTER THREE

contrary. The first hint that Hal's reign as king will not be what Falstaff hopes came in response to the old rascal's plea, 'Do not thou, when thou art king, hang a thief'. The prince's seemingly jocular reply is, as previously noted, a double entendre: 'No, thou shalt'. Moreover, it is followed by a clear indication that thieves *will* continue to be hanged—as is later borne out by the hanging of Bardolph, Falstaff's erstwhile factotum (*Henry V*, 3.6.97–112). More pointed, however, is Hal's warning when speaking in the guise of his father the King, to Falstaff pretending to be the Crown Prince:

> There is a devil haunts thee in the likeness of an old fat man; a tun of man is thy companion. Why dost thou converse with that trunk of humours, that bolting-hutch of beastliness, that swollen parcel of dropsies, that huge bombard of sack, . . . that reverend Vice, that grey Iniquity, that father Ruffian, that Vanity in years? Wherein is he good, but to taste sack and drink it? Wherein neat and cleanly, but to carve a capon and eat it? Wherein cunning, but in craft? Wherein crafty, but in villainy? Wherein villainous, but in all things? Wherein worthy, but in nothing?
> (*1 Henry IV*, 2.4.435–47)

Though easily dismissed as just comical raillery, is this not perilously close to the objective truth? Wherein *is* he good? Wherein *worthy*? But if the answer is as given: 'in nothing' (and though spoken as if by the King, it *is* Hal that frames and pronounces the entire denunciation), this appraisal makes the basic puzzle all the more perplexing: Why *does* the Crown Prince, who one presumes could have his pick of companions, hang out with *Falstaff* of all people? This question is never explicitly addressed—beyond, that is, what Hal indicates in his first and only soliloquy, interpreted in light of everything that follows.

At this point in their staged colloquy, however, the false knight feigns perplexity: 'Whom means your grace?' The true Prince answers: 'That villainous, abominable misleader of youth, Falstaff, that old white-bearded Satan' (ibid., 2.4.449–51). And though Hal in the persona of his father had said nothing about banishment, Falstaff seems to intuit the moral of this indictment, and concludes his defence of himself by arguing against it (while throwing all their other associates under the gun carriage, as it were):

> No, my good lord, banish Peto, banish Bardoll, banish Poins, but for sweet Jack Falstaff, kind Jack Falstaff, true Jack Falstaff, valiant Jack Falstaff, and therefore more valiant being as he is old Jack Falstaff, banish not him thy Harry's company, banish not him thy Harry's company. Banish plump Jack and banish all the world. (Ibid., 2.4.461–67)

No doubt Falstaff, ever the indulger of congenial assumptions, chose to regard the Prince's terse reply—'I do; I will'—as if spoken only in jest, or (less plausibly) as still in the guise of King Henry IV. It is his destiny to be disappointed, indeed, to die of it. Though he would have his friends believe he expires of a broken heart, his love for young Henry so cruelly unrequited (*Henry V*, 2.1.88),[20] it is far more likely from despair upon the collapse of his house of cards, putting an end to all his grandiose expectations.

Prince Hal almost never addresses Falstaff in terms other than those of disparaging raillery, usually of his girth: 'fat-witted', 'fat guts', 'fat kidneyed rascal', 'fat rogue', 'fat paunch', 'chops', 'ribs', 'tallow', 'damned brawn', 'whoreson round man', 'natural coward', 'woolsack', 'sweet creature of bombast', 'impudent embossed rascal', 'Whoreson candlemine'. Hal's creativity in noxious epithets is especially inspired by Falstaff's lying account of the Gad's Hill episode: 'thou clay-brained guts, thou knotty-pated fool, thou whoreson obscene greasy tallow patch'; and, 'this sanguine coward, this bed-presser, this horse-back-breaker, this huge hill of flesh—' (*1 Henry IV*, 2.4.219–21, 235–37). For the most part Falstaff seems grandly indifferent to being addressed in such abusive terms as the Prince uses—*exclusively*, it should be noted—though he does once complain of slender Hal's 'most unsavoury similes' (ibid., 1.2.76). Moreover, on the two occasions when Falstaff invites a confirmation that the Prince holds him in special regard, Hal is noncommittal (cf. ibid., 3.3.135–36; 5.1.121–24). As previously noted, the kindest words the Prince ever uses with respect to Falstaff are addressed to what he presumes to be the corpse of his 'old acquaintance', and they hardly attest to deep affection: 'Poor Jack, farewell. / I could have better spared a better man. / O, I should have a heavy miss of thee / If I were much in love with vanity'. (Whereas, 'if not . . .') Hal then adds, 'Death hath not struck so fat a deer today, / Though many dearer in this bloody fray' (ibid., 5.4.102–7). '*Many dearer*'—it hardly matters to whom.

Although Falstaff is lavish in bestowing terms of endearment on the Prince when in his presence, such is not always the case when out. More significant, however, is the fact that 'sweet Jack Falstaff, kind Jack Falstaff, true Jack Falstaff' never performs any service for Hal in recompense for those that Hal does him (e.g., paying his bar tab, covering up his misdeeds, securing military commissions, inter alia)—other than provide a source of amusement, that is, while serving unbeknownst as the centrepiece of the Prince's 'shrouded sun' strategy (for which the old scrounger can hardly claim credit). Nor does he do better by anyone else; whenever he pretends to be furthering someone else's good, it is only the more readily to exploit him, or her. Apparently, the reciprocity that practically defines genuine friendship is utterly alien to him.

The Falstaff formula. As even an inattentive reader would surely suspect, my unflattering descriptors of Falstaff and his actions—while hardly as imaginative as those Shakespeare has provided Hal, whence I take my cue—are intended to imply that, if one strips away the morally spurious charm of his wit and considers him objectively, there is less than little good to be seen in him, but a whole lot of harm. Consequently, I regard Hal's public repudiation of him as not only fully justified, but practically obligatory. Moreover, I'm confident that the philosopher-poet would agree since he provided a pattern of evidence pointing directly to this conclusion, especially in this second part of *Henry IV*.[21] For every scene in which Falstaff appears testifies against him morally, and therefore politically.

For example, as the centrepiece of the play, there is the comedy of Falstaff pressing manifestly unfit men, practically a sequence of cartoon characters, to fill the ranks of the company he is commissioned to raise, while leaving Bardolph to extract bribes for dismissing the fit (3.2.238–40). The travesty is so patent it moves the obtuse old Justice Shallow to protest: 'Sir John, Sir John, do not yourself wrong, they are your likeliest men, and I would have you served with the best' (249–51).[22] As typical of his talent, Sir John palms off the objection with some witty sophistry, though one proposition does tacitly raise a question worth considering. For he defends his choice of skinny Master Shadow with 'give me this man, he presents no mark to the enemy—the foeman may with as great aim level at the edge of a penknife' (260–62). While no one would suspect Falstaff of ever leading from the front, still one must wonder how a target of such prodigious bulk manages to escape unscathed from battles which virtually annihilate the rest of his company.

Having satisfied his profitable recruitment objectives, he confidently plots recurring to the hospitality of his foolish admirer, musing to himself, 'and now has he land and beefs. Well, I'll be acquainted with him if I return, and't shall go hard but I'll make him a philosopher's two stones to me. If the young dice be a bait for the old pike, I see no reason in the law of nature but I may snap at him' (322–26).

Then there is the soliloquous self-indictment Shakespeare supplies Falstaff wherein he reveals his plan to use this same Justice Shallow (who so fondly misremembers their school days together), along with his servants who model their deportment on that of their master, as fodder for comedy whereby to ingratiate himself with his main meal-ticket, who (he implies) is easily entertained:

> I will devise matter enough out of this Shallow to keep Prince Harry in continual laughter the wearing out of six fashions, which is four terms, or two actions, and a shall laugh without intervallums. O, it is much that a lie with a slight oath, and a jest with a sad brow, will do with a fellow that never had the ache in his shoulders! O, you shall see him laugh till his face be like a wet cloth ill laid up! (5.1.75–82)

So, as Shakespeare makes him privately admit, Falstaff's wittiness is *not* simply the generous overflowings of a humorous spirit; he quite deliberately uses his clever jests and novel oaths to ingratiate himself with his primary source of support, as well as to annoy his critics and placate those he exploits. However, it seems the fat sponger's relationship with Hal had begun to cool as his verbal ingenuity wore thin, and occasionally crossed the line (recall Hostess Quickly's telling of the Prince's bloodying Falstaff's head for some particularly offensive remark about the King; 2.1.86–90).

If there is any injustice in what Henry has said or done upon the occasion of publicly severing all connection with his erstwhile companions, it would be his blaming them, and Falstaff in particular ('The tutor and feeder of my riots'), for having 'misled' him. Whereas, we know that frequenting the company of lowlifes was intrinsic to Hal's 'shrouded sun' strategy from the beginning, that it was his way of crafting that 'sullen ground' against which he may glitter all the brighter when at last he chose to discard the 'loose behaviour' he had adopted. So that, ironically, old Sir John unknowingly spoke the truth when he countered the Lord Justice's accusation of misleading the young Prince: 'The young Prince hath misled *me*' (1.2.143–44). In any event, this 'having misled a prince' need not be interpreted as the King's justification for seeing the fat swindler and his followers arrested and imprisoned; with exception of the page and possibly Justice Shallow (but who may be dimly aware that his 'loan' will be treated as a bribe), the whole gang deserves to be in jail on their own demerits, scofflaw Falstaff especially.[23]

Moreover, as noted earlier, Henry can hardly admit that his having been debauched by bad company was all an act—the offensiveness of which rumour amplified, as he knew it would (*1 Henry IV*, 3.2.18–28)—without ruining the political effect of his seemingly miraculous transformation, analogous to that of Saul into Paul on the road to Damascus. For it is treated as nothing less by the two ecclesiarchs who wonder over it in the opening scene of *Henry V* ('like an angel came / And whipped th'offending Adam out of him'; 1.1.28–29). Given the danger posed, not only to Henry but to the whole kingdom, by his right to the Crown being disputable, there is ample justification for an essentially harmless piece of theatre designed as the first step in addressing this threat. After all, the danger is nothing less than the chaos of civil war, what Hobbes characterized as a return to the 'State of mere Nature' wherein the human condition becomes one of continual fear, and danger of violent death, and the life of men, solitary, poor, nasty, brutish, and short.

Still, there remains something puzzling about the Prince's choosing to hang out with Falstaff and his admirers. With all the dregs of society to choose from, why did Hal light upon this particular crew? Might Falstaff have played an active part in getting chosen, ever on the lookout for a future payoff? If so, what did he have to offer besides his irreverent wit? Worldly wisdom? There is not a single 'teaching' characteristic of the old fraud—whether regarding Church or State, Virtue or Family—that is not repudiated by Hal in deed, if not in so many words. Here someone might protest, 'He learned from Falstaff to regard everyone and everything as merely means to furthering his own ends'. Without agreeing that this is Hal's universal policy, he revealed in his first soliloquy that this was his *antecedent* posture towards the denizens of the Eastcheap tavern; he didn't await learning it from Falstaff. Lessons in sophistical argument? Not likely, since Falstaff's efforts never mislead anybody not already a natural fool, and are indulged by Hal only because they're so absurdly funny. Rhetorical expertise? As if the Prince, who could so powerfully rebut his father's accusation of consorting with the enemy (*1 Henry IV*, 3.2.129–59), needed any tutoring in oratory, much less from a clown whose speeches, apart from their drollery, are quite pedestrian. Well then, might Hal have wished to learn how to be witty himself? He might, and if so, he would have come to the right place—provided, that is, Falstaff's kind of wittiness is teachable, rather than a natural bent perfected over a lifetime of mocking the world and everyone in it, the better to think well of himself. In any case, Hal's subsequent career as King provides precious little evidence of his using humour to further his ends.

This is not surprising, as being a joker does not comport well with a political leader's maintaining an appropriate dignity. Hal's father illustrated that point by contrasting his own behaviour with that of his predecessor:

> Thus did I keep my person fresh and new,
> My presence like a robe pontifical,
> Ne'er seen but wondered at; and so my state,
> Seldom but sumptuous, showed like a feast
> And won by rareness such *solemnity*.
> The skipping King, he ambled up and down
> With shallow jesters and rash bavin wits,
> Soon kindled and soon burnt; carded his state,
> Mingled his royalty with cap'ring fools,
> Had his great name profaned with their scorns [etc.]
> (*1 Henry IV*, 3.2.55–63)

Henry V will make no such mistakes. Apart from the odd sarcasm or irony (cf. *Henry V*, 3.6.145–49), one may comb his speeches for jokes and come up almost empty-handed. The single conspicuous exception proves the rule: his banter in wooing the French princess, a *private* conversation *designed* to show that he's not all serious business and discipline, but has a relaxed, light-hearted, fun-loving side as well.

Having eliminated the other possible reasons for the prince choosing to consort with Falstaff, one is left with a single primary motive: the fat old ruffian is the ideal foil for the 'shrouded sun' strategy, and is so precisely because—as all decent, law-abiding subjects of the King would agree—there is nothing good to be said for him, and much bad. As the Lord Chief Justice admonishes, 'the truth is, Sir John, you live in great infamy' (1.2.135–36). And the further truth is, he is as a consequence fully deserving of whatever comeuppance he may suffer. Conversely, Hal doesn't *owe* Falstaff anything, whether for his serving unknowingly as Hal's foil, or for serving knowingly as the Prince's jester: he's been well compensated, month by month, for that. Most likely it is his comedic talent that accounts for the Prince's choosing to while away time with such a bounder. For to give the devil his due: Falstaff *is* endlessly amusing, partly for what he himself 'invents', partly for what is 'invented on him'. And since Hal is committed to a 'shrouded sun' strategy, he would see no reason not to enjoy himself in carrying it out. The Prince is as capable as anyone else of relishing the fun the old pretender provides. Hal's own sense of humour is evident in his agreeing to Poins's Gad's Hill escapade merely for the sake of the jest, namely, 'the incomprehensible lies that this same fat rogue will tell us'. Young Henry differs from most people in this one vital respect, however: he can enjoy without enjoyment clouding his judgment.

As a salvation army of critics attest (the merest minuscule of which I've cited), this assessment of the propriety of Hal's dealing with Falstaff is a minority view, to say the least. Apparently most people see the old rogue as more or less hard done by. Why is that? Is it not simply because he has made them laugh—that is, brought their souls the *effortless pleasure* of comedy? To be sure, his world, like ours, provides plenty to laugh at, and still more that a witty man can construe as laughable, especially if not overly scrupulous as to what he mocks or lampoons. Falstaff has lynx eyes for whatever and whoever can be made the butt of a joke, himself included. As his creator makes Sir John privately admit, 'A good wit will make use of anything; I will turn *diseases* to commodity' (1.2.249–50).[24] Add to this the delight of clever repartee and unique similes, of feigned obtuseness, of absurd braggadocio matched with clever self-deprecation, all issuing from a fat body with an insatiable thirst for sack, and there one pretty much has the Falstaff formula—or rather, Shakespeare's formula for crafting this wonderfully funny character. As he has the comical knight himself boast, 'The brain of this foolish-compounded clay, man, is not able to invent anything that intends to laughter more than I invent, or is invented on me; I am not only witty in myself, but the cause that wit is in other men' (1.2.5–9).[25]

The inventive use of language is Falstaff's special forte, and accounts for much, indeed almost all, that audiences and readers find amusing. For example, he has been fashioned with a rare talent for crafting humorous 'hypothetical-conditional' propositions ('if *x*, then *y*'), proposing preposterous identities for someone, usually himself, should, or should not, a certain condition (equally absurd, supposedly) obtain: 'If manhood, good manhood, be not forgotten on the face of the earth, then I am a shotten herring' (*1 Henry IV*, 2.4.122–24); 'if I fought not with fifty of them, I am a bunch of raddish' (ibid., 2.4.179–80); 'if I tell thee a lie, spit in my face and call me horse (ibid., 2.4.186–87); [if whatever] 'I am the veriest varlet that ever chewed with a tooth' (ibid., 2.2.22–23); 'If thou dost it half so gravely . . . , hang me up by the heels for a rabbit sucker or a poulter's hare' (ibid., 2.4.423–25); '[if] I have not forgotten what the inside of a church is made of, I am a peppercorn, a brewer's horse' (ibid., 3.3.7–8); 'if I be not ashamed of my soldiers, I am a soused gurnet' (ibid., 4.2.11–12).[26] The verbal ingenuity with which he boasts and cajoles, invents hilarious lies and when caught out attempts to cover them over with even more hilarious lies, is both entertaining and perversely endearing.

For surely there *is* something perverse in finding his characteristic behaviour not only amusing, but *endearing*—as so clearly do the myriads of people who regard the fat villain with affection, and even admiration. Is this not at least a *bit* puzzling? What is there in human nature that allows for this generous indulgence, if not tacit approval, of a character such as Falstaff?[27] Charmed by his foibles—his ineptitude in carrying through his shoddy schemes, his supposedly 'low but solid realism' (e.g., about honesty, or the value of honour), and especially by the wittiness of the self-evident sophistry with which he pretends to justify himself—most people are inclined to overlook whatever actual transgressions he commits (presuming they give them a second thought). And yet, there is no natural law obliging one to approve, even slightly, of somebody's words and deeds simply because he makes one laugh. One can both despise and laugh. But that goes against the grain of our moral instincts. Because we enjoy laughing at funny things, whoever causes a person to laugh has provided him a benefit gratis (i.e., the pleasure of amusement, one of life's enhancements). And benefits freely bestowed naturally oblige one to be grateful.[28] Thus one more readily forgives a humorous villain, even endeavours to see (or imagine, or presume) some good in him, and to interpret his deeds more favourably than one otherwise would.

Falstaff is an exemplary beneficiary of precisely such a misapplied sense of justness, indeed, an unusually 'pure' example. For transgressions constitute his entire repertoire of actions; there are no good deeds to weigh in the balance. What has Falstaff done upon which he, or anyone, could base a claim that he 'deserves better' than he gets? Or why his continuing to behave as he has in the past should continue to be tolerated? Mislead a hundred and fifty unfit ragamuffins to slaughter, while he—this fat target—somehow manages to escape without a scratch? Use his recruiting commission to extract bribes from those who can afford to pay? Exploit the trust of those who mistakenly believe he is their friend? Falsely promise to marry an aging pub-keeper in order to bilk her out of everything she owns? One searches in vain for his having done any good . . . *other*, that is, than make people laugh, a talent which, *within the plays*, he exploits for purely selfish ends. Meanwhile, we viewers and readers of those same plays are free to enjoy unadulterated whatever we find humorous in his escapades, insulated as we are from their pernicious consequences.

In the case of Falstaff, however, all objective criticism of him hardly matters to most people. They are grateful for the pleasure he has brought them, which they presume to be a harmless pleasure, and gratitude is simple justice. But also, they will have laughed *with* him, perhaps as much and as often as *at* him, and to that extent are complicit in mocking whatever they laughed at—whether or not it is rightly and truly laughable. Having no wish to think ill of themselves, they resist considering critically what provoked their laughter. So, prejudiced by self-love, they approve of their reaction more or less unthinkingly, and judge matters accordingly: *rideo, ergo ridiculat*—'I laughed; therefore it is laughable'—a judgment ratified by so many others laughing likewise.

Shakespeare fully understood that such would be the case, since *exposing* this typical human response to the comedic—of which *he*, we tend to forget, is the actual source—is essential to the philosophical teaching he has embedded in this play for the sake of the few who might look to him for wisdom. That is the serious purpose behind making his funniest character be without a single morally redeeming quality.[29] It is a quite remarkable—even if, perhaps, somewhat mischievous—tour de force. He easily could have compromised. He could have had Falstaff perform at least one act of courage, say, or of generosity, or fidelity, or helpfulness—some simple display of selflessness or justness or honesty, some one moral peg to which his admirers might attach their esteem. But our philosopher-poet declined to do so. Instead, he imparted to his brilliant creation a ruthless consistency, such that those who insist upon not merely enjoying but *approving* this character are left dependent upon the ingenuity of their own rationalizations. Whereas, those who care to reflect on this normal impulse to subordinate one's reason to one's amused spirit can learn an important truth about human nature: laughter can corrupt judgment. And it's a truth of far greater scope and consequence than simply the matter of fairly judging Falstaff and Henry's treatment of him: every day of everyday life proves, over and again, that most people allow moral leeway to transgressors of responsible, decent behaviour whom they find humorous or otherwise entertaining.

Most of us readily acknowledge both the power of comedy and the propriety of using it to expose folly and absurdity, pretention and incompetence, prejudice and imposture, among other failings. We not only enjoy laughing at examples of human foolishness and vice; we believe that exposing them to ridicule is, or at least can be, an effective way to reveal the truth about them. Even if this involves no more than replacing an excessively 'idealized' notion of something or someone with a view that is more 'realistic', there can be a gain in clarity, a clearer view of the truth. However, to the extent people's laughter implicates them, they do not so readily recognise that comedy can also distort, and even *conceal* the truth, that its power is *not* strictly dependent on the *truth*, and that like all power it can be abused—that people's sense of humour can be exploited, even turned against them insofar as it prejudices their capacity for balanced judgment. In the present case, it leads many to reproach if not condemn Hal for his public repudiation of Falstaff upon becoming King Henry V, while completely ignoring the reason for his action (in the unlikely event they have any understanding of it, or of the political problem he is confronting).[30]

'It is certain that either wise bearing or ignorant carriage is caught, as men take diseases, one of another; therefore let men take heed of their company'. In truth, *these* are the wisest words Shakespeare makes Falstaff speak (oblivious to their reflexive significance, of course). Insofar as his example would influence others, what is apt to be its effect? Falstaff serves as a parody of the civil disorders that plagued the father's reign, and which the son inherited along with the Crown. Seeing to their correction is necessarily his most urgent business, for there would be no possibility of 'busying giddy minds with foreign quarrels' unless and until domestic tranquility and prosperity has been firmly reestablished.[31] The new King's public repudiation of Falstaff and all he stands for is the first step towards that end, and his serving this purpose is the old rogue's one patriotic contribution to the England of Henry V.

Doubtless the creator of this funny fat man took satisfaction in the theatrical success of what so many regard as an adorable clown, an inexhaustible source of the kind of seemingly harmless entertainment people seek from comedy. Falstaff has become firmly established as one of our premier Poet's favourite creations. Moreover, that very 'success'—having made Falstaff so terribly *funny*—is essential to his serving Shakespeare's *philosophical* purpose of teaching those who care to learn this important truth about comedy: that whoever aspires to wisdom must train himself to think before he laughs, lest he prejudice his ability to judge all things fairly.[32] No doubt the person who mistakes wittiness for wisdom, flippant irreverence for moral clarity, and exuberant bonhomie for genuine friendship may persuade himself that Falstaff is superior to Prince Hal, and so carry that prejudice forward into the final chapter of the *Henriad*. Is it conceivable that such could be Shakespeare's view?[33]

CHAPTER FOUR

A CURIOUS MIRROR OF CHRISTIAN KINGS

The Brief Glorious Reign of King Henry V

> A Commander of an Army in chiefe, if he be not Popular, shall not be beloved, nor feared as he ought to be by his Army; and consequently cannot performe that office with good successe. He must therefore be Industrious, Valiant, Affable, Liberall and Fortunate, that he may gain an opinion both of sufficiency, and of loving his Souldiers. This is Popularity, and breeds in the Souldiers both desire, and courage, to recommend themselves to his favour; and protects the severity of the Generall, in punishing (when need is) the Mutinous, or negligent Souldiers.
> —Hobbes, *Leviathan*, chap. 30, para. 28

The following commentary treats Shakespeare's *Henry V* in terms of five general topics. First, its beginning with a pair of perplexed ecclesiarchs in a private conspiratorial conversation about the new King—a scene which contrasts so dramatically with the one they anticipate: a formal conclave of the King and his Court. Second, the conspiracy to kill the King, puzzling both as to the conspirators' motivation and to the King's timely learning of it. Third, Henry's strategy whereby to make good his claim to be the rightful King of France. Fourth, assessing Henry as a man and as a king. Fifth, the Battle of Agincourt, with particular attention to the King's notorious order to kill the French prisoners.

I conclude the story of Henry, however, with an 'Alternative Epilogue' that is inspired by, but ranges beyond, the text of Shakespeare's play. It is the result of my accepting his tacit invitation to imagine what might have been.

The seemingly miraculous transformation of roguish Prince Hal into virtuous King Henry dominates the opening scene of a play that thereafter is dedicated primarily to depicting the splendid character of this warrior monarch and the glorious achievements of his reign. Since the idea of Henry's having contrived such a sensational metamorphosis is entirely Shakespeare's invention, we must assume that it has some special importance in the philosopher-poet's account, even though his Chorus silently passes over it to focus attention instead on another apparent miracle: the English victory at Agincourt, the first and most celebrated of the series of military successes Henry achieved in his attempt to impose his will upon France.

In its prologue, the Chorus proclaims that a stage as vast as a kingdom would be required for a story of such magnificense as that of 'warlike Harry'. The play, however, actually begins with a scene that would fit comfortably in the average kitchen. For the story opens upon a conspiratorial conversation between two ranking churchmen, the Archbishop of Canterbury, highest ecclesiastical authority in England, and the Bishop of Ely. They are discussing a profound threat to the property, hence to the power, of the Church. It is the revival of a bill first proposed in Parliament during the reign of the present King's father, but not then passed since it would have further disturbed an already unsettled polity.[1] The bill mandated the confiscation of all so-called 'temporal lands' that successive generations of laypersons had donated to the Church, presumably in the hope—which doubtless the clergy encouraged—of thereby gaining favour with God. Such lands now amounted to the 'better half' of all the property that the ecclesiastical community possessed, and upon which it paid no tax to the Crown.

The scale of this mere half is staggering. One might suppose a lesser man would blush to admit it: an amount sufficient to support fifteen earls, fifteen hundred knights, over six thousand esquires, as well as a hundred almshouses (why are these needed, given the Church's vast resources?), with a thousand pounds per annum income left over for the King's own treasury. The proposal's attractiveness to supporters of the secular authority is self-evident, and the popularity of the bill is attested by its being once again 'urged by the Commons' (1.1.71).[2] Thus the question the prelates are considering is, what can be done to thwart the bill's becoming law, which would emasculate the country's religious establishment.[3]

As these two lords of the Church appreciate full well, the new King holds the key. So, how does he stand towards the proposal? The Archbishop expresses an optimistic view: 'The King is full of grace and fair regard'. Ely affirms what does not automatically follow: 'And a true lover of the holy Church'. This prompts Canterbury to muse at length on the *suddenness* of young Henry's extraordinary transformation, almost as if blessed by a divine visitation.

> The courses of his youth promised it not.
> The breath no sooner left his father's body
> But that his wildness, mortified in him,
> Seemed to die too; yea, at that very moment,
> Consideration like an angel came

> And whipped th'offending Adam out of him,
> Leaving his body as a paradise
> T'envelope and contain celestial spirits.

If there is a Biblical parallel, at least for the abruptness of the change, it happened on the road to Damascus. The full scope of Henry's change, however, is actually unprecedented, as the Archbishop's continuation makes clear:

> Never was such a sudden scholar made,
> Never came reformation in a flood
> With such a heady currence scouring faults,
> Nor never Hydra-headed wilfulness
> So soon did lose his seat, and all at once,
> As in this king.

The faults Canterbury has in mind were not those of Saul, but manifestations of the Prince's apparent 'Hydra-headed wilfulness'.[4] Ely's response to his superior's reminder of what has so astounded high and low alike is, predictably, platitudinous: 'We are blessed in the change'. However, there is more cause for the Archbishop's amazement than Henry's sudden transformation in disposition and moral character. It is signaled by his 'Never was such a *sudden* scholar made'. For Henry has with equal suddenness revealed himself to be *knowledgeable* in a range of accomplishments that can only excite wonder.

> Hear him but reason in divinity
> And, all-admiring, with an inward wish
> You would desire the King were made a prelate.
> Hear him debate of commonwealth affairs,
> You would say it hath been all in all his study.
> List his discourse of war, and you shall hear
> A fearful battle rendered you in music.
> Turn him to any cause of policy,
> The Gordian knot of it he will unloose,
> Familiar as his garter, that when he speaks,
> The air, a chartered libertine, is still,
> And the mute wonder lurketh in men's ears
> To steal his sweet and honeyed sentences.
>   (1.1.24–50)

Apparently the Archbishop—an habitué of London by reason of usually residing at Lambeth Palace rather than at his diocesan residence in Canterbury—is informing his provincial colleague of matters he is presumed to be unaware of, namely, the King's mastery of theology, of politics, of warfare, of practical analysis, and of rhetoric.

If we may at all trust his lordship's report, this is a far greater mystery: how could young Henry have acquired such a depth of expertise in such a range of subjects? For unlike the sudden switch in his outward demeanor and moral posture—strange to be sure, but not such as to seem practically impossible; there have been others who have suddenly 'seen the light', decided to reform themselves, then done so. But unlike, say, a religious conversion, the acquisition of knowledge is a laborious, time-consuming affair. There are no shortcuts to scriptural expertise, prudential wisdom, political sagacity, and military acumen. As Canterbury notes, mastery of any *one* of these subjects would seem to require that it be 'all in all his study'. How, then, could Henry manage to become so prodigious in such an array of esoteric matters, given that as a youth he reputedly wasted all his time and energy in riotous escapades? A worthy puzzle, without doubt—and entirely of Shakespeare's making.

The Archbishop ventures that the prince was somehow instructed by experience, despite the low-life company he kept.

> So that the art and practic part of life
> Must be the mistress to this theoric:
> Which is a wonder how his grace should glean it,
> Since his addiction was to courses vain,
> His companies unlettered, rude, and shallow,
> His hours filled up with riots, banquets, sports,
> And never noted in him any study,
> Any retirement, any sequestration
> From open haunts and popularity.
> (Ibid., 51–59)

The Bishop of Ely replies with a botanical analogy apparently intended as explanatory of the Crown Prince's choice of companions, and perhaps exculpatory as well ('The strawberry grows underneath the nettle, / And wholesome berries thrive and ripen best / Neighboured by fruit of baser quality'). Whatever may be true about strawberries, the Bishop's analogy has only the most oblique pertinence to the Prince's preferred pastimes and associates, and offers no insight at all regarding the primary puzzle. For however salubrious his material environment, a youth's becoming knowledgeable is not like puberty, something that naturally happens as he 'ripens' into a man. Nor is a person, however intelligent, likely to achieve a refined understanding of anything important simply through daily intercourse with others who are not only as ignorant as he is, and happy to stay that way, but of questionable intelligence to boot. The obliging Bishop, addressing the fact that acquiring advanced knowledge in subjects remote from everyday experience requires study, resorts further to botany: 'And so the Prince obscured his contemplation / Under the veil of wildness, which, no doubt, / Grew like the summer grass, fastest by night, / Unseen, yet crescive in his faculty'. Bizarre as this analogy is, it does manage to point to the only reasonable possibility: Prince Hal burnt the midnight oil. But it offers the clergymen no insight as to *why* the Prince might wish to 'obscure his contemplation' from the world.

Privy as we are to Hal's 'shrouded sun' strategy, we understand the need for concealment lest awareness of his intellectual seriousness compromise his pose as a wild wastrel given over entirely to 'riots, banquets, sports'. But knowing that much does nothing to dissipate the real mystery. Even if we presume Shakespeare's Henry to be a quick study, we must nonetheless presume that he *did* study, and so made time for it, possibly also for tutelage, or at least discussion with discrete others. So, prompted by the Archbishop's puzzlement, spelled out in such detail amidst this conspiratorial conversation with his fellow prelate, are we meant to surmise the existence of one or more dialogical partners never expressly identified as such? Warwick perhaps?[5]

Canterbury accedes to the Bishop's speculation that the Prince was a scholar in private, since it would seem nature allows for no other way: 'It must be so, for miracles are ceased, / And therefore we must needs admit the means / How things are perfected'. Suffice it to say, young Henry's scheme for astonishing the world upon ascending the throne has succeeded beyond hope, at least to judge by the wonder expressed by the good Archbishop.[6] Does he also, perhaps, arouse a certain trepidation? A king who is genuinely a pious Christian—or convincingly seems so—and who is, moreover, well grounded in Scripture and theological arguments, might have rather strict expectations about appropriate clerical behaviour, say, or his own view of the proper relationship between Church and Crown. And if he is also, as Canterbury attests, a rigorous analyst, and a shrewd dissector of policy implications in particular, it would not be easy to pull the wool over his eyes.

The two prelates having registered their satisfaction in the moral reformation of the new King, and pondered the mystery of his even more wonderful intellectual competence, Ely returns their conversation to the urgent question at hand: 'How now for mitigation of this bill / Urged by the Commons? Doth his majesty / Incline to it, or no?' The Archbishop is guardedly optimistic: 'He seems indifferent, / Or rather swaying more upon our part / Than cherishing th'exhibitors against us'. And with good reason, as Canterbury now explains.

> For I have made an offer to his majesty,
> Upon our spiritual convocation,
> And in regard of causes now in hand

> Which I have opened to his grace at large,
> As touching France, to give a greater sum
> Than ever at one time the clergy yet
> Did to his predecessors part withal.
> (Ibid., 75–81)

Better to donate half a cup voluntarily than be compelled to render up a whole cupful and the cup to boot. Bishop Ely asks the obvious question: 'How did this offer seem received, my lord?' The Archbishop replies, 'With good acceptance of his majesty'. However, his lordship was not able to lay out in full the basis of the case he was prepared to make regarding Henry's title to 'certain dukedoms, / And generally to the crown and seat of France, / Derived from Edward, his great-grandfather'. For though the King showed an interest in hearing the evidence, they were interrupted by a report that the French ambassadors had arrived and craved an immediate audience. Whereupon the King departed in order to receive this embassy, for contentious 'causes' pertaining to France and certain of her dukedoms had already been raised by Henry (as we learn in the succeeding scene; 1.2.247–49), and presumably the ambassadors bring the French response.

It is these 'causes' that provide the Church the opportunity to ingratiate itself with the King by an unprecedented display of patriotic generosity in financing what could amount to an undertaking of enormous magnitude. Moreover, it is not merely money that Canterbury is prepared to offer, but also legal justification and moral encouragement for a foreign adventure that—not incidentally—would necessitate Henry's leaving domestic arrangements undisturbed. No doubt Canterbury congratulates himself for having devised such a shrewd strategy for circumventing the dangerous confiscatory Commons bill, since that measure would be shelved, if not consigned to limbo, were the country to gird for war with its ancient foe. But it soon becomes clear that his shrewdness is subordinate to that of Henry. For the King did *not* terminate their conversation in order to meet immediately with the French ambassadors. Rather, he intends that the Archbishop be obliged to lay the details of his case—'the severals and unhidden passages' that would validate Henry's title to the Crown of France irrespective of the so-called Salic law—not in private, but in the presence of his whole council. Likewise, the unprecedented offer of financial assistance.

The second scene leaves no doubt about that. When Westmorland asks whether the French ambassador should be called in, Henry replies, 'Not yet, my cousin: we would be resolved, / Before we hear him, of some things of weight / That task our thoughts concerning us and France'. For this purpose he bids Canterbury be summoned first. After politely acknowledging the Archbishop's pious salutation, the King proceeds straight to business, stressing the gravity of the matter at issue while nonetheless apparently deferring to the prelate's scholarship, all expressed in terms emphasizing his own piety:

> My learned lord, we pray you to proceed
> And justly and religiously unfold
> Why the law Salic that they have in France
> Or should or should not bar us in our claim.
> And God forbid, my dear and faithful lord,
> That you should fashion, wrest or bow your reading
> Or nicely charge your understanding soul
> With opening titles miscreate, whose right
> Suits not in native colours with the truth.
> For God doth know how many now in health
> Shall drop their blood in approbation
> Of what your reverence shall incite us to.
> Therefore take heed how you impawn our person,
> How you awake our sleeping sword of war:
> We charge you in the name of God take heed.
> (1.2.9–23)

Thus the King saddles the Archbishop with the moral culpability for what he emphasizes could result in a bloody war with France, entailing the loss of untold numbers of innocent lives ('what *you* incite us to', 'how *you* impawn our person', 'how *you* awake our sleeping sword'): 'For we will hear, note, and believe in heart / That what you speak is in your conscience washed / As pure as sin with baptism' (ibid., 30–32). This is the first use we're shown of a tactic which Henry hereafter resorts to repeatedly: that of deflecting responsibility for the destructive consequences of his own actions onto others.[7]

Canterbury's explicit acceptance of responsibility in this case is everything Henry could hope for, and then some. For it includes an unqualified recognition of Henry's claim to the *English* Crown: 'Then hear me, gracious sovereign, and you peers / That owe yourselves, your lives and services / To this imperial throne'. The Archbishop then proceeds to lay out at tedious length not a positive case for Henry's claim to the Crown of France (nor need he, since as a direct descendant of Edward III, the basis of Henry's claim would be familiar to Englishmen),[8] but the negative case for why the Salic law, allegedly barring inheritance via the female line, is no valid obstacle to that claim. He argues, first, that the Salic lands to which it solely applies are in Germany, not France. Second, that the law is not of the antiquity the French claim, since it was laid down, not by King Pharamond of France (as the French would have it) but four centuries later by

Charlemagne after he had subdued the Saxon occupants of those lands and introduced French settlers. Here the Archbishop reveals himself no arithmetician.[9] Third, that the French themselves have several times recognised the legitimacy of incumbents, including that of their present king, whose claim to the French throne—usurped from Great Edward nearly a century previous—is via various female connections.

Whether or not in his enthusiasm he realizes it, Canterbury is sailing close to the wind here, not only with his mention of 'usurpation', but even more so with his insistence that kingdoms *can* be legitimately inherited via the female line. For given that admission, Henry's claim to the throne is arguably inferior to that of Edmund Mortimer, fifth Earl of March, who is a direct descendant of Lionel Duke of Clarence, *third* son of Edward III via Lionel's daughter Philippa, Edmund's grandmother (whereas Henry's grandfather, John of Gaunt, Duke of Lancaster, was Edward's *fourth* son).[10] Whatever the case, the Archbishop's explanation of *why* the Salic law was set down makes no sense: 'holding in disdain the German women / For some dishonest manners of their life, / [Charlemagne] Established then this law, to wit, no female / Should be inheritrix in Salic land'. But if the chastity of the German women with whom the French men cohabit is suspect, and therefore the children they bear not necessarily fathered by their ostensible husbands, then there is no reason to preclude only *female* offspring from inheritance. Since the 'learned' Archbishop's scholarship is clearly suspect on this point, it is reasonable to suspect that it may be on others as well.[11]

When Canterbury at last brings to an end his convoluted and otherwise problematic presentation, Henry pins him in place with one direct question, leaving no room for equivocation: 'May I with right and conscience make this claim?' (ibid., 96). The Archbishop, intent on maneuvering the King and his Court into this foreign adventure, obliges with an answer that goes well beyond the clarity Henry solicited: 'The sin upon my head, dread sovereign'. And not content to let his analysis speak for itself, he then proceeds—rather un-Christian-like—to exhort Henry to prove himself a man worthy of his lineage: 'Gracious lord, / Stand for your own, unwind your bloody flag, / Look back into your mighty ancestors. / Go, my dread lord, to your great-grandsire's tomb, / From whom you claim; invoke his warlike spirit [etc.]'. Bishop Ely, taking his cue from the Archbishop, offers further incitement of Henry's spirit, while—not incidentally—ratifying, as if indisputable, his right to the English throne: 'Awake remembrance of these valiant dead, / And with your puissant arm renew their feats. / You *are* their heir, you sit upon their throne [etc.]'. Now members of the Council also take up the hue and cry, first Exeter ('rouse yourself / As did the former lions of your blood'), then Westmorland ('your grace hath cause, and means, and might; / . . . Never king of England / Had nobles richer and more loyal subjects' (ibid., 122–27).

Neither the churchmen nor these councillors seem aware that they are laboring to persuade Henry of something to which he is already firmly committed—that, as his father had privately advised with almost his dying breath, the young King fully intends 'to busy giddy minds / With foreign quarrels'. But he is happy to allow the appearance that others have pressed this risky undertaking upon him, while he pretends a prudent reluctance. Even better, that the *Church* is so in favour of this adventure that it is willing, indeed eager, to contribute largely to financing the adventure. For so Canterbury pledges: 'In aid whereof we of the spiritualty / Will raise your highness such a mighty sum / As never did the clergy at one time / Bring in to any of your ancestors'. Of course, as Henry knows, this offer is in lieu of the mass expropriation of Church property threatened by the bill once again being urged by the Commons. A cynic might even suspect that the King had something to do with the revival of that bill. In any event, he has made no promise that he would never in the future approve such a bill—after, say, he has solidified his right to the English throne in the hearts of his people by conquests in France.

For the present, however, Henry professes to see only practical difficulties with the project: 'We must not only arm t'invade the French, / But lay down our proportions to defend / Against the Scot, who will make road upon us / With all advantages'. If he is trolling for reassurance, Canterbury is happy to oblige. For whatever an archbishop's opinion on such matters is worth, he is sure that the lords of the northern marches will be adequate to keep out 'pilfering borderers'. Henry persists in objecting: 'We do not mean the coursing snatchers only, / But fear the main intendment of the Scot, / Who hath been still a giddy neighbor to us'. Somewhere along the way Henry has done some reading, for he cites what can be read about England's sufferings at the hands of the Scots whenever great-grandfather Edward took his army to France. Again it is the Archbishop who will not be denied, insisting that England had then experienced more fear than actual harm, and he reminds Henry that on one occasion the English forces in the north not only defeated a Scottish invasion, but captured the king who led it.

At this point, Westmorland and Exeter again weigh in. The former (whose estates lie in the north, hence are among the most exposed to Scottish predation) cites some proverbial wisdom: 'If that you will France win / Then with Scotland first begin'. However, Exeter (whose holdings are farthest from Scotland) not surprisingly takes a more sanguine view of the danger: 'While that the armed hand doth fight abroad / Th'advised head defends itself at home'. His contribution inspires a lengthy discourse by Canterbury on the divinely ordained *qualitative* division of labour in the human case as in that of the honey bee, which he somehow supposes validates a *quantitative* division of forces ('Divide your happy England into four, / Whereof take you one quarter into France / ... / If we with thrice such powers left at home [etc.]'; ibid., 215–18).

It is most unlikely that the King's political judgment was in any way affected by the Archbishop's arguments. But he doubtless found it useful to have the supreme head of the English Church be heard publicly validating both the rightness and the practicality of his imperial ambition, as well as commit to underwriting it financially. That accomplished, he bids the French embassy be called in, announcing,

> Now are we well resolved; and by God's help
> And yours, the noble sinews of our power,
> France being ours, we'll bend it to our awe
> Or break it all to pieces. Or there we'll sit,
> Ruling in large and ample empery
> O'er France and all her almost kingly dukedoms.
> (Ibid., 223–28)

'*Almost kingly* dukedoms'! Needless to say, all those 'noble sinews' in the council chamber and throughout England fairly salivate at the prospect of their own enrichment. So shortly the Chorus will declaim: 'For now sits expectation in the air / And hides a sword from hilts unto the point / With crowns imperial, crowns and coronets, / Promised to Harry and his followers'.

Henry has already been informed that the French ambassadors have been sent, not by their King, but by his heir apparent, the Dauphin. It is not clear whether this embassy has the French King's approval; the haughty tone and substance of the message being conveyed almost surely does not—it is 'pure Dauphin' (cf. 2.4.23–41, 127–31). Aware of the insulting substance of what they have been commissioned to say, they first inquire whether they may speak 'the Dauphin's meaning' freely and frankly; or would Henry prefer it be indicated only obliquely and ambiguously, as is not uncommon in diplomacy. Since it is insulting even to pose such a choice explicitly, one suspects that this too is in accord with the Dauphin's instructions. Unruffled, Henry blandly assures his guests, 'We are no tyrant but a Christian king, / Unto whose grace [lucky for you] our passion is as subject / As are our wretches fettered in our prisons: [some simile!] / Therefore with frank and with uncurbed plainness / Tell us the Dauphin's mind' (1.2.242–45).

And so they do. The message they bear is a response to Henry's recent revival of a claim to 'certain dukedoms' ceded by treaty to his great-grandfather, Edward III, some forty years dead. As Henry is well aware, to resurrect these moribund claims now is—practically speaking—asking for trouble. The Dauphin's reply is everything he could have wished.

> The Prince our master
> Says that you savour too much of your youth
> And bids you be advised. There's naught in France
> That can be with a nimble galliard won;
> You cannot revel into dukedoms there.
> He therefore sends you, meeter for your spirit,
> This tun of treasure, and in lieu of this
> Desires you let the dukedoms that you claim
> Hear no more of you. This the Dauphin speaks.
> (Ibid., 250–58)

The King asks Exeter, 'What treasure, uncle?' Have the French sent a barrel of gold to buy off the English, as they have done so often in the past? Not this time. For the 'treasure' on offer is—notoriously—a tun of tennis balls. One may suppose that Henry has no difficulty maintaining his composure in the face of this insulting gift, being more gratified than the French ambassadors could possibly imagine. Thus the irony in his reply: 'We are glad the Dauphin is so pleasant with us. / His present and your pains we thank you for'. As he continues, however, his words become more menacing.

> When we have matched our rackets to these balls
> We will in France, by God's grace, play a set
> Shall strike his father's crown into the hazard.
> Tell him he hath made a match with such a wrangler
> That all the courts of France shall be disturbed
> With chases. And we understand him well,
> How he comes o'er us with our wilder days,
> Not measuring what use we made of them.

Thus, Prince Hal's 'shrouded sun' strategy is still paying dividends. Reports of his (supposedly) wasted youth have filtered abroad, prejudicing views of England's new king. Simply by virtue of his lineage and England's martial history, older heads may be more reserved in their judgment than is the Dauphin (cf. 2.4.50–52). But few people are likely to anticipate in him another Black Prince, despite his robust response to his counterpart's provocative gift.

> But tell the Dauphin I will keep my state,
> Be like a king and show my sail of greatness,
> When I do rouse me in my throne of *France*.

> For *that* have I laid by my majesty
> And plodded like a man for working-days,
> But I will rise there with so full a glory
> That I will dazzle all the eyes of France,
> Yea, strike the Dauphin blind to look on us.
>   (1.2.260–81)

As in his dealing with the Archbishop, here too Henry is careful to craft his reply in pious terms: 'But this lies all within the will of God, / To whom I do appeal, and in whose name / Tell you the Dauphin I am coming on / To venge me as I may'.[12]

It is of some interest, however, that reports of Prince Hal's delinquent youth seem to have shaped common opinion in the French Court, although at least one member of that Court—the Constable—seems better informed than the rest, and than the Dauphin in particular (of whom, it would seem, he is no admirer). Their prickly confrontation will be examined in due course.

The Dauphin's ambassadors having been sent safely on their way, the King turns straight to the matter at hand: 'Therefore, my lords, omit no happy hour / That may give furtherance to our expedition, / For we have now no thought in us but France, / Save those to God that run before our business' (1.2.301–4). Surely we are meant to notice that throughout this long court scene, Shakespeare's Henry lets pass no opportunity to express his piety. Likewise in the balance of the play. This is but one respect in which he would seem to anticipate Machiavelli's advice to princes:

> This has to be understood: that a prince, and especially a new prince, cannot observe all those things for which men are held good, since he is often under a necessity, to maintain his state, of acting against faith, against charity, against humanity, against religion. And so he needs to have a spirit disposed to change as the winds of fortune and variations of things command him, and . . . not depart from good, when possible, but know how to enter into evil, when forced by necessity.
>
> A prince should thus take care that nothing escape his mouth that is not full of the above-mentioned five qualities and that, to see him and hear him, he should appear all mercy, all faith, all honesty, all humanity, all religion. And nothing is more necessary to appear to have than this last quality. Men in general judge more by their eyes than by their hands, because seeing is given to everyone. Everyone sees how you appear, few touch what you are.[13]

Strictly speaking, Henry V is not a 'new prince' as Machiavelli defines it in the second sentence of his infamous handbook; but neither does he fully qualify for the main consequence of being an hereditary prince 'in which the blood line of their lord has been prince for a long time': that of unquestioned legitimacy. Henry is ever aware that his own status is compromised by the manner in which his father became king, as is clear in his prayer to 'the God of battles' prior to Agincourt: 'Not today, O Lord, / O not today, think not upon the fault / My father made in compassing the crown' (4.1.289–91). Thus the importance of extracting an official recognition of his legitimacy from the country's highest churchmen. Not for nothing is Henry 'a true lover of the holy Church'. Still, their stamp of approval cannot alter the known facts of the case: that his is but a collateral bloodline of that previously regarded as hallowed. If he does in fact enjoy *God's* approval, this will have to be established by plausible indications of divine favour.

The discovery of a conspiracy to kill the King on the very eve of his army's setting sail for France is one such indication. Or so Henry would have it understood: 'We doubt not of a fair and lucky war, / Since God so graciously hath brought to light / This dangerous treason lurking in our way / To hinder our beginnings' (2.2.185–88). Admittedly, God works in mysterious ways His wonders to perform, hence we may be left with an insoluble mystery as to *how* in this instance He ensured that the King would in the nick of time learn of the threat upon his life. Presumably, it was not by some dream or vision, much less out of a burning bush. Henry never so much as hints that the Almighty speaks to him directly, as to a prophet. Who or what, then, were the means 'God' used to warn the young King that three trusted associates were conspiring to murder him? Shakespeare's Henry must know, but he isn't telling—us, for sure, nor possibly anyone else.

At least no one else is more forthcoming than is the King himself. This includes the trusty Chorus, who first alerts us to the mischief afoot.

> The French, advised by good intelligence
> Of this most dreadful preparation,
> Shake in their fear, and with pale policy
> Seek to divert the English purposes . . .
> But [England,] see, thy fault France hath in thee found out,
> A nest of hollow bosoms, which he fills
> With treacherous crowns; and three corrupted men, . . .
> Have, for the gilt of France,—O guilt indeed!—
> Confirmed conspiracy with fearful France,
> And by their hands this grace of kings must die,
> If hell and treason hold their promises.
> (2.0.12–29)

So, according to this choral preface, the French, 'advised by good intelligence' of the planned invasion, are quaking in their boots, and seek to subvert the threat by the removal of its leading spirit: war-loving King Henry V. To this end, they have suborned three prominent members of the English aristocracy, who promise to kill the King in exchange for French gold. The Chorus does not apprise us that their plot fails because Henry gets wind of it in time—much less, then, does it provide any indication how he does so. On the other hand, what it says about the conspirators' motivation is puzzling. How would these assassins intend to enjoy the proceeds of their treachery? How escape punishment? What about the consequences for their families? Where would they live? Do they plan to flee to France, leaving behind their English titles and estates? The French bribe would have to be enormous to make that a tempting proposition.

Be all this as it may, we learn in the course of a brief conversation amongst three of the King's intimates—his uncle, Thomas Beaufort, Duke of Exeter; Ralph Neville, Earl of Westmorland; and the King's brother John, Duke of Bedford—that Henry is aware of the three conspirators' treachery, and has taken steps to foil it. According to young Bedford, 'The King hath note of all they intend, / By interception, which they dream not of' (2.2.6–7). Apparently John also knows something about how Henry intends to 'stage' their exposure, and is not altogether comfortable with it ("Fore God, his grace is bold to trust these traitors'). But neither he nor the other two interlocutors give any indication that they know quite *how* Henry learned of the conspiracy, other than it was by some 'interception'. Moreover, to judge by Exeter's indignant denunciation of Lord Scroop—'That he should for a foreign purse so sell / His sovereign's life to death and treachery!'—these trusted members of the King's Council apparently accept that the conspirators' motivation was exclusively mercenary, puzzling though this would seem to be.

In light of what follows, the wish of the Chorus that 'warlike Harry' might have 'A kingdom for a stage, and princes to act, / And monarchs to behold the swelling scene' is, ironically, to be granted. For this is pretty much what Shakespeare's Henry contrives on this occasion, foreshadowed from the moment we first meet him, stage-managing his ascent to the throne of England. Likewise thereafter, he shrewdly crafts scene upon scene, with his princely brothers and nobles in supporting roles and all the courts of Europe a captivated audience. Thus did he stage the two episcopal lords' appearance before his Council, knowing beforehand the script they would follow. So, too, this dramatic exposure of the conspirators.

The King enters, attended by the three traitors with whom he is making small talk. He asks their opinion whether the powers he has assembled are adequate to 'cut their passage through the force of France' (as if this could still be a question on the eve of the army's sailing). Lord

Scroop answers, 'No doubt, my liege, if each man do his best'. What a perfect opening for Henry's rejoinder, his every line suffused with the irony he apparently so savours:

> I doubt not that, since we are well persuaded
> We carry not a heart with us from hence
> That grows not in fair consent with ours,
> Nor leave not one behind that doth not wish
> Success and conquest to attend on us.
> (2.2.20–24)

This provides the other two conspirators an opportunity to display their hypocrisy as well. Anticipating one of the highest accolades Machiavelli bestows on a prince, Cambridge professes, 'Never was monarch better feared and loved / Than is your majesty'.[14] Grey, for his part, assures Henry, 'your father's enemies / Have steeped their galls in honey and do serve you / With hearts create of duty and of zeal'. The King professes to have therefore 'great cause of thankfulness', and adds what should seem rather odd to those with no reason to suspect some ironic pertinence: 'And shall forget the office of our hand / Sooner than quittance of desert and merit / According to their weight and worthiness'.

Turning then to Exeter, the King bids him release the man arrested the previous day for slandering the sovereign while 'under the influence'. Henry must know his quarry well, for this act of leniency prompts more hypocrisy, and precisely of the sort that will suit the charade he has planned: first Scroop ('That's mercy, but too much security. / Let him be punished, sovereign, lest example [etc.]'); then Cambridge ('... punish'); and Grey ('You show great mercy if you give him life, / After the taste of much correction'). But the King sticks by his decision.

> Alas, your too much love and care of me
> Are heavy orisons 'gainst this poor wretch.
> If little faults proceeding on distemper
> Shall not be winked at, how shall we stretch our eye
> When capital crimes, chewed, swallowed, and digested,
> Appear before us?
> (Ibid., 52–57)

Then, apparently moving on to other business but in a forgetful state of mind, he asks who are the commissioners that he has (just this day!) appointed for something to do with 'our French causes'. Whereupon the three conspirators step forward to receive their 'commissions', which actually are letters informing them that they are discovered. Each turns pale at the shock, confesses his guilt, and—what else—appeals to the King's mercy. Having so neatly set this up, Henry's response is predictable: 'The mercy that was quick in us but late / By your own counsel is suppressed and killed: / You must not dare, for shame, to talk of mercy, / For your own reasons turn into your bosoms'.

The King then proceeds to castigate them one by one. First Cambridge, who owed to royal favour both his earldom and the means to support it: 'and this man / Hath for a few light crowns lightly conspired / And sworn unto the practices of France / To kill us here in Hampton'). Then Grey, who 'hath likewise sworn'. But it is Lord Scroop of Masham, whose treason so especially scandalized Exeter ('the man that was his bedfellow') who is the recipient of the bulk of Henry's cold fury, or apparent fury (cf. 1.2.243–44): 'thou cruel, / Ingrateful, savage and inhuman creature, / Thou that didst bear the key of all my counsels / That knewst the very bottom of my soul', and so on for another fifty accusatory lines, concluding with an implicit warning to all those present:

> Such and so finely boulted didst thou seem:
> And thus thy fall hath left a kind of blot
> To mark the full-fraught man and best endued
> With *some* suspicion. I will weep for thee,
> For this revolt of thine, methinks, is like
> Another fall of man.
> (2.2.137–42)

Taken at his word, Henry here declares to all present that he will never again trust any man implicitly or unqualifiedly; that he will instead presume that every man, however seemingly virtuous, may nonetheless be tempted to the sin of disloyalty if the price is right. However, we should notice that while Henry has railed at such length upon Scroop, according him perverse pride of place in the conspiracy, the reason he has done so (supposedly) is because this 'kind Lord of Masham', the picture of all virtue, violated Henry's personal trust most of all. That is, the King does not accuse him of being the ringleader of the conspiracy.

Their crime exposed, Henry orders the trio arrested and made to answer to the full force of the law. And so they are. Whereupon Scroop and Grey repent their 'fault' and ask forgiveness for it, but not for their persons; rather, they declare themselves resigned to suffer the penalty of death, and so do not beg to escape it, at least not explicitly. Since they offer no alternative explanation for their treason, the accusation that their motive was mercenary stands by default. Cambridge's response, however, contrasts with theirs: 'For me, the gold of France did not seduce, / Although I did admit it as a motive / The sooner to effect what I intended' (ibid., 155–57). The King declines to probe further what Cambridge really 'intended' to 'effect'. Instead, he persists in attributing to all three traitors simple greed as their motive.

Yet, Henry would have it understood that they '*sold*' not only their 'king to slaughter', but also 'His princes and his peers to servitude, / His subjects to oppression and contempt, / And his whole kingdom into desolation' (ibid., 171–74). Accordingly, they are to be put to death, not because of their attempt on *his* life (ever the good Christian, he forgives his enemies: 'Touching our person seek we no revenge'), but because of all the rest: 'we our kingdom's safety must so tender, / Whose ruin you have sought'. How strange is this? He speaks as if France were threatening to conquer England! And, moreover, would likely succeed if only he were eliminated, whereupon the regime would disintegrate and the whole country fall into '*ruin*'! But as it is, God in His good time has 'brought to light / This dangerous treason', such that now the King and his army may set 'Cheerily to sea', confident that they are embarking on 'a fair and lucky war'.

The more one thinks about this episode, the more bizarre it seems. But Henry's staging of the conspirators' exposure is so dramatically engaging, the sheer poetry of his rhetorical denunciation so captivating, its pell-mell pace so demanding of one's complete attention, and the denouement both conclusive and transitional—'Bear them hence. Now, lords, for France' (in effect, 'so much for that, now let's get on with the main business')—that one is allowed no opportunity to think about what one has just witnessed. If, however, one does review this 'official' version, it is profoundly puzzling.

First of all, as already noted, the notion that the three conspirators had agreed to kill the King simply in return for French gold is implausible on the face of it. How could they do so without any risk of detection; a king's person is always guarded, his food and drink likewise. And escaping detection would seem the prerequisite of their enjoying the promised reward while continuing to live in England, secure in their titles and estates. But if, on the other hand, they were willing to kill him more or less openly—and the fact that there are three assassins involved might suggest some sort of assault is planned—how do they intend to escape the usual consequences of regicide: relentless pursuit, capture, torture, and execution? After all, the King has brothers, ready and able to take up the Crown, not to mention other kin, friends, and adherents. The conspirators would have to have arranged a foolproof scheme to flee abroad, abandoning their personal estates, and possibly their families. How much gold would it take to make that prospect attractive? There must be more to the story than the official version allows.

And of course there is. But apparently in the interest of adding some intellectual challenge for thoughtful readers, Shakespeare has chosen to suppress it almost entirely. Almost. He has, however, allowed Cambridge to hint that there *is* more: 'For me, the gold of France did not seduce, / Although I did admit it as a motive / The sooner to effect what I intended'. As Shakespeare knows full well (for it is complete in Holinshed), the 'effect' Cambridge 'intended' was the replacement of King Henry V by King Edmund I—with an eye, however, to the Crown eventually devolving upon his own son. As noted previously, Henry's claim to the throne was arguably inferior to that of Edmund Mortimer, fifth Earl of March. Edmund's father, Roger Mortimer, was childless Richard II's designated heir, and quite properly so since he was a direct descendant of Edward III's third son, Lionel, Duke of Clarence via his daughter Philippa, Roger's mother and Edmund's grandmother. Hence, when Roger Mortimer was killed by Irish rebels, occasioning Richard's leaving England to subdue the rebellion, Edmund (then but six or seven) stood next in line. So, immediately upon usurping Richard's throne, Bolingbroke took the boy into his own household for 'safekeeping'. And there young Edmund remained throughout most of Henry IV's reign, effectively under house arrest, though well treated and raised on friendly terms with the King and his family.[15]

However, Edmund had a sister, Anne Mortimer, who had married the Earl of Cambridge by whom she had a son, Richard, whose father was sure would be Edmund's heir.[16] For though Edmund was then but a young man in his twenties, Cambridge somehow knew that 'the earle of March, for diverse secret impediments, [was] not able to have issue'.[17] Edmund's sister Anne died young, whereupon Cambridge married Maud Clifford (ca. 1414), providing him a connection with the still powerful Percy clan. Thus, when agents of France sought out someone who had access to the King, and whom they might bribe to kill him, Cambridge was more than just willing to take the 'great summe of monie' they offered (not merely 'a few light crowns'), since he had his own fish to fry.

Of course, replacing Henry with Edmund would not be simply a matter of eliminating Henry. A large swath of the nobility, beginning with the King's brothers and uncles and cousins, as well as other adherents would have to be suppressed as well. And that would require the support of many more malcontents and adventurers than just Cambridge's two co-conspirators. We may presume he was aware of their existence, and had plans to draw them in. This suggests that, prior to Henry's initial success in the attempt to bend France to his will—thereby gaining him a popularity verging on adoration—the Lancastrian dynasty was far from solidly established. When Sir Thomas Grey assured Henry that his father's enemies had all changed from bitter to sweet and were now zealous in his service, this well-connected Northumberland knight doubtless knew this was far from true.

In short, were the conspiracy to kill Henry successful, England might well be plunged into a civil war of the sort that did eventually result from these rival Plantagenet claims, already well known to Shakespeare's contemporary audiences and readership as the Wars of the Roses, subject of his first tetralogy. The young King is fully aware of what the Cambridge-led conspiracy actually aimed to accomplish: to replace him with Richard's supposedly legitimate successor, Edmund Mortimer, fifth Earl of March. Thus, Henry's seemingly impertinent hyperbole about the threat the conspiracy posed to 'his princes and peers', endangering his whole kingdom with 'desolation' and 'ruin', is ironically *true*. Still, he can only glance at this real threat, as it is not in his interest to acknowledge that his claim to the throne is disputable. So he prefers to promote the fiction that the conspirators were motivated solely by money. And they, too, have an interest in going along with this version, especially Cambridge, since to admit publicly what they hoped to achieve by their plot would endanger the very people whose fortunes they sought to promote—not only Edmund Mortimer and Cambridge's son Richard, but other family members and associates who might be suspected of being implicated.[18]

Still, the second puzzle remains: how did Shakespeare's Henry learn of this conspiracy—or if one prefers, by what means did God ensure that he did so? The sources to which our philosopher-poet had access provide no answer. His principal source (Holinshed) says merely, 'the night before the daie appointed for their departure, [Henry] was crediblie informed' that the three conspirators, 'being confederate together, had conspired his death'.[19] Having only this tantalizing titbit to play with, Shakespeare was free to use the mystery of the conspiracy's discovery to imagine a solution which he might weave into his story. What are its main elements?

First, the French—or, to speak more precisely, someone in France—has indeed offered bribes to these three conspirators to kill King Henry. While the Chorus is far from a wholly reliable authority, we may assume that neither is it a purveyor of outright lies; it tells us, 'The sum is paid, the traitors are agreed'. And although Cambridge denies that 'the gold of France' was his real motive, he admits he took it because it would be useful 'to effect what [he] intended'. No surprise, that; money has countless uses, especially in furthering political aims. Moreover, the amount on offer must have been quite substantial, given that the French would presume that no one would undertake such a risky business otherwise—certainly not for 'a few light crowns', though Henry's implying that the conspirators were cheaply bought has the psychological effect of aggravating their offence.

Second, because we get no confirmation in the French Council scenes of this (failed) attempt to buy the death of Henry at the hands of a few unscrupulous fellow countrymen, we may presume that it was not a decision of that Council, or at least not with the French King presiding. This, too, is hardly surprising; no sitting king with an ounce of sense would authorize the assassination of his opposite number, thereby inviting a reciprocal attempt. On the other hand, it is believable that the Dauphin (as Shakespeare portrays him) is just foolish and shameless enough to instigate such a cynical plot. For all of his bravado, he may have found unsettling his 'tennis ball embassy' being served back at him with such threatening scorn. And presumably he would have no difficulty commanding the means to fund the scheme. Moreover, the Chorus tells us that the French have 'good intelligence' about the English preparations to invade. There is no reason to suppose that they, and the Dauphin in particular, are not well informed on other matters as well, including who among the English nobility might be disaffected from the new Lancastrian regime.

How then, in Shakespeare's casting of the story, is it most likely that Henry learned of the conspiracy? Doubtless he also has spies providing *him* 'good intelligence' about whatever the *French* were doing to counter his planned invasion.[20] And his agents may simply have penetrated the French end of the plot—perhaps aided by the judicious application of *English* gold—and thereby learned the identity, route, and timetable of couriers passing between the two countries, hence effecting the 'interception' Prince John spoke of. But a more intriguing hypothesis is the possibility that a French insider supplied Henry, either through his known agents or independently, with more particular information about this conspiracy. Presuming that the assassination scheme is the Dauphin's doing, there seems to be one well-placed member of the French Court who, if he learned of the plot, would take special delight in foiling it, and who moreover would believe that doing so was the honourable thing: 'Charles Delabreth, High Constable of France', who heads the list of French nobles reported killed at Agincourt (4.8.92–93). His rivalry with, and contempt for, the Dauphin is evident every time they appear together. Why else has Shakespeare made such a point of showing this (which has no basis in his sources)?

The first such occasion is during the first scene set in the Court of the French King Charles VI, who orders those attending him to make all preparations to defend their fortified towns against the threatening invasion, bearing in mind the death and destruction wrought by English armies of a previous generation. But the Dauphin insists this should be done with 'no show of fear' of England, since 'she is so idly kinged / Her sceptre so fantastically borne / By a vain, giddy, shallow, humorous youth, / That fear attends her not'. In short, there is little to worry about this time. However, his assessment is immediately contradicted by the Constable: 'O peace, Prince Dauphin! / You are too much mistaken in this king. / Question your grace the late ambassador, / With what great state he heard their embassy, / How well supplied with noble counsellors [etc.]'.[21] It is of interest that the Constable *has* questioned one of those ambassadors, though they were sent by the

Dauphin. Evidently the French Crown Prince undertakes some enterprises on his own authority, and evidently the Constable makes a point of monitoring such initiatives. Whether on the basis of having questioned the Dauphin's ambassadors, or through some other source of information, he has concluded that King Henry's 'vanities forespent / Were but the outside of the Roman Brutus, / Covering discretion with a coat of folly'. Are we to presume this is just a lucky guess? Whatever the case, the Dauphin rudely rejects Delabreth's strangely accurate surmise: 'Well, 'tis not so, my lord High Constable; / But though we think it so, it is no matter' (2.4.23–42).

When next we see the two together at Court—Harfleur having meanwhile surrendered, not least because the relief sought of the Dauphin was withheld (3.3.44–47)—each man seems determined to outdo the other in urging action on the French King. And while both resort to hyperbole, there is a marked difference in how they express their exasperation. The Constable, while insisting that 'for the honour of our land' they must fight the English, focuses upon the surprising martial virility of their foe (3.5.15–26). Whereas the Dauphin is preoccupied with mainly sexual implications: 'Shall a few sprays of us, / ... our fathers' luxury, / ... put in wild and savage stock'; and 'Our madams mock at us and plainly say / Our mettle is bred out, and they will give / Their bodies to the lust of English youth, / To new-store France with bastard warriors' (ibid., 5–7, 28–31). The French King is finally persuaded to go on the offensive, and orders his assembled nobles to bear down hard on his English counterpart: 'you have power enough, / And in a captive chariot into Rouen / Bring him our prisoner'. The Constable responds with enthusiasm, confident that when Henry sees how badly mismatched his bedraggled band is in confronting the full flower of the French army, he'll sue to ransom himself. This prompts the French King to instruct, 'Therefore, Lord Constable, haste on Montjoy, / And let him say to England that we send / To know what willing ransom he will give' (ibid., 53–63).

We are allowed to witness Montjoy's discharge of his assignment. The message he delivers bears scant resemblance to that which his King ordered sent.

> Thus says my king: 'Say thou to Harry of England, though we seemed dead, we did but sleep.... Now we speak upon our cue, and our voice is imperial. England shall repent his folly, see his weakness, and admire our sufferance. Bid him therefore consider of his ransom, which must proportion the losses we have borne, the subjects we have lost, the disgrace we have digested, which in weight to re-answer, his pettiness would bow under. For our losses, his exchequer is too poor; for th'effusion of our blood, the muster of his kingdom is too faint a number; and for our disgrace, his own person kneeling at our feet but a weak and worthless satisfaction. To this add defiance, and tell him, for conclusion, he hath

betrayed his followers, whose condemnation is pronounced'. So far my king and master, so much my office. (3.6.117–35)

Now, was it the Constable who drafted this extravagant, impossible demand? That seems unlikely, since we can compare it, point for point, with the one which Montjoy subsequently delivers, expressly affirming *this* one *is* from the Constable. Certainly the first ransom demand bears no resemblance to the temper of the anxious King Charles, though the herald, who was not present when the King issued his order, might believe that it does originate with him. However, he is sent a second time to inquire as to Henry's willingness to ransom himself. Unlike the first ultimatum, whose vulgar and demeaning character is poetically indicated by being in prose, the second is in verse.

> Once more I come to know of thee, King Harry,
> If for thy ransom thou wilt now compound,
> Before thy most assured overthrow:
> For certainly thou art so near the gulf
> Thou needs must be englutted. Besides, in mercy,
> The Constable desires thee thou wilt mind
> Thy followers of repentance, that their souls
> May make a peaceful and a sweet retire
> From off these fields, where, wretches, their poor bodies
> Must lie and fester.
>   (4.3.79–88)

Henry, doubtless noticing the radical difference in tone and substance from Montjoy's earlier message, pointedly asks, 'Who hath sent thee *now*?' The herald answers, 'The Constable of France'. The point is, the ransom inquiry we know to be the Constable's is not only a genuine solicitation, but courteous, considerate, and pious—in a word, *chivalrous*. No one would say that about Montjoy's earlier recitation. Who, then, should we suppose drafted it? Is it not cut from the same cloth as the speech that was crafted for his tennis-ball ambassadors: 'This the Dauphin speaks' (1.2.258)?

However, the clearest indication of the mutual animosity between the Dauphin and the Constable, and the disdain the latter has for the former, is provided on the very eve of battle. The scene is the French camp in the wee hours of the morning; various nobles are discussing their equipment while champing at the bit to begin the day's action. The Constable boasts that his armour is the best in the world, which the Duke of Orleans graciously concedes while soliciting in turn the praise due his horse. The Constable readily complies, 'It is the best horse of Europe' (3.7.5). As this is said in the hearing of the Dauphin, one suspects that it is intended to provoke him. He immediately confirms that he takes an inordinate pride in *his* horse, launching into extravagant praise of the beast, even proclaiming, 'my horse is my mistress' (3.7.44). This leads into a series of increasingly bawdy, insulting, hence acrimonious exchanges between the two, only terminating when the Dauphin leaves to arm himself. Upon his departure, Lord Rambures observes, 'He longs to eat the English', to which the Constable rejoins, 'I think he will eat all he kills'—the first of a series of sarcasms expressing skepticism of the Prince's self-proclaimed valour (3.7.90–112).

When next we see the two antagonists together, they are with the French battalions confronting the greatly outnumbered English army. The Constable, ostensibly the overall commander of French forces, addresses the assembled warriors, not so much out of concern to inspire them to acts of bravery as to apologize that their foe is so contemptible, a 'poor and starved band' whose numbers are so depleted that there will be scant opportunity for distinguishing acts of heroism (4.2.14–36). Lord Grandpré then enters, asking, 'Why do you stay so long, my lords of France?' followed by a graphic account of how pathetic the enemy appears. Whereupon the Dauphin taunts the Constable, as if he delayed attacking the enemy out of pity for their abject condition, who responds, 'I stay but for my guidon'. Then, substituting a trumpet banner for the purpose, he orders the attack.

The French assault fails, their ranks are broken, with men fleeing in disorder. It is in the wake of this debacle that we observe for the last time the two rivals together, along with three other leading nobles, all bewailing their situation. The Dauphin professes suicide: 'O perdurable shame! Let's stab ourselves'. The Duke of Bourbon, however, suggests instead that they die fighting: 'Let us die instant. Once more back again, / And he that will not follow Bourbon now, / Let him go home and with his cap in hand [etc.]'. The Constable answers the call: 'Disorder, that hath spoiled us, friend us now! / Let us on heaps go offer up our lives'. Orleans supposes they may still snatch victory: 'We are enough yet living in the field / To smother up the English in our throngs / If any order might be thought upon' (4.5.7, 11–21). The Dauphin is silent. We know the outcome of this last effort. Orleans and Bourbon are taken prisoner, and the Constable is killed. But the Dauphin is neither killed nor captured. Did he go home, 'cap in hand'? In any event, he is seen nor heard no more.[22]

So, what can one conclude? Nothing with certainty—as is typical of the puzzles that Shakespeare weaves into his plots. The conspiracy to murder Henry is a nice case in point. First of all, one must recognise that the 'official version' which King Henry propagates (as distinct from what Shakespeare himself would have gleaned from Holinshed) *is* puzzling. How could a French bribe of whatever amount tempt highly placed noblemen, with such substantial stakes in England, to assassinate the King? And of utmost importance, how did Henry learn of the threat in time to foil it?

One might also wonder why there is not the slightest reference in the French Court scenes to either the scheme or its failure. In addressing such questions, one is led to ask who likely instigated the plot, what was its true purpose, and how was it betrayed.

I have marshaled circumstantial evidence which suggests to me that Shakespeare has cast the Dauphin as the likely instigator; that the Constable who despised him and monitored his activities—and who would regard such an assassination as not merely unchivalrous, but profoundly ignoble and inconsistent with national honour, not to mention mortally dangerous to his own King—was the most likely source of warning; and that the conspirators accepted the French bribe, not primarily for the sake of personal enrichment, but to help fund an anti-Lancastrian rebellion. But whether or not my speculations are valid, and whether a reader finds my evidence for them persuasive, or inadequate, or amenable to an entirely different interpretation, the *questions* I am addressing cannot be gainsaid: they are posed by the text, and tacitly oblige the reader to address them himself.[23]

The attempt to conquer France and unify it with England under a single Crown presents a political challenge of the first order: 'But when one acquires states in a province disparate in language, customs, and orders, here are the difficulties, and here one needs to have great fortune and great industry to hold them'.[24] How, then, does Henry plan to succeed in what he knows full well will be an especially difficult undertaking?

The first thing to notice about Henry's method is his use of rhetoric as a weapon; in particular, vivid, 'brutal' threats—words chosen with the tactical intention of making the blood run cold, but with the strategic intention of minimizing, if not obviating, the need for brutal deeds. Why else issue such threats? We get our first indication of this from Exeter, who (we must presume) carries out his embassy to the French Court according to his king's instructions. Indeed, his threat as to 'what follows' should the French King not voluntarily resign his Crown and kingdom offers a mild foretaste—complete with the self-exonerating rationale—of Henry's own threat against Harfleur. One may suspect Henry himself to be the author.

> Deliver up the crown and [so] take mercy
> On the poor souls for whom this hungry war
> Opens his vasty jaws; and on your head
> Turning the widows' tears, the orphans' cries,
> The dead men's blood, the pining maidens' groans,
> For husbands, fathers and betrothed lovers
> That shall be swallowed in this controversy.
>   (2.4.103–9)

In his warning to the Governor of Harfleur, Henry actually shifts the blame in two opposing directions, as it were. First, onto the savage nature of his soldiers, capable of 'mowing like grass / Your fresh fair virgins and your flowering infants'—and which once unloosed, he claims, are utterly beyond his control: 'We may as bootless spend our vain command / Upon th'enraged soldiers in their spoil / As send precepts to the leviathan / To come ashore'.[25] But at the same time, he would also blame the Governor and the other men of Harfleur: 'What is't to me, when you yourselves are cause, / If your pure maidens fall into the hand / Of hot and forcing violation?'—'Your fathers taken by their silver beards, / And their most reverend heads dashed to the walls, / Your naked infants spitted upon pikes' (3.3.13–38). He concludes by reiterating who he claims must bear responsibility for such atrocities: 'Will you yield and this avoid? / Or, guilty in defence, be thus destroyed?'[26]

'*Guilty* in *defence*'? Is not the right of self-defence a basic principle of natural justice? Surely we ought to insist that it is. But whatever its moral propriety, there is little *practical* purpose served by *invoking* such a right except in circumstances where *justifying* one's actions matter. Generally speaking, this means within some political association in which all relevant parties are subject to the judgment of a single sovereign authority—precisely what is absent in the case of parties at war. Thus, sophistical as may be King Henry's attributing the *blame* to the men of Harfleur for whatever his 'enraged soldiers' may do should the city not be voluntarily surrendered, protesting the moral deficiency of his argument does not resolve the practical quandary with which he has confronted the Harfleurians—indeed, it has no bearing on it whatsoever. As Hobbes teaches, a 'RIGHT, consisteth in the liberty to do, or to forbeare'.[27] For what it's worth, the men of Harfleur have the natural *right* to defend their city to the death, if they so choose; the question is whether they *should* so choose, or instead 'forbeare'.

Their dilemma is as ancient as that posed by the Athenian ultimatum to the Melians during the Peloponnesian War.[28] And though one may admire the courage of the Melians for choosing the opposite horn than did the Harfleurians, one may still doubt their wisdom in doing so. When one's defensive situation is or will soon become utterly hopeless, and surrender promises survival, it is not unreasonable to conclude that further resistance is foolhardy, being pointless. Of course, often in actual circumstances the choice is not so clear; sometimes resistance could be successful—but only if undertaken. For instance, sometimes a besieging army may become so depleted by disease that the siege must be abandoned (as was nearly the case historically at Harfleur).[29] Or, outside assistance might arrive in time to save the day, perhaps inspired by the very tenacity of the resistance.[30] The Melians held out to the bitter end, hoping for aid from Sparta—vainly, as it turned out. Whereas the Governor of Harfleur learns in time that the 'succours' sought of the Dauphin would not be forthcoming, and so he answers Henry's ultimatum, 'dread King, / We yield our town and lives to thy soft mercy' (3.3.44–48).

'Soft mercy'—thus the Governor incidentally points to the second principle Henry adopts in his campaign to conquer France: treating its civilian population with consideration. His policy is on display, and not least for the instruction of other cities he may assault, in dealing with the inhabitants of Harfleur upon their surrender. Henry turns over the city to the Duke of Exeter, instructing him to 'Use mercy to them all' (3.3.54).[31] Shortly thereafter, we hear the policy, including its rationale, expressed by the King himself. The occasion is his learning that Exeter (who, in order to accompany the King on his march towards Calais, must have turned over the keeping of Harfleur to his lieutenant)[32] has caused Bardolph—adherent of the late Sir John Falstaff, and ipso facto a familiar of Prince Hal—to be hanged 'for robbing a church'.

Fluellen, who is the conveyor of this news, describes the villain as having a red face covered with carbuncles, 'if your majesty know the man' (3.6.100–101). One would not guess he did from Henry's aloof reply.

> We would have all such offenders so cut off; and we give express charge that in our marches through the country there be nothing compelled from the villages, nothing taken but paid for, none of the French upbraided or abused in disdainful language; for when lenity and cruelty play for a kingdom, the gentler gamester is the soonest winner. (3.6.106–12)

As Henry makes explicit, he demands that his army adhere to this policy, not primarily as a matter of justice, but because it facilitates conquest[33]— much as it did Caesar's conquest of France, according to Machiavelli.[34] Moreover, the less destructive the means of winning the prize, the more value the prize retains. All this and whatever else might be said, the fact remains that Henry's policy *is* more merciful, hence more decent, than that of a scorched-earth, and as such would be infinitely preferred by the civilian inhabitants of the country—which is the objective reality whence derives the policy's strategic advantage.

The third strand of Henry's acquisition strategy aims to solidify his military conquest by matrimonial means. For beyond doubt his marriage to the French princess *is* first and foremost a *means* to this political end. But it is equally beyond doubt that the marriage was insufficient in and of itself for the accomplishment of Henry's aim; that, rather, the marriage is conjunctive to the antecedent military subjugation. For the Chorus tells us that upon Henry taking up position for the siege and assault on Harfleur, the French King did 'offer him / Katherine his daughter and with her, to dowry, / Some petty and unprofitable dukedoms' (3.0.29–31). But Henry did not bring an army to France in order to extort a marriage proposal, with or without some petty dukedoms to sweeten the deal. As he will later acknowledge to the girl herself, it is not she alone he loves: 'I love France so well that I will not part with a village of it; I will have it all mine' (5.2.173–75). And while he does profess to love her dearly, he admits that he'll not die of a broken heart should she reject him (ibid., 150–53). But of course, practically speaking, her rejecting him is not really an option—a fact of which she surely is well aware. Moreover, it is most unlikely that she would wish it otherwise; not for nothing did she set about learning English well before Henry had achieved a position in France whence he could dictate anything. Perhaps the prospect of taking a soldier for a husband, and in taking a soldier taking a king, is not without its appeal?

But whatever may be her, or his, personal feelings about the matter, the French Princess's becoming Henry's queen is essential to gaining broad acceptance among the French people for the new political order. Thus, when Henry speaks of her as his 'capital demand' in the peace negotiations (ibid., 95–97), that is the ironic truth, and not to be gainsaid by anyone, including her.[35] Still, it would be best were it generally known that she submitted willingly to his proposal. Thus the importance of Henry's wooing of her, even if the outcome is a foregone conclusion.[36] The main point is the intention that she 'prove a good soldier-breeder', such that they together, 'between Saint Denis and Saint George, compound a boy, half French, half English, that shall go to Constantinople and take the Turk by the beard' (ibid., 203–7). The French may then regard that boy, Henry's *successor*, as one of their own, even as the English will do likewise. Notice, however, the King apparently intends to pass on to his son the same advice he received from his father: 'Be it thy course to busy giddy French minds with foreign quarrels, that action hence borne out may waste the memory of the former days'.

It is also worth noting that the French Queen expressly endorses, without prompting, Henry's own rationale—though with a subtle warning:

> God, the best maker of all marriages,
> Combine your hearts in one, your realms in one!
> As man and wife, being two, are one in love,
> So be there 'twixt your kingdoms such a spousal
> That never may ill office or fell jealousy,
> Which troubles oft the bed of blessed marriage,
> Thrust in between the paction of these kingdoms
> To make divorce of their incorporate league;

> That English may as French, French Englishmen,
> Receive each other. God speak this amen.
>
> (5.2.353–62)

Her admonition is entirely appropriate, as there is apt to be any number of still potent French lords, with grievances yet green, that will be inclined to stir up what trouble they can for a marriage of kingdoms they do not regard as a blessing.

This does not include, however, the powerful Duke of Burgundy, whom Henry expressly 'salutes' for his having 'contrived' to bring together both Courts for the purpose of negotiating a peace settlement (5.2.5–7). Though posing as a neutral, we may presume the Duke knows full well that any peace will be on the English King's terms or not at all. It would seem, then, that the Duke favours the arrangement most agreeable to Henry—perhaps having received prior assurance that, under the suzerainty of Henry as king of France, he will exercise a practical autonomy in his province.[37]

Burgundy's behaviour on this occasion suggests that Henry's strategy included a fourth strand: covertly recruiting at least one powerful French ally.[38] For some reason, Burgundy was not among the French at Agincourt. Lest this detail be overlooked, Shakespeare subtly directs attention to it by expressly identifying 'Anthony, Duke of Brabant', one of the many French nobles who fell there, as 'brother to the Duke of Burgundy' (4.8.97–98; cf. 3.5.42). And notice, in what is clearly a prepared speech to the 'Great Kings of France and England', Burgundy alleges to them an '*equal* love' and duty; he does not, that is, acknowledge a superior obligation to the present King of France.

And yet, he is so eloquent in describing the damage that years of war have visited upon 'fertile France' ('best garden of the world'), returning it to a savage state, and similarly its populace: 'And as our vineyards, fallows, meads and hedges, / Defective in their natures, grow to wildness, / Even so our houses and our selves and children / Have lost . . . / The sciences that should become our country' (5.2.54–58).[39] The effect of his rhetorical display is to emphasise the importance to France of achieving peace ('Dear nurse of arts, plenties and joyful births') as to make it worth virtually any price. Hence, it practically solicits the sort of response Henry gives it: 'If, Duke of Burgundy, you would the peace / Whose want gives growth to th'imperfections / Which you have cited, you must buy that peace / With full accord to all our just demands' (5.2.68–71).

Doubtless, these four elements of the strategy whereby Henry attempts to graft onto his existing state another 'disparate in language, customs, and orders' would meet with Machiavelli's approval. But since the young English King died before his conquest of France was consolidated, we do not know whether he would have acted as the Florentine advises in order to deal with the many difficulties such an annexation presents: 'the greatest and quickest remedy would be for whoever acquires it to go there to live in person. This would make that possession more secure and more lasting'. Why so?

> For if you stay there, disorders may be seen as they arise, and you can soon remedy them; if you are not there, disorders become understood [only] when they are great and there is no longer a remedy. Besides this, the province is not despoiled by your officials; the subjects are satisfied with ready access to the prince, so that they have more cause to love him if they want to be good and, if they want to be otherwise, more cause to fear him. Whatever outsider might want to attack that state has more hesitation in doing so; hence, when one lives in it, one can lose it [only] with the greatest difficulty.

But given Henry's experience of his father's reign and the first years of his own, it seems unlikely he would suppose that England and Wales would long remain peaceful, orderly, united, and secure under an absentee king.[40] Such being the case, it would preclude making France his primary residence and seat of government. What, then, would be his alternative? According to Machiavelli:

> The other, better remedy is to send colonies that are, as it were, fetters of that state, to one or two places, because it is necessary either to do this or to hold them with many men-at-arms and infantry. One does not spend much on colonies, ... and one offends only those from whom one takes fields and houses in order to give them to the new inhabitants—who are a very small part of that state. And those whom he offends, since they remain dispersed and poor, can never hurt him, while all the others ... are afraid to err from fear that what has happened to the despoiled might happen to them.[41]

Trying to hold such an acquisition by garrisoning it with soldiers—the third alternative—is expensive, and a chronic irritation to the native population; hence, 'keeping guard in this way is as useless as keeping guard by means of colonies is useful'. To repeat, we cannot know what Shakespeare's Henry intended in this regard, but we do know how the historical Henry proceeded after he had taken Harfleur: he turned it into a second Calais.

> It was to be the first example of Henry's new policy of colonization in Normandy, a development which changed the character of the war being fought in France, and which marked off the new phase of the conflict with France from that of the fourteenth century, characterized as that

had been by a military policy of raids and, not infrequently, physical destruction. Henry was doing something significant. Within a week or two of the fall of Harfleur, he was to invite merchants and those, such as victuallers, whose presence had a military justification, to come to the town, where they would be given houses to live in and outlets for their trade in return for undertakings to set up a permanent residence. Harfleur was too important to remain a dead town. A substantial English presence would help revive its fortunes, assure its permanent defence, provide the English with the rapid and regular supply of their military needs on campaign, and help bring about the establishment of an English settlement in Normandy which . . . was to be the hallmark of the history of the duchy for the coming thirty-five years or so.[42]

To what extent Shakespeare was cognisant of this is impossible to say, but he could hardly have been unaware that a long-term English presence in Normandy began with the occupation of Harfleur, and ended only with 'the loss of France' during the disastrous reign of Henry VI (of which the Chorus speaks in the Epilogue).

So much, then, for Shakespeare's portrayal of *how* Henry V attempted to make himself king of both England and France in deed, as he and three predecessors had claimed to be in word. But what about the propriety of the attempt itself? Does it amount to nothing less than armed robbery, as some of his critics claim?[43] We cannot know how seriously the philosopher-poet took the historical Henry's claim to the French Crown, either morally or legally. He has *his* King and Council treat the issue as if the sole basis for the French rejection of that claim rested on the so-called Salic law barring inheritance via female descendants (which would preclude the English claim, since it derived from Edward III's mother).

Nothing of what is shown of the French deliberations, however, provides any confirmation of this. Stranger still, perhaps, Exeter makes no reference to the, supposedly bogus, Salic law in presenting Henry's case to Charles VI and his Council. He simply asserts that by all lawful authority—that of heaven, and of nature, and of nations—the French throne is rightfully Henry's by virtue of his pedigree, of which Exeter provides a schematic for the French King to 'overlook':

> And when you find him evenly derived
> From his most famed of famous ancestors,
> Edward the Third, he bids you then resign
> Your crown and kingdom indirectly held
> From him the native and true challenger.
> (2.4.90–95)

Of course, Shakespeare is fully aware that the French royalty would not have resigned the Crown in Henry's favour on the basis of *any* merely legalistic argument, Salic law or no Salic law. And as previously discussed, this law—which supposedly barred inheritance via the female line—*is* awkward for Henry, since he is the *direct* heir 'evenly derived' from Great Edward (via his *fourth son*, John of Gaunt, Duke of Lancaster) only if the heir via the *daughter* of his *third* son (namely, the fifth Earl of March) is disallowed on some equivalent of the Salic law. We may suppose Shakespeare meant us to savour this contradiction in Henry's claims to be the legitimate king of *both* France and England.

But regardless of the merit of Henry's claim, what are we to think of his attempt to make it good by conquest? Perhaps more to the point, what most likely is Shakespeare's view? Or has he not clearly tipped his hand by having the Welsh captain Fluellen so amusingly liken Henry to 'Alexander the Pig'? Not clearly enough, I submit, as a serious explication and analysis of the parallels between these two famous conquerors would show—'If you mark Alexander's life well' (4.7.31), and Henry's likewise.[44] Of course, for anyone who simply opposes military conquest per se, regardless of whom, by whom, and for whatever reason, no justification of Henry's ambition is possible. But neither, then, can such a person regard as justified the origin of virtually any polity from the beginning of civilization, since what Hobbes calls 'Naturall force' is the historical basis of each and every one.[45] As for the alternative, there are severe limitations on the quality of life possible within human associations no larger than that of extended families, most especially with respect to the cultivation of knowledge. Supposing both the laws of heaven and of nations to be inconclusive if not irrelevant to the issue, on what basis, then, is Henry's aspiration to be condemned? That the French nobility has a natural right to rule the French commonality, those 'lackeys and peasants' of which the Constable speaks so disdainfully?[46] Is it so obvious that the average French peasant would *not* be better off, and so come to prefer English overlords once he had adequate exposure to their different attitude towards their underlings? Given an experiential basis for comparison, might not ordinary French men and women rather be ruled by a man such as Henry—who does, after all, have a genealogical claim to their throne—than by any of the French nobility we meet in the play?

What kind of man is Shakespeare's Henry? The question has a special importance in his case, as it bears on the strategy whereby he seeks to establish his unqualified *legitimacy* as king of England; that is, to gain universal recognition of a practically indisputable *right* to rule such as would oblige the willing obedience of his subjects. True, he is of royal lineage himself, the eldest son of the preceding King, and directly descended from King

Edward III—and thus, not incidentally, from Edward's mother, Isabella, daughter and heir of Philip IV of France. He's not just anybody. And like all English kings before him, he does embed himself within the protocols and trappings of kingship, all the 'general ceremony' of which he speaks so disdainfully in his one soliloquy. For Henry is under no illusion about its limitations. Having posed to himself the question, 'And what art thou, thou idol ceremony', he in effect concludes, 'Nothing truly substantial' (4.1.237, 254–63)

> No, thou proud dream
> That play'st so subtly with a king's repose,
> I am a king that find thee, and I know
> 'Tis not the balm, the sceptre and the ball,
> The sword, the mace, the crown imperial, . . .
> The throne he sits on, nor the tide of pomp
> That beats upon the high shore of this world,
> No, not all these, thrice-gorgeous ceremony . . .

. . . will suffice to put his legitimacy beyond all question, since his *right* to use these symbols and paraphernalia of kingship is tainted by his father's sin of usurpation.[47] As noted previously, it is this abiding worry that dominates Henry's prayer to the 'God of battles' on the eve of Agincourt, harkening back to the reign of Richard II—and, not incidentally, thereby attesting to the 'legitimacy problem' as the unifying theme of the whole *Henriad* tetralogy: 'Not today, O Lord, / O not today, think not upon the fault / My father made in compassing the crown' (ibid., 289–91)[48]

Henry remains keenly aware that the Crown he inherited is not free and clear of this encumbrance upon his title. Moreover, that this liability has practical consequences was made perfectly evident by the recurring civil strife of his father's reign, and was proved once again by the conspiracy so recently thwarted at Southampton. Consequently, he is determined to rectify this defect in the foundation of his claim to his subjects' allegiance. Because the means whereby he endeavours to do so are primarily *personal*, at least initially, his nature and character as well as his actions and accomplishments take on an importance out of all proportion to that of his predecessors. Presuming he is successful in expunging this blot on his own escutcheon, he then would face the more difficult task of transforming his personal right to rule into one that is *institutional*, such as will outlast him as its founder.

That Henry is not merely shrewd, but highly intelligent, that he knows his own mind and keeps his own counsel, is evident in all we are shown of his words and deeds. He is famously courageous—physically brave to the point of fearless—but intellectually bold as well. The innovative spirit of which he assures his bride-to-be regarding the conventions and expectations of the given world has applications far more important than the parochial rules of kissing: 'O Kate, nice customs curtsy to great kings. Dear Kate, you and I cannot be confined within the weak list of a country's fashions. We are the makers of manners, Kate, and the liberty that follows our places stops the mouth of all find-faults' (5.2.266–70).

There is no indication that he's inclined to either luxury or pleasure-seeking; what he professes in his prebattle exhortation at Agincourt must be largely true, for he is addressing men who would know if it wasn't: 'I am not covetous for gold, / Nor care I who doth feed upon my cost; / It earns me not if men my garments wear: / Such outward things dwell not in my desires' (4.3.24–27). Judging by what he claims in wooing his future queen, his manner of life has been that of a simple soldier, Spartan even, devoid of the common social graces and refinements characteristic of his class (such as dancing and versifying; 5.2.133–37—thus the unintended irony of the Dauphin's taunt; 1.2.252–54). He obviously is a skilled rhetorician despite his professing to the French princess, 'I have no cunning in protestation, only downright oaths, which I never use till urged, nor never break for urging' (5.2.144–46). He would be seen as trustworthy, just, firm in his resolve, a man of his word, 'Who never promiseth but he means to pay' (cf. *1 Henry IV*, 5.4.42). Doubtless, some would call his temper 'hard', and this would be true insofar as a certain hardness is implicit in his emotional detachment from the destructive consequences of his pursuit of political goals, especially whatever 'collateral damage' this causes other people. He has long since accommodated himself to the fact that political creation entails destruction. After all, he didn't make the world and its necessities; he simply works upon the world as he finds it. He is frequently characterized as 'machiavellian', which is also true—indeed, so obviously true that one might imagine Shakespeare's having *The Prince* by his side as he crafted the play—though this is not necessarily the damning indictment many of his modern critics apparently treat it as being.[49]

But is it conceivable, then, that 'warlike Harry' could well and truly be 'the mirror of all Christian kings', as the Chorus claims (2.0.6)? Or is this a Shakespearean joke? For we know his Henry prays, not to the Prince of Peace, but to the God of Battles. If he is any sort of Christian, it's of a militant, 'muscular' cast, one who thinks of himself as first and foremost a soldier . . . perhaps well suited for a world of warring religions? We know he seeks in a wife 'a good soldier-breeder', that he wishes for a son who would take an army—not to the Holy Land to recapture Jerusalem, but to Constantinople with the intention of defeating the Turks, thereby ending the threat to Christian Europe (5.2.203–7). Perhaps, then, Shakespeare's Chorus speaks the ironic truth: Henry would indeed be a suitable mirror for all

Christian kings. It is hard to know with certainty just what is Shakespeare's overall assessment of his Henry,[50] but we can be sure that the philosopher-poet is neither a sentimentalist nor a utopian. It is quite possible that—reflecting upon the abbreviated career of the historical Henry, whose fate might as readily have been otherwise—Shakespeare may have seen in the man a potential for achievements far beyond those actualized.

Despite inheriting the English throne from his father, a sitting king, and whatever lingering influence his partaking of a supposedly sacred bloodline might contribute to his acceptance by his people, Henry never expressly claims the *right to rule* on this basis. Doubtless he welcomed the realm's highest churchmen acknowledging him as England's lawful king, but he never speaks in a mode even remotely similar to that which came so naturally to Richard II prior to his fall: 'Not all the water in the rough rude sea / Can wash the balm off from an anointed king; / The breath of worldly men cannot depose / The deputy elected by the Lord' (*Richard II*, 3.2.54–57). Henry's language 'bespeaks' an outlook on the world radically different from that of Richard. However, it is equally at odds with the dominant mentality of the French—a difference that Shakespeare is at pains to emphasize in *Henry V.*

The French elite openly express their disdain, not to say outright contempt, for those they regard as their inferiors, whether French plebian or anyone English. Thus the Constable's sarcasm at the idea of Henry being permitted to advance through France unopposed: 'let us quit all / And give our vineyards to a barbarous people'. The Dauphin, with his characteristic French sensitivity to sexual implications, laments that the seed of French fathers, 'put in wild and savage stock', should be suffered to 'overlook their grafters'. The Duke of Britain (i.e., of Brittany/Bretagne) is equally scandalized at the thought that 'Normans, but *bastard* Normans, Norman bastards' are being allowed to 'march along / Unfought' (3.5.2–12). Having to admit that an army of such base lineage has once again triumphed over the flower of French chivalry redoubles the pain of their defeat at Agincourt. The profound *shame* of it dominates their reaction. The Dauphin exclaims, 'Mortal reproach and everlasting shame . . . O perdurable shame! Let's stab ourselves'. Bourbon likewise: 'Shame, and eternal shame, nothing but shame! Let us die instant', rather than 'Like a base pandar hold the chamber-door / Whilst by a slave no gentler than my dog / His fairest daughter is contaminated' (4.5.4–16).

The attitude of the French aristocracy towards their own commoners comes out most clearly just before and then after the Battle of Agincourt. In addressing his army prior to the engagement, the Constable regrets that the opposing army amounts to such a 'poor and starved band' that it will not provide sport enough for all his 'French gallants'. As for the 'superfluous lackeys and peasants' who hang around the margins of the French battalions, propriety precludes allowing them to share in the little glory that the coming battle promises to afford (4.2.24–31). The Constable's prebattle exhortation obviously invites comparison with that of King Henry (to be examined anon), but the material point is this: the French nobility claim as their natural right a monopoly on military activity and the honours gained thereby. So, whereas over five-sixths of the twelve thousand that made up the English army were commoners (4.3.3–4; cf. 74–76), the French army was overwhelmingly composed of upper-class men-at-arms. This is clear from the casualty report Henry reads: 'So that in these ten thousand they have lost / There are but sixteen hundred mercenaries [what Holinshed calls 'the meaner sort']; / The rest are princes, barons, lords, knights, squires / And gentlemen of blood and quality'. The proportional relationship of these figures (roughly, six to one) are the inverse of the English dead: four men 'of name, and of all other men but five-and-twenty' (4.8.88–91, 104–7).

The French nobility's fastidious attention to social rank is nicely epitomized by Montjoy when he comes a third time. Henry facetiously asks, 'How now, what means this, herald? . . . Com'st thou again for ransom?' Montjoy replies, 'No, great King':

> I come to thee for charitable license
> That we may wander o'er this bloody field
> To look our dead and then to bury them;
> To sort out our nobles from our common men.
> For many of our princes—woe the while!—
> Lie drowned and soaked in mercenary blood;
> So do our vulgar drench their peasant limbs
> In blood of princes.
> (4.7.70–77)

In reviewing the evidence of the French nobility's social sensibilities, one notices that they, like Richard II in his glory days, invest 'blood', *lineage*, with an almost supernatural significance. And this despite a plenitude of contrary natural evidence: they regard the English as base-born, a bastard race little better than barbarians—and yet this supposedly mongrel tribe has *repeatedly* bested the 'purebred' French nobility in what they profess to be their defining métier: martial excellence (cf. 2.4.48–64). Still, they prefer to regard their cultural refinement as proof of their natural superiority—a refinement epitomized by food and drink: the English 'eat like wolves' their 'great meals of beef' (3.7.149–50), washed down with crude 'barley-broth' (i.e., ale), whereas the French have made cookery an art, and their 'blood [is] spirited with wine' from the vineyards of their more salubrious climate (3.5.16–22).

In marked contrast to the preeminent representatives of the French aristocracy, Shakespeare's King Henry, like Julius Caesar, cultivated 'the common touch'. Employed judiciously, hence sparingly (as his father advised; *1 Henry IV*, 3.2.46–59), this works to bind the lower classes to him while nonetheless preserving a social distance that will ensure his word is law. And the example he thereby sets dampens the natural haughtiness of the nobility. Being himself the son of a great duke who made himself king, he necessarily has been familiar since childhood with the ways and perspectives of his country's political elite. This is implicitly confirmed dozens of times in the *Henriad*—and often enough explicitly, as when he imitates this father dressing him down for the questionable company he keeps (ibid., 2.4.421–68). But in the guise of the scapegrace Prince Hal, companion of Falstaff and his seedy crew, he also learned the language, manners, and morals of the lower orders of English society, along with how they view their betters. Thus he acquired the 'synoptic perspective' that Machiavelli implicitly claims for himself in the Dedicatory Letter of *The Prince*.[51]

> For just as those who sketch landscapes place themselves down in the plain to consider the nature of mountains and high places and to consider the nature of low places place themselves high atop mountains, similarly, to know well the nature of peoples one needs to be a prince, and to know well the nature of princes one needs to be of the people.

Whatever the merits of his dubious analogy, Machiavelli's handbook of advice for actual and aspiring princes makes clear that a competent prince must know thoroughly the *natures* of *both* princely types and common people—not just how they appear from a distance—since he necessarily must be able to deal with both. Practically speaking, this requires first-hand familiarity with both perspectives.

This is precisely what Henry has made it his business to acquire. Knowing how to relate to his fellow nobles was never to be much of a problem, and is even less so after his ruthlessly dispatching the conspirators. What especially distinguishes him, however, is how skilfully he bonds with the commoners, and with his soldiers in particular. Of course, the fact that he leads from the front, hence shares fully their danger, is fundamental. But the effect of his example is reinforced by his rhetoric, which invites his men to identify with him and share his cause, softening while still preserving the distinction between him and them—ruler and ruled—as in his rallying cry at Harfleur: 'Once more unto the breach, *dear friends*'. Similarly, he softens yet preserves the distinction between his nobles and his commoners (which since at least his great-grandfather's day had never been so strict and stark as with the French), and he does so in a way that is flattering to both. The former are urged to set the standard for the latter: 'On, on, you noble English, / ... / Be copy now to men of grosser blood / And teach them how to war'. Whereas the commoners are encouraged to believe that they have enough natural nobility in them to measure up to that standard:

> And you, good yeomen,
> Whose limbs were made in England, show us here
> The mettle of your pasture; let us swear
> That you are worth your breeding—which I doubt not,
> For there is none of you so mean and base
> That hath not noble lustre in your eyes.
> (3.1.25–30)[52]

Shakespeare's Henry is no democrat, but he clearly courts popularity with his commoners. Insofar as that popularity is evident to one and all, it serves as a counterpoise to the power of his nobles. Having digested the lessons of his father's troubles with the Percys and others, he is determined to avoid them himself—much as Machiavelli advises:

> He who comes to the principality with the aid of the great maintains himself with more difficulty than one who becomes prince with the aid of the people, because the former finds himself prince with many around him who appear to be his equals, and because of this he can neither command them nor manage them to suit himself.... Besides this, one cannot satisfy the great with decency and without injury to others, since the great want to oppress and the people want not to be oppressed. Furthermore, a prince can never secure himself against a hostile people, as they are too many; against the great, he can secure himself, as they are few.[53]

As noted before, strictly speaking Henry is not a *new* prince. Nor was he elevated to his position through popularity; he did inherit his Crown. But neither is he the beneficiary of a long and well-established family dynasty, much less one whose right to rule was grounded on a belief in divine right, publicly accepted by both the 'great' and the 'people'. Thus, the practical problem he inherited along with the Crown—as I have been at pains to emphasize—is that of establishing in the minds of his own subjects not merely the *fact* that he rules, but that he does so with incontestable moral *legitimacy*. And the tack he has taken might have come straight from the notorious Florentine:

> But when a prince who founds on the people knows how to command and is a man full of heart, and does not get frightened in adversity, does not fail to make other preparations, and with his spirit and his orders keeps the generality of people inspired, he will never find himself deceived by them and he will see he has laid his foundations well.[54]

History has proven countless times that ordinary people naturally admire such a man, and willingly accept his leadership. And the venue in which one can most readily and unmistakably prove oneself 'full of heart' and 'fearless in adversity', a man among men, and show both his resourcefulness and his strength of soul, is that of war. No wonder, then, that this is, literally, the central teaching of Machiavelli's *The Prince*.

> Thus, a prince should have no other object, nor any other thought, nor take anything else as his art but the art of war and its orders and discipline; for that is the only art which is of concern to one who commands. And it is of such virtue that not only does it maintain those who have been born princes but many times it enables men of private fortune to rise to that rank; and on the contrary, one sees that when princes have thought more of amenities than of arms, they have lost their states. [Richard II comes to mind.] . . .
>
> Therefore, [a prince] should never lift his thoughts from the exercise of war, and in peace he should exercise it more than in war. This he can do in two modes, one with deeds, the other with the mind. And as to deeds, besides keeping his armies well ordered and exercised, he should always be out hunting, and through this accustom the body to hardships [cf. *2 Henry IV*, 4.4.13–14]. . . .
>
> But, as to the exercise of the mind, a prince should read histories and consider in them the actions of excellent men, should see how they conducted themselves in wars, should examine the causes of their victories and losses, so as to be able to avoid the latter and imitate the former [cf. *Henry V*, 1.2.146–54]. Above all he should do as some excellent man has done in the past who found someone to imitate who has been praised and glorified before him, whose exploits and actions he always kept beside himself, as they say Alexander the Great imitated Achilles; Caesar, Alexander; Scipio, Cyrus.[55]

Moreover, should a prince be *victorious* in war—better still, victorious against overwhelming odds; best of all, a great *conqueror*, an Alexander, a Caesar—he will be venerated by people as virtually a demigod.[56] Thus was Henry (according to the Chorus) upon returning to England after his victory at Agincourt. Met on the very beach by throngs of 'men, with wives and boys' shouting their praises, he proceeds to London,

> Where that his lords desire him to have borne
> His bruised helmet and his bended sword
> Before him through the city. He forbids it,
> Being free from vainness and self-glorious pride,
> Giving full trophy, signal and ostent
> Quite from himself to God. But now behold, . . .

How London doth pour out her citizens.
The Mayor and all his brethren in best sort,
Like to the senators of th'antique Rome
With the plebeians swarming at their heels,
Go forth and fetch their conquering Caesar in.
                    (5.0.17–28)

Henry, ever the master of political stagecraft, knows that report of his refusal to parade through the city with his beaten helmet and sword preceding him (as would be customary), and instead to attribute his victory solely to God, will quickly spread through the town and into the country, amplifying the people's veneration of him. And however 'modestly' he pretends otherwise, he knows the crowds are cheering him, not God. Still, the fact that he and his tired, ragged band, though greatly outnumbered (and *how* greatly will only increase with the telling; cf. 4.3.50) nonetheless managed—'miraculously'—to emerge victorious will be interpreted as evidence of divine approval of his kingship. Needless to add, this is the sort of thing that poets memorialize for the delight and inspiration of current and later generations.[57]

Shakespeare's King Henry is no more a democrat than is Shakespeare himself, but if one credits at all the claims of the Chorus, the King's behaviour during the night preceding the battle displays a certain egalitarian sensitivity.

           O now, who will behold
    The royal captain of this ruined band
    Walking from watch to watch, from tent to tent,
    Let him cry 'Praise and glory on his head!'
    For forth he goes and visits all his host,
    Bids them good morrow with a modest smile,
    And calls them brothers, friends and countrymen. . . .
    With cheerful semblance and sweet majesty,
    That every wretch, pining and pale before,
    Beholding him plucks comfort from his looks.
    A largess universal, like the sun,
    His liberal eye doth give to every one,
    Thawing cold fear, that mean and gentle all
    Behold, as may unworthiness define,
    A little touch of Harry in the night.
                    (4.0.28–47)[58]

He 'visits *all* his host', offering cheer and comfort to '*every* wretch'; his liberal eye displays 'a largess *universal* to *every* one', to 'mean and gentle *all*';

all are addressed as 'brothers' and 'friends' and 'fellow countrymen'. The contrast this presents to how the French leaders occupied themselves that night could hardly be more diametrical. Though to be fair, the French army is fresh, and the opposite of disheartened; and since it is composed almost entirely of nobility, there are no 'mean' as well as 'gentle' whose spirits might need bucking up. Rather, 'Proud of their numbers and secure in soul', well might they cast dice for the ransoms they anticipate winning from English noblemen, who (they presume) will be eager enough to surrender, given half a chance.

The King having concluded his nocturnal round of encouraging his discomfited host, he apparently desires a more candid sampling of his men's opinions and feelings than he could obtain in his own royal person. Thus he borrows old Sir Thomas Erpingham's cloak, and in this disguise has a twilit conversation with three ordinary soldiers who are not optimistic as to what the dawning day has in store for them. Henry's initial contribution, for all of its irony, indicates his awareness of the extent to which he shares a nature with the men he leads:

> I think the King is but a man, as I am: the violet smells to him as it doth to me; the element shows to him as it doth to me; all his senses have but human conditions; his ceremonies laid by, in his nakedness he appears but a man; and though his affections are higher mounted than ours, yet when they stoop they stoop with the like wing. Therefore when he sees reason of fears as we do, his fears, out of doubt, be of the same relish as ours are. (4.1.102–10)

There is a more problematic portion of this predawn conversation, however, concerning the moral responsibility of a ruler who leads his subjects into war.

One of the men (Bates) wishes both he and the King were elsewhere, even were it in the Thames up to their necks, given the likely fate that awaits them where they are now. The disguised Henry does not agree, claiming to suppose the King would not wish to be anywhere but where he is. To this implausible view, Bates replies, 'Then I would he were here alone; so should he be sure to be ransomed, and a many poor men's lives saved'. Again Henry objects: 'Methinks I could not die anywhere so contented as in the King's company, his cause being just and his quarrel honourable'.

This provokes another of the trio (Williams) to demur, 'That's more than we know', ruefully adding, 'But if the cause be *not* good, the King himself hath a heavy reckoning to make'—at the throne of God, presumably—given the likely costs in men's lives, whose deaths have ill consequences for others as well: 'their wives left poor behind them', their debtors unpaid, and 'their children rawly left'. The problem, as this soldier sees it, is that 'few die well that die in battle, for how can they charitably dispose of anything when blood is their argument? Now if these men do not die well it will be a black matter for the King, that led them to it, who to disobey were against all proportion of subjection' (4.1.129–46). Was not a similar line of thought implicit in Henry's emphatically warning Canterbury to 'take heed' in urging war: 'For never two such kingdoms did contend / Without much fall of blood, whose guiltless drops / Are every one a woe, a sore complaint / 'Gainst him whose wrongs gives edge unto the swords [etc.]' (1.2.24–27)?

Henry's response to William's veiled protest treats the question as if the only matter at issue concerned the state of a man's soul upon dying. That is, he ignores entirely the this-world consequences for dependents and others affected by the man's death. And he argues by analogy, using a pair of hypothetical cases from civilian life, one featuring a son who perishes at sea while on his father's business, the other a servant killed by robbers while transporting his master's money. Should either of these men die with a soul still heavy with sin, surely one would not (he suggests) charge the father or the master with being 'the author of [their] damnation'. Likewise, then (he claims), 'the King is not bound to answer the particular endings of his soldiers', for in all three of these cases, 'they purpose not their death when they purpose their services'. Strictly speaking, that is true of course. But there is at least a great practical difference between civilian callings in which the risk of death is small, and danger not purposefully sought, and one is free to avoid it so far as one can—between that, and a profession which is the opposite in all of these respects.

Indeed, an admission that such is the case is implicit in Henry's suggesting that his army is bound to contain its fair share of lawbreakers who have joined up to escape civilian justice.

> War is [God's] beadle, war is his vengeance; so that here men are punished for before breach of the King's laws in now the King's quarrel. . . . Then if they die unprovided, no more is the King guilty of their damnation than he was before guilty of those impieties for the which they are now visited. Every subject's duty is the King's, but every subject's soul is his own.[59] Therefore should every soldier in the wars do as every sick man in his bed, wash every mote out of his conscience; and dying so, death is to him advantage; or not dying, the time was blessedly lost wherein such preparation was gained. (4.168–81)

This might be good advice for everyone, but clearly it has a special pertinence to soldiers in the midst of war—'*every* soldier', notice, not merely former lawbreakers—who as a matter of their profession should (according to

Henry) regard themselves as being as near to death as is someone mortally sick. Whereas the son and the servant are not necessarily closer to death than other healthy civilians.[60]

Suffice it to say, the disguised Henry's argument absolving the King of responsibility for his men's fate should they die in battle smacks not a little of sophistry. But the real *puzzle* about it is: *why does he bother to make it?* He had already declared that the cause for which the King risked his and their lives was just and honourable. Why not leave it at that? What difference does it make whether or not these three particular soldiers believe this to be true—which Henry doesn't attempt to show in any case! As Bates acknowledges, 'we know enough if we know we are the King's subjects. If his cause be wrong, our obedience to the King wipes the crime of it out of us' (4.1.130–33). Much less would there seem to be any reason for Henry to spend the wee hours of the morning before battle attempting to persuade these three men of what is, essentially, a 'theoretical' proposition: why the King is not responsible for the fate of his soldiers' souls should they die in battle (meanwhile, ignoring all the practical consequences for their wives, children, and other dependent survivors, to say nothing of abbreviating the soldiers' own lives). One can hardly imagine a less appropriate occasion for the King to prove that he can, as Canterbury claimed, 'reason in divinity' like a prelate (1.1.38–40). It's not as if these three soldiers can take any comfort from a doctrine that lessens the scope of their commander's responsibility for leading his men into the jaws of death. Nor could he expect them now to 'spread the word', or that their doing so would have any useful effect. This is very strange. What explains it? Is Henry laboring to persuade himself? Or is this simply Shakespeare's way of showing Henry's conversancy with the standard doctrine of 'the just war'? That seems most unlikely, given its dramatic implausibility. I remain puzzled.

Once more left alone, Henry offers nary a clue as to why he bothered to argue his case when and to whom he did, though the encounter does provoke his musing upon what, supposedly, *differentiates* a king from common men, who are all too ready to shift the entire responsibility for the condition of their lives onto their sovereign: 'We must bear all. O hard condition, / Twin-born with greatness, subject to the breath / Of every fool whose sense no more can feel / But his own wringing!' (4.1.230–33). True enough, perhaps. But surely Shakespeare intends for us to see an irony here: this master of publicly shifting responsibility for his own actions onto others complains in private of commoners doing likewise onto him—perhaps confirming by this human, all too human, inclination his common humanity in spite of himself?

Henry claims that a king can never enjoy the 'infinite heart's ease' readily available to a private man, and that all he gets in return for everything he gives up is 'ceremony', which is largely useless and empty of meaning. He must be speaking of a king 'in the precise sense' of the word: a ruler who rules exclusively in the interest of the ruled, and whose only 'pay' is honour and modest wealth, neither of which he much prizes.[61] But what of the opportunity kingship provides a magnanimous man to exercise his extraordinary virtue? For though not *payment*, it is not without *value*. Admittedly, most so-called kings would not qualify as true kings in this precise sense. Richard II, for example, would not. Would the historical Henry V? Perhaps he might, if one credits Holinshed's summary appraisal of the man.[62] But would *Shakespeare's* Henry V?

What might call it into question is the conclusion of this, his sole soliloquy in the play: 'The slave, a member of the country's peace, / Enjoys it, but in gross brain little wots / What watch the King keeps to maintain the peace, / Whose hours the peasant best advantages' (4.1.278–81). Henry, however, has led his nation into *war*—albeit, perhaps, in part as a means of maintaining domestic peace by busying 'giddy minds with foreign quarrels'.[63] Whatever one may make of this ambiguous fact, Henry's soliloquy provides some basis for judging his rhetoric—that is, for assessing to what extent it is 'mere rhetoric'. In particular, one would not suppose he has an especially high view of most ordinary soldiers, despite the impression created by his public pronouncements. Thus, one may at least partly discount the muting of social distinctions in his various exhortations, such as was evident in his addressing his troops before Harfleur, and even more prominent in Henry's famous prebattle speech at Agincourt—the speech which (courtesy Shakespeare) has won him such lasting renown, especially the most famous lines the poet provided him.

> This story shall the good man teach his son,
> And Crispin Crispian shall ne'er go by
> From this day to the ending of the world
> But we in it shall be remembered,
> We few, we happy few, we band of brothers.
> For he today that sheds his blood with me
> Shall be my brother; be he ne'er so vile,
> This day shall gentle his condition.
> And gentlemen in England now abed
> Shall think themselves accursed they were not here,
> And hold their manhoods cheap whiles any speaks
> That fought with us upon Saint Crispin's day.
> (4.3.56–67)

'We', and 'we', once more 'we', and again 'we', and 'us'—this, notice, is *not* the royal 'we'. It is the ordinary 'we', referring to an undifferentiated plurality of persons (cf. 1.2.260). The same fraternal identification is implicit in Henry's earlier professing, 'if it be a sin to covet honour / I am the most offending soul alive'.[64] Hence, he does not wish their army was more numerous since that would mean his own share of the honour to be won would be diminished: 'I would not lose so great an honour / As one man more, methinks, would share from me' (4.3.28–32)[65]—as if the total honour were a great pie that will necessarily be apportioned *equally* among those present, such that the fewer there are to share it, the larger each one's own portion. As if! Moreover, in the very midst of his seemingly egalitarian exhortation, Henry tacitly concedes that some of the participants' portion will necessarily be 'more equal' than others, subtly confirming thereby the priority of his nobles:

> Old men forget; yet all shall be forgot
> But he'll remember, with advantages,
> What feats he did that day. Then shall our names,
> Familiar in his mouth as household words,
> Harry the King, Bedford and Exeter,
> Warwick and Talbot, Salisbury and Gloucester,
> Be in their flowing cups freshly remembered.
> (Ibid., 49–55)

Veterans know this to be the truth of the matter: it is the leaders who are remembered by name, and ordinary soldiers are honoured by their association with them (cf. 3.6.66–80). Similarly, when Henry receives the report of Englishmen killed in this famous battle, he will distinguish those four men 'of name' from the twenty-five 'other men' (4.8.104–7).[66] Still, this mode of speaking serves well both nobles and commoners, for it reminds the nobles that the 'media' of their fame are the commoners, who are not to be despised lest the value of that fame be compromised.

What kind of king is Shakespeare's Henry? Certainly not of an egalitarian stripe, any more than was Alexander or Caesar; yet nonetheless, a workingman's king who does not spare himself, who works as tirelessly at being a king that others must reckon with as he expects his common soldiers do at being warriors worthy of the name. Thus he bade the Dauphin's ambassadors tell their master:

> I will keep my state,
> Be like a king and show my sail of greatness,
> When I do rouse me in my throne of France.
> For *that* I have laid by my majesty
> And plodded like a man for working-days,
> But I will rise there so full of glory

That I will dazzle all the eyes of France,
Yea, strike the Dauphin blind to look on us.
(1.2.274–81)

He would have himself be seen as a man more concerned with substance than style. Likewise just prior to the Battle of Agincourt, he bids the herald Montjoy:

Tell the Constable
We are but warriors for the working-day;
Our gayness and our gilt are all besmirched
With rainy marching in the painful field.
There's not a piece of feather in our host[67]
(Good argument, I hope, we will not fly),
And time hath worn us into slovenry.
But by the mass, our hearts are in the trim.
(4.3.108–15)

Again, this is not the royal 'we'. Henry speaks here as a fellow warrior among warriors, a warrior's warrior who happens also to be their king, and who promises to share their fate. Twice in the presence of his troops he insists he'll not allow himself to be ransomed, should he and they be defeated; rather, he intends to fight to the death: 'My ransom is this frail and worthless trunk' (3.6.152); and 'Come thou no more for ransom, gentle herald. / They shall have *none*, I *swear*, but these my joints, / Which if they have as I will leave 'em them / Shall yield them little' (4.3.122–25).[68]

In short, Shakespeare portrays Henry V as every inch a warrior king, willing and able to 'perform himself the office of captain', quite as Machiavelli contends a prince ought to, by virtue of making it his profession, and so having 'no other object, nor any other thought, nor taking anything else as his art but the art of war and its order and discipline'.[69] Henry warns the Governor of Harfleur that he will do what he threatens, vowing 'as I am a soldier / A name that in my thoughts becomes me best' (3.3.5–6). So, too, in his softer mood, wooing the French princess as 'a plain soldier', who like the sun and unlike the moon 'shines bright and never changes, but keeps his course truly. If thou would have such a one, take me; and take me, take a soldier; take a soldier, take a king' (5.2.150, 164–66).[70]

Moreover, warlike Harry would qualify as 'a *wise* prince' by Machiavelli's criterion, in that he relies on an army that is composed entirely of his own subjects, with no admixture of either mercenaries or 'auxiliaries' (i.e., soldiers whose first loyalty is to some other prince).[71] We are meant to notice, however, this is not necessarily a matter of common ethnicity; Henry's army is composed of soldiers representing four distinct nationalities.[72]

And while it is not without its frictions (3.2.121–37; 5.1.14–80), it is united by its allegiance to him. However, the fact that all of his soldiers speak some dialect of English is of great practical importance—as is made clear by reflection on the comical confusions that arise in Katherine's attempt to learn English (3.4.47), and on the frustrations Henry later experiences in wooing a girl who doesn't understand half of what he says (not that it matters much in her case, since—as noted—she's bound to be his, whatever she thinks of his wooing).

Agincourt! The battle, like the name, is irrevocably associated with this warrior king of virtually legendary proportions, England's Henry the Fifth. Originally, this association was due almost entirely to the fact that his famous victory there on a late October day in 1415 seemed practically miraculous, given the depleted condition of his army, the apparently overwhelming superiority of the forces arrayed against it, and the relatively light casualties suffered by the English side.[73] In more recent times, however, the status of Henry and his victory has been rendered somewhat questionable by a chorus of criticism, even outright condemnation, ignited mainly by one command he issued when the outcome of the battle was still in doubt: his order to kill the French prisoners (most of whom, presumably, had surrendered on the understanding their lives would be spared, and set free upon payment of some ransom). Nor was this, strictly speaking, an isolated case. Shortly after issuing that command, Henry spied French cavalry gathering on a nearby hill, and ordered his herald to warn them either to come down and fight or 'void the field'; and that if they did neither, the King and his forces would chase them off: 'Besides, we'll cut the throats of those we have, / And not a man of them that we shall take / Shall taste our mercy' (4.7.54–64). Once again, Henry's brutal rhetoric must have turned the trick, as the next we hear of the French is their herald Montjoy confirming, 'The day is yours' (4.7.85). The King's apparently ruthless handling of armed opposition is in marked contrast to his humane, one might even say Christian, manner of dealing with the mainly complaisant French population.[74]

Thought about, however, Shakespeare's presentation of the episode is a bit puzzling, especially in light of its treatment in his sources. The King's order is brevity itself: 'But hark, what new alarum is this same? / The French have reinforced their scattered men. / Then every soldier kill his prisoners! / Give the word through' (4.6.35–38). With that the scene ends. No further explanation for the order is provided at the time, though its laconic terseness clearly suggests a battlefield emergency, the 'new alarum' signaling that the French are apparently reorganizing for a fresh attack (cf. 4.5.17–21). What else *could* it mean?

However, Shakespeare intentionally complicates the episode by having his invented captains, Fluellen and Gower (neither of whom could be privy to Henry's thinking), 'explain' his command after the fact. The effect of their suppositional account for the King's giving the order simply aggravates its moral offensiveness. For these two captains presume it was in revenge for a French raid on the English encampment left in charge of servant boys, and they laud their King for exacting it:

> 'Tis certain there's not a boy left alive, and the cowardly rascals that ran from the battle ha' done this slaughter. Besides, they have burned and carried away all that was in the King's tent, wherefore the King most worthily hath caused every soldier to cut his prisoner's throat. O, 'tis a gallant king! (4.7.5–10)

Gower's account (ignoring his muddling together the killing of the boys with the pillaging of the King's baggage) actually makes Henry's action seem irrational as well as grossly unjust—as if he ordered the killing of French prisoners, who had nothing to do with the atrocity, in retaliation for the killing of the English boys by some 'cowardly rascals' who happen also to be French. While this sort of thing is all too common in wars, viewed in the cold light of a later day it never reflects well on the perpetrators. And if Gower's misconstrual of Henry's action were not sufficiently damaging to his King's reputation (though, to be sure, not in the eyes of these two), it is further darkened by Fluellen's elliptical reminder that it violates a long-recognised convention of chivalry: 'Kill the poys and the luggage! 'Tis expressly against the laws of arms' (ibid., 1–2)—as it is to kill enemy combatants who surrender on the understanding they will be given quarter.

Despite what these two confused captains suppose, however, Shakespeare makes it clear that the King's notorious order had nothing to do with the slaughter of the boys left in camp with the baggage, since Henry learns of that only *after* he has dealt with the emergency which actually prompted the command. News of the boys' fate *does*, however, provoke the anger in which he *subsequently* warns the French to 'void the field' or he'll butcher the prisoners he presently holds, as well as any more he takes (which implies that the former were *not* all killed as a result of his prior order). But what, then, *does* explain his earlier precipitous command to 'kill the prisoners'? For all the hand-wringing and sanctimony Henry's action has since brought forth from his critics, this is *not* a difficult puzzle to solve: he judged it a military necessity in the circumstances, and a fair appraisal of his situation bears him out.

Though the initial French attack had been repulsed, with the survivors retreating in disorder (4.5.6, 17–18), Henry's tired army has been further exhausted by the fighting, his archers have likely spent their supply of arrows,[75] and for all the French casualties, the English are still greatly outnumbered—as the Duke of Orleans urges, seconding the Constable's and Bourbon's intention to attempt a fresh assault: 'We are enough yet living in the field / To smother up the English in our throngs' (4.5.19–20). Obviously that attempt to salvage success was carried out, for Bourbon and Orleans are taken prisoner, and the Constable is killed. So, at the time Henry orders the word passed for 'every soldier kill his prisoners'—having heard some 'new alarum' (presumably the signaling of French trumpets announcing the Bourbon-led attack[76])—an English victory was by no means assured. The King can hardly spare soldiers to guard prisoners, who for all their vaunted 'honour' and Fluellen's 'rules of war', cannot be counted on not to seize discarded weapons and turn on their captors should a second French assault seem to be making headway. Given how desperate his situation remained, what else was Henry to do? Every English life, including his, was still at risk. What other course consistent with prudent generalship was possible?

However, because Shakespeare is dramatizing a famous, albeit controversial historical event, assessment of *his* Henry's actions and those of the *historical* Henry are especially apt to become entangled. There is a strong temptation to use modern historians' accounts of the Battle of Agincourt to critique the King's conduct in *Henry V*, not only in order to understand why he issued the command, but more particularly what in all likelihood resulted from it. Nor need the temptation be resisted insofar as various historians' re-creations of Henry's situation match in their essentials Shakespeare's depiction—and almost all of them do.

Despite there being little support among reputable historians, it seems that many literary critics nonetheless succumb to the temptation to judge both Henrys—history's and Shakespeare's—anachronistically by modern rules of warfare (such as the Geneva Conventions, however vaguely understood). Whereas, one respected military historian, sorting through the welter of conflicting and uneven testimony, reconstructs the event thus:

> Henry's caution was justified. Soon after midday, the Duke of Brabant, arriving late, half-equipped, with a tiny following, charged into [the English] ranks. He was overpowered and led to the rear. But this gallant intervention inspired at least two French noblemen in the third division, the Counts of Masle and Fauquemberghes, to marshal some six hundred of their followers for a concerted charge.[77] They could clearly be seen massing, two or three hundred yards from the English line, and their intentions were obvious. At about the same time, moreover, shouting from the rear informed the English of a raid by the enemy on the baggage park, which had been left almost unguarded.

It was these events which precipitated Henry's notorious order to kill the prisoners. As it turned out, the charge was not delivered and the raid was later revealed to have been a mere rampage by the local peasantry, under the Lord of Agincourt.[78] The signs were enough, however, to convince Henry that his victory, in which he can scarcely yet have believed, was about to be snatched from him. For if the French third division attacked the English where they stood, the archers without arrows or stakes, the men-at-arms weary after a morning of hacking and banging in full armour, all of them hungry, cold and depressed by the reaction from the intense fears and elations of combat, they might easily have been swept from the field. They certainly could not have withstood the simultaneous assault on their rear, to which, with so many inadequately guarded French prisoners standing about behind them on ground littered with discarded weapons, they were likely also to have been subjected. In these circumstances, his order is comprehensible.[79]

It strikes me that 'comprehensible' is too tepid an endorsement of Henry's action, given circumstances such as those described. Would not a failure to protect his army from the threat these prisoners posed not only be militarily foolish to the point of idiocy, but morally irresponsible in the extreme? Thousands of *English* lives are at stake, which surely must be granted Henry's first priority.

Another historian, judging the event in the context of its time, concludes: 'Not an attractive episode, but it is necessary to say that it was condemned neither by contemporaries nor by the laws of war. Examples of exactly similar actions by French, Portugese [*sic*], German, Italian, and Burgundian commanders can be collected to show that such inhuman conduct was excused in the hard-pressed'.[80] To put Henry's decision in a broader context, another scholar who exonerates the King ('because Henry believed that the battle had not been won and danger persisted, . . . his order to kill the prisoners probably did not violate medieval legal standards'), cites a pertinent doctrine established in more recent times:

> Those of us who consider Henry's order to be barbaric may need to revisit the law in force during the American Civil War. The well-known Lieber's Code, the military law promulgated by President Lincoln . . . , which was generally admired for its humanitarian and enlightened nature, allowed the denial of quarter on grounds of necessity . . . : 'a commander is permitted to direct his troops to give no quarter, in great straits, when his own salvation makes it impossible to cumber himself with prisoners'.[81]

There is one detail about the battle that does not figure in Shakespeare's version, but possibly had a bearing on the historical King's decision: 'It is notable that, while regretting the loss of noble prisoners, no contemporary

French chronicler criticized the morality of Henry's action. Was this because the French had unfurled the "oriflamme", or special, red war banner, taken as a sign of "guerre mortelle" during which no quarter was to be granted, and that this convention was used by Henry to justify the death of prisoners taken by the English on this occasion?'[82] If the French did in fact so signal, might it have been in response to Henry's adamant refusal to consider a ransom for himself?

About the actual *consequence* of Henry's order, however—that is, how many French prisoners were in fact killed—there is less but still some substantial agreement among historians. There are those who assume it must have been thousands: 'The order [to kill the prisoners] is probably responsible for the high number of French killed rather than taken prisoner, and there were cries of protest in the army at the loss of so many valuable ransoms'.[83] Others are skeptical:

> Henry ... came back to England with well over 1000 prisoners, perhaps even more, men who may be regarded as the survivors of the massacre, for relatively few prisoners would have been taken after that time. In addition to these men, many others were left behind in Calais, some of them having already changed hands as a result of cash transactions. It is likely, then, that at the moment Henry gave the order for the prisoners to be killed, they numbered 2000 or more men, mostly well armoured although by then without weapons or head-piece. How could the king ever expect such numbers to be killed in the brief time which would elapse before the anticipated charge took place? Would such a large number of men meekly submit to being put to death?[84]

More than one historian has suggested that, for reason of sheer practical difficulty, the number actually killed has 'probably been exaggerated':

> The chroniclers record that the killers spared the most valuable prisoners and were called off as soon as Henry assured himself that the French third division was not going to attack after all. We may take it therefore that the two hundred archers whom he detailed [to do the killing] were heavily outnumbered by their victims, probably by about ten to one. The reason for wanting them killed, however, was that they were liable to rearm themselves from the jetsam of battle if it were renewed. Why did they not do so when they saw themselves threatened with death ... ? Is it realistic to imagine ... these proud and warlike men passively awaiting the arrival of a gang of their social inferiors to do them to death—standing like cattle in groups of ten for a single archer to break their skulls with an axe?
> It does seem very improbable, and all the more because what we know of twentieth century mass-killing suggests that it is very difficult

for small numbers of executioners, even when armed with machine-guns, to kill people much more defenceless than armoured knights quickly and in large numbers. What seems altogether more likely, therefore, is that Henry's order, rather than bring about the prisoners' massacre, was intended by its threat to terrorize them into abject inactivity.... Some would have been killed in the process, and quite deliberately, but we need not reckon their number in the thousands, perhaps not even in hundreds.[85]

Another skeptic, and one by no means over-enamoured of Henry, concludes:

Unless le Fèvre and Waurin were completely wrong in their estimate of two hundreds archers assigned to the job [of killing], then it is simply not credible that there were more than three or four hundred prisoners at this stage of the battle—at the very most. The suggestion that there were thousands massacred is not only without direct evidence, it conflicts with the eyewitness evidence that we do have.[86]

One is inclined to agree that the number of French prisoners peremptorily killed cannot have been as great as some contemporary accounts claim, which squares with the multitude of evidence suggesting that the number ransomed were well over a thousand, and perhaps twice that many.

In Churchill's judgment, 'Agincourt ranks as the most heroic of all the land battles England has ever fought'. And, temporarily at least, 'the victory at Agincourt made [Henry] the supreme figure in Europe'. However, Churchill continues, 'glory was, as always, dearly bought. The imposing empire of Henry V was hollow and false.... When Henry revived the English claims to France he opened the greatest tragedy in our medieval history. Agincourt was a glittering victory, but the wasteful and useless campaigns that followed more than outweighed its military and moral value, and the miserable, destroying century that ensued casts its black shadow upon Henry's heroic triumph'.[87]

True enough, perhaps. Still, need things have turned out as they did? The effects of Fortune frustrate our effort to understand the strategy whereby Henry planned, not only to integrate France into his existing principate, but also to restore an unproblematic legitimacy to the kingship he inherited. Both the augmented domain and the refounded sovereignty might then be passed on to his successor 'free and clear'. The play's choral Epilogue but glances at various dimensions of his problem:

Small time, but in that small most greatly lived
This star of England. Fortune made his sword

> By which the world's best garden he achieved,
> And of it left his son imperial lord.
> Henry the Sixth, in infant bands crowned King
> Of France and England, did this king succeed,
> Whose state so many had the managing
> That they lost France and made his England bleed.

The crucial fact is alluded to only tacitly by this reminder that Henry V reigned but a 'small time'. Why so? Because Fortune also *stilled* his sword. Henry died young, not in battle—as well he might have, leading from the front—but of a disease he chanced to acquire in the course of campaigning (dysentery, most likely). He died, that is, before he could consolidate his conquest of France; before he could solidly establish, and the French people experience, the new manner and order of his rule; before the 'boy, half French, half English' that he and Queen Katharine had 'compounded' (perhaps merely the first of several) could be brought to maturity under his watchful eye, trained and hardened to his eventual responsibilities, known to and accepted by his future subjects; and before Henry had overseen a judicious leavening of English loyalists become strategically established within France.

Thus, his is a cautionary tale attesting to the sometimes profound consequences of the unpredictable in politics, how and why the wild card of Fortune precludes its being reduced to an exact science. Had Henry V—the indispensable man in this case—lived to the age of his famous great-grandfather (Edward III died at sixty-nine), or even of his paternal grandfather (John of Gaunt was fifty-nine when he died), not only could Henry have put his and his heir's status as King of England beyond dispute, and thus the Wars of the Roses which 'made his England bleed' would never have occurred;[88] but also, the parts of the Anglo-French state would have had a quarter-century of his expert management whereby to become accommodated to their new relationship, and his acquisitions would not have been bungled away, as they were under the many-headed regency of his infant successor. Does not Shakespeare's clever Epilogue, along with other hints woven into his text, invite one to imagine what might have been?

An Alternative Epilogue

Imagining What Might Have Been

> Though nothing can be immortall, which mortals make; yet, if men had the use of reason they pretend to, their Commonwealths might be secured, at least, from perishing by internall diseases. For by the nature of their Institution, they are designed to live, as long as Mankind, or as the Lawes of Nature, or as Justice it selfe, which gives them life. Therefore when they come to be dissolved, not by externall violence, but intestine disorder, the fault is not in men, as they are the *Matter*, but as they are the *Makers*, and orderers of them.
> —Hobbes, *Leviathan*, chap. 29, para. 1

Was Henry's attempt to conquer France the epitome of an extravagant, vainglorious, immoral, and ultimately futile ambition, as not a few of his modern critics claim? Or could he have succeeded in achieving what his invasion began: to make good his claim to be the rightful King of France as well as of England, and by uniting the two realms end the chronic conflict between them? Why not? A bold ambition, to be sure, and doubtless difficult to accomplish. But he had at least one factor in his favour: no part of France was a republic. For all of its provincial variety, it was a nation whose various provinces—'all her almost kingly dukedoms'—were long accustomed to princely rule. And as Machiavelli teaches:

> When cities or provinces are used to living under a prince, and his bloodline is eliminated—since on the one hand they are used to obeying, and on the other they do not have the old prince—they will not agree to make one from themselves and they do not know how to live free. So they are slower to take up arms, and a prince can gain them with greater ease and secure himself against them. But in republics there is greater life, greater hatred, more desire for revenge; the memory of their ancient liberty does not and cannot let them rest.[1]

In judging the practicality of his enterprise, one should bear in mind that the 'reverse' had already been done. That is, the Norman French had successfully conquered Anglo-Saxon England three and a half centuries earlier—as Shakespeare subtly reminds us by having the fifteenth-century French nobility complain so bitterly of the mongrel descendants of that conquest: 'Normans, but bastard Normans, Norman bastards'; 'Shall a few sprays of us, / The emptying of our fathers' luxury, / Our scions, put in wild and savage stock, / ... overlook their grafters?' The very same. Though neither Henry nor any of his Court ever refer to themselves as anything but English, their progenitors were indeed Normans.[2]

William 'the Conqueror', though a Norman—and previously known as William 'the Bastard'—had claimed to be the heir of childless King Edward the Confessor, whose mother was the daughter of Count Richard I of Normandy and the sister of his successor, the powerful Richard II. She was also the great-aunt of William. Thus William's lineal claim to the English throne was not unlike Henry's to that of France as the great-great-grandson of the French princess who bore Edward III. Moreover, childless Edward the Confessor had years earlier designated William as his heir (supposedly), whereas on his deathbed he recognised Harold Godwineson as his successor (supposedly). But William was no more to be denied by the murky status of legal claims than was Henry. In the fateful year of 1066, he invaded England to seize what was 'rightfully' his, leading an army across the channel in the direction opposite to that of Henry, landed at Hastings, where—blessed by fortune—he defeated the forces Harold had marshaled to repulse him. Three centuries and ten kings later, William's direct descendant, Richard II, was unquestionably the *legitimate* ruler of England, and Henry Bolingbroke a usurper. How did *that* happen!

The Normans, though composing scarcely more than one percent of the population they ruled, successfully imposed themselves on the country, first, through sheer force of arms. As they steadily expanded their hold over the land, William's Normans by virtue of their intensive training and organizational discipline quickly proved themselves militarily superior to the native population—rather as their descendants had proven superior to the French in over a half century of warfare prior to Henry's day (cf. 1.2.101–24, 2.4.48–64). But also instrumental to the Normans' successful subjugation of England were their extraordinary feats of building. For the original earth-and-timber 'motte and bailey' forts, foci of loyal Norman villages, were rapidly superseded by impregnable castles, which, along with their immense cathedrals, made clear to the native inhabitants that the Normans were there to stay.

Moreover, the conquerors brought to England an expertise in administration, epitomized by the Domesday survey that William commissioned within twenty years of his conquest. (Given the historical Henry's renowned attention to the details of governing, one can readily imagine that he would see the value of a similarly detailed accounting of his new French possession, and so have ordered it made.) And not least significant, the Norman experience proved that neither geographic separation nor linguistic diversity were not insuperable obstacles to a successful *annexation* of a conquered territory (for their power base remained Normandy well into the twelfth century). The Normans established French as the language of government throughout Anglo-Saxon England, obliging the natives to learn it as the price of protecting and advancing their own interests. And so it remained for the better part of three centuries. Likewise, Henry might have imposed English as the common language of a united kingdom.[3]

Julius Caesar, who also made his fortune by conquering France, is apparently Henry's model.[4] Caesar's subjecting 'Gaul', *omnes* its *tres partes*, to the Roman *imperium* was the basis of his near idolatry amongst the plebs of Rome, and this led eventually (after his defeat of Pompey's challenge) to a more or less grudging acceptance by most of his fellow patricians.[5] The chorus reports how, in like manner, Londoners met King Henry upon his homecoming after Agincourt.

> But now behold . . .
> How London doth pour out her citizens,
> The Mayor and all his brethren in best sort,
> Like to the senators of th'antique Rome
> With the plebeians swarming at their heels,
> Go forth and fetch their conquering Caesar in.
> (5.0.22–28)

The fact that Caesar was not only a general with a string of splendid victories to his credit, often against daunting odds, but also Rome's most skilled rhetorician (rivaled only by Cicero) as well as the plebs' most generous benefactor, doubtless facilitated his rise to political supremacy. Shakespeare's Henry likewise well understands how to wield the power of speech, both as a means of inspiring his subjects and of demoralizing his opponents. Nor is he averse to his followers believing that they will profit from his success (cf. 2.0.8–11, 2.3.53–54)—as did the many who shared in the ransoms resulting from the historical Henry's victory at Agincourt, the first of several. His glorious accomplishments in France, which his mastery of staging exploited to the full (according to Shakespeare's portrayal), established beyond question his personal legitimacy as King of England. But what about of France?

The Gauls, having experienced the benefits of living under Roman law and the Pax Romana, became within a couple of generations reliable supporters of the empire (sporadic local rebellions notwithstanding). Perhaps many inwardly regarded submission to one's conqueror not so much as a personal humiliation, but as practically a 'law of nature' inasmuch as the entire natural order—and not least of all, human life—confirms that the strong prevail and the weak submit. Seen in that light, the conqueror has earned the right to rule the conquered, who ought to concede that right and so willingly obey, at least so far as the return for obedience is security for life, liberty, and property under the rule of law.[6] After all, for the vast majority of people this is simply the best to be hoped for from political life, *whoever* their rulers be. And doubtless many Gauls welcomed the opportunity to join the 'strong' side; in imperial times, the enlisted ranks of some Roman legions consisted wholly of Gauls. Hence, Henry might reasonably expect the French commonality of his day, just as did their Gaulish forefathers in that of the Caesars, to become accustomed to rule partly by foreigners, especially if treated as citizens equal to their English counterparts (as the French queen urged, to which Henry added his 'amen'; 5.2.361–62). The Romans had done likewise to conquered peoples who accepted their new reality.[7]

Henry's greater problem, however, is that of reestablishing the legitimacy of the monarchy he inherited. And of doing so, moreover, in such a way that his successors will not be obliged to prove themselves in the manner he did, but will be acknowledged as the rightful rulers simply by virtue of acceding to the kingship, albeit of a new kind. For it would be a kingship whose legitimacy was based neither strictly on genealogy (much less on the inheritance of supposedly sacred blood) nor on personal charisma (as in Henry's own case).

To imagine how he might have managed this, one must extrapolate from the few textual clues, viewed in light of the political situation he had created, and 'piece out' the rest as would seem most plausible. I need hardly remind the reader who regards such flights of fancy vain, or otherwise annoying, he is free to close the book at this point and move on to something worthier of his time. But readers more indulgent, or idle, may find the following effort amusing, or otherwise rewarding. The license for the attempt I borrow from the Prologue:

> And let us, ciphers to this great account,
> On your imaginary forces work.
> Piece out our imperfections with your thoughts
> For 'tis your thoughts that now must deck our kings.
> Carrying them here and there, jumping o'er times,
> Turning th'accomplishment of many years
> Into an hour-glass.

However, I must emphasize, first, the notion that Shakespeare may have seen grander possibilities in the historical King Henry and his situation is, of course, speculation; but some such idea, I mean to suggest, is not unlikely since this sort of imagining about the past, so-called counterfactual history, arises quite naturally. Who can fail to wonder 'what might have been' had 'this Star of England' lived out the natural span allotted human life? Second, the hypothesis I propose pertains to Shakespeare's Henry V, not to the historical figure. The two are connected only insofar as (per hypothesis) the philosopher-poet saw in the stature achieved by the historical figure a potential for political innovation that this fabled king did not necessarily envision himself—though one should not rule out the possibility that he did. We cannot know what Henry would have attempted, much less what he might have achieved, given another twenty-five or thirty years. Third, Henry's historical situation would obviously admit of more than one response to the problem of establishing a new basis for a legitimate monarchy. I have attempted to imagine one that seems viable, given the constraints of that situation, and of the practical necessity of managing the transition from the kind of regime he inherited, now rendered questionable, to a regime whose legitimacy its subjects would view as self-evident. The reader might find it enlightening to attempt the same exercise himself. Fourth, the main purpose of the following sketch is simply to make plausible the notion that there was a way that Henry could have solved the legitimacy problem for succeeding generations of his countrymen. I claim no originality for the form of kingship, or aristocracy, which I here adumbrate; as anyone familiar with our tradition of political philosophy will readily recognise, I have simply appropriated the ideas of its greatest exemplars, and adapted them to Henry's situation—the sort of enterprise which, whatever else, the philosophers must have intended by troubling to write their books.

It may prove useful to begin, however, by reviewing the *problem* of legitimacy as was laid it out in chapter 1. As a matter of *practicality*, the root of the problem attending the very idea of legitimacy consists in its being not simply, nor even primarily, a rational matter. For rationally considered, the most *truly* 'legitimate' rulers are those who would be *good* rulers, possessing the qualities requisite to best fulfilling the responsibilities of political rule: to defend the polity from both internal and external threats, to administer justice, and to make and enforce laws and policies that serve the common good. But given their strictly formal character, these *objective* criteria—derived exclusively from the ruling task itself—will not suffice for people in general, since it is far from self-evident as to what substantially they require in a given case, or who in particular they designate (while excluding all others). Whereas, practically speaking, *acceptance* of a ruler's legitimacy requires that the criteria indicating it be easily *recognised* and *applied* by the many ruled. For this is the political significance of legitimacy: it facilitates civil peace and stability by obviating the most dangerous threat to civil peace, namely, quarrels over who ought to rule.

In practice, then, the *subjective* recognition of legitimacy in the minds of the ruled must be conceded priority over whatever objective criteria might be disclosed by strictly rational analysis. And insofar as these rational criteria do not of themselves generate the required subjective consensus (though they figure in virtually everyone's own conception of a *good* ruler), some other criterion of legitimacy—something credible as conveying a right to rule, yet easily recognisable by all who are expected to acknowledge and respect it—must serve instead. This need raise no difficulties provided there is some readily recognisable criterion that reliably *correlates*, at least approximately and usually, with the objective criteria. But apparently there is not.

Consequently, there is a latent source of political discord inherent in the very idea of political legitimacy: in the interests of civil peace and stability, the *right* to rule, legitimacy, is necessarily treated as separate from *good* rule, and moreover granted absolute priority inasmuch as the breakdown of civil order threatens everyone with regressing to an existence that is hardly better—indeed, if Hobbes is correct, can even be worse—than that of beasts in the state of nature. But though subordinated, the concern for good rule, for rule that is both competent and just (however controversial the judging of such qualities may be), never expires. And so the possible tension between these two claims on subjects' allegiance—the 'right to rule' versus 'good rule'—remains a potential source of civil discord. For should the discrepancy between people's conception of *good* governance and their perception of their ruler's *actual* governance become great enough, an increasing number of people will be inclined to challenge that ruler's continuing right to rule, regardless of his admitted legitimacy—as Richard II learned to his regret.

Viewing the situation through Shakespeare's portrayal, the problem confronting Henry V (had he lived to face it) would be that of establishing a regime in which the risk of this tension growing to a dangerous level is minimized. In practical terms, this means conceiving some form of rulership whose legitimacy is relatively transparent, while also offering reasonable assurance that whoever occupies the position of ruler will be at least minimally competent and just, which would in turn reinforce his legitimacy: a virtuous circle. Should such a conception be once established as a functioning regime, its legitimating principles and procedures will tend to gain in credence, in 'legitimacy' themselves, with use; the longer they are in place and serve their purpose tolerably well, the more solidly will they become established in people's minds as 'right and proper'. And, correspondingly, the more suspect will alternative claims be regarded. Hence the great importance of *time*, prerequisite of *tradition*, in legitimating a polity, strengthened by the psychical effects of legal forms, ceremonies, manners, symbols, modes of respectful address, and engagements of personal honour (pledges of allegiance, oaths of obedience).

With respect to the most challenging *practical* problem, that of regime *transformation*, here too might Henry take some inspiration from Caesar. Like Caesar, Henry courted 'popularity' with all the people he ruled, but especially with the common people. Yet it is clear that neither man was a democrat—far from it. Henry lets pass no opportunity to indicate that he is 'special', as successful founders invariably are. His exceptionality is attested not only by his exemplary piety, but in his accomplishing seeming miracles such as would suggest a favoured relationship with the Higher Powers. There is, for example, his utterly transforming himself in character and disposition virtually overnight (or so it seemed); and his acquiring recondite knowledge in diverse fields, apparently without study; and uncovering plots against him by means which the plotters 'dream not of'; and, of course, achieving military victories in the face of seemingly insuperable odds.

What is arguably his most important asset, however, is that he regards himself—and rightly so—as capable of reforming people's mores and manners, the regimes of their very souls. For this is the broader significance of his admonishing his Queen-to-be, 'O Kate, nice customs curtsy to great kings. Dear Kate, you and I cannot be confined within the weak list of a country's fashion. We are the makers of manners' (5.2.266–69). Partly by the charm of his rhetoric, more through the influence of his example, and foremost through the veneration people bear him—never forgetting that he commands the means to silence the unpersuaded and punish the recalcitrant—he has the power to cultivate, over time, whatever 'national character' he deems suitable for the citizen-subjects of whatever form of regime he would endeavor to establish. Needless to say, such a capability is invaluable for he who would introduce a new mode of social order.

In imagining the form of his new regime, it is essential to bear constantly in mind that 'warlike Harry' is, as he both claims and proves, first and foremost a soldier. He has a martial nature; his soul is that of a natural warrior. This has not only shaped his primary range of experiences—which, it is worth stressing, entailed mastering much more than the skills, tactics, and self-discipline required for battle. Beyond that, it has also determined what sorts of men he trusts and respects, whose company he enjoys, and whom he understands—from the inside out, as it were. He knows full well the importance of military competence for accomplishing what only military force can, the most vital being, of course, protection of the polity from external threats; but also, securing whatever resources are necessary to ensure its continuing strength and prosperity. But he appreciates as well that true military competence recognises the limitations and inefficiencies of force, how sometimes 'the gentler gamester is the soonest winner'. Moreover, since anyone's becoming a successful *general* officer requires learning whatever is entailed in moving and maintaining large armies of men, complete competence is not simply a matter of mastering sound military strategy. As the historical Henry was taught by long experience directing the suppression of the Welsh rebellion—and as his subordinates will have learned in the months of elaborate preparations for their successive invasions of France[8]—it includes knowledge of communication, transport, equipage, logistics, and not least of all, *finance*. That is, it presumes expertise in organization, in management, and in the monitoring of performance: the same sort of expertise as is required to oversee and administer a more or less rationally ordered polity.

As for public perceptions, Henry would know better than most in what high regard men of proven martial virtue are held by ordinary citizens and subjects—especially if such men display conspicuous self-discipline and austerity, eschew luxury and swagger, and seem suitably modest regarding their own excellence and achievements. Such men by their reputation, reflected in their very demeanor, naturally elicit the respect that is their due. For most people, aware of how much they themselves value comfort and safety and liberty, do naturally accord respect to men of strength and courage who voluntarily forgo such things and opt instead for a life of strict discipline and some privation, and of hardship and mortal danger when service to the polity requires it. Nonetheless, what people feel is not apt to be unalloyed adoration. Rather, it is a complex passion compounded partly of admiration and gratitude, perhaps even a certain wonder; but also of envy, and not least of all, of fear to offend (fortunately so, as this is essential to their governability).

For these and lesser reasons, Henry, no democrat, would favour a monarchy based upon a military aristocracy (as to a large extent had long been the case in England and Wales, as in France and elsewhere). It would, however, be a military aristocracy with a difference, one whose composition is determined not primarily by lineage, but by proven excellence. For Henry has had enough experience in dealing with soldiers of all types to know that among the ranks of his 'good yeomen' and their officers (the Gowers and Fluellens, the Jamys and Macmorrises) are to be found warriors who truly *do* have 'noble lustre in their eyes'—that is, have quite as much natural soldierly potential as exists among the established nobility. The freshly crowned King's final words to Falstaff express the general principle of justice upon which he would base a new regime: 'We will, according to your strengths and qualities, / Give you advancement'.[9]

Thus he would introduce, over time, important changes in the social order of his realm. So far as possible, these changes would be, or be made to seem, simply needed 'reforms' of existing practices. Thus, as before, all able-bodied men would be required to train regularly in martial skills at least one day a week (typically Sunday, after church service); something like this had been more or less the English practice since Edward I issued his edict forbidding the playing of any other sports on Sunday in order that men would practice their archery.[10] As a consequence, yeomen and peasants would constitute an effective militia that could serve as an auxiliary force to the core of professional soldiers. And there are other benefits to this practice having to do with self-respect and manliness, patriotism and civic spirit, discipline and bodily fitness.

But prior to this becoming a part of men's routine—and vital to both its producing a truly useful reserve army, and respect for the military calling—each winter, shire by shire, *all* young men between the ages of (say) sixteen and nineteen, regardless of family background, would undergo intensive military training under the supervision of experienced professionals. This would, in effect, amount to a doubling for these youths of the traditional 'forty days' owed under bygone feudalism. Not only would this training provide the young men a solid foundation of competence for their lifelong military responsibilities, it would also allow their trainers to ascertain which of the youths seemed well suited to become professional soldiers themselves. Each year, those so identified, regardless of their antecedents, would be allowed to join the body of esquires presently apprenticing under the existing soldiery. Should they choose to do so, that is. For it is imperative, *first*, that such a career be freely chosen if there is to be much prospect of a man's excelling at it; thus, any esquire who, having tasted the professional soldier's life and found that it suits him not, would be free to resign and return to civilian life (cf. 4.3.35–39). *Second*, that it be open to all who qualify without regard to the social status of their families.

These two provisos would be essential to Henry's establishing a new basis of legitimacy, while at the same time minimizing the possibility of there ever arising a dangerous tension between the 'right to rule' and 'good rule' (as brought on Bolingbroke's usurpation). For in this new arrangement, it would be people's confidence—one might call it 'faith' or 'trust'—in the integrity and proficiency of their rulers that would be the principal constituent of those rulers' legitimacy. This faith would not be groundless, much less blind; but neither would it be based on approval of how well the rulers govern, at least not primarily. For people generally, then as now, lack the competence to make valid assessments of the quality of governing.[11] Rather, people's trust in the soldiers who have risen to the upper ranks of government would be the result of personal familiarity with the kind of men who are recruited as esquires, and with how they live thereafter (all men having trained *with* some future soldiers, and been trained *by* their seniors).

Thus, the class of esquires would be, in effect, the foundation of the new regime, for its ultimate rulers would all have begun their professional lives as members of it. And because there is no predicting which of these youths might eventually ascend to the highest rank, all esquires would be subjected to the same rigorous training and education (in place of the uneven, 'hit or miss' training of esquires in times past). Needless to say, there would still be a heavy emphasis on physical training, but aimed more at developing an overall bodily hardihood (as manifested by the historical Henry) than at martial skills per se, much less at any sort of athletic specialty. However, this bodily regimen would be matched with an equally demanding training of the mind. All esquires would receive schooling in the mathematical disciplines, particularly geometry. For not only does geometry have direct military applications (e.g., in disposing and maneuvering forces, in designing and assaulting fortifications, in directing mining and sapping operations, inter alia; cf. 3.2.54 ff.), it trains the mind in logical rigour.[12] And with an eye towards these young men's possible futures, each must be fully literate, and not simply for all of the usual practical reasons. The reading and rereading of good literature of any sort refines a person's manners and taste (all the more needed, given the coarsening influences inherent in military life). And it is vital that they be imbued with a pride in their polity's past by studying its history, especially its triumphs (such as Agincourt), and be able to view it in the context of the history of other nations, past and present; but also to acquaint themselves with what lessons, military and otherwise, have been learned the hard way (cf. 1.2.146).

Just as a novice's training in other trades is through apprenticeship to an expert craftsman, so too the skills of the soldier. There are various ways this could be adapted to the training of the esquires. For example, throughout their period of education, each could be assigned for a year to a particular experienced soldier, who would be for that period his tutor and supervisor, and whom the cadet would accompany and perform whatever menial tasks were required of him (as have esquires traditionally). But this would not be left, as in the past, to private arrangements (i.e., upper-class fathers placing their sons in other upper-class households). Since esquires are drawn from all classes, their assignments to particular tutors would be by lot. At the end of a year, each would be reassigned to another soldier, and so on through a four-year apprenticeship. The only restriction on these assignments would be that no soldier can be the supervisor of his own son or nephew, should it be the case (as is more likely than not) that any of his sons or nephews are selected to become esquires.

AN ALTERNATIVE EPILOGUE   191

Gradually, then, Henry—uniquely capable of effecting profound political change by virtue of his exalted status, reflective of his exceptional qualities and accomplishments—could transform the ruling nobility as a class from one that is merely accidental, determined by the fortunes of family descent, to one that is natural inasmuch as membership would reflect, primarily, personal merit. But the King is a realist. He knows that if there is to be a sufficient number of suitable men willing to commit to the strenuous life of a soldier, and if the commoners are to regard the nobles as truly, and *deservedly*, 'above' them, the latter must as a measure of their higher status, rarer qualities, and graver responsibilities enjoy a more privileged life—not luxurious, but clearly superior in its equipage, dress, and manners to that normal for commoners. Thus they must have the means to support their higher station. And for this purpose, Henry has an ace in the hole, so to speak: that bill favoured by the Commons in the time of his father, and whose revival was so worrisome to the clerical elite early in his own reign. Recall, it proposed the expropriation of all so-called 'temporal lands' that previous generations of laypersons had donated to the Church, and which had amassed to the point that such alienated property comprised the 'better half' of all that the ecclesiastical community possessed. According to the Archbishop, its annexation would be sufficient to support fifteen earls, fifteen hundred knights, over six thousand esquires, as well as a hundred almshouses (with a thousand pounds per annum income left over for the King's own treasury). Enough, that is, to equip a whole new aristocracy. The expropriated land would become part of the royal demesne, from which Henry could from year to year award appropriate estates, or augment existing holdings, to such of his soldiers as prove themselves deserving.

Moreover, this proposal has the added advantage that it would severely curtail clerical power—a generally desirable outcome, given the abuses to which history has repeatedly shown it to be subject. Restricting the ecclesiastical establishment to numbers and resources sufficient for their legitimate spiritual and pedagogical responsibilities, with livelihoods to match, is essential to ensuring that whoever is king be truly sovereign within his realm. For surely Hobbes is right, based on reasoning that is and always has been self-evident to anyone capable of realistic political thinking: men cannot faithfully serve more than one master. Thus the very existence of a bifurcated authority is a chronic invitation to civil confusion, unrest, and outright conflict. So, while there are many benefits to a polity's having a single established religion—as a primary source of civic unity by virtue of a shared cosmology and common morality, preached weekly to noble and commoner alike—the professional clergy charged with nurturing and maintaining religion must nonetheless be subordinate to the civil sovereign, recognising his ultimate authority not only with respect to appointments and functions, but regarding doctrine as well.

It is especially important that the clergy not be seen as having any independent power over the fate of men's souls. For as Hobbes warns:

> The maintenance of Civill Society, depending on Justice; and Justice on the power of Life and Death, and other lesse Rewards and Punishments, residing in them that have the Soveraignty of the Common-wealth; It is impossible a Common-wealth should stand, where any other than the Soveraign, hath a power of giving greater rewards than Life; and of inflicting greater punishments, than Death.

However, Hobbes continues, insofar as the promise of '*Eternall life* is a greater reward than *life present*, and *Eternall torment* a greater punishment than *death of Nature*',[13] the power of so promising and threatening must not be allowed to run counter to civil authority. The only guarantee that this will not happen is for the king to be acknowledged as head of the Church as well as of the State, Defender of the Faith as well as of the polity.

Would Shakespeare's Henry be able to accomplish, *peaceably*, such a major transformation in the composition of his society, including—most importantly—to defend its rightness doctrinally? It is hard to imagine anyone better qualified than the very monarch whose Archbishop marveled, 'Hear him but reason in divinity / ... / You would desire the King were made a prelate'. (Be careful what you wish for, Canterbury.) Add to his scriptural-theological acumen an analytical ability to unravel any 'Gordian knot of policy', and a talent for fashioning such 'sweet and honeyed sentences' as would charm birds out of trees, one may suppose that a solidly ensconced King Henry V might well have managed more easily and safely what Shakespeare knew Henry VIII accomplished at great cost and risk over a century later.

With Henry acknowledged, not merely as beyond dispute the rightful King, but as a favourite of God and adored by men, he could undertake a radical refashioning of the very kingship he inherited, with the intention of passing on to his son (or whomever) a Crown whose legitimacy is based neither in divine right (as was Richard II's) nor in personal charisma (as was his own). Although the Tudors continued to invoke the verbal formulas of divine right, few people who mattered could seriously credit a doctrine which Bolingbroke's successful usurpation empirically proved to be, for all practical purposes, false. Charisma, on the other hand, cannot be institutionalized; and it would be unrealistic to the point of absurdity to foist on people a regime in which each sovereign was expected to prove his personal legitimacy in the same manner as did Henry. So, these alternatives eliminated, what possible kind of kingship might Henry work to establish, given that its incumbent must be subjectively viewed as legitimate by those he rules, but also be, and be believed to be, generally competent for the role—all the more important inasmuch as ruling *well* tends to confirm a ruler's legitimacy.

It would be a kingship based upon a royal council whose membership was restricted to a small number of senior officers, no more than a dozen (say), whose entire careers bespoke their prudence, patriotism, and firm commitment to the rationale of the regime. Henry would make the initial selection himself. Thereafter, his successors would nominate replacements as deaths and retirements made replenishment necessary, but subject to the confirmation of present council members, since they would have the strongest interest in ensuring that the regime continues to be overseen by men who, like themselves, cared most to preserve it according to its founding principles. Just as have a king's councillors in the past—as portrayed in the second scene of *Henry V*—the members of the Council would serve as advisers to the sitting king, possibly with special responsibilities distributed amongst them (e.g., for finance, public works, education, diplomacy, and so on). This Royal Council would also serve as the supreme judiciary, and oversee such lower courts as were necessary to administer a uniform system of justice throughout the polity. For as Henry acknowledged in reappointing his father's Lord Chief Justice—'Happy am I, that have a man so bold / That dares do justice on my proper son'—administering equal justice, 'without fear or favour', is his foremost domestic responsibility.

Most important, it would be a requirement that a present king's choice of his successor be ratified by this council—or rejected in the unlikely event (given the very possibility of such a rejection) that there was a broad agreement amongst its members that his choice was clearly unsuitable. Moreover, in the event (also unlikely) that a duly anointed king were to prove grossly incompetent or unjust, the council would have the authority to force his abdication and choose a successor. A similar arrangement would pertain in case a sitting king became permanently incapacitated. And should a king have chosen a son to succeed him (as would be expected, though lacking a son perhaps a nephew, as did Caesar, or someone wholly unrelated) but die before the chosen person reach maturity (as did Henry), the council would choose from among its members a regent to rule in his stead until such time as the council judged the late king's choice ready to assume sovereignty—and preparing him for that day would be the regent's primary duty.

Given such an arrangement, the legitimacy of successive kings would grow and solidify with each passing generation. For though people might regard the reign of one king to be better than that of another, they would presume each to be at least satisfactory, confident that the council would intervene should the situation prove otherwise. Thus, both the subjective legitimacy of sitting kings and an assurance of their objective competence would be grounded in the top rung of a martial aristocracy: a Royal Council consisting of senior soldiers whose superior qualities were self-evident, the entire population knowing how they achieved their positions and what their responsibilities are.

'Thus far, with rough and unable pen', have I further 'pursued the story', attempting to imagine how 'this Star of England', had Fortune allotted him a normal span of years, might have come to be memorialized—not primarily for the miraculous victory he achieved at Agincourt, prelude to a failed attempt to make him and his heirs master of France as well as England—but as the begetter of an Anglo-French kingdom, and architect and founder of a new kind of regime, one in which a king's legitimacy carried a sufficient warrant for his competence. I do not suppose such a legacy would have permanently erased for subsequent generations of Henry's peoples the distinction between the *right* to govern and *good* government. Like all political arrangements, it would be subject to eventual decay, human nature being as it is. But it is conceivable that its longevity might have rivaled that of the regime founded by William the Conqueror, if not that of Lykurgus.

Notes

Prologue

1. A second caveat is required with respect to the effect of the play in performance. It tends to produce comparably divergent reactions amongst audiences on those infrequent occasions when the *whole* play is performed just as Shakespeare wrote it. That is, performed with no abridgment of the text, and in particular no deleting of any speech or deed of Henry's that might seem to reflect poorly on him; nor with the play being performed as in effect a parody of martial heroism, typically with some relocation in time or place in an attempt to make it seem more relevant (as has recently become fashionable).

2. Thomas Carlyle can be treated as speaking for them in his lecture 'The Hero as Poet'. He adduced approvingly the view of the eminent German scholar and translator of Shakespeare: 'August Wilhelm Schlegel has a remark on [Shakespeare's] History Plays, *Henry Fifth* [*sic*] and others, which is worth remembering. He calls them a kind of National Epic'. Carlyle goes on to speak of the *beauties* to be found in Shakespeare's works, including *Henry V*: 'That battle of Agincourt strikes me as one of the most perfect things, in its sort, we anywhere have of Shakspeare's [*sic*].... There is noble Patriotism in it,—far other than the "indifference" you sometimes hear ascribed to Shakspeare. A true English heart breathes, calm and strong, through the whole business; not boisterous, protrusive; all the better for that. There is a sound in it like the ring of steel' (as quoted in Bate, *Romantics on Shakespeare*, 254). In his assessment of the historical accuracy of Shakespeare's portrayal of the man, J. A. R. Marriot writes, 'In *Henry V* Shakspeare [*sic*] got his chance of depicting an ideal Christian Knight; a ruler who was at once powerful and successful; a man whom we may both love and admire' (*English History in Shakspeare*, 136).

3. Hazlitt comes to mind. He lamented Shakespeare's valorizing the historical Henry, portraying him as 'the king of good fellows', whereas he was in fact scarcely deserving of the honour. As for his popularity: 'How then do we like him? We like him in the play. There he is a very amiable monster, a very splendid pageant. As we like to gaze at a panther or a young lion in their cages in the Tower, and catch a pleasing horror from their glistening eyes, their velvet paws, and dreadless roar, so we take a very romantic, heroic, patriotic, and poetical delight in the boasts and feats of our younger Harry, as they appear on stage and are confined to lines of ten syllables; where no blood follows the stroke that wounds our ears' (Bate, *Romantics on Shakespeare*, 365).

4. There are exceptions, of course, most notably John E. Alvis, who writes in 'Spectacle Supplanting Ceremony: Shakespeare's Henry of Monmouth':

> The tetralogy form can also accommodate the gradual unfolding of a political project from its moment of conception, through stages of adjustment and revision, to completion and valedictory flourish. That we may appreciate the daring and momentous project espoused by Henry Monmouth, Shakespeare allows us to see how the goal he reaches in the last play of his tetralogy is conceived in the first. We might characterize Henry's purpose as the depreciation of traditional ceremony in favor of innovative spectacles. (107)

Because Shakespeare's English history plays provide such vivid illustrations of Hobbes's political teaching, especially of the dangers that threaten civil life when the 'Sovereign Power' is disputed, I have used selections from *Leviathan* to annotate the chapters which follow. That his seminal work lends itself so readily to this use is not, I believe, pure coincidence. According to John Aubrey, in *The Life of Mr Thomas Hobbes of Malmsbury*, 'Before Thucydides, he spent two years in reading romances and plays, which he has often repented and said that these two years were lost of him—wherein perhaps he was mistaken too, for it might furnish him with copy of words'. I also have never been persuaded that Hobbes did not profit from his reading of plays (which almost certainly included those of Shakespeare), having noticed too many subtle indications to the contrary. One example not all that subtle begins chapter 6 of *The Elements of Law*:

> There is a story somewhere, of one that had pretended to have been miraculously cured of blindness, wherewith he was born, by St. Alban or some other St., at the town of St. Alban's; and that the Duke of Gloucester being there, to be satisfied of the truth of the miracle, asked the man, What colour is this? who by answering, It is green, discovered himself, and was punished for a counterfeit: for though by his sight newly received he might distinguish between green, and red, and all other colours, as well as any that should interrogate him, yet he could not possibly know at first sight, which of them was called green, or red, or by other name. By this we may understand, there be two sorts of knowledge, whereof the one is nothing else but sense, or knowledge original; [the other] the experience men have of the proper use of names in language.

The 'somewhere' of this 'story' is Shakespeare's *2 Henry VI* 2.1.58–134. According to the editor of the 3rd Arden edition of the play, the miracle story 'is not found in Hall or Holinshed but is in Grafton (1.630), where the source, Sir Thomas More, is acknowledged' (195n2.1; cf. 79–82). But in the original version, Gloucester is credulous and joyful to learn of the miracle. Whereas Shakespeare transforms the Duke into a skeptic who exposes the fraud.

5. As Pamela Jensen observes by way of beginning her fine essay 'The Famous Victories of William Shakespeare: *The Life of Henry the Fifth*': 'I know of no other Shakespearean play whose commentators are as concerned about the author's political judgment as this one. Virtually all the principal *dramatic* questions raised by *Henry V* resolve themselves into *political* questions. Above all, they ask, what does Shakespeare think about the king he portrays? And, as a related question, what ought *we* to think about him?' (235–36).

6. So Anthony Brennan prefaces his useful *Twayne's New Critical Introductions to Shakespeare: Henry V* by noting, 'Where the play had once been a reliable, unproblematical, and not especially challenging tapestry of famous events it gradually became an exciting, complex, ambiguous and disturbing account which seemed fully responsive to current political anxieties. The reputations of many of Shakespeare's plays have been modified in this century but in none has the transformation been quite as complete as in *Henry V*' (xi).

7. I have discussed this interpretive principle at some length in the prologue to *Philosophy and the Puzzles of 'Hamlet'*.

Chapter One

1. Foreword to Steel, *Richard II*, vii. And as Steel observes, 'Richard II was the last of the old order, the last king ruling by hereditary right, direct and undisputed from the Conqueror' (1).

2. For so the quarto editions entitle it, whereas it appears in the folio as simply *The life and death of King Richard the Second*; likewise the plays about Kings John and Richard III. As for the period and the play about it, Lily B. Campbell, in *Shakespeare's Histories: Mirrors of Elizabethan Policy*, begins her treatment of Richard's reign thus:

> When Halle wrote his chronicle . . . , he opened it with a section which he entered as 'An introduccion into the devision of the two houses of Lancastre and Yorke'. The section began with the quarrel between Mowbray and Bolingbroke in the presence of Richard II, which to Halle seemed the inception of the struggle that later devastated England as the Wars of the Roses. Late in Elizabeth's reign, Sir John Hayward wrote a book about *The First Part of the Life and Raigne of King Henrie the IIII*, in which he devoted one hundred and 36 pages out of a total of one hundred and 49 to Richard II. He later justified his extensive treatment of the deposition and murder of Richard II in a supposed life of Henry IV by explaining that he had to write of Richard II insofar as his follies were 'either causes or furtherances of the fortunes of the other', and claimed that he followed Halle in commencing his story where he did. Shakespeare's play of *Richard II* will be better understood if we remember that he began the action exactly where Halle began his 'introduccion', with the quarrel between Mowbray and Bolingbroke before the King. (168)

3. All textual references are to Forker, 3rd Arden ed. The amount of scholarly literature on this play is quite considerable. Over eight hundred pieces were published in just the four-plus decades following 1944, according to Josephine A. Roberts's *Richard II: An Annotated Bibliography*, a number that had swollen to nearly three thousand by the time Forker wrote his introduction. As I presume is obvious, it is practically impossible for anyone to have read all of it. I have consulted a reasonable sampling, including several of the most influential accounts pertinent

not only to *Richard II* but also to the subsequent plays of the *Henriad* (e.g., those of E. M. W. Tillyard, Lily B. Campbell, Derek Traversi, Harold C. Goddard, Robert B. Pierce, Ernst H. Kantorowicz, and Graham Holderness, inter alia, as identified when specifically cited), as well as authors who have undertaken to compare Shakespeare's version of English history with more modern treatments, such as J. A. R. Marriot (*English History in Shakspeare*), Peter Saccio (*Shakespeare's English Kings*), and John Julius Norwich (*Shakespeare's Kings*). Of all the sources I have considered, I have found four interpretive efforts to be especially helpful: Allan Bloom's 'Richard II' and Louise Cowan's 'God Will Save the King', both in *Shakespeare as Political Thinker*; Pamela K. Jensen's 'Beggars and Kings: Cowardice and Courage in Shakespeare's *Richard II*'; and the chapter on *Richard II* in Tim Spiekerman's *Shakespeare's Political Realism: The English History Plays*. Together, these authors provide such a thorough exposition of, among other important matters, the various biblical parallels Shakespeare wove into *Richard II*—the Cain-Abel story; the passion of Jesus; and especially the elaborate conceit comparing the Edenic story of man's loss of moral innocence to Englishmen's loss of political innocence with the fall of Richard—that I need say little more about it beyond registering my general agreement. I do, however, differ substantially on several issues of sufficient importance as to justify (in my mind, at least) offering my own interpretive effort.

4. Cf. 2.1.228–34; 4.1.2–4, 327–29. The poetic quality of the language Shakespeare lavished on this play—one of only four crafted entirely in verse, with an abundance of rhyming couplets—itself requires comment. It has been analyzed in detail by John Baxter, in *Shakespeare's Poetic Styles: Verse into Drama*. He writes:

> *Richard II* is a precursor of Shakespeare's great tragedies, not because it discovers the melancholic character (Richard) confronting the necessity of action, or the character of amoral efficiency (Bolingbroke) confronting the necessity of moral and spiritual sanctions, but because it discovers an adequate style or range of styles for presenting 'men in their causative character' [Coleridge's phrase for what effective drama must do]; it discloses a range of stylistic mastery, unprecedented in Shakespeare's career before 1595, that is capable of encompassing, without falsifying, a full complexity of human experience; it offers a clear prognosis of the mature and urbane style of Shakespeare. (55)

Forker agrees, beginning his introduction to the 3rd Arden edition with the observation, "*Richard II* marks an exciting advance in the development of Shakespeare's artistry. Its unusual formality of structure and tone as well as the impressive eloquence of its style seem to have been crafted to express the mystique of kingship more emphatically than any of the earlier histories" (1).

5. The later tumultuous scene in Parliament of charges and denials, challenges and counterchallenges, especially regarding the Duke of Gloucester's death (4.1) has a historical basis. According to Holinshed, on this occasion Sir John Bagot, then a prisoner, 'disclosed manie secrets, unto which he was privie'. About the Duke's murder, however, he testified that once when he and the Duke of Norfolk were riding together, Mowbray asked him 'what he knew of the manner of the duke of Glocester [*sic*] his death' (409–10; all quoting of Holinshed's *Chronicles* regarding

Richard II's reign is from vol. 3 of Geoffrey Bullough, *Narrative and Dramatic Sources of Shakespeare*, hereafter cited as 'Bullough'; in subsequent chapters, Holinshed references are to vol. 4 of Bullough's series):

> [Bagot] answered that he knew nothing at all: but the people (quoth he) doo say that you have murthered him. Whereunto the duke sware great othes that it was untrue, and that he had saved his life contrarie to the will of the king, and certeine other lords, by the space of three weeks, and more; affirming withal, that he was never in all his life time more affraid of death than he was at his comming home againe from Calis at that time, to the kings presence, by reason that he had not put the duke to death. (3:409–10)

Shakespeare perhaps hints at this testimony by having Mowbray reply to Bolingbroke's charge, 'For Gloucester's death, / I slew him not, but to my own disgrace / Neglected my sworn duty in that case' (1.1.132–34).

6. So it would seem, based on the—admittedly slight—textual evidence (as distinct from the historical record): Richard entrusted Mowbray with the responsibility of fetching the future queen from France (initially at his own expense, no less), as well as with disbursing payment to the garrison at Calais. Seen from the other side, Mowbray is regarded by Gloucester's widow as working hand in glove with Richard in arranging the murder of her husband (along with other such 'sins so heavy in his bosom / That they may [she hopes] break his foaming courser's back'; 1.2.46–53). Mowbray's behaviour in responding to Bolingbroke's appeal is that of a fearless man confident of his innocence, and eager to prove himself 'a loyal gentleman'—certainly no traitor to Richard—by defeating and killing his accuser on a field of honour (1.1.142–51). And according to the Lord Marshal, he arrives on the appointed day sprightly and bold' (1.3.3).

7. H. M. Richmond may be taken as representative of critics who see a 'kinder, gentler' Richard in Shakespeare's portrayal, and who accordingly credit the reduction in Henry's term of banishment as a sincere instance of 'the most graceful gestures of kingly mercy . . . in consideration of the grief of Bolingbroke's father, Gaunt' (*Shakespeare's Political Plays*, 126)—this despite Richard's behaviour in the very next scene, first, hinting that it's doubtful Henry will *ever* be 'call[ed] home from banishment' (1.4.20–22, which squares with what we know from historical sources, as did Shakespeare: that within six months of Gaunt's death Richard *extended* Henry's banishment *for life*); and second, that in private with his closest associates he wished for Gaunt's immediate death (1.4.59–60)!

8. The willingness with which other warlike men bowed to Henry's leadership in their common rebellion is sufficient testimony to his martial bona fides; and Bishop Carlisle's report of Mowbray's demise does likewise for him: 'Many a time has banished Norfolk fought / For Jesu Christ in glorious Christian field [etc.]' (4.1.93–101). According to Bruce, *Usurper King*, 'while Henry had excelled in the jousts at St. Inglevert, Mowbray had won fame at Smithfield' (165).

9. Shakespeare would have read in Holinshed's *Chronicles* of the commotion attending Bolingbroke's departure into exile: 'A woonder it was to see what number of people ran after him in everie towne and street where he came, before he tooke the sea, lamenting and bewailing his departure, as who would saie, that when

he departed, the onlie shield, defense and comfort of the commonwealth was vaded and gone' (Bullough, 394).

10. According to Holinshed, King Richard 'entred into the field with great triumph, . . . accompanied with all the peers of the realm, and in his companie was the earle of saint Paule, which was come out of France in post to see this challenge performed. The king had there above ten thousand men in armour, least some fraie or tumult might rise among his nobles, by quarreling or partaking' (Bullough, 392). The fullest account of this episode that I'm aware of, synthesized from all the contemporary and near-contemporary accounts, is that of Bruce in *The Usurper King*. As most modern readers are unlikely to appreciate the enormity of Richard's aborting the long-scheduled trial, it is worth quoting at some length:

> But beneath the surface pageantry its real meaning was grim: since God was expected to help the just, whoever succumbed in battle was guilty of treason according to the law, and if not killed in the lists would be handed over to the executioner in a terrible and humiliating procedure. . . . So, although in appearance resembling the tournaments Henry so loved, the spirit of the duel at Coventry would be very different, its object being, not sport, but death for the weaker contestant. (162–63)

Nor should the significance of the elaborate preparations and pageantry hedging this august public event be underestimated.

> When the Court of Chivalry at Windsor set a date four months ahead for the duel between Henry and Mowbray it was not out of kindly desire to give the combatants a chance to arrange their affairs before facing death, but to a quite callous reason: what was to be a form of public execution was also an entertainment, a Roman holiday staged as a magnificent spectacle. Time was needed for painters and embroiderers to adorn the area with flags, to ornament the pavilions of the contestants with their heraldic badges (Henry's patterned all over with Lancastrian red roses, Mowbray's perhaps with mulberries); for carpenters to build the lists, the barriers and the spectators' stands; and for the king to name the privileged audience. At the royal order messengers must be dispatched with invitations to foreign nobles across the sea and to summon all bishops, lords and members of his council throughout England. Most important of all, time was needed for the contestants to equip themselves in dazzling apparel.
>
> Since nothing, even in Henry's lavish collection of jousting gear, was good enough for such an exceptional occasion he sent to Italy for a new suit of armour from his old friend, the Duke Gian Galeazzo of Milan, with whom he had corresponded ever since his pilgrimage to the Holy Land. The Count of Virtues lived up to his name: excited by the approaching drama, Galeazzo invited Henry's emissary to choose from the ducal armoury himself, and sent him back to England accompanied by four Milanese armourers to adjust the intricate pieces of steel and leather, and to strap Henry into them on the day of the duel. Meanwhile, Mowbray's envoys had been engaged in buying his armour in the Holy Roman Empire, German and Italian armourers being currently reputed the best in Christendom. (164)

What must have been the reaction, then, both of the protagonists and of the vast audience upon the king's last-second cancellation of such a carefully orchestrated and long-anticipated event?

11. In the historical case, each man was given fifteen days to put his affairs in order, and equip himself for life abroad. Thus Bolingbroke arranged for the 'letters patents' empowering his attorneys to act for him during his absence—which, as York complains, Richard subsequently revoked (2.1.201–4; cf. 2.3.129–30).

12. As Hobbes teaches, 'Vain-glorious men, such as estimate their sufficiency by the flattery of other men, or the fortune of some precedent action, without assured ground of hope from the true knowledge of themselves, are enclined to rash engaging; and in the approach of danger, or difficulty, to retire if they can: because not seeing the way to safety, they will rather hazard their honour, which may be salved with an excuse; than their lives, for which no salve is sufficient' (*Leviathan*, chap. 11, para. 12).

13. As so it must have on the historical occasion Holinshed recounts (Bullough, 393):

> The duke of Hereford was quicklie horssed, and closed his bavier, and cast his speare into the rest, and when the trumpet sounded set forward couragiouslie towards his enemie six or seven pases. The duke of Norfolke was not fullie set forward, when the king cast downe his warder, and the heralds cried, Ho, ho. Then the king caused their speares to be taken from them, and commanded them to repaire againe to their chaires, where they remained two long houres, while the king and his councell deliberatlie consulted what order was best to be had in so weightie a cause.

Doubtless the fact that Shakespeare incorporated this episode virtually unaltered from Holinshed's history explains the rather easy acceptance of its propriety by the majority of commentators on the play. They fail to recognise how aberrant was the *historical* Richard's behaviour on this ceremonial occasion of highest formality, and what its significance proved to be—which Shakespeare saw clearly. So, too, does Allan Bloom:

> Richard, despite his fears that the result of the combat will inculpate him, is constrained by the rules of honor to permit it. But this aborted combat on St. Lambert's Day in the lists at Coventry is the last trial by combat England will ever see. When Richard recognizes that the risks are too great for him and halts it, he unwittingly brings the era of chivalry, the era of Christian knights inaugurated by the first Richard, the Lion-Hearted, to its end. By Act IV the challenges of the lords have become empty bluster and a parody of what they had been. They will never be committed to a test. ('*Richard II*', 60–61)

Alexander Leggatt likewise sees the larger significance of the Coventry episode, and draws out the sense in which here, too, 'all the world's a stage'. He stresses the fact that the various participants to the event 'are not just asserting their own wills but working through a larger order which they implicitly accept. The elaborate technical preparations for the lists at Coventry confirm this effect. The ritual builds, the symmetry intensifies—to a startling anticlimax: '... Stay, the king has thrown his warder down'.

> As the ritual is at once decorous and a bit tedious, its violation is at once a shock and a relief. The gesture itself is part of the language of the occasion, but its timing makes it theatrical. It is splendid theatre, but it is theatre at the cost of ceremony..., and what is most disturbing is that the violation has come right from the centre. The King, custodian of order, has himself broken the order of a formal occasion. The structure is not smashed from without, like the vials and branches of the Duchess's speech; the shock that destroys it comes from its very centre, and it collapses inwards.
>
> The moment is a striking image of Richard's responsibility for the disorder of his kingdom and the later collapse—so sudden and complete—of his own rule. (*Shakespeare's Political Drama*, 61)

Richard's erratic behaviour on this high ceremonial occasion—suddenly reversing a decision long since taken and accepted by everyone as definitive and practically irrevocable, who then plan accordingly—is of a piece with that which he displays upon arriving back from Ireland to find that his Welsh army has disbanded and disbursed. It bespeaks the same irresolution and failure of nerve, oscillating radically between bravado and despair—in short, the same fragility and weakness of soul.

14. Basing her account on eyewitness testimony, Bruce reports, 'the moment the spectators had eagerly awaited was to end in anticlimax, for the king rose to his feet, cried loudly, "Ho! Ho!" and cast down his warder into the list to stop the battle. There was amazement on all sides'. No doubt. And when two hours later the judgment of banishment was pronounced on both protagonists, 'it caused such an uproar of protest that men could not hear each other speak' (*Usurper King*, 168).

In his chapter on Richard's reign, David Hume observes, 'The weakness and fluctuations of Richard's counsels appear no where more evident than in the conduct of this affair. No sooner had Hereford left the kingdom, than the king's jealousy of the power and riches of that prince's family revived; and he was sensible, that, by Glocester's [sic] death, he had only removed a counterpoise to the Lancastrian interest, which was now become formidable to his crown and Kingdom' (*History of England*, 2:313).

15. Since continuance of their 'home-bred hate' is a significant addition to the oath as recounted in Holinshed—'the king called before him both the parties, and made them to sweare that one should never come in place where the other was, willinglie; nor keep any companie to gather in any forren region' (Bullough, 393–94)—one must assume that Shakespeare intends something by it.

16. Graham Holderness is one of the comparatively few Shakespeare scholars who subjects this episode to anything like a detailed analysis. In his monograph on the play (*Critical Studies*), he states the problem fairly enough:

> In law, the king was entirely within his rights to do this [i.e., halt the combat], but legal authority is hardly sufficient to explain why Richard should choose such a moment and such a manner for something he could have done equally well at the very opening of the proceedings—by denying the knights

the right to battle, and judging the case himself. Why let things go so far? Is it a sudden decision made in a moment of guilty panic? Or is Richard possessed by the fear that Bolingbroke might win, and the king's own complicity in Gloucester's murder thereby be revealed? Such explanations would appeal to those who see Richard as weak, indecisive and perpetually haunted by the guilt attaching to his uncle's murder. Or is it a deliberate, carefully planned and decisive intervention? (33)

Holderness then proceeds to argue for this latter interpretation—and, I should add, does so as plausibly as anyone could—basing it on his understanding of the historical context that Shakespeare would have presumed his audience was familiar with. Thus, Holderness contends that Richard's action is part of an attempt 'to curtail the nobility and to arrogate greater authority to the crown—a king who is moving, in other words, towards the royal absolutism of the Tudor and Stuart monarchs', and that he is 'showing them who is master by the simple expedient of putting an abrupt stop to their little game' (34). *Little game?*—a curious characterization of what is ostensibly a duel to the death. Moreover, Richard himself is already as deeply implicated in this 'game' as a king could possibly be: 'we shall see / Justice design the victor's chivalry'. There is no finessing the fact that he authorized it, that he set in motion the elaborate material and technical arrangements. And that, consequently, his halting it when he does will not seem 'masterly' so much as evidence of indecisiveness, infirmity, and irresolution born of concerns one can only imagine, none of which would reflect well on Richard. Certainly the rationale he subsequently provides should not lay to rest anyone's darker suspicions, since it would have obviated authorizing the trial in the first place. And that he doesn't even take sole responsibility for it, but palms it off as the collective decision of his council, hardly seems the act of one who is determined to show the nobility 'who is master here'. We may agree that Richard's abrupt cancelling of the trial has the effect of undermining the chivalric-ceremonial order of society, but that he does this as a matter of policy is most unlikely, given what we see of his temperament in the balance of the play.

In short, I believe Holderness misreads Richard's character as Shakespeare portrays it, much as he does Bolingbroke's. Failing to note that *Shakespeare's* Henry (in contrast to Holinshed's) has determined to 'repeal himself' *before* his father dies, hence before there is any Lancastrian estate to inherit, Holderness prefers to accept at face value Henry's repeated profession that he returns only to claim what is rightfully his. In keeping with his 'nobility versus monarchy' interpretation, Holderness would have us see Henry as simply 'a figure in many ways typical of his time, his class and his profession'; one whose speech 'is stiff with the punctilious pride of the aristocrat'; that 'Northumberland's language is not Bolingbroke's, and it is a mistake to transpose the patent machiavellianism of the former to the political consciousness of the latter' (62–63). Thus Holderness asks rhetorically, is Bolingbroke's becoming Henry IV 'the culmination of a long, protracted campaign of political aspiration? Or does he find himself almost unexpectedly catapulted to power, unprepared and tongue-tied by the sudden accession of responsibility?' (67). I submit that a more careful reading of the play answers the former question with an emphatic 'Yes', and with an equally emphatic 'No' the latter. Consequently, far from simply a representative of the nobility in its struggle to maintain its privileges in the face an encroaching monarchy, Shakespeare's Henry from the outset aspired to *be* the monarch, and a strong one in every way that Richard was weak.

17. Alvin Kernan, who coined the now widely used name for the second tetralogy, summarizes the historical significance of the period portrayed by the *Henriad*:

> In historical terms the movement from the world of Richard II to that of Henry V is the passage from the Middle Ages to the Renaissance and the modern world. In political and social terms it is a movement from feudalism and hierarchy to the national state and individualism. In psychological terms it is from a situation in which man knows with certainty who he is to an existential condition in which any identity is only a temporary role. In spatial and temporal terms it is a movement from a closed world to an infinite universe. In mythical terms the passage is from a garden world to a fallen world. In the most summary terms it is a movement from ceremony and ritual to history and drama. ('The Henriad', 3)

18. In his catalogue of 'Instrumental Powers', Hobbes includes several pertinent to Bolingbroke's success, among them: 'Reputation of power, is Power; because it draweth with it the adhaerence of those that need protection. So is Reputation of love of a mans country, (called Popularity,) for the same Reason' (*Leviathan*, chap. 10, paras. 5–6).

19. Robert B. Pierce notes that Northumberland's 'oily flattery' differs markedly from his son's mode of addressing Henry, that 'Hotspur's bluntness to the rising Bolingbroke' signals the contrast of character between father and son that proves so important to the plot of *1 Henry IV* (*Shakespeare's History Plays*, 169n5).

20. The episode obviously reminds one of how Henry II dealt with 'the Becket problem'. But does it not also refer obliquely to the indirect way in which Elizabeth disposed of Mary Queen of Scots? Parallels were frequently drawn between the reign of Richard II and that of Elizabeth, especially the alleged influence of 'flatterers' in the courts of both monarchs. Campbell documents in detail the many, mainly invidious, comparisons that were made between the 'follies' of Richard's reign and those of Elizabeth's, almost from its beginning (*Shakespeare's Histories*, 168–212). Martin Coyle notes in his useful *Critical Guide* to the play, '*Richard II* is unique insofar as it is the only play of Shakespeare's that we know was demonstrably subject to some form of censorship', referring to the deletion of the deposition scene from all quartos published during Queen Elizabeth's lifetime. Coyle adds that the play 'is also unique, and this is probably a related point, in that it is the only play by Shakespeare that seems to have been involved directly in contemporary political events' (14)—meaning, of course, the notorious Essex rebellion of 1601, adherents of the Earl having arranged for a performance of the play on the day prior to the abortive attempt to capture or unseat the Queen.

J. E. Neale provides a detailed account of the episode, including Shakespeare's peripheral involvement: 'Some of Essex's hare-brained followers bribed Shakespeare's company, with a *douceur* of forty shillings, to play the deposing and killing of King Richard II at the Globe Theatre on the Saturday afternoon; and after dining together a company of them crossed the river to witness this ominous performance' (*Queen Elizabeth*, 371). In her account of the event, Campbell adds, 'The actors protested that the play was by then "so old and so long out of use" that it would attract but a small audience' (*Shakespeare's Histories*, 188)—or so one of them later testified: 'members of the Chamberlain's company were arraigned and questioned, though Shakespeare was apparently not involved and none of the actors were punished'. Campbell continues:

> The facts that Hayward's account of the deposing of Richard II and the usurpation of Henry IV was a matter of prime consideration in determining Essex's fate, and that a play 'of King Henry the Fourth, and of the killing of Richard the Second' was used by Essex's friends as a curtain-raiser to his rebellion have provided us with a clearly authenticated account of the Elizabethan recognition of history as a political mirror potentially dangerous. . . . ['Hayward' refers to Sir John Hayward, who in 1599 published a book, dedicated to the Earl of Essex, entitled *The First Part of the Life an Raigne of King Henrie the IIII*, of which, as noted previously, 'the first 136 pages of the 149 were devoted to reciting the history of Richard II and the reasons which led to his deposition by Henry IV' (182–83).]
> In the 1601 trial of Essex these matters were again threshed out. Cecil accused the earl of having for five or six years plotted to become king and affirmed that the proof of his intentions was in 'the book written on Henry IV., making this time like that of Richard II., to be reframed by him as by Henry IV.' The trial also elicited evidence concerning the playing of the play about Richard II on the eve of the rebellion. (188–89, 190)

Essex, like Bolingbroke, courted 'popularity', but relevant as well is the fact that Essex 'was descended from the Duke of Gloucester whose murder lies behind the action of [Shakespeare's] play and through him traced a line of descent to the throne' (Coyle, *Critical Guide to Richard II*, 21). In short, it is not difficult to understand Elizabeth's famously declaring to William Lambarde, her Keeper of the Tower Records, 'I am Richard II. know ye not that', complaining, 'this tragedy was played 40^{tie} times in open streets and houses' (20).

21. Surely one of the more curious features of this play is the lack of any reference to the fact that there was already an acknowledged heir to childless Richard: until his death in 1398 while serving as the King's lieutenant in Ireland (which occasioned Richard's Irish expedition), it was Roger Mortimer, fourth Earl of March and great-grandson of Edward III through his mother Philippa, who was the sole heir of Edward's *third* son, Lionel Duke of Clarence. He may, accordingly, have been proclaimed Richard's heir as early as 1385. Upon Roger's death, his claim to the throne passed to his son, Edmund, the fifth Earl of March, who may have been expressly recognised by Richard as the heir presumptive in 1398 (though he was but a small child at the time). What makes this 'omission' so odd is the fact that Shakespeare is fully aware of the Mortimer claim, since it figures explicitly in the next play of the tetralogy (*1 Henry IV*, 1.3.143–46); he was, however, misled by his source, Holinshed, to confuse the claimant with his uncle, also named Edmund.

22. Bolingbroke shows a similar concern for public justification when ordering the execution at Bristol of the 'caterpillars' Bushy and Green: 'yet to wash your

blood / From off my hands, here in the view of men / I will unfold some causes of your deaths' (3.1.5–7). He doesn't seem overly concerned that at least half of the causes he alleges are almost surely false, and implausible to boot; he apparently presumes that the general populace will believe almost anything nefarious attributed to this unpopular pair.

23. Katharine Eisaman Maus suggests that the preceding lines, which are obviously 'meant to recall a coronation ceremony', are effectively a parody of undoing something that in principle 'cannot be undone':

> By referring to this ritual at the moment of his deposition, Richard implies that giving up the crown is an impossible act, a kind of absurdity. Moreover, reversing the ceremonies... suggests a special scandal. In medieval and early modern Europe,... reversing beneficent ceremonies supposedly evoked their diabolical opposites. One called up devils by reciting Scripture passages backward, or bound oneself to Satan by performing an inversion of baptismal rites. Richard's enthusiastic self-dramatization of his plight does not quell doubts about the legitimacy of the usurpation, but encourages those doubts. (Preface to *Richard II*, 418)

24. As is well known, her entire role is a dramatic invention, the actual Queen being but a girl of ten or thereabouts at the time of Richard's downfall. It seems, however, that Shakespeare chose to invest her with the qualities of Richard's first wife, Anne of Bohemia, whose marriage to him 'became legendary for its romantic happiness' (according to the 3rd Arden editor, 174).

25. It is mainly from this point on, it seems to me, that Shakespeare's Richard can be fairly characterized as the 'Poet-King' that Walter Pater famously contended he is 'from first to last, in light and gloom alike' (*Appreciations: With an Essay on Style*, 112).

26. Most knowledgeable critics agree that the fall of Richard, both historically and in Shakespeare's plays, marks some sort of major change in English political life, though there is no unanimity as to quite what sort and whether for good or ill. Pierce sees it thus: 'Richard's deposition begins a cycle of guilt and punishment that ends only with the triumph of Henry Tudor at the end of *Richard III*. As a result, it is natural that this play should emphasize the prospect of a chain of inherited guilt that will destroy the whole order of the kingdom' (*Shakespeare's History Plays*, 149). Leggatt contends, 'Nor is Richard the only loser. Kingship is the play's central idea, and when it becomes relative, not absolute, other absolutes fall with it' (*Shakespeare's Political Drama*, 74). Cowan is more specific: 'That the kings Richard II and Henry V are entirely different sorts of rulers almost every reader will acknowledge; but that kingship itself is a very different sort of thing in the two plays is less often argued. The world of Richard is ceremonial, chivalric, medieval, poetic, essentially static; whereas the world of Henry is pragmatic, modern, competitive, dynamic. The King in one is God's steward, in the other a man among men' ('God Will Save the King', 87). Rabkin, on the other hand, contends that *Richard II* is a tragedy, not because of what in particular it depicts, but simply because it partakes of Shakespeare's general view of politics: 'Every political play that he wrote, without exception, shows the state in crisis.... And because politics is the art of managing

the social world in which we live and attempting to solve its insoluble problems, Shakespeare's politics is tragic. . . . Shakespeare's politics is tragic precisely because he will not allow us the luxury of evading action, because he shows us why we must act in history, and err' (*Shakespeare and the Common Understanding*, 81).

27. Obviously, the Bishop means to bring to mind the words of Jesus: 'Every kingdom divided against itself is brought to naught, and every city or house divided against itself shall not stand' (Matthew 12:25, as per the Geneva text). Despite the scriptural authority for Carlisle's jeremiad, Cowan plausibly contends, 'It is from his moral wisdom that the Bishop gives this impassioned warning rather than from a religious conviction that God will punish the sinners who oppose Richard. Raising "this house against this house" will prove the "woefullest division" that man has ever known—because of the nature of man and of society, not because of God's vengeance' ('God Will Save the King', 78).

28. The popularity of Henry's usurpation was attested by his reception as he travelled to London with Richard as his prisoner. According to Holinshed:

> He was received with all the joy and pompe that might be of the Londoners, and was lodged in the bishops palace, by Paules church. It was a woonder to see what great concursse of people, & what number of horsses came to him on the waie as he thus passed the countries, till his coming to London, where (upon his approach to the citie) the mayor rode foorth to receive him, and a great number of other citizens. Also the cleargie met him with procession, and such joy appeared in the countenances of the people, uttering the same also with word, as the like not lightlie beene seene. For in everie towne and village where he passed, children rejoised, women clapped their hands, and men cried out for joy. But to speake of the great numbers of people that flocked together in the fields and streets of London at his comming, I here omit; neither will I speake of the presents, and welcommings, lauds, and gratfications made to him by the citizens and communaltie. (Bullough, 405)

29. Salisbury enters at 3.2.64. Since *Richard II* is entirely in verse, stichometric analysis is a valid adjunct of interpretation (although the absence of the 'Deposition Scene' from the early quartos distorts the results with respect to those texts—to say nothing of its impoverishing the play both dramatically and philosophically). By line count, the exact centre (line 3.2.70) falls in the middle of Salisbury's report, which occurs in the tenth of the nineteen scenes, as the text is divided in most modern editions (such as the Arden used here).

30. According to Holinshed (Bullough, 400), the force Salisbury was able to gather was no less than *forty thousand*! As for the inconsistency between Salisbury's 'twelve thousand' and Richard's 'twenty thousand', this may be meant to indicate something about Richard's state of mind, but I'm inclined to chalk it up to a compositor's error, the spelling of the two words being close enough for one to be misread in a handwritten manuscript. In any case, the discrepancy matters little to the plot, as on either number Richard's forces would be a match for Henry's (cf. 2.1.286).

31. Shakespeare has Worcester conveniently 'misremember' this fact in subsequently claiming that among Henry Bolingbroke's many strokes of good fortune

was Richard's being 'So long in his unlucky Irish wars / That *all in England* did repute him dead' (*1 Henry IV*, 5.1.53–54).

32. As Richard laments in captivity, 'Was this face the face / That every day under his household roof / Did keep ten thousand men?' (4.1.281–83). His foolish liberality is but one of several cardinal sins he commits, at least according to the gospel of Machiavelli (*The Prince*, chap. 16, para. 3):

> And so, if one wants to maintain a name for liberality among men, it is necessary not to leave out any kind of lavish display, so that a prince who has done this will always consume all of his resources in such deeds. In the end it will be necessary, if he wants to maintain a name for liberality, to burden the people extraordinarily, to be rigorous with taxes, and to do all those things that can be done to get money. This will begin to make him hated by his subjects, and little esteemed by anyone as he becomes poor; so having offended the many and rewarded the few with this liberality of his, he feels every least hardship and runs into risk at every slight danger. . . .
>
> And there is nothing that consumes itself as much as liberality: while you use it, you lose the capacity to use it; and you become either poor and contemptible or, to escape poverty, rapacious and hateful. Among all things a prince should guard against is being contemptible and hated, and liberality leads you to both.

I incline to the judgment of Wyndham Lewis in his well-named study, *The Lion and the Fox: The Rôle of the Hero in the Plays of Shakespeare*: 'Over all the plays of Shakespeare is the shadow of Machiavelli' (15).

33. According to the folio's stage directions, the King is accompanied by 'Gaunt, Bushy, Bagot, Green, & others'; the quarto text does not specify what 'nobles' accompany the King, but given their prominence in the rest of the play, it is natural to assume that these three are included.

34. Leggatt comments on the cavalier attitude Richard displays here and elsewhere in the play:

> Cheerfully admitting that his court has been too lavish, he comes up with ingenious ways of raising money—farming the realm, issuing blank charters—but what really counts is the casualness with which he talks of these things. . . . His airy manner is in itself a devastating criticism of him. . . . The flippant manner we glimpse in the first scene . . . deepens into shocking callousness at the impending death of Gaunt: 'Now put it, God, in the physician's mind / To help him to his grave immediately!' . . . The initial joke is in the manner of Richard III. But while that Richard's inhumanity was the result of a conscious philosophy and a controlled strategy, this one seems flippant and unthinking. The speed with which he seizes the estate as soon as he hears of Gaunt's death is tactless to the point of stupidity. (*Shakespeare's Political Drama*, 63)

Pierce also notes this about Richard's manner: 'His flippant cynicism with his coterie about his kinsman Bolingbroke and Gaunt (I.iv) is less evil than Richard III's ironic scorn at family bonds only because Richard II is weaker. He is an amateur playing at professional villainy' (*Shakespeare's History Plays*, 161).

35. I have left this last line attributed to Green, as per the quarto and followed by the 2nd Arden. The folio attributes it to Bushy, which makes little sense. The 3rd Arden editor gives it to Bagot on the grounds that it 'renders the dialogue more dramatic' in that 'the alteration preserves a psychological distinction between Bagot and his two friends, he being more insistent on taking leave than they' (290n147). Given the analysis I am presenting here, this editorial improvement is tempting—but for that reason is best resisted.

36. Scroop having arrived in the wake of Salisbury with a report of how throughout the land even the young and old flock to Bolingbroke's standard, Richard irately responds with the lines here quoted. He then misinterprets Scroop's ironic reply ('Peace they have made with him indeed'), and continues to disparage those 'villains, vipers damned without redemption / Dogs easily won [etc.]', then apparently differentiating the three favoured commoners (Bushy, Bagot, and Green) from the one noble (the Earl of Wiltshire), he characterizes them as 'Snakes, in my heart-blood warmed, that sting my heart! / Three Judases' (3.2.129–32). Realizing his mistake, Scroop urges the King to 'uncurse their souls. Their peace is made / With heads, and not with hands. Those whom you curse / Have felt the worst of death's destroying wound'. Apparently Scroop assumed that all four of those named were together, and so met the same fate. Aumerle, however, must have known otherwise, for he asks specifically, 'Is Bushy, Green, and the Earl of Wiltshire dead?' Scroop replies, 'Ay, all of them at Bristol lost their heads'. Because Aumerle did not initially leave with Richard but joined him later—thus old York had expected still to find him where and when he came to collect the Queen, only to be informed that his son had just left (2.2.86)—Aumerle may before sailing have learned the whereabouts of the three he named. And by the time that 'Bolingbroke / Hath seized the wasteful King', even gardeners are aware that 'the Earl of Wiltshire, Bushy, Green' have been 'plucked up, root and all' (3.4.52–55).

37. Notice, the Welsh captain does not tell Salisbury from *whom* he was 'well assured' that King Richard is dead. In fact, he may not know from whom the claim originated, but merely that it was passed on by a trusted friend, who heard it from another friend, who heard it from a 'reliable source'—the way rumours typically spread.

38. There is an intriguing claim in Holinshed (whence Shakespeare may have drawn inspiration) concerning 'what secret malice king Richard had conceived against the duke of Hereford being in exile, whereof the same Bagot had sent intelligence unto the duke into France, by one Roger Smart, who certified it to him by Piers Buckton, and others, to the intent he should the better have regard to himselfe' (Bullough, 410).

39. According to Anthony Steel's history of Richard's reign (*Richard II*), 'Bagot managed to escape from Bristol into Cheshire, where he was captured but ultimately pardoned, though not for some years' (265). The 3rd Arden editor (Forker) asserts that Bagot 'escaped to Ireland after Bolingbroke's invasion and, although later arrested, was released' (*Richard II*, 176n12). This squares with the account in Shakespeare's primary source, Holinshed ('Bagot got him to Chester, and so escaped into Ireland'; Bullough, 398). But Shakespeare uses his source materials

rather freely when subordinating strict historical accuracy better serves his dramatic and philosophical purposes. One example, previously mentioned, is his transforming Richard's Queen from a ten-year-old child into a mature woman. Another is his portraying Henry (contra Holinshed) as having embarked to return to England even *before* his father had died. Still another is his treating the Duchess of York as the natural mother of Aumerle (she was his stepmother, though Shakespeare may have been unaware of this), and as her and York's only child (whereas Aumerle had a younger brother, Richard, of whom Shakespeare was fully aware, since he figures as one the trio of traitors executed in *Henry V*; 2.0.23).

40. These details of the text have obviously confused Geoffrey Bullough (354), among others, including the 2nd Arden editor, Peter Ure, who supposes from what Henry says at 2.3.163–64 that Bagot is in fact placed at Bristol, contrary to his announced intention (at 2.2.140) to head for Ireland; and so Ure accounts for this imaginary contradiction as 'due to sheer carelessness' on Shakespeare's part (78)—and this despite there being no Bagot to be executed along with Bushy and Green once Henry actually arrives at Bristol (3.1.2)! And Ure presumes that Henry's reference to Glendower was merely for the sake of adding 'a bit of local colour', since 'the suggestion that Bolingbroke fought Glendower in 1399 is unhistorical'; he adds that Shakespeare may have had a confused recollection of subsequent events Holinshed recounts (93). But Shakespeare makes no such 'suggestion', and gets the history right in the following play (*1 Henry IV*). The speech he here provides Henry has an altogether different purpose, as I hope my analysis makes clear.

41. I have discussed this relationship at some length in the final section of my earlier Shakespeare book, *Of Philosophers and Kings*, 251–68.

42. *The Prince*, chap. 18, para. 3, 69.

43. Holinshed: 'whereby it was evident, that the king meant [Bolingbroke's] utter undoing' (Bullough, 395). It would seem that Shakespeare has chosen the case of Richard II to provide a powerful validation of one of Machiavelli's most important pieces of advice to a prince, derived from one of his most notorious claims about ordinary human nature: 'But above all, [the prince] must abstain from the property of others, because men forget the death of a father [!] more quickly than the loss of a patrimony' (*The Prince*, chap. 17, para. 4). The fact that Richard's seizure of Bolingbroke's rightful inheritance is not really what provokes the latter's illegal return from exile *in Shakespeare's version* (a point that doubtless escapes many of its viewers and readers, and is a clear departure from Holinshed's account) does not affect its disturbing implications for the rest of England's propertied class. As the historian M. H. Keen writes, in *England in the Later Middle Ages*:

> To many who were already alarmed by the novel courses of Richard's government the seizure of the Lancastrian estates seemed the last straw. No man or family appeared to be secure in his property; the sacred right of inheritance was threatened. Lampoons and satires on the courtiers bore witness to a wave of popular resentment, and wild rumours were beginning to circulate. Richard was planning to make Dublin his capital and to tyrannize his English subjects from a distance; unheard of taxes were to be imposed; noblemen were going to be murdered and their estates farmed by Wiltshire for the king's profit. (269)

44. For an insightful analysis of why this is so, see Jensen, 'Beggars and Kings', 115–20.

45. If he is to be taken at his word, Henry was certainly lion enough to shed blood if success required it, expressly threatening to 'lay the summer's dust with showers of blood / Rained from the wounds of slaughter'd Englishmen' (3.3.43–44). And to be sure, Richard's prophecy of great bloodshed 'ere the crown [Henry] looks for live in peace' is ultimately fulfilled during Henry's troubled reign (as depicted in the two succeeding plays of the tetralogy). But this should not obscure his minimizing the violence with which he dispossessed a legitimate king.

46. In his account of language, Hobbes specifies four 'Speciall uses of Speech', the third of which is 'to make known to others our wills, and purposes, that we may have the mutuall help of one another' (*Leviathan*, chap. 4, para. 3). Bolingbroke's solicitation of allies to assist him in securing his Lancastrian inheritance would seem an apt illustration. Thus Northumberland: 'The noble Duke hath sworn his coming is / But for his own; and for the right of that / We all have strongly sworn to give him aid. / And let him never see joy that breaks that oath!' (2.3.148–51; cf. 3.3.104–14). To each of his special uses, Hobbes specifies 'foure correspondent Abuses'. Thus, to the third use corresponds 'when by words they declare that to be their will, which is not' (*Leviathan*, chap. 4, para. 4). Again, Bolingbroke provides the perfect example (3.3.196–99).

47. *The Prince*, chap. 18, para. 6.

48. As Norman Rabkin writes in *Shakespeare and the Common Understanding*, '*Richard II* is all problem':

> Written in a day so close to insurrection that its performance had to be blocked by the state, . . . Shakespeare's first mature essay into the mimesis of historical crisis could hardly have been anything but problematic.
>
> As always, the problem shapes the structure of the play. The question that *Richard II* poses is the question of what to do about a king whose continuance on the throne is essential to the continued order of a state governed by hereditary monarchy, but who is manifestly unfit personally for what is required of him. . . .
>
> In one respect *Richard II* sets the terms for all the political plays Shakespeare will write after it: political success, defined in whatever terms the play's situation requires, will always be complementary to qualities of the human spirit incompatible with it. Shakespeare does not scorn such success—the harmonious commonwealth is an ideal he teaches us to value as few other writers do—but he makes us fully aware of the cost of achieving it. (188–89, 95)

49. Plato, *Republic*, 412c–414b. Precisely what is meant in this context by 'strongest' or 'most powerful' is a taxing question in its own right, as it is neither reducible to nor independent of the other two qualities (prudence and patriotism); and for it to be analytically meaningful, it must be distinguished from the strength or power inherent in controlling the levers of political rule (cf. 338c–d).

50. Cf. ibid., 346e–347d, 519c–520e.

51. Since most people *do* regard ruling as a privilege, but disagree as to the relevant grounds on which it is rightly claimed, the *practical* problem for the political philosopher is that of designing a regime in which these various claims and concerns are given some recognition, and harmonized so far as possible. One such solution is the form of regime that Aristotle simply calls 'regime' (*politeia*); cf. *Politics*, 1282b14–1284a2.

52. *Republic*, 347b; Hobbes, *Leviathan*, chap. 10, para. 7.

53. Cf. *Republic*, 431d–e, 433c, 434b, 521a–b; Aristotle, *Politics*, 1281a12–38, 1302a17–34.

54. A version of the problem is implicit in Hobbes's distinction between 'worth' and 'worthiness':

> WORTHINESSE, is a thing different from the worth, or value of a man; and also from his merit, or desert; and consisteth in a particular power, or ability for that, whereof he is said to be worthy: which particular ability, is usually named FITNESS, or *Aptitude.*
>
> For he is Worthiest to be a Commander, to be a Judge, or to have any other charge, that is best fitted, with the qualities required to the well discharging of it; and Worthiest of Riches, that has the qualities most requisite for the well using of them; . . . Again, a man may be Worthy of Riches, Office, and Employment, that neverthelesse, can plead no right to have it before another; and therefore cannot be said to merit or deserve it. For Merit praesupposeth a right, and that the thing deserved is due by promise. (*Leviathan*, chap. 10, paras. 53–54)

To illustrate with the simplest example: in a democracy, the loser of an election may be objectively the worthiest candidate, but that confers no right to be acknowledged the 'rightful/legitimate' ruler.

55. Here one might object that, since civil peace and stability are obviously political concerns of first importance, they should figure in the philosopher's supposedly rational determination of objective criteria of legitimacy in the first place. However, the concern for producing and maintaining civil peace only arises as a separate consideration because the criteria derived strictly from a rational analysis of the task of ruling well do not suffice to produce subjective legitimacy in the vast majority of the ruled—this being a measure of the difference between a philosopher and everyone else. And this fact, the insufficiency of the rational criteria to be broadly persuasive and easily applied, must be registered in order to understand why the practical problem of political legitimacy is complicated, and not perfectly solvable even 'in principle', much less in practice.

56. If there is one major respect in which Shakespeare saw in English political history a challenge to the wisdom of Machiavelli, it is in regard to this, the infamous Florentine's most infamous (albeit commonly misunderstood) claim: 'and in the actions of all men, and especially of princes, where there is no court to appeal to, one looks to the end. So let a prince win and maintain his state: the means will always be judged honorable, and will be praised by everyone' (*The Prince*, chap. 18, para. 6, 71). As Shakespeare's two tetralogies seem designed to show, establishing stable rule isn't that simple. Indeed, he portrays England in

the fifteenth century as practically a laboratory for investigating the problem. Thus, I agree with Paul Cantor, in 'Shakespeare's *Henry V*: From the Medieval to the Modern World', that Shakespeare 'found the phenomenon of a new prince more problematic than Machiavelli did', and that 'the disjunction between political legitimacy and political power—between a genuine claim to rule and a genuine ability to rule—is a formula for tragedy throughout Shakespeare's political plays, and especially his English histories'.

57. Consequently, the challenge for distinctly *political* philosophy is that of determining which compromise is best: which is simply and absolutely best, given the most felicitous circumstances; and which is best relative to various particular sets of lesser circumstances.

58. Spiekerman concludes, 'Richard's fate, simply put, is a direct consequence of his belief in his divine right to rule, which *causes* him to abuse his power and renders him *unable* to maintain it' (*Shakespeare's Political Realism*, 70; my emphases). In the absence of a strictly deterministic psychology, I find this a bit *too* 'simply put'— as if all this would necessarily be so with any ruler who believed he was divinely chosen to rule—and thus is not sufficiently appreciative of the cunning with which Bolingbroke secretly engineers Richard's inability to defend himself. While I agree with most of his analysis of the play, and particularly with much of his criticism of the divine right doctrine, I believe Spiekerman oversimplifies the problem of legitimacy by (in effect) making this doctrine the real villain of the piece: 'Divine right provides the curious combination of the highest political principles with the lowest practical result' (73). Would one wish to say this about King Solomon? 'The Bishop of Carlisle gives the briefest statement of the perfect insularity divine right affords the king: "what subject can give sentence on his king / And who sits here that is not Richard's subject?"' (73). Before one accepts this damning indictment of divine right doctrine for the 'absolutism' with which it insulates the sovereign, one should recall that, on the surface, this is also Hobbes's teaching, based solely on natural laws that (according to him) are themselves simply dictates of *reason* (cf. *Leviathan*, chap. 18, paras. 6–7).

Hobbes, however, is not only a truly *political* philosopher of the first rank, but moreover a writer of unsurpassed cleverness. He confronts his readers with a comprehensive paradox that goes unnoticed by most of them. For while he spends some twenty chapters establishing that there are no legitimate bases on which a subject can object to the quality of a sovereign's rule (not conscience, not private property, not breach of contract, not whatever)—since to do so is flirting with rebellion, hence with the chaos of civil war, hence with a return to the state of mere Nature where every man is enemy to every man, etc., etc.—he then spends ten chapters providing the one thing needful for doing that very thing: a template for judging the quality of a sovereign's rule. I have explored the implications of this and dozens of other wonders of this amazing book in *The Platonian Leviathan*.

59. Allan Bloom succinctly states the core issue of the play:

> In spite of what some critics say, there can be little doubt that Shakespeare teaches us that Richard is a sort of legitimate tyrant who deserves to be deposed. Moreover, he chooses to present the divine right of kings as the underpinning of Richard's rule and thereby teaches us that the principle

is responsible for his tyrannical deeds. Richard never understands the real conditions of rule and believes he is unaccountable. This does not mean that Shakespeare holds there to be nothing divine in kingship; nor does it mean that Shakespeare believed that once Richard's undisputed title to rule vanishes, there could ever be an unproblematic legitimacy in this world. But that is precisely the burden of the play: legitimacy is a problem, and Richard, God's vicar, is an artificial contrivance which disguises rather than resolves the problem. ('*Richard II*', 59–60)

60. Speaking more precisely, it might rather be called 'The Tudor-Stuart Doctrine', since 'divine right' per se only became *expressly* invoked well over a century after the events depicted in this play (which, not incidentally, provides such a devastating exposé of the doctrine's liabilities). In this respect, attributing to Richard and other characters a belief in the doctrine amounts to an anachronism. But it is a harmless anachronism inasmuch as something very like this doctrine had been *implicit* in the legitimizing of English kings for centuries. Thus, Shakespeare's having various characters articulate their belief that legitimate kings rule through the grace of God does not misrepresent history, and doing so allows for the general problem of legitimacy to be more clearly focused for purpose of analysis.

61. When Bolingbroke appeals Mowbray before the King, his principal accusation concerns his uncle Gloucester's death, that Mowbray:

> ... like a traitor coward,
> Sluiced out his innocent soul through streams of blood—
> Which blood, like sacrificing Abel's, cries
> Even from the tongueless caverns of the earth
> To me for justice and rough chastisement.
> And by the glorious worth of my descent,
> This arm shall do it, or this life be spent!
> (1.1.102–8)

Richard is bound to be both stung and threatened by this accusation, presuming he fully understands himself to be Henry's real target (as he surely does).

62. Hobbes reasons as follows in *Leviathan*, chap. 15, paras. 26–28:

> But some things there be, that can neither be divided, nor enjoyed in common. Then, The Law of Nature, which prescribeth Equity, requireth, *That the Entire Right; or else, (making the use alternate,) the First Possession, be determined by Lot.* For equall distribution is of the Law of Nature; and other mean of equall distribution cannot be imagined.
>
> Of *Lots* there be two sorts, *Arbitrary,* and *Naturall.* Arbitrary, is that which is agreed on by the Competitors: Naturall, is either *Primogeniture,* (which the Greek calls $K\lambda\eta\rho\text{o}\nu\text{o}\mu\text{í}\alpha$, which signifies, *Given by Lot*;) or *First Seizure.*
>
> And therefore those things which cannot be enjoyed in common, nor divided, ought to be adjudged to the First Possessor; and in some cases to the First-Borne, as acquired by Lot.

In the marginal annotations, distribution by Lot is identified as the thirteenth Law of Nature, both Primogeniture and First Seizing as the fourteenth.

63. The one complication—whether primogeniture is understood as restricted to male heirs (e.g., as according to the so-called Salic law) or whether a claim to the royal power can be conveyed via a female line—turns out to figure prominently in the disputes that trouble the final century of Plantagenet rule.

64. Hobbes, a proponent of rational kingship, has thought through its practical problems more rigorously than have most of its critics. He addresses this particular objection in *Leviathan*, chap. 19, para. 9:

> It is an inconvenience in Monarchie, that the Soveraigntie may descend upon an Infant, or one that cannot discerne between Good and Evill: and consisteth in this, that the use of his Power, must be in the hands of another Man, or some Assembly of men, which are to governe by his right, and in his name; as Curators, and Protectors of his Person, and Authority.... And then the Law of Nature hath provided this sufficient rule, That the Tuition shall be in him, that hath by Nature most interest in the preservation of the Authority of the Infant, and to whom least benefit can accrue by his death, or diminution. For seeing every man by nature seeketh his own benefit, and promotion; to put an Infant into the power of those that can promote themselves by his destruction, or dammage, is not Tuition, but Trechery.

65. The fact that here Shakespeare departs from his historical source (Holinshed) in order to cast Henry as scheming to return even *before* the death of his father also serves to emphasize the pattern of crucial events dependent on timing.

66. Thus Machiavelli's *The Prince*, chap. 25, para. 2: 'he is prosperous who adapts his mode of proceeding to the qualities of the times; and similarly, he is unprosperous whose procedure is in discord with the times.... And so the cautious man, when it is time to be impetuous, does not know how to do it, hence comes to ruin: for if he would change his nature with the times and with affairs, his fortune would not change' (99–100).

67. Conquest is the actual origin of most commonwealths, as Hobbes implicitly shows in chapter 20 of his *Leviathan*, '*Of Dominion* PATERNALL *and* DESPOTICALL' (cf. *Platonian Leviathan*, chap. 19). In his 'Review and Conclusion', Hobbes is again explicit: 'Conquest, is not the Victory it self; but the Acquisition by Victory, of a Right, over the persons of men.... He that is taken, and put into prison, or chaines, is not Conquered, though Overcome; for he is still an Enemy, and may save himself if hee can: But he that upon promise of Obedience, hath his life and liberty allowed him, is then Conquered, and a Subject; and not before' (para. 7).

According to Francis Bacon's history of Henry VII, the Right of Conquest was one strand on which Henry Tudor claimed legitimacy after defeating the last Plantagenet, Richard III, at the Battle of Bosworth Field. The other two were his own (questionable) lineage via the Beaufort line of John of Gaunt's Lancastrian descendants, reinforced by his marriage to the daughter of Edward IV of the Yorkist line (supposedly bringing together the red rose and the white); and ratification of his succession by act of Parliament.

68. The first line of the 'Introduction' to his *Leviathan*. I have discussed the radical implications of this conflation of art and nature in chapter 18 of *The Platonian Leviathan*.

69. Hobbes contends that this is also the basis of God's authority, hence of divine right: 'To those therefore whose Power is irresistible, the dominion of all men adhaereth naturally by their excellence of Power; and consequently it is from that Power, that the Kingdome over men, and the Right of Afflicting men at his pleasure [as, e.g., He did Job], belongeth Naturally to God Almighty; not as Creator, and Gracious; but as Omnipotent' (*Leviathan*, chap. 31, para. 5).

70. The problems with both divine right and natural force (or conquest) as bases of legitimacy are further illuminated by comparing them with the view that has now almost entirely replaced them: that legitimacy derives from the consent of the governed, expressed periodically in free elections. There can be no question but that this doctrine has proven successful, and is a great political accomplishment; there are at least a dozen important democracies in which it is practically inconceivable that any significant faction would even attempt to unseat by extralegal means the duly elected leaders, much less succeed in doing so. But several further observations are pertinent. (1) The most stable of these polities have had their democratic institutions in place for a long time, and so benefit from tradition, custom, and habit as well as from the explicit rationale justifying this conception of legitimacy. (2) All avail themselves of such additional support as is provided by ceremonies, pledges of allegiance, symbols, modes of respectful address, etc. And there may be other cultural and historical factors that contribute to the success of these regimes. Recent history provides a plethora of evidence that simply instituting democratic forms and procedures does *not*, in itself, establish more or less immediately such a powerful subjective legitimacy as to place the supposed 'people's choice' beyond challenge. (3) The very flexibility that contributes so much to the strength of this conception—that everyone knows there *is* an orderly and fairly expeditious way to change rulers: periodic elections, hence there is no need to resort to violence—undercuts somewhat the 'majesty' with which such leaders are viewed. They come and they go; here today, gone tomorrow. Some of the consequences of this are not salutary. (4) Official rationale to the contrary notwithstanding, the gulf between legitimate rule and good rule remains (and in my opinion, increasingly widens).

71. Cf. Hobbes, *Leviathan*, chap. 38, para. 1.

72. Leggatt notes how Richard accelerates his own undoing: 'As though trying to keep control even of his ruin, Richard falls faster than anyone can push him. He anticipates moves against him before they have been made' (*Shakespeare's Political Drama*, 66).

73. As everyone knows who has ever seriously tried, accounting for the *natural* basis of all human power is one of the more challenging problems for political philosophy. And in the absence of such an account, claims such as Thrasymachus's are empty tautologies (that justice is merely the advantage of the stronger, by which he means the rulers who make the laws; *Republic*, 338c–339b). To understand the constituents of the *natural* power or strength which underlie the gaining and sustaining of *political* power, one might consult Hobbes's analysis in *Leviathan*, chap. 10, paras. 1–15.

74. For a detailed exposition of this important aspect of the play, see Jensen, 'Beggars and Kings', 129–38.

75. I have more fully discussed the psychical implications of Sokrates's radical political innovations—profoundly paradoxical as applied to the regime of his city, but not at all paradoxical when applied to that of the soul (cf. 368d–e)—in *The War Lover: A Study of Plato's 'Republic'*, 233–44. Cf. also Nietzsche, *Beyond Good and Evil*, aph. 9.

76. Richard's 'how sour sweet music is' is a concluding instance of a curious linguistic feature of this play: the frequency with which these terms figure: 'sweet' (23 times) and 'sour' (9)—often, as here, directly juxtaposed. Gaunt's 'Things sweet to taste prove in digestion sour' (1.3.236) might serve as a summary observation concerning his son Bolingbroke's usurpation. And bearing in mind Henry's future relations with the Northumberland clan, one can see a special pertinence to Scroop's observation that 'Sweet love' may turn to 'the sourest and most deadly hate' (3.2.135–36).

77. Even the report of Richard's former groom, of how the well-named horse Barbary now bears Henry as proudly as it ever bore Richard—much as the fickle public that once cheered Richard now cheers Henry (5.5.77–92, 5.2.7–30; note esp. l.36)—contains an echo of Plato. For the Platonic Sokrates explicitly likened the polity itself to a large noble horse, and implicitly likened competent rulers to expert riders and trainers (*Apology*, 30e, 25b; cf. *Republic*, 328a, 335b–c, 601c).

E. K. Chambers is one of a small minority of Shakespeare scholars who recognises the Platonic character of Shakespeare's political thought. As he wrote in some introductory comments to his edition of *Richard II* (published in 1891; as quoted in Coyle, *Critical Guide to Richard II*):

> At bottom Shakespeare is always a student, and these plays are the outcome of a student's reflection on grave questions concerning the well-being of a nation. For Shakespeare, as for Thucydides, History becomes at once a judgment of the past and a forecast of the future; no longer merely a tale of 'forgotten, far off things', it is an 'eternal possession', and a potent factor in determining the conduct of life. Thus *Richard II* and the rest are studies in kingship, wherein, to those who can read, the poet has laid bare his mind upon the problems of government in the form which they appeared to our ancestors. His answer to them is one which Plato might have applauded. He finds the true foundation of regal authority neither in an imaginary divine right nor in the will of a parliamentary assembly: the genuine king and leader of men is he who best understands and sympathizes with the needs and aspirations of his people, and is best fitted to guide them in the working out of their proper destiny. . . .
>
> On the delineation of Richard all the resources of Shakespeare's genius have been poured: it is a work of art and love. We have presented to us the portrait of a finely tempered man, gifted and graced in mind and body. He 'looks like a king' for beauty and majesty, with his fair face in which the blood comes and goes. His marvellous wealth of eloquent imaginative speech irradiates the play. . . . This beautiful, cultured king, for all his delicate halftones of feeling and thought, is a being devoid of moral sense, treacherous,

unscrupulous, selfish; he murders his uncle, robs his cousin, and oppresses his people; he trails the fair name of England in the dust; even in the days of his captivity he regrets his follies, but scarcely regards his crimes. It is not in moral sense only that he is deficient, but in moral and intellectual fibre; like Plato's 'musical man' he has 'piped away his soul with sweet and plaintive melodies' [cf. *Republic*, 411a–b].... In prosperity he yields himself to flatterers; in adversity he puts an idle confidence in a supposed God-given commission to reign. (96–97, 99)

Chapter Two

1. Many would second Schlegel's flat declaration that 'Falstaff is the crown of Shakspeare's [*sic*] comic invention', that he is 'the most agreeable and entertaining knave that was ever portrayed'. Hazlitt largely agreed, suggesting that 'the character of Falstaff . . . is perhaps the most substantial comic character that ever was invented'. Like Schlegel, Hazlitt provides a plausible analysis of what makes Falstaff so endearing, on which basis he concludes, 'we never could forgive the Prince's treatment of Falstaff' (both authors as quoted in Bate, *Romantics on Shakespeare*, 360).

2. Christopher Allmand begins his well-regarded biography, *Henry V*, by observing, 'The historian can be more confident about the place which witnessed the birth of the boy who would one day become Henry V than he can be about its date. He was born, as a financial document of Henry VI's reign informs us, in the chamber of the gatehouse tower of Monmouth castle. . . . As to the date, there is no absolute certainty about it, although either 9 August or 16 September always features. The year, however, remains unresolved: was it 1386 or 1387?' (7).

3. Mary was the younger of the two heiresses of Humphrey de Bohun, Earl of Hereford and Essex. The elder, Eleanor, was married to young Bolingbroke's uncle, Thomas of Woodstock (Duke of Gloucester, eventually murdered on the orders of Richard II, as his widowed Duchess complains so bitterly to brother Gaunt in the second scene of *Richard II*). According to Bruce, Woodstock had attempted to acquire the entire Bohun estate by persuading Mary to enter a convent, but 'his intentions were speedily frustrated by Gaunt, who on 27 July 1380 bought Mary's marriage from the king for 5000 marks' (*Usurper King*, 24). It was by virtue of this marriage that Henry inherited the earldoms of Hereford and Northampton.

4. McFarlane, in *Lancastrian Kings and Lollard Knights*, judges that 'Henry V's . . . own library was for his time, rank and other tasks, remarkably well stored and, it was believed, much read. A list of 110 volumes in his possession at his death has been preserved; this includes much law, a good many of the fathers, Seneca's letters, Cicero's *Rhetoric*, some history, and some logic. But it does not exhaust the known content of his shelves'. He borrowed chronicles of the Crusades, and according to the poet Lydgate, Henry was 'given to the study of ancient histories'. According to McFarlane, 'His copy of Chaucer's *Troilus* still survives. Well-read, if not a scholar, Henry is the first king of England whose state papers, written in his own hand, have been preserved for us' (116–17). Moreover, these papers are always in English: 'Though he could read, write, and speak Latin and French—and that

for pleasure—Henry was the first king of England who preferred to conduct business in the vernacular and to encourage its use by others' (119).

5. Allmand, *Henry V*, 11. Particularly noteworthy is the fact that brother Humphrey, Duke of Gloucester, was the patron of Tito Livio, who in 1437–38 composed what might be regarded as the 'official' biography of Henry V, based as it was on material supplied by Humphrey. Thus it became the primary source for the main events of King Henry's life. Tito's work was translated into English in 1513, but by someone who blended into it other material from various sources, including most of the vignettes about Henry's wild youth. It is this augmented version of Tito's vita on which Holinshed relied.

6. Seward, *Henry V*, 4.

7. This is disputed by Juliet Barker, who rejects the contemporary French source that claims it (*Agincourt*, 385n14) and contends instead that 'he was one of the young men chosen for the customary honour of being knighted on the eve of the coronation. Knighthoods conferred on such occasions were highly prized because they occurred so rarely and because they were accompanied by unusual pageantry and religious ritual. The ceremony took place in the tower of London' (26).

8. According to the chronicle known as *The Brut* (began sometime after 1272, then extended to 1333, translated into English ca. 1400, with a second continuation written around 1430 which extends the account from 1377 to 1419), the twelve- or thirteen-year-old boy was distressed at the predicament of the captive king. Upon the occasion of this first meeting with his father after returning from Ireland, 'Henry, the son and heir of the said Duke, came to his father and knelt down before him and welcomed him, as he ought to do; and therewith his father charged [him] the next day to come from the king and wait upon him. Then this young knight Henry brought the king to his chamber with a sorrowful heart, for cause he should depart from his godfather and sovereign king, for he loved him entirely. . . . And so on the next day after, Henry took his leave of the king with a heavy heart and went to his father' (as quoted in McFarlane, *Lancastrian Kings and Lollard Knights*, 121).

9. Ibid., 121–22. Shakespeare may have surmised something to this effect from Holinshed's report of Henry V's reinterring Richard's body, as well as from Fabyan's *Chronicle*. Hence the prayer our philosopher-poet supplied Henry, which is almost entirely concerned with making amends for Richard's deposition and death (*Henry V*, 4.1.290–302).

10. Keen explains the special significance of this: 'Henry *viva voce* claimed the throne by blood and conquest; parliament ratified what had happened afterwards by recognising Henry's heir as heir to the throne' (*England*, 277). Nevertheless, as Keen observes, 'The usurpation injected into the political life of the kingdom a new and perilous force working in favour of disruption' (287). This was part of what Bolingbroke bequeathed to his successor: 'Henry V did, in fact, provide better government than Henry IV had, but before the period of his great successes he had to deal with an ugly legacy of disaffection from his father's time' (296).

11. Allmand, *Henry V*, 22–23.

12. There are enough similarities in the lives of Alexander of Macedon and Henry of Monmouth to suspect that Shakespeare means for his Captain Fluellen's comical comparison of Henry to 'Alexander the Pig' to suggest that a

valid comparison could be drawn—'if you mark Alexander's life well' (*Henry V*, 4.7.31)—despite the disparity of their achievements. This interpretive possibility is strengthened by other allusions to Alexander in *Henry V*, such as Canterbury's 'Turn him to any cause of policy / The Gordian knot of it he will unloose' (1.1.45–46; cf. 3.1.19). For not only did both Princes display remarkable military precocity at approximately the same early age, both were also entrusted with sovereign political responsibilities. Like Henry in Wales, Alexander at the age of sixteen was left in charge of Macedonia in his father's absence, and tasked with subduing the hill tribes on its northern border. And yet Alexander, like Henry, had an uneasy relationship with his father, which likewise was aggravated by Court intrigues. As a result of their subsequent achievements, both princes had to cope with ruling disparate peoples, and did so with tolerable success. In the course of achieving their respective conquests, both resorted to a similar policy; having given a city the option to submit or face utter destruction, each carried through his threat (Alexander at Thebes, Henry at Caen), with the result that subsequently threatened cities surrendered peacefully rather than suffer a like fate. And both kings died young—Alexander at age 33, Henry at 35 (or thereabouts)—whereupon their respective conquests began to unravel.

13. Seward, *Henry V*, 20.
14. According to Barker, the wound was serious indeed:

> A way had to be found of extracting the arrow that had entered his face on the left side of his nose. The shaft was successfully removed but the arrowhead remained imbedded six inches deep in the bone at the back of his skull. Various 'wise leeches' or doctors were consulted and advised 'drinks and other cures', all of which failed. In the end it was the king's surgeon, a convicted (but pardoned) coiner of false money, John Bradmore, who saved the prince and the day. He devised a small pair of hollow tongs the width of the arrowhead. . . . The wound had to be enlarged and deepened before the tongs could be inserted and this was done by means of a series of increasingly large and long probes made from 'the pith of old elder, well dried and well stitched in purified linen cloth'. When Bradmore judged that he had reached the bottom of the wound, he introduced the tongs at the same angle as the arrow had entered. . . . 'Then by moving it to and fro, little by little (with the help of God), I extracted the arrowhead'. He cleansed the wound by washing it out with white wine and placed into it new probes made of wads of flax soaked in a cleansing ointment, which he had prepared from an unlikely combination of bread sops, barley, honey and turpentine oil. These he replaced every two days with shorter wads until, on the twentieth day, he was able to announce with justified pride that 'the wound was perfectly well cleansed'. A final application of 'dark ointment' to regenerate the flesh completed the process.
>
> The pain the prince must have suffered in the course of this lengthy operation is unimaginable. (*Agincourt*, 29–30)

It is curious that the one portrait we have of Henry V is in the left profile, yet shows no sign of this wound. Of course, painters have been known to graciously ignore blemishes, and otherwise enhance the appearance of their subjects; most sitters would not insist, as reputedly did Cromwell, that they be painted warts and all.

15. Holinshed is not precise: 'The prince that daie holpe his father like a lustie young gentleman: for although he was hurt in the face with an arrow, so that diverse noble men that were about him, would have conveied him foorth of the field, yet he would not suffer them so to doo, least his departure from amongst his men might happilie have stricken some feare into their harts: and so without regard of his hurt, he continued with his men, & never ceassed, either to fight where the battle was most hot, or to incourage his men where it seemed most need' (Bullough, *Narrative and Dramatic Sources of Shakespeare,* vol. 4, 191; quotes from Holinshed's *Chronicles* in this chapter and those that follow are to this volume, and are cited simply as 'Bullough' followed by the page therein).

16. Allmand, *Henry V,* 26–27.

17. Financial difficulties plagued Henry throughout much of his reign: 'for the first six years... he was on the verge of bankruptcy. The customs on wool, the king's principal source of revenue, fell as low as £20,000 during 1402-7 compared with £46,000 during Richard II's reign. Henry's income averaged less than £90,000 a year—Richard's had averaged £116,000—and he needed at least £140,000 even in peacetime' (Seward, *Henry V,* 13). Cf. also Keen, *England,* 287–89.

18. Holinshed gives two versions of the Archbishop's capture; Shakespeare chose to use the morally more questionable one. See Bullough, 271–74.

19. Seward reports, 'The *Brut* says that the king was immediately smitten by leprosy, while miracles began to be worked at the archbishop's tomb. Only the papal schism saved the king from excommunication'. As he became ever more grossly disfigured, Henry himself came to share the view that he was being divinely punished (*Henry V,* 22, 27).

20. As Keen writes, 'After 1405, Henry IV never again had to face a full-scale domestic rebellion. His troubles were not by any means over yet, for Glendower in Wales was still dangerous; Harlech and Aberystwyth were still in rebel hands three years later. It was not till 1409 that it was clear the Welsh revolt was under control' (*England,* 286).

21. Allmand, *Henry V,* 33–34. Not surprisingly, then, the old rebel became a figure of legend. He is thought to have died ca. 1415, and is buried who knows where.

22. 'A close study of those in the Prince's service would show that the war was the cause for the entry of many into that service, as well as the reason for them remaining in it. It tells us something about the Prince that from an early age he liked soldiers whose loyalty he was ready to reward' (ibid., 36). Moreover, according to Barker, 'he was also prepared to promote Welshmen who had proved their worth and loyalty, despite parliamentary enactments to the contrary.... Talent, rather than status and connections, was the key to advancement in Henry's administration' (*Agincourt,* 32). Also, 'Within a few days of his accession, Henry dispatched Thomas, earl of Arundel to Wales with special powers to receive former rebels into the king's grace and to grant them pardons at his discretion. The results were spectacular'. So, for example, 'Six hundred inhabitants of Merionethshire appeared before Arundel admitting that they deserved death as traitors but asking for mercy; when he granted them a communal pardon on Henry's behalf, they fell on their knees and thanked God for the magnanimity of their king'. Henry had sworn to

provide 'equal justice for all in Wales. It was a policy that clearly won him friends in that principality, judging by the huge numbers of Welshmen who signed up for the Agincourt campaign' (46–47).

23. One of the best accounts of the Lancastrian dynasty, I believe, remains E. F. Jacob's *The Fifteenth Century: 1399–1485*. In it he offers the following summary judgment:

> By the time the prince returned to Westminster, Aberystwyth being securely in English hands again, he had learned something about garrisons left in semi-hostile territory and about victualing and maintaining outposts such as these. He had been able to judge of the inadequacy in Wales of short campaigns in force, fought with troops who, though salaried, were anxious to get home; he had learned the value of speed, and the importance of good supplies and had acquired some knowledge of siege-craft. By 1408 he had taken part in practically every important engagement; in 1406 he had been given command over the whole Welsh front, north and south Wales and the Marches, with power to receive and pardon all rebels, and his new command had brought him into touch with the best soldiers of his day . . . and with the knights on whom he had to rely for the administration and defence of the Marcher counties. (102–3)

Thus Jacob notes, 'the later dramatic figments, such as the Boar's Head tavern with all its engaging scallywags, will have to go. By 1413, the prince was already a hard-bitten leader with experience of campaigning under conditions where the personal influence of the commander rather than the cash at his disposal was responsible for holding the troops together; a leader with a shrewd knowledge of men and an important following among the nobility' (126).

24. Keen, *England*, 289. For all the challenges to Henry's legitimacy in the first decade of his reign, Keen notes, 'There is no hint of direct sympathy with Ricardian or March legitimism in the records of any of Henry IV's parliaments. The attitude of the commons reflects rather an as *per* opposite feeling, anxiety that the succession should be unequivocally entailed on Henry's descendants. Their attitude seems to have been rather like that of the later Elizabethan commons, who constantly petitioned the queen to marry or recognise a successor. The motivation in both cases was the same: fear of the civil disorder that might follow a disputed succession' (291).

25. Lady Swynford, ex-governess of Bolingbroke's sisters, mother of his 'Beaufort' half brothers, mistress and finally the wife of his father, John of Gaunt, Duke of Lancaster, must have been on good terms with his son. She reportedly had 'such a gift for organizing noble households that she was eventually in her old age . . . put in charge of the future Henry V's establishments' (Bruce, *Usurper King*, 45).

26. Barker, *Agincourt*, 17.

27. Prince Hal's favouritism towards the House of Burgundy would later pay major dividends when as King he laid claim to the throne of France—some hint of which Shakespeare provides in the final act of *Henry V*.

28. The Prince, according to Holinshed, 'got knowledge that certeine of his fathers servants were busie to give information against him, whereby discord

might arise betwixt him and his father: for they put into the kings head, not onelie what evill rule (according to the course of youth) the prince kept to the offense of manie: but also what great resort of people came to his house, so that the court was nothing furnished with such a traine as dailie followed the prince. These tales brought no small suspicion into the kings head, least his sonne would presume to usurp the crowne' (Bullough, 193). See also Jacob, *Fifteenth Century*, 115–16.

29. This was clearly intended as a thumb in King Henry's eye. Cf. Keen, *England*, 291.

30. When Hal became King, Thomas, Duke of Clarence, was the one member of their extended family that was never admitted to the inner circle of court; and far from enjoying favour, he was soon stripped of offices he had held under Henry IV. Barker writes: 'The manner of Clarence's death in 1421 mournfully demonstrated that he could not be trusted to act in the best interests of either the king or the kingdom. In his anxiety to outdo his brother's success at Agincourt, he overruled wiser and more experienced soldiers to attack a much larger French army without waiting for his archers to arrive. The resulting battle of Baugé was the greatest military disaster of Henry's reign' (*Agincourt*, 388n17).

31. Bruce, *Usurper King*, 57–58.

32. Bullough, 280.

33. As Peter Saccio succinctly observes, 'Henry came to the throne extensively experienced in politics, administration, and warfare: few kings have been so well trained for their job' (*Shakespeare's English Kings*, 66). 'Administration' should be emphasized, since it is overshadowed in popular esteem by his military talents. 'In complete contrast to his father, financial prudence, economy and strategic planning were to be his watchwords'. He took a personal hand in managing his assets in Cornwall and Chester, greatly increasing his net revenue from those sources; similarly, his reconquest of Wales produced a threefold increase from that region. 'Such financial wisdom could not help but endear the prince to the same parliaments that groaned over his father's mismanagement of money' (33).

34. Holinshed offers this summary of the Prince's life prior to becoming king:

> Thus were the father and sonne reconciled, betwixt whom the said pickthanks had sowne division, insomuch that the sonne upon a vehement conceit of unkindnesse sproong in the father, was in the waie to be worne out of favour. Which was the more likelie to come to passe, by their informations that privilie charged him with riot and other uncivill demeanor, unseemelie for a prince. Indeed he was youthfullie given, growne to audacitie, and had chosen him companions agreeable to his age [!]; with whome he spent the time in such recreations, exercises, and delights as he fansied. But yet (it should seeme by the report of some writers) that his behaviour was not offensive or at least tending to the damage of anie bodie; sith he had a care to avoid doing of wrong, and to tedder his affections within the tract of virtue, whereby he opened unto himself a redie passage of good liking among the prudent sort, and was beloved of such as could discerne his disposition, which was in no degree so excessive, as that he deserved in such vehement manner to be suspected. (Bullough, 195)

35. Seward, *Henry V*, 33. He continues, 'The otherwise hagiographic *Gesta* admits that, "Passing the bounds of modesty, he was the fervent soldier of Venus as well as of Mars; youthlike he was fired by her torches". . . . Yet there is no record of any bastards'.

> Prince Henry is supposed to have had other amusements, including the odd pastime of disguising himself and then beating up and robbing his own household officials though there is no mention of this before the sixteenth century. . . . We know that his brothers, Thomas and Humphrey, were involved in a midnight brawl at a tavern in Eastcheap where they were drinking on 23 June 1410 and the uproar was such that the mayor and the sheriffs had to be called to restore order; Thomas was involved in a similar disturbance the following year. Yet there is no evidence that Henry was ever Falstaff's 'good shallow young fellow'. (33)

David Hume credits the stories of the Prince's riotous living, and presumes that it was confined to the final two years of his father's reign when 'the active spirit of young Henry, restrained from its proper exercise, broke out in extravagances of every kind'. But Hume evidently based part of his understanding of Henry on Shakespeare's portrait. For example, that Henry retained his father's Chief Justice, William Gasgoigne, who had previously offended him; and that 'it was the dying injunction on the late king to his son' to (as Shakespeare has him express it) 'busy giddy minds / With foreign quarrels' (*History of England*, 2:352, 354, 358). According to McFarlane, however, Gascoigne was in fact promptly dismissed (*Lancastrian Kings and Lollard Knights*, 123). And there is no record of the dying king offering any advice to his heir other than that regarding his own haunting fear: 'that the struggle between himself and Richard would be repeated by his own two elder sons, Henry and Thomas'; accordingly, he warned the Prince of the dire consequences of allowing this to happen (Bruce, *Usurper King*, 221–22).

36. McFarlane, *Lancastrian Kings and Lollard Knights*, 123. One might add that much about the supposed life of Shakespeare is likewise of dubious authenticity—escapades 'remembered', or concocted, well after the famous philosopher-poet's death. Bullough provides a convenient summary of madcap escapades alleged of the Prince, and of what use Shakespeare made of them:

> The Chronicles, from Thomas Walsingham to Stow, described at least six legendary incidents relating to his misbehavior, most of them going back directly or indirectly to stories told by the 4th Earl of Ormonde and included by the English translator of Titus Livius's *Life of Henry V*: (1) the robbing of the Receivers; (2) the riot in Eastcheap; (3) the striking of the Lord Chief Justice and the committal of the Prince to prison; (4) the Prince's coming to Court strangely dressed and carrying a dagger; (5) the Prince's visit to his dying father during which he took away the Crown; (6) his dismissal of his former companions after the Coronation. To these *Famous Victories* added (7) the new King's commendation of the Lord Chief Justice . . . In the Chronicles the first three incidents took place at indefinite dates, the rest towards the end of Henry IV's reign when the King was already ill. Shakespeare made

some use of Nos. 1, 3, 5, 6, and 7, omitting for good reason to show the striking of the Lord Chief Justice or the dagger incident. (159–60)

True, Shakespeare did not *show* Hal assaulting the Lord Chief Justice, but it is several times referred to in part 2 of *Henry IV* (1.2.55–56, 93–96; 5.2.80).

37. Indeed, they had already shown their appeal in the popular potboiler from which Shakespeare appropriated several comic ideas and characters, *The Famous Victories of Henry the fifth*—author anonymous, registered (and presumably performed) some six years prior to the registration of Shakespeare's play. With respect to these borrowings, the comments of Bullough are apropos: 'It can hardly be doubted that in writing *Henry V* Shakespeare was affected both positively (to accept) and negatively (to reject and replace) material found in the original *Famous Victories*. But he transmuted almost everything that he touched' (349). More to the point, Shakespeare subsumed all these comical escapades under Hal's strategy for dealing with the 'legitimacy' problem he anticipated inheriting.

38. For instance, as Bullough notes, 'Shakespeare does not let Prince Henry pursue Glendower into the mountains and bring about his downfall. His Prince is too busy with Falstaff and the Percies for that. In fact, Prince Henry had been nominally governor of North Wales and the Marches since 1400, when he was only thirteen, and Henry Hotspur was chief of his Council. . . . Shakespeare thus diminishes the importance of Glendower and with it the administrative experience of Prince Hal, who during his father's illness acted as head of the King's ministers in 1410 and was so energetic that the poet Hoccleve, who had a post in the Council office, urged him not to hold business meetings on holy-days' (165–66).

39. In disputing this claim, some might cite Shakespeare's villainous portrayal of Richard III as similarly 'fictitious'. But in that case, he chose to follow his sources (Thomas More, Hall, Holinshed, etc.), arguably the best available, with tolerable fidelity. Thus, Ricardians' quarrel with this portrayal is not in the first instance with Shakespeare, though they may rightly insist that it is he who has so indelibly imprinted it in people's minds.

40. The text of *King Henry IV Part One* used throughout is the 3rd Arden edition, David Scott Kastan, ed. *1 Henry IV* was a hit from the start. As Peter Ackroyd, in *Shakespeare: The Biography*, observes, 'the presence of Falstaff rendered [the *Henry IV*] plays so popular [that] the first part of *Henry IV* was reprinted more frequently than any other of Shakespeare's plays, . . . with three reprintings in the first year of publication' alone. But no serious textual issues have resulted from all these editions, as the second and third printings of the 1598 quarto are the basis of all the rest. In his editorial introduction, Kastan notes about the production of these two, 'considerable care for the text is . . . evident' (109); moreover, 'the manuscript [from which they were set] seems to have been unusually clean' (117).

41. Shakespeare has Worcester call attention to this nickname's particular suitability: 'My nephew's trespass may well be forgot; / It hath the excuse of youth and heat of blood, / And an adopted name of privilege; / A hare-brained hotspur governed by a spleen' (5.2.16–19). Casting Henry Percy Jr. as roughly an age-mate of Prince Hal—whereas in reality he was actually a couple of years older than Hal's father—is another liberty the philosopher-poet has taken with factual history in the name of a higher purpose, at once dramatic and philosophic.

42. Accordingly, not a few writers register disapproval of Henry for what they interpret as the implicit duplicity in his relations with the Boar's Head crew. J. A. R. Marriot doubtless speaks for many who would have preferred being allowed to take the comic scenes at face value:

> Henry V is the son of the 'vile politician' Bolingbroke. A vein of 'policy' and calculation runs through his character and distinguishes his career. He reveals the hereditary taint (if taint it be) quite plainly in his first soliloquy' (140). Most people, I think, will feel that this revelation ... is not quite an agreeable one. We had hoped that the riotous fun with Falstaff was wholly spontaneous; sheer high spirit without a touch of vice; ebullient enjoyment of the priceless gifts of youth and physical well-being. But alas! it is, after all, shrewd political calculation worthy of a vile politician like his father. . . . The self-consciousness of the first soliloquy seems to take the edge off the Falstaff scenes. (*English History in Shakspeare*, 141)

A. C. Bradley likewise regards this as grounds for criticizing the Prince:

> Henry IV. describes him as the noble image of his own youth; and, for all his superiority to his father, he is still his father's son, the son of a man whom Hotspur called 'a vile politician'. . . . Just as he went to war chiefly because, as his father told him, it was a way to keep factious nobles quiet and unite the nation, . . . this same strain of policy is what Shakespeare marks in the first soliloquy in *Henry IV.*, where the prince describes his riotous life as a mere scheme to win him glory later. It implies that readiness to use other people as a means to his own ends which is a conspicuous feature in his father; and it reminds us of his father's plan of keeping himself out of people's sight. (*Oxford Lectures on Poetry*, 257)

43. Cf. Leggatt's analysis:

> Hal's promise to imitate the sun takes us back to *Richard II*; but while Richard, as rightful king, was naturally identified with the sun, Hal can only promise to *imitate* it—to produce, as his father did, a good performance in the role of king. In that admission there is a satisfying honesty, and the rest of the speech has the same clear-eyed quality. . . . Timing, the essential art of the actor, [is] the art of knowing when to make one's move. . . . Hal is not explicit about when he plans to make his self-revelation. . . . But he knows that for his strategy to work he must move 'when men think least I will', exploiting the element of surprise. (*Shakespeare's Political Drama*, 89)

44. Cf. Plato, *Republic*, 580b–c.

45. Here Shakespeare's liberties with the historical time line contribute to various confusions. First, that the period during which the Prince was altogether at leisure to lead a dissipated lifestyle—if ever he did—was during the last eighteen months of Henry IV's reign, after he had been replaced on the

council by his brother Thomas (i.e., late 1411). And yet because this development is treated as having preceded the Battle of Shrewsbury (July 1403), one is left with the impression that Hal behaved as Shakespeare portrays him throughout most his father's reign.

46. The word 'persona' comes from Latin, and it originally meant a 'mask' such as that worn by actors in Greek and Roman drama, whence it is extended to mean a role played by any actor or representative, or by anyone playing a part. Thus Hobbes: 'And from the Stage, hath been translated to any Representer of speech and action, as well in Tribunalls, as Theaters. So that a *Person*, is the same that an *Actor* is, both on the Stage and in common Conversation; and to *Personate*, is to *Act*, or *Represent* himselfe, or an other; and he that acteth another, is said to beare his Person, or act in his name' (*Leviathan*, chap. 16, para. 3). The Lord Chief Justice exemplifies the idea in defending himself before now King Henry V for having committed then Prince Hal to prison for having struck 'The image of the King whom I presented' while 'in my very seat of judgment': 'I then did use the person of your father; / The image of his power lay then in me' (*2 Henry IV*, 5.2.73–74, 79–80).

47. As is well known, here Shakespeare was misled by his sources, who were confused by there being two 'Edmund Mortimers'. The fifth Earl of March, designated heir of Richard, was a child at this time, and safely held in the King's custody. Hotspur's brother-in-law is this child's uncle, after whom he was named; this Edmund Mortimer died in 1409, either during or shortly after the English siege of Harlech.

48. According to Keen, 'The battle was one of the hardest fought of the age; and little groups of combatants were still struggling on the field when darkness fell. But by that time Hotspur had fallen, and both Worcester and Douglas were the king's prisoners; on the next day, the rebel army had disappeared and the king was the clear victor' (*England*, 284).

49. Ironically, the leaders of the second rebellion acknowledge these principles, and rely on them to ensure their own success, or at least Hastings and the Archbishop do. Lord Bardolph is skeptical that they can count on Northumberland, and doubts that without him their twenty-five thousand are sufficient to defeat the forces of the King. Hastings argues that they are:

For his divisions, as the times do brawl,
Are in three heads: one power against the French;
And one against Glendower; perforce a third
Must take us up. So is the unfirm King
In three divided, and his coffers sound
With hollow poverty and emptiness.

Consequently, the Archbishop adds, 'That he should draw his several strengths together / And come against us in full puissance / Need not be dreaded' (*2 Henry IV*, 1.3.70–78).

50. This, at least, is how the action is depicted in *Henry IV*. One gets a small indication of how the mythical treatment of Prince Hal's youth—substituting hijinks with Falstaff for his service on the Welsh frontier—affects the story Shakespeare

tells. Compare Shakespeare's account with that told by a modern historian, E. F. Jacob: 'Henry Percy was moving upon Shrewsbury with all speed to capture the prince of Wales *at his headquarters* [!], and the king must get there first. On 20 July Henry IV entered the town, and Hotspur, with a force estimated at fourteen thousand, on learning of the king's advance, withdrew with his uncle Thomas Percy along the Whitchurch road, a couple of miles to the northwest' (*Fifteenth Century*, 51; emphasis added).

51. This was generally the posture among the martial societies of the Plains Indians. At communal gatherings warriors were expected to stand and boast about their past deeds of valour, thus keeping alive the memory of their victories and allowing their listeners to share in the enjoyment thereof. Among other consequences, this encourages young men to attempt heroic deeds themselves, so that they too may have something to boast of on such occasions. The practice of modern militaries to award decorations for bravery that may be worn on one's dress uniform, publicly advertising past heroism, partakes of the same rationale.

52. It is of some interest that when Percy's widow urges Northumberland not to keep his commitment to stand with the Archbishop and the Lord Marshal in the second phase of the rebellion, neither her berating of him for deserting her husband nor his rejoinder mention anything about an illness having prevented his participation in the first phase.

> The time was, father, that you broke your word
> When you were more endear'd to it than now;
> When your own Percy, when my heart's dear Harry,
> Threw many a northward look to see his father
> Bring up his powers; but he did long in vain.
> Who then persuaded you to stay at home?
> There were two honours lost, yours and your son's. . . .
> O miracle of men!—him did you leave,
> Second to none, unseconded by you,
> To look upon the hideous god of war
> In disadvantage, to abide a field
> Where nothing but the sound of Hotspur's name
> Did seem defensible: so you left him.
> Never, O never, do his ghost the wrong
> To hold your honour more precise and nice
> With others than with him!
> (*2 Henry IV*, 2.3.10–41)

In replying, Northumberland denies nothing of what Lady Percy has said, but merely pleads, 'Fair daughter, you do draw my spirits from me / With new lamenting ancient oversights'. *Oversights?* To this textual evidence one may add Rumour's informing us that the Earl 'Lies crafty-sick' while he awaits news from the battle at Shrewsbury, whereas his porter directs Lord Bardolph to seek the Earl in his orchard where he has gone for a walk (ibid., Induction; 2.3.46–47; 1.1. 4–6).

53. To what extent this truly matters to Henry, as opposed to the men he exhorts, will be addressed in a subsequent chapter.

54. With respect to Hal's eulogy over Falstaff, Northrop Frye's characterization seems to me simply an amusing exaggeration of the essential truth: 'he gives what he thinks is the dead Falstaff an obituary speech that one might make about a dog that has been run over, but still there are traces of affection in it' (Sandler, *Northrop Frye on Shakespeare*, 79).

Treating the matter more seriously, J. Dover Wilson observes in *The Fortunes of Falstaff*, as excerpted in Eugene M. Waith's *Shakespeare: The Histories*, 'There is genuine sorrow here; Falstaff has given him too much pleasure and amusement for him to face his death without a pang. But the tone, which may be compared with Hamlet's when confronted with Yorick's skull, is that of a prince speaking of his dead jester, not of friend taking leave of familiar friend; and what there is of affection is mainly retrospective'. Moreover, in comparing his eulogy of Falstaff with that which Hal gives Hotspur: 'Can there be any reasonable doubt which seemed to Shakespeare the more important? The overthrow of Hotspur is the turning point not only of the political plot of the two Parts but also in the development of the Prince's character. . . . The epitaph on Hotspur contains not a word of triumph; its theme is the greatness of the slain man's spirit, the tragedy of his fall, and what may done to reverence him in death' (148–49).

In discussing the two eulogies, John E. Alvis challenges the common interpretation of Hal's relationship with each man:

> He delivers a gracious farewell speech to his fallen rival wherein he expresses the hope that Hotspur's honors may mount to heaven while his shame sleeps in the grave. To honor him and cover his shame Hal places his official plumes upon the mangled face of the dead rebel. The gesture is touching and delicate in contrast to the contemptuous obsequy he proceeds to make for Falstaff, who lies beside Percy pretending to be dead. Harry's true friend is not Falstaff but Hotspur . . . the warm esteem any man of honor feels for another. Hotspur was almost Hal's equal, and he *was* equal in the intensity of his devotion to honor'. ('Spectacle Supplanting Ceremony', 113)

It is surely true that a genuine lover of honour with any self-understanding cannot despise another such lover without undermining the value of that which he himself pursues. But I am dubious that Hal *is* an honour lover (as opposed to treating honour as an instrumental good). I incline, rather, to the summary judgment so well expressed by Tim Spiekerman: that Prince Hal's 'concern for honor is ultimately instrumental or prudential, a means to another end. Hal is not really devoted to honor at all—and his political success . . . can in large part be explained by his ability to ignore its claims while understanding its power' ('Making of a Politician', 200).

55. Let a pronouncement from the irrepressible Harold Bloom suffice (from *Shakespeare: The Invention of the Human*):

> Can there be an audience that will not learn from this, in a society still given to military fantasies? Are there any societies not so given, past or present? Falstaff, like his reluctantly charmed admirer, Dr. Samuel Johnson, urges us to clear our minds of cant, and Falstaff is even freer of societal delusions than was the Grand Cham, Johnson. Shakespeare, we can surmise from his life

as well as from his work, had a horror of violence, including the organized violence of warfare. *Henry V* hardly exalts battle; its ironies are subtle but palpable. 'Honor' is the sphere of Hotspur, and of Hal who slays Hotspur and thus usurps the throne of this 'Air. A trim reckoning!' (295–96)

56. Hobbes's discussion of the issues raised by Falstaff, and by Prince Hal's response 'in deed', is worth considering here:

> Desire of Praise, disposeth to laudable actions, such as please them whose judgement they value; for of those men whom we contemn, we contemn also the Praises. Desire of Fame after death does the same. And though after death, there be no sense of the praise given us on Earth, as being joyes, that are either swallowed up in the unspeakable joyes of Heaven, or extinguished in the extreme torments of Hell: yet is not such Fame vain; because men have a present delight therein, from the foresight of it, and of the benefit that may redound to their posterity: which though they now see not, yet they imagine; and any thing that is pleasure in the sense, the same also is pleasure in the imagination. (*Leviathan*, chap. 11, para. 6)

57. There is little dispute as to whether Falstaff is shameless, hence indifferent to allegations of hypocrisy. What is at issue is 'why so'. There are those who contend it is a consequence of clear-sightedness. One of the more moderate proponents of this view is Allan Bloom, in *Love and Friendship*:

> [Falstaff's] salvation for himself and his audience is that he is screamingly funny. And, although there is much slapstick in him, the humor does not stop at that but touches on the great themes traditional to comic liberation—the gods, the city, and the family. He is a criminal not only because his uncontrolled tastes lead him in that direction, but also because he is a critic of the conventions.
> This is perhaps enough to explain the shrewd Hal's attraction to Falstaff. From his earliest youth Hal seems to have known that the official versions of what is good and evil, noble and base, are defective and can hamper political activity....
> Falstaff is the only inhabitant of the Boar's Head who has self-knowledge, and that seems to be irresistibly charming, at least for a time, to Hal....
> Falstaff has a touch of nobility in him ... [;] he could have made a political career for himself.... His failure to do so could be understood as the usual tale of a promising man undone by unbridled passions. But it is equally plausible that he has turned to that life of his, which he so evidently enjoys, because he sees through or beyond the political careers of the nobles. His reflections on the vanity of honor as opposed to the reality of life give some indication of the kind of critique he has made of such aspirations. (402–4)

This view borders on the bizarre. As if Falstaff's hedonistic life of self-satisfied indulgence, mainly of the body—the easy life of letting go—is *actually superior* to the self-mastery required for the pursuit of martial glory or political honor! Bloom treats Falstaff's vulgar hedonism (for he's certainly no Epicurean, pursuing a life of *refined* pleasures) as if it were a *consequence* of some deep insight into the (assumed) insubstantiality of the conventions regulating decent political life—rather than vice versa: a critic of those conventions because they would obstruct his self-indulgence.

58. With much subtlety and circumspection, Hobbes allows for this vital truth especially pertinent to the better sort of men: 'No man is bound by the words themselves, either to kill himselfe, or any other man; And consequently, that the Obligation a man may sometimes have, upon the Command of the Soveraign to execute any dangerous, *or dishonourable* Office, dependeth not on the Words of our Submission; but on the Intention; which is to be understood by the End thereof. When therefore our refusall to obey, frustrates the End for which Soveraignty was ordained; then there is no Liberty to refuse: otherwise there is" (*Leviathan*, chap. 21, para. 15; emphasis added). I have analyzed the profound, indeed comprehensive, implications of this allowance in chapter 13 of *The Platonian Leviathan*.

59. Thus Hobbes contends, 'There be some things Honourable by Nature; as the effects of Courage, Magnanimity, Strength, Wisdom, and other abilities of body and mind' (*Leviathan*, chap. 28, para. 19). And, 'There be some signes of Honour, (both in Attributes and Actions,) that be Naturally so; as amongst Attributes, *Good, Just, Liberall*, and the like; and amongst Actions, *Prayers, Thanks*, and *Obedience*' (chap. 31, para. 10). Similarly, some things are naturally *dishonourable*; so, whereas some actions are 'Naturally signes of Honour, others of Contumely, these later (which are those that men are ashamed to do in the sight of them they reverence) cannot be made by humane power a part of Divine worship' (ibid., para. 39).

60. Again, I have discussed in detail the importance to the polity of properly managing the 'economy of honour' in chapter 13 of *The Platonian Leviathan*.

61. Shakespeare has his Westmorland remind us of Bolingbroke's former martial prowess in rebutting Mowbray's claim that his father would have bested Henry had King Richard allowed the trial by combat to take place: 'You speak, Lord Mowbray, now you know not what. / The Earl of Hereford was reputed then / In England the most valiant gentleman' (*2 Henry IV*, 4.1.130–32).

62. We are allowed to observe directly Falstaff's corrupt recruiting practices during his visit to Justice Shallow in part 2 of *Henry IV* (3.2.92–282). The fact that the scene is a comic exaggeration of practices all too common in Elizabethan times, as has often been claimed, hardly amounts to an apology for Falstaff's behaviour.

63. There are some who profess to admire Falstaff's careless cynicism here—William Empson, for example: 'What is recalled is the most unbeatable of all Falstaff's retorts to Henry—"they'll fill a pit as well as better; tush, man, mortal men, mortal men". Falstaff has just boasted that he took bribes to accept such bad recruits ("I have misused the King's press damnably"—and the audience would not think him a coward here, but that it took a lot of nerve to be so wicked) and he boasts later that he got them killed to keep their pay . . . but this makes his reply all the more crashing, as from one murderer to another: "that is all you Norman lords want, in your squabbles between cousins over your loot, which you make an excuse to murder English people"' (*Essays on Shakespeare*, 52). Empson's defence of Falstaff is entirely fitting, that is, Falstaffian.

64. And yet, the possibility that Prince Hal did indeed provide some such 'gilding' of Falstaff's participation would seem borne out by the Lord Chief Justice's servant informing his master what could only have been bruited on the basis of some seemingly reliable authority: that Falstaff 'hath since done good service at

Shrewsbury' (*2 Henry IV*, 1.2.61–62). This gossip the Lord Justice apparently accepts at face value: 'Your day's service at Shrewsbury hath a little gilded over your night's exploit on Gad's Hill' (1.2.147–48).

65. A. C. Bradley, in his essay 'The Rejection of Falstaff'—which, though now more than a century old, remains to my mind the most persuasive defence of Falstaff—regards such 'objectivity' as impertinent: 'Yes, it makes an ugly picture when you look at it seriously. But then, surely, so long as the humorous atmosphere is preserved and the humorous attitude maintained, you do not look at it so. . . . You do not exactly ignore [Falstaff's misdeeds], but you attend only to their comic aspect. This is the very spirit of comedy, and certainly of Shakespeare's comic world, which is one of make-believe, . . . a world in which gross improbabilities are accepted with a smile, and many things welcomed as merely laughable which, regarded gravely, would excite anger and disgust. The intervention of a serious spirit breaks up such a world, and would destroy our pleasure in Falstaff's company' (270). True. But nonetheless, must we not invoke a serious spirit if we are to justly assess Henry's rejection of Falstaff?

66. *The Prince*, chap. 7, para. 4.

Chapter Three

1. Campbell is surely correct that it is the 'immortal' character of Falstaff which has been 'largely responsible for keeping the [*Henry IV* plays] alive in the hearts of posterity' (*Shakespeare's Histories*, 213). As such, one must credit the character with preserving the philosophical lesson Shakespeare has embedded in this pair of plays. That said, the enduring popularity of the two plays is due primarily to their effectiveness in live performances, wherein even mediocre actors can milk the Falstaff character for laughs aplenty.

2. This 'singing-man of Windsor' is a notorious crux. A. R. Humphreys, editor of the edition *of King Henry IV Part Two* used here (2nd Arden), devotes a short appendix (III) to its possible meaning. He suggests that it may be an elliptical allusion to the first plot against Hal's father as a usurper, and adds, 'Any reference to Henry IV as a pretender involved in a dethronement of the true king would certainly qualify Falstaff for a broken head' (234–35).

3. Thus the title of W. H. Auden's perceptive essay on Falstaff, 'The Prince's Dog', in *The Dyer's Hand and Other Essays*, which begins:

> At a performance, my immediate reaction is to wonder what Falstaff is doing in this play at all. At the end of *Richard II*, we were told that the Heir Apparent has taken up with a dissolute crew of 'unrestrained loose companions'. What sort of bad company would one expect to find Prince Hal keeping when the curtain rises on *Henry IV*? Surely, one would expect to see him surrounded by daring, rather sinister juvenile delinquents and beautiful gold-digging whores. But whom do we meet in the Boar's Head? A fat, cowardly tosspot, old enough to be his father, two down-at-heel hangers-on, a slatternly hostess and only one whore, who is not in her earliest youth either; all of

them seedy, and, by any worldly standard, including those of the criminal classes, all of them *failures*. Surely, one thinks, an Heir Apparent, sowing his wild oats, could have picked himself a more exciting crew than that. As the play proceeds, our surprise is replaced by another kind of puzzle, for the better we come to know Falstaff, the clearer it becomes that the world of historical reality which a Chronicle Play claims to imitate is not a world which he can inhabit.

In Auden's judgment, Falstaff's 'true home is the world of music', as he found at last in Verdi's opera (183).

4. Peto, the messenger who informs the Prince that the King is at Windsor fielding worrisome news from the North, also reports that he 'met and overtook a dozen captains, / ... knocking at taverns, / And asking every one for Sir John Falstaff' (apparently in regard to the same military emergency). These captains manage to track their quarry to Hostess Quickly's establishment in Eastcheap, for the Prince and Poins no sooner leave than Bardolph enters, urging Falstaff, 'You must away to court, sir, presently. A dozen captains stay at door for you' (2.4.354–56, 368–69). What could possibly account for this faker's continuing military status other than the widespread belief that he is the Prince of Wales's boon companion, and so must be indulged with some minor command responsibility despite his manifest incompetence, cowardice, and avarice? As we see when Hal first succeeds to the kingship, even his own brothers are under the impression that everyone 'must now speak Sir John Falstaff fair', whatever one's personal opinion of the man (cf. 5.2.33).

5. By a scholarly tradition, this has come to be known as 'The Boar's Head', apparently a well-known tavern of Shakespeare's day; however, the only trace of textual evidence for this attribution is highly elliptical: Hal asks Poins when plotting their exposure of Falstaff's 'true colours', 'Where sups he? Doth the old boar feed in the old frank?' (2.2.138–39).

6. For the sake of consistency, I here follow the spelling of the 3rd Arden editions of *1 Henry IV* and of *Henry V* ('Westmorland').

7. Here one might recall Falstaff's rejoinder to Westmorland, who was urging haste to join the King prior to the battle looming at Shrewsbury: 'Well, to the latter end of a fray and the beginning of a feast / Fits a dull fighter and a keen guest' (*1 Henry IV*, 4.2.77–78).

8. If Prince Hal might be said to favour any of his brothers, the textual evidence seems to suggest it is John Bedford, Duke of Lancaster. Hal praises him for his eagerness at the Battle of Shrewsbury after John refuses to escort him from the field, instead rushing off with Westmorland to continue fighting: 'By God, thou hast deceived me, Lancaster; / I did not think thee lord of such a spirit. / Before I loved thee as a brother, John, / But now I do respect thee as my soul'. The King then tells of John's having held off Hotspur, whereupon Hal comments, 'O, this boy lends mettle to us all' (*1 Henry IV*, 5.4.14–23). And when the battle is over and won, the Prince and Lancaster are shown walking together, the elder brother complimenting the younger on this, his first taste of battle (5.4.128–29). Finally, as noted in the preceding chapter, Hal passes to John the 'honourable bounty' of releasing the prestigious prisoner Douglas, and John thanks him for this 'high courtesy' (5.5.18–33).

By contrast, Thomas, Duke of Clarence, is altogether absent from part 1 of *Henry IV*, and is merely a mute presence in two scenes of *Henry V* (1.2 and 5.2). His only substantial contributions in the entire second tetralogy are the few lines he speaks in this scene (4.4) and the one that follows, and the acerbic warning he directs to the Lord Chief Justice when in company with his brothers they meet after Hal has become Henry V: 'Well, you must now speak Sir John Falstaff fair, / Which swims against your stream of quality' (5.2.33–34). Reviewing those few lines, however, one might detect the slightest hint of an inclination to show his elder brother in an unfavourable light. However, Thomas may actually be *Henry's* favourite son. It could only have been with his approval that Thomas replaced Hal on the King's Council (*1 Henry IV*, 3.2.32–33).

9. For a period beginning in the mid-sixteenth century, it was the Turkish practice that whichever son of a sultan's many wives succeeded to the sultanate, he immediately had all of the other sons executed (strangled by a silken cord, supposedly). Prior to that, the many brothers and half brothers and their respective supporters were expected to fight it out. Over the centuries, the later policy of fratricide evolved into one of comfortable imprisonment for life.

10. Historically, relations between Hal and Thomas were decidedly cool. There is a smattering of evidence that the latter hoped and schemed to replace the former as Henry IV's heir. For his part, Hal never entirely trusted him. Barker writes: 'The most significant person to be excluded from Henry V's inner circles and favour was his brother Thomas, duke of Clarence. Despite the fact that for the first eight years of Henry's reign Clarence was next in line for the throne, he was never appointed regent, never received a major independent military command and was never given a significant position of trust. . . . His treatment is in marked contrast to that meted out to his two younger brothers' (*Agincourt*, 44). Thomas was in Aquitaine when news reached him of his father's death, and was unable to return home in time to participate in the coronation of his elder brother.

11. Thus, when Shakespeare has King Henry address the Earl of Warwick as 'cousin Nevil', and remind him of his having heard Richard II prophesy that Northumberland would betray Henry as he had betrayed Richard (3.1.66–71), Shakespeare is twice mistaken: Richard Neville was not then Earl of Warwick, nor was any Earl of Warwick present on that occasion, at least as Shakespeare himself portrayed it (cf. *Richard II*, 5.1.55–59).

12. The Earl of Warwick already had achieved some standing prior to his service in Wales, as he was one of four nobles who bore ceremonial swords in the coronation procession of Henry IV (Allmand, *Henry V*, 16). But while overseeing the campaign to pacify Wales, Henry Jr. (as noted before) acquired 'a tightly knit group of tried and trusted councilors, retainers and servants, most of whom were to serve him for the rest of his life':

> Foremost among these were two young soldier aristocrats who had much in common with the young prince and became his loyal retainers. Thomas Fitzalan, earl of Arundel, was five years older, Richard Beauchamp, earl of Warwick, four: both, like Henry himself, were sons of the so-called Appellant earls, who had challenged Richard II's autocratic style of government and reaped a bitter harvest in consequence. Arundel's father had been executed, Warwick's sentenced to life imprisonment, Henry's exiled: all had their estates forfeited by

Richard II and, after his deposition, restored by Henry IV.... Warwick, who distinguished himself at the battle of Shrewsbury, was rewarded by being made a Knight of the Garter at the age of twenty-one. (Barker, *Agincourt*, 31)

Desmond Seward also notes that as King, Henry V 'was fortunate in possessing a ready-made reservoir of corps commanders in his nobility' (*Henry V*, 56), with Warwick being especially prominent among them. About the Earl, Seward writes (with his characteristic tinge of disdain):

> He was an avaricious knight errant with a taste for the spectacular; in 1408 he had performed a long, round-about pilgrimage to Jerusalem, a species of grand tour during which he stayed with Charles VI at Paris, with the Doge of Venice and with the Grand Master of the Teutonic knights in Prussia, fighting in tournaments whenever possible—most notably a ferocious duel on foot against Pandolfo Malatesta. At the same time he was a steady and resourceful commander in the field and an excellent administrator. The king had so much respect for Warwick that he appointed him a governor and tutor of his son. (94–95)

13. He does play a substantial, though still minor, part in *1 Henry VI*, the first play in the earlier tetralogy.

14. His son and heir voices a similar lament as he gazes upon the crown resting on the pillow of his dying father (4.5.20–27), and again in the wee hours before the Battle of Agincourt. Part of the King's melancholy musing—'Wilt thou upon the high and giddy mast / Seal up the ship-boy's eyes, and rock his brains / In the cradle of the rude imperious surge [etc.]' (3.1.18–20)—apparently inspired a particularly significant chapter in Melville's *Moby-Dick*, 'The Mast-Head' (chap. 35, note esp. the concluding four paragraphs).

15. Presumably only an incorrigible cynic would suspect this to be the real reason Hal assaulted the man in the first place: that he might stage this act of exemplary contrition and justice.

16. In his *Lectures on Shakespeare*, W. H. Auden suggests that Henry's study is more narrowly focused: 'Why, essentially, does Hal associate with Falstaff and his companions? Not just for the surprise of his "reformation", but because he must possess a knowledge of human weakness. Court manners hide too much. Let people take liberties and they'll give themselves away. Then he can rule them' (110).

17. The phrase is that of Machiavelli, describing the effect of Cesare Borgia's unique manner of terminating the employment of Remirro de Orco (*The Prince*, chap. 7, para. 4).

18. Marriot asks rhetorically, 'Can we approve, can we ever forgive the abrupt repudiation of Falstaff', adding, 'his words strike a chill not only into Falstaff but into all who for the last three hundred years have listened to them' (*English History in Shakspeare*, 148–49). Leggatt observes, 'His rejection of Falstaff is the final touch in Hal's shaping of his career, the moment that symbolizes his last surrender of his former self. Yet it also brings to a head whatever misgivings we may have about Hal's strategy: many have found the human cost, to Hal as well as to Falstaff, intolerable. Others, with varying degrees of enthusiasm, have called it necessary' (*Shakespeare's Political Drama*, 99). That Hal found it all that 'costly' may be doubted.

19. Thus, Nuttall observes, 'The Prince's real revolution is not his switch from wild young man to ruler but his turning inside out of English history. The transformation of Hal is indeed made very visible in the play, but at the same time Shakespeare teaches us, gently, that there may never have been any change at all in Hal himself. Hal was never a wild young man. . . . Inheriting a throne tainted by his father's act of usurpation, he redirects the aggression of his countrymen from baronial in-fighting to a consolidated assault on a foreign power, France, thereby achieving glory' (*Shakespeare the Thinker*, 158).

Derek Traversi, in *Shakespeare from 'Richard II' to 'Henry V'*—an insightful book not least because it treats the second tetralogy as the whole it is—explains Hal's 'seeming' somewhat differently: 'From the outset, the supreme quality inherited by Hal from his father and raised by his own practice to new levels of shrewd consistency is *detachment*: a *detachment* from traditional conceptions'—including ordinary conceptions of human relationships:

> In a very important sense, there is in Hal's behaviour no true 'conversion' at all. The detachment which [is] his distinguishing quality . . . determines from the first moment his attitude in the tavern scenes of the two *Henry IV* plays. . . . Falstaff and his companions are . . . no more than living examples of the consequences of 'misrule', of the anarchy which his father's action has, against his own intentions, promoted but which he has never, with his outlook confined as it is to the narrow sphere of courtly intrigue, properly understood. Henry V, unlike Bolingbroke, *will* understand it, because he has surrounded himself with it, has with set purpose gone so far as to *live* it in his own person; but when the time comes for his tavern friends to be discarded, that action will come easily to a man who has from the first declared his intention of turning away from them as soon as he has extracted, from his contact with them and by intimate observation, the knowledge he requires of men as they are. (5–6)

Hal's capacity for 'detachment' is of primary importance, I believe, for understanding both his disposition and his behaviour throughout the *Henriad*. My only reservation about Traversi's characterization of Hal's 'tavern life' is that it does not give sufficient weight to its importance as a basis for his 'shrouded sun' strategy, which in turn is crafted to kick-start his campaign to establish the legitimacy of his kingship by the public disavowal of his previous lifestyle.

20. Many of Falstaff's admirers apparently accept Hostess Quickly's testimony on this point, despite the lack of evidence that Falstaff's 'care' for the Prince is anything other than utilitarian, not to say mercenary (and despite the evidence of Dame Quickly's rosy powers of misjudgment; cf. 2.4.379–81). Thus, Marriot: 'Falstaff had attached himself to Hal, not for what he could get out of the Prince, but because he loved the lad' (*English History in Shakspeare*, 150). Has Marriot forgotten *why* Falstaff had ridden hard—on whosever's horse was at hand—to accost Henry in the coronation procession? And thus Auden:

> As the play proceeds, we become aware, behind all the fun, of something tragic. Falstaff loves Hal with an absolute devotion. 'The lovely bully' is the son he never had, the youth predestined to the success and worldly glory

which he will never enjoy. He believes that his love is returned, that the Prince is indeed his other self, so he is happy, despite old age and poverty. We, however, can see that he is living in a fool's paradise, for the Prince cares no more for him as a person than he would for the King's Jester. He finds Falstaff amusing but no more. (*Dyer's Hand and Other Essays*, 191)

And thus Frye: '[Falstaff's] other weakness is his very real fondness for Prince Hal' (Sandler, *Northrop Frye on Shakespeare*, 75). Allan Bloom apparently concedes what I claim the textual evidence shows, but nonetheless rejects my conclusion: 'Falstaff, of course, profits from the association with the heir apparent.... But Hal's utility is not enough to account for the kind of attachment Falstaff expresses.... He has a sort of erotic attraction to this promising youngster in whom he would like to see himself reproduced' (*Love and Friendship*, 404–5). In all these cases and the like, might wish be father to the thought? That is, the wish to find something redeeming about the fat rascal such as would justify one's affection for him (something to the effect of, 'well, at least he really loved Hal')?

21. A. C. Bradley's 'Rejection of Falstaff' (1902) doesn't dispute my claim that *Shakespeare* sided with Hal against Falstaff (as do I), but argues that we are both mistaken for doing so. The basic thesis of Bradley's analysis is argued primarily in light of Henry V's actions in rejecting Falstaff:

> For the natural conclusion is that Shakespeare *intended* us to feel resentment against Henry. And yet that cannot be, for it implies that he meant the play to end disagreeably; and no one who understands Shakespeare at all will consider that supposition for a moment credible. No; he must have intended the play to end pleasantly, although he made Henry's action consistent. And hence it follows that he must have intended our sympathy with Falstaff to be so far weakened when the rejection-scene arrives that his discomfiture should be satisfactory to us; that we should enjoy his sudden reverse of enormous hopes (a thing always ludicrous if sympathy is absent); that we should approve the moral judgment that falls on him; and so should pass lightly over that disclosure of unpleasant traits in the king's character which Shakespeare was too true an artist to suppress. Thus our pain and resentment, if we feel them, are wrong, in the sense that they do not answer to the dramatist's intention. But it does not follow that they are wrong in a further sense. They may be right, because the dramatist has missed what he aimed at. And this, though the dramatist was Shakespeare, is what I would suggest. In the Falstaff scenes he overshot his mark. He created so extraordinary a being, and fixed him so firmly on his intellectual throne, that when he sought to dethrone him he could not. The moment comes when we are to look at Falstaff in a serious light, and the comic hero is to figure as a baffled schemer; but we cannot make the required change, either in our attitude or our sympathies.... [For] the Falstaff of the body of the two [*Henry IV*] plays, the immortal Falstaff, [is] a character almost purely humorous, and therefore no subject for moral judgments. (259–60)

This last claim I regard as simply wrong, and directly contrary to what I believe Shakespeare is using these plays to teach. Bradley wants to have it both ways: for

Falstaff, as an 'almost purely humorous' dramatic character, to be immune to our moral evaluation; and yet, for us to blame Henry for condemning Falstaff as a being every bit as subject to moral judgment as himself.

Concerning expressly 'the question of the rejection of Falstaff by the Prince on his accession to the throne', Bradley asks: 'What do we feel, and what are we meant to feel, as we witness this rejection? And what does our feeling imply as to the characters of Falstaff and the new King?' (249):

> They will depend on our feelings about Falstaff. If we have not keenly enjoyed the Falstaff scenes of the two plays, if we regard Sir John chiefly as an old reprobate, not only a sensualist, a liar, and a coward, but a cruel and dangerous ruffian, I suppose we enjoy his discomfiture and consider that the King has behaved magnificently. But if we *have* keenly enjoyed the Falstaff scenes, if we enjoyed them as Shakespeare surely meant them to be enjoyed, and if, accordingly, Falstaff is not to us solely or even chiefly a reprobate and a ruffian, we feel, I think, during the King's speech, a good deal of pain and some resentment; and when, without further offence on Sir John's part, the Chief Justice returns and sends him to prison, we stare in astonishment. (251)

Here Bradley has set up a false dichotomy, as if having 'keenly enjoyed' the Falstaff scenes, 'as surely Shakespeare meant them to be enjoyed', we should, or must, resent Hal's final treatment of him. Whereas, for Shakespeare to make the *philosophical* point which this pair of plays are designed to teach requires *both* the intense enjoyment of the comedic Falstaff *and* the recognition that, if his behaviour is soberly considered, it is morally inexcusable, and that (consequently) Hal's treatment of him is appropriate and justified.

22. Neale cites this episode as actually 'a good burlesque' of practices all too common of the age in which Shakespeare wrote the play (*Queen Elizabeth I*, 291).

23. Some further support for my contention that, whatever his affection for his fat funny man, Shakespeare did not really approve of him, is implied by an intriguing possibility Stephen Greenblatt presents in *Will in the World: How Shakespeare Became Shakespeare*. For Greenblatt makes a convincing case that the character Falstaff is to some considerable extent based on a particularly obnoxious and resentful contemporary of Shakespeare, Robert Greene, alleged author of the notorious *Greene's Groatsworth of Wit*, a pamphlet in which he speaks scathingly of 'an upstart Crow, beautified with our feathers, . . . [who] is in his own conceit the only Shakescene in a country'. Thus Greenblatt:

> To recognize this proximity between Greene and Falstaff is not only to see how 'foul and ugly' were the origins of Shakespeare's golden, capacious, and endlessly fascinating character. To be sure, Greene was tawdry enough—a drunk, a cheat, and a liar whose actual horizons were pathetically narrow compared to his grandiose projections. . . . What Falstaff helps to reveal is that for Shakespeare, Greene was a sleazy parasite, but he was also a grotesque titan, a real-life version of the drunken Silenus in Greek mythology or of Rabelais' irrepressible trickster, Panurge. . . . Falstaff captured Greene's binging and whoring, his 'dropsical' belly, his prodigal wasting of

his impressive talents, his cynical exploitation of friends, his brazenness, his seedy charm. He captured too the noisy, short-lived fits of repentance for which Greene was famous, along with solemn moralizing that swerved effortlessly into irreverent laughter. (218–19)

Does not this description of Robert Greene provide a useful focusing lens for evaluating Falstaff—despite Greenblatt's rhetorical effort to radically distinguish the two (the latter being 'golden, capacious, and endlessly fascinating')? Incidentally, Greene's wife was called 'Doll'.

24. Most people are aware, at least tacitly, that wittiness requires intelligence—'quick wits'—which fact in itself lends some credibility to a witty man's opinions and preferences. And all the more so if his views contrast with conventional beliefs and pieties whose inconsistencies and other limitations he humorously exposes. Beyond that, some people *prefer* to believe that Falstaff is essentially correct in disparaging what he does (e.g., martial honour, law-abidingness, respect for property), and in his general approach to life (that of a self-centred, self-satisfied hedonist). They excuse his transgressions on the grounds that he is 'honest with himself', as if that were all that mattered, and as if his supposed 'honesty' amounted to genuine self-knowledge. Shakespeare's Richard III is also 'honest with himself'.

25. Inspired by claims such as this, several scholars have noted some conspicuous parallels between Shakespeare's Falstaff and Plato's Sokrates (as I discussed in *Of Philosophers and Kings*, 266–67, 390–91). Most conspicuous is the similarity in the descriptions of the physical process of each man's dying (*Phaedo*, 117e–118a; *Henry V*, 2.3.21–25). Also, both men were accused of being 'misleaders of youths' and masters of sophistry (Sokrates of 'making the weaker argument the stronger' [*Apology*, 18b–c, 19b–c, 23d]; Falstaff of 'wrenching the true cause the false way' [*2 Henry IV*, 2.1.108–9]). And both claim to be a cause of 'wit' in others, but in different senses of the word: comic wittiness versus intellectual conceiving (Sokrates famously characterized himself as an intellectual midwife, assisting others to give birth to their ideas; *Theaetetus*, 149a–151c). Beyond these details, Allan Bloom, in *Love and Friendship*, suggests that the 'Hal-Falstaff relationship is not entirely unlike the one between Socrates and Alcibiades' (407). Not *entirely* unlike, perhaps, but crucially.

It seems to me that Shakespeare established the Falstaff-Sokrates parallels in order to highlight the *contrast* between the two characters, Falstaff being the antithesis of Sokrates in every important respect. While the *bodily* experience of their dying was similar, the states of their respective *souls* could hardly have been more different, the slightly delirious Falstaff crying out "God, God, God!' three or four times' (*Henry V*, 18–19), whereas a perfectly lucid Sokrates chides those at his bedside for wailing their grief, and—ironist to the end—bids his old friend Krito discharge the debt owed Asklepius for 'curing' him of life. According to no less a witness than Alkibiades, Sokrates always remained sober, was truthful, chaste, hardy, brave, and steadfast in battle even when his own ranks were broken (*Symposium*, 217e–221d; cf. *Laches*, 181b). Whereas Falstaff is a notorious coward and womanizer, a boastful liar and con artist, often drunk or sleeping off the effects of having been so. Sokrates is invariably shown by Plato to be attempting to bring out the best in the youths he associates with (while also showing why some powerful men resented his influence; cf., e.g., *Meno*, 94e). Whereas Falstaff, to the extent Shakespeare allows him any influence, might justly be called a 'villainous misleader of youth'. It should be no surprise, then, that Hal, knowing the amusing old fraud for what he is, utterly repudiates him in the end. Plato's Alkibiades, by contrast, remained attached to Sokrates, and criticizes himself for not following the philosopher's example more strictly (cf. *Symposium*, 215d–216c, 222c).

26. It is worth noting that all of the foregoing examples come from part 1 of *Henry IV*.

27. Auden suggests, 'Overtly, Falstaff is the Lord of Misrule; parabolically, he is a comic symbol for the supernatural order of Charity as contrasted with the temporal order of Justice symbolized by Henry of Monmouth' (*Dyer's Hand and Other Essays*, 198).

28. So the wise Hobbes teaches (*Leviathan*, chap. 11, para. 7; chap. 15, para. 17).

29. When Lord Russell Gower wished to surround his life-size bronze memorial to Shakespeare with dramatic characters emblematic of the four dimensions of his genius, he chose Falstaff to represent Comedy (along with Lady Macbeth for Tragedy, Hamlet for Philosophy, and Prince Hal for History). Who would care to quarrel with his choice for Comedy? Originally sited (1888) near the Stratford-upon-Avon parish church, the ensemble has since been moved to a small park adjacent to a major roadway entering the town.

30. Bradley argues, 'what troubles us is not only the disappointment of Falstaff, it is the conduct of Henry'.

> It was inevitable that on his accession he should separate himself from Sir John, and we wish nothing else. It is satisfactory that Sir John should have a competence, with the hope of promotion in the highly improbable case of his reforming himself. These arrangements would not have prevented a satisfactory ending: the King could have communicated his decision, and Falstaff could have accepted it, in a private interview rich in humour and merely touched with pathos. But Shakespeare has so contrived matters that Henry could not send a private warning to Falstaff even if he wished to, and in their public meeting Falstaff is made to behave in so infatuated and outrageous a manner that great sternness on the King's part was unavoidable. And the curious thing is that Shakespeare did not stop here. If this had been all we should have felt pain for Falstaff, but not, perhaps, resentment against Henry. But two things we do resent. Why, when this painful incident seems to be over, should the Chief Justice return and send Falstaff to prison? . . . The other is the King's sermon. He had a right to turn away his former self, and his old companions with it, but he had no right to talk all of a sudden like a clergyman; and surely it was both ungenerous and insincere to speak of them as his 'misleaders', as though in the days of Eastcheap and Gadshill he had been a weak and silly lad. . . . He ought in honour long ago to have given Sir John clearly to understand that they must say goodbye on the day of his accession. And having neglected to do this, he ought not to have lectured him as his misleader. It was not only ungenerous, it was dishonest. It looks disagreeably like an attempt to buy the praise of the respectable at the cost of honour and truth. And it succeeded. Henry *always* succeeded. ('Rejection of Falstaff', 253–54)

Bradley seems not to understand that his preferred manner of rupture would utterly annihilate the effect Hal had planned from the very beginning—an effect which is literally fundamental to his strategy for dealing with the problem of legitimacy that he inherited with the Crown, a problem that threatens the vital interests of everyone in the realm. He cannot take Falstaff (of all people) into his confidence, requiring that *he* fake the public spectacle Henry has been so long preparing, and which to be effective must have permanent consequences. Hal's repudiation *has* to be public and unequivocal if he is to put a stop to Falstaff's trading on people's presumption that he enjoys the new King's favour. But even more to the point, Bradley ignores the plethora of evidence that Falstaff *deserves* punishment—in fact, upon a dispassionate review of his misdeeds, it seems to me that he and his dissolute crew get off lightly. And as John Dover Wilson argues in rebutting Bradley's view, Henry lectures Falstaff, *not* 'like a clergyman', but like the Lord Chief Justice whom he has just enlisted as his adviser (*Fortunes of Falstaff*, 121–22).

31. Of the historical Henry, Barker writes:

> The king might penalize those who had rebelled against his authority, but he was also prepared to punish those who abused it. Henry was demonstrably carrying out his oath to do right and equal justice for all in Wales. It was a policy that clearly won him friends in the principality, judging by the huge numbers of Welshmen who signed up for the Agincourt campaign.
>
> The same was true for the rest of his kingdom. Violence against persons and property, riots and disorder were endemic in medieval England. The principal reason for this was not that society was naturally more criminal, but rather an inability to obtain justice, which encouraged those who perceived themselves to be victims to seek redress or revenge themselves. . . .
>
> By sheer force of personality, Henry succeeded in establishing and keeping the king's peace to a degree that was unprecedented, especially for a monarch who spent much of his reign absent from his kingdom. In doing so, he earned himself a reputation that extended far beyond the shores of England and even eclipsed his military successes in contemporary eyes. 'He was a prince of justice, not only in himself, for the sake of example, but also towards others, according to equity and right'; wrote the Burgundian chronicler, Georges Chastellain, 'he upheld no one through favour, nor did he allow wrong to go unpunished out of kinship'. (*Agincourt*, 47, 50)

32. Cf. Plato, *Republic*, 388e, 452d, 499c, 518a–b, 606c.

33. Leggatt makes a collateral point:

> [We] have through the two parts [of *Henry IV*] an interplay of genres, History and Comedy moving side by side, sometimes working together, frequently going their own ways. The concerns of history we have seen: order and rebellion in the state, public achievements on the battlefield and elsewhere, the gaining and losing of reputation, the manipulation of appearances. The end is the orderly exercise of power. The concerns of the comic world are money (in small quantities), drink (in large quantities), food, song, sex, and laughter. There is no particular end. . . . But this is comedy

> seen not as a certain kind of story but as a certain attitude to life—a concentration on the common and material, and a stance that is light-hearted, irresponsible, and self-gratifying. Falstaff stands for all of this, and this is what Hal must reject in order to prove himself the king the world of history needs. One way of looking at the ending is to say that, while the two genres coexist peacefully for much of the play, Comedy finally steps into the path of History and is crushed.... Shakespeare in *Henry IV* both exploits the spirit of comedy and examines it. The examination ... goes beyond the spirit of Falstaff alone; but it naturally centres on him. (*Shakespeare's Political Drama*, 99–100)

Leggatt sees what few other critics do: 'There is in fact a critique of comedy going on throughout the play.... Comedy is, in *Henry IV*, the medium by which characters misunderstand each other'. Thus, as Leggatt rightly concludes, 'Comedy, then, can be a barrier to understanding' (102). And, 'As Bergson warned us in his classic essay, laughter is like sea-foam, light and sparkling, "But the philosopher who gathers a handful to taste may find that the substance is scanty, and the aftertaste bitter". It is the pause to analyze, to look closely at the cause of laughter, that makes the laughter die. Shakespeare does this increasingly throughout *Henry IV*. It is generally observed that in Part 2 Falstaff is losing his immunity to time, feeling age and disease creeping up on him' (104).

Indeed, by the conclusion of *2 Henry IV*, it is clear that not only has Hal turned against Falstaff, so has Shakespeare: even while milking the Eastcheap world for the comic relief it could afford, he deftly laid the justification for the new King's total repudiation of it. But that said, is there not some merit in Bradley's contention that, though Shakespeare's objective appraisal of Falstaff is as I've argued, he nonetheless overshot his mark, creating a character that escapes his control (cf. nn. 21 and 30, above). And that as a consequence, we can, and *should*, condemn Henry's public rejection of the old scapegrace as unfeeling and unnecessarily brutal. While I certainly do not agree with this conclusion, I have a collateral sympathy with his questioning of Shakespeare inasmuch as I wonder whether in this case his *dramatic-entertainment* purpose, which succeeds only too well, is (consequently) too much at odds with his *philosophic* purpose: to *demonstrate* the *dangerous power* of comedy, its capacity to distort rational judgment. For this philosophic purpose to be 100 percent successful, he must create a character that is utterly hilarious (hence provides 'to the max' the painless pleasure of comedy, unquestionably one of life's joys), but who if viewed objectively has absolutely no redeeming qualities whatsoever other than his supple wit (which he uses carelessly), and who is actually quite pernicious. However, the problem may remain: can a fair-minded person's objective appraisal of Falstaff utterly ignore the pleasure he has provided, not only to us but sometimes to his victims as well? Personally, I believe so; being witty does not entitle a witty person to special moral leeway—a witty bastard is still a bastard—but everyday life confirms that almost all people, in practice, grant that it does. And this is a truth that Shakespeare uses Falstaff to teach. But is this effort a complete success? Or has he attempted a bridge too far?

Chapter Four

1. When this policy was carried out by Henry VIII over a century later, the effect was much as had earlier been feared. It led to the most serious threat to his reign, the rebellion that styled itself 'the Pilgrimage of Grace'. In the time of Henry IV and Henry V, the popularity of the proposed measure was partly a reflection of the growing influence of the puritanical Lollards, fervent critics of the established Church and the lavish lifestyle of some of its clergy.

2. As John E. Alvis observes in his richly insightful 'Spectacle Supplanting Ceremony: Shakespeare's Henry of Monmouth':

> The politically traumatic deposition of a legitimate king leaves a rent in the social fabric which must be patched with cloth of any color. Something must be done to restore the power of the monarchy since its moral authority has suffered perhaps irreparable harm. Bolingbroke appears to have given more thought to this problem than has been generally credited him. He leaves to his son a piece of legislation which, if properly administered, promises a means to domestic order without war. Bolingbroke's tax bill upon ecclesiastical property could provide added strength to the throne far in excess of a simple increase in revenues. In view of his other bequest—to make war as a diversion of domestic unrest—Bolingbroke appears not to have fully grasped the possibilities afforded by his own policy. However, Shakespeare dwells upon details that bring these possibilities to our attention. . . .
>
> Nothing attests power so manifestly as creation. By making a new nobility the king would demonstrate his power and by the same act provide for its continuation. . . . The risk of alienating worldly churchmen could be more than balanced by the gain of depriving prelates like Scroop of the means for sustaining revolts, and, in any event, new lords living off former church lands could be expected to side with the king against any troublesome bishops. Shakespeare knew of just such a social revolution from the successful policy of Henry VIII. (125–26)

Ultimately successful, yes. However, Alvis ignores the fact, first of all, that Henry VIII had inherited the Crown from his father, who had reigned for nearly a quarter century, and had himself been King for over a quarter century before undertaking this revolution. Consequently, he was far more solidly established on the throne than was Henry IV upon his initial ascension. And, secondly, that even so the later Henry's mass expropriation of Church property provoked the most serious threat to his throne (cf. the previous note).

3. According to Holinshed's *Chronicles*, 'This bill was much noted, and more feared among the religious sort, whom suerlie it touched verie neere, and therefore to find remedie against it, they determined to assaie all waies to put by and overthrow this bill' (Bullough, 377).

4. Cf. Plato, *Republic*, 590a–b.

5. Shakespeare would have read in Holinshed's summary comments on Henry as King, 'Everie honest person was permitted to come to him, sitting at meale,

where either secretlie or openlie to declare his mind. High and weightie causes as well betweene men of warre and other he would gladlie heare, and either determined them himself, or else for end committed them to others. He slept verie little, but that verie soundlie' (Bullough, 407). It is unlikely that Henry adopted these practices only upon ascending the throne.

6. The Duke of Exeter attests to the continuing effect of Henry's 'shrouded sun' strategy in the course of his embassage to France: 'And be assured you'll find a difference, / As we his subjects have *in wonder* found, / Between the promise of his greener days / And these he masters now' (2.4.134–37).

7. Thus his reply to the Dauphin's ambassadors ('tell the pleasant Prince . . . *his* soul / Shall stand sore charged for the wasteful vengeance [etc.]' [1.2.282–84]). And the ultimatum he has Exeter deliver to the French court ('take mercy / On the poor souls for whom this hungry war / Opens his vasty jaws; and on *your* head [etc.]' [2.4.101–9]). Again, in threatening the Governor of Harfluer ('What is't to me, when *you* yourselves are the cause, / If your pure maidens fall into the hand / Of hot and forcing violation? [etc.]' [3.3.19–21]). He uses a variant of this tactic even in arguing with three of his own soldiers before the Battle of Agincourt ('the King is not bound to answer the particular endings of his soldiers, [etc.]' [4.1.55–84]). Later, victorious, he insists that the restoration of peace depends solely on French acceptance of his terms (5.2.68–76).

Bernard J. Dobski, in 'Friendship and Love of Honor: The Education of Henry V', credits this tactic to Falstaff: 'It is not for friendship then, but for a kind of dialectical mastery, that the Prince serves as apprentice to this bawdy vintner. . . . What he learns is *the* Falstaffian calling card—how to use speech to evade or conceal personal responsibility' (160).

8. Great-grandfather Edward's mother was the French Princess Isabella, daughter of King Philip IV of France, whose three sons each died without leaving a male heir.

9. According to Canterbury, the French did not acquire 'the Salic land' until Charlemagne conquered it in AD 805, which was—according to his calculation—*421* years after King Pharamond died in AD 426. How he (or whoever) managed to subtract 426 from 805 and get 421 instead of 379 is a puzzle. The fact that the mistaken answer *adds* 21 to 400, rather than subtracting it, may somehow 'figure'. As the numbers come straight from Holinshed's account (Bullough, 378), responsibility for the miscalculation cannot be established with certainty, but since Shakespeare has incorporated a pattern of logical mistakes in the Archbishop's argument, we can be pretty sure the culpability is not his, and that he intentionally declined to rectify the error.

10. Shakespeare was well aware of this fact (as doubtless were many of his contemporaries), since it figures importantly in earlier plays of the second tetralogy (cf. *1 Henry IV*, 1.3.144–57). And it is essential to understanding the Wars of the Roses as depicted in the first tetralogy.

11. The fact that Shakespeare lifted this supposed rationale more or less directly from Holinshed's account of the Archbishop's testimony is irrelevant to its invalidity. Nor should we suppose that Shakespeare was unaware of its flaws, since supplying Canterbury—so intent on persuading Henry to attack France (rather than the English Church)—with a flawed case suited the author well.

12. It soon becomes clear that Shakespeare has cast the Dauphin as a perfect foil to his King Henry, rather as was Hotspur to his Prince Hal, in both cases tampering substantially with the historical record to create the fit. For as Hotspur was not actually an age-mate of Hal but of his *father*, so the Dauphin was not the picture of boastful vanity prior to the battle, nor the abject creature in defeat, since—as Holinshed makes clear—he was not present at Agincourt.

13. *The Prince*, chap. 18, paras. 5–6. 'Men in general judge more by their eyes than by their hands, because seeing is given to everyone. Everyone sees how you appear, few touch what you are'. Might Machiavelli's political maxim explain the curious prominence in this play of references to 'hands', 'fingers', 'touching', 'fists', and such? This family of terms figures more than four dozen times. Most mentions—like Machiavelli's—are metaphorical usages, which come so naturally to us, such as those (the first) by Canterbury: 'And in regard of causes now in hand / . . . / As touching France' (1.1.77–79). The first English words the French princess learns are 'de hand', followed by 'de fingres', then 'de nails' (3.4.5–16, 39–40). In threatening the Governor of Harfleur, Henry refers repeatedly to the 'bloody' and 'foul' hand of the English soldiery once unleashed (3.3.12, 20, 34). And, not surprisingly, he more than once refers to 'the hand of God' (2.2.191; 3.6.168). Three times a character swears by his hand (2.1.31; 3.2.94, 112), another 'By the white hand of my lady' (3.7.94)—rather unusual oaths, it would seem. But not as odd as Henry's ironic assurance to the three conspirators prior to their learning that he knows of their plot: '[We] shall forget the office of our hand / Sooner than quittance of desert and merit / According to their weight and worthiness' (2.2.33–35)—apparently an elliptical allusion to Psalms 137:5. Even the comic episode involving Henry's glove fits this pattern.

14. Shakespeare uses Cambridge's sycophancy to point directly to the chapter of *The Prince* that is especially pertinent to this scene (i.e., 17): 'of Cruelty and Mercy, and Whether It's Better to Be Loved Than Feared, or the Contrary', in which Machiavelli contends:

> A prince, therefore, so as to keep his subjects united and faithful, should not care about the infamy of cruelty, because with very few examples he will be more merciful than those who for the sake of too much mercy allow disorders to continue. . . . And of all princes, it is impossible for the new prince to escape a name for cruelty because new states are full of dangers.
>
> From this a dispute arises whether it is better to be loved than feared, or the reverse. The answer is that one would want to be both the one and the other; but because it is difficult to put them together, it is much safer to be feared than loved, if one has to lack one of the two. . . .
>
> The prince should nonetheless make himself feared in such a mode that if he does not acquire love, he escapes hatred, because being feared and not being hated can go together very well. This he will always do if he abstains from the property of his citizens and his subjects, and from their women; and if he also needs to proceed against someone's life, he must do it when there is suitable justification and manifest cause for it.
>
> I conclude, then, . . . that since men love at their convenience and fear at the convenience of the prince, a wise prince should found himself on what

is his, not on what is someone else's; he should only contrive to avoid hatred, as was said.

Still, it should be emphasized what Machiavelli said *first*: that it is *best* is to be *both* loved and feared, which is admittedly 'difficult', but *not* impossible.

15. According to Seward, Hal while still Crown Prince 'showed both subtlety and rock-like self-confidence in his treatment of the man who was potentially the most dangerous in the realm, the Earl of March'.

> So fearful had the king [i.e., Henry IV] been of the very existence of Richard II's rightful heir that he always kept him in custody. Instead the prince freed the seventeen-year-old earl, attaching him to his own household in much the same way he himself had once been attached to Richard II's—his father was too ill to demur. This ostensibly conciliatory approach, very carefully calculated, was to appear in Henry's dealings with the other magnates when he ascended the throne. (*Henry V*, 30)

16. As it turns out, the youth was twice blessed in this manner. For Cambridge's elder brother was the childless Duke of York (Aumerle in *Richard II*), who fell at Agincourt. Thus his title also passed to Cambridge's son, who thereupon became Richard of York, claimant to the crown by virtue of his descent from Lionel, Duke of Clarence, via his great-grandmother Philippa and his uncle Edmund. As such, he led the Yorkist challenge to the Lancastrian King Henry VI, son of Henry V. The result was the Wars of the Roses, which Shakespeare treats in the first tetralogy.

17. Holinshed's *Chronicle* (Bullough, 386). This is such a curious piece of information, one must suspect that Henry IV had something to do with ensuring Edmund's incapacity. Whatever the 'incapacity', it didn't prevent his marrying Anne Stafford (also a descendant of Edward III), though he had been forbidden to marry without royal permission (though he did somehow receive papal permission from Pope John XXIII, one of three popes contending for the title at the time). Henry punished Edmund with an enormous fine (10,000 marks), which he had to borrow heavily to pay (from Lord Scroop, among others), and so was smarting from Henry's discipline when approached by the conspirators.

18. As Shakespeare would have read in Holinshed (ibid., 385–86):

> The king thought that suerlie all treason and conspiracie had beene utterlie extinct; not suspecting the fire which was newlie kindled, and ceassed not to increase, till at length it burst out into such a flame, that catching the beames of his house and familie, his line and stock was cleane consumed to ashes. Diverse write that Richard earle of Cambridge did not conspire with the lord Scroope & Thomas Graie for the murthering of king Henrie to please the French king withal, but onelie to the intent to exalt to the crowne his brother in law Edmund earle of March as heire to Lionell duke of Clarence: after the death of which earle of March, for diverse secret impediments, not able to have issue, the earle of Cambridge was sure that the crowne should come to him by his wife, and to his children, of hir begotten. And therefore (as was thought) he rather confessed himselfe for need of monie to be corrupted by

the French king, than he would declare his inward mind, and open his verie intent and secret purpose, which if it were espied, he saw plainlie that the earle of March should have tasted of the same cuppe that he had drunken, and what should have come to his owne children he much doubted. Therefore, ... he feined that tale, desiring rather to save his succession than himself, which he did indeed: for his sonne Richard duke of Yorke not privilie but openlie claimed the crowne, and Edward his sonne both claimed it, & gained it. ... Which thing if king Henrie had at this time either doubted, or foreseen, had never beene like to have come to passe.

19. Ibid., 384.
20. This, too, Shakespeare would have read in Holinshed: 'In time of warre such was his providence, bountie and hap, as he had true intelligence, not onlie what his enemies did, but what they said and intended: of his devises and purpose few, before the thing was at point to be done, should be made privie' (ibid., 407).
21. Machiavelli explains the special significance of this item. He begins chapter 22 of *The Prince*: 'The choice of ministers is of no small importance to a prince; they are good or not according to the prudence of the prince. And the first conjecture that is to be made of the brain of a lord is to see the men he has around him'. Hobbes, *Leviathan*, chap. 25, para. 16, is also obliquely relevant.
22. That is, Shakespeare chose to leave his disappearance a mystery, though he would have read in Holinshed, 'either for melancholie that he had for the losse at Agincourt, or by some hidden disease Lewes Dolphin of Viennois, heire apparant to the French king, departed this life without issue.
23. Modern historians, with access to sources of which Shakespeare was unaware, provide an answer as to how Henry learned of the conspiracy. Seward gives the following account as simply 'matter of fact':

On 1 August the Earl of March came suddenly to Porchester Castle from where the king was directing the embarkation. He demanded an audience and revealed that his brother-in-law, the Earl of Cambridge, had tried to enlist him in a plot to overthrow Henry. He was to be denounced in a proclamation as 'Henry of Lancaster, usurper of England'. As Cambridge later explained in a confession, 'I purposed to have had the aforesaid earl [of March] into the land of Wales without your consent, to confer upon the earl the sovereignty of this land. ...' Henry Percy, Hotspur's son, not yet restored to his grandfather's earldom, was to cross the border into England with a Scots army and raise the North, while a Davy Howell was to hand over the royal castle in Wales, where Owain's old followers were waiting to rise. ... It was the old alliance of Percy, Mortimer and Glen Dŵr.
There had been long discussions between March, Lord Clifford—who refused to be drawn into the conspiracy—and the other two ringleaders, Sir Thomas Grey [cousin to Henry Percy], and Lord Scroop [nephew of Archbishop Scroop, whom Henry IV had executed after the rebellion of 1405]. ... A plan to fire the invasion fleet was rejected. Finally it was decided to assassinate King Henry on the very day that March had his audience. (*Henry V*, 47)

However, Christopher Allmand treats the episode as still shrouded in some mystery:

> At the end of July a plot, seemingly to kill the king, was betrayed by Edmund Mortimer, earl of March. . . . What kind of plot it was intended to be, what it aimed to do, and what brought the plotters to the point of seeming desperation has long puzzled historians. Was it a dynastic plot, centring on Edmund Mortimer? Possibly, but unlikely, since it was Mortimer himself who revealed the conspiracy. [However, only after being aware of it for at least ten days, it should be added, leaving the impression that he may simply have lost his nerve in the end. That Henry waited until August 9 to issue Mortimer a full pardon suggests that he, too, found this delay suspicious.] Or was it a revival, a kind of 're-run' of 1405, of the Mortimer-Glen Dŵr-Percy alliance which led to the planned tripartite division of England and Wales in that year? . . . Was it, as some contemporary writers presented it, a betrayal of the king's military interest in France, paid for by the French as a last-ditch attempt to prevent the invasion of their country, a conspiracy which followed the very recent visit to Winchester of the French king's ambassadors? (*Henry V*, 74)

There must be *something* to the French bribery version if we are to account for the version in Holinshed: 'These prisoners upon their examination, confessed, that for a great sum of monie which they had received of the French king, they intended verily either to have delivered the king alive into the hands of his enimies, or else to have murthered him before he should arrive in the duchie of Normandie' (Bullough, 384–85).

The most detailed account of the conspiracy that I'm aware of—and, I should imagine, among the most controversial—is that of Ian Mortimer in *1415: Henry V's Year of Glory*, 284–319. He contends that Scroop (which he spells 'Scrope') may not have actually been a party to the conspiracy, but associated with the others simply in order, if possible, to dissuade them from what they were contemplating, and in any event to discover their plans, with the intention of ultimately revealing them to the king.

> In all this, Lord Scrope's behaviour and testimony concerning his own actions is consistent with the way that Edward, duke of York, had gathered information about the Epiphany Rising in 1400. York had attended the secret meetings of the conspirators without telling the king for more than two weeks; and when they had been about to act, York had sent an urgent message to the king, warning him. [However, in this case, too, might York have had a last-minute failure of nerve?] Scrope's evasive and ambiguous answers were clearly designed to lead Cambridge and Gray into revealing more information about their plans. . . . Still there were things that Scrope did not know, as the earl of Cambridge pointed out; and so he still had good reason to stay in with the conspirators. But he was not one of them. (299)

> Being so close to the king, and so important, Scrope was presumed to have been the leader of the conspiracy; and being so often in France, it was presumed that he must have been bribed by the French. . . . From this distance in time, and with the original records available to us, we can see that Scrope

> had not had any dealing with the French other than his official diplomatic ones, and was not part of the conspiracy at all. (307)

For his part, Edmund Mortimer was in on the conspiracy up to his neck, but apparently got cold feet.

> The earl of March was due to ride to Cranbury . . . to meet the earl of Cambridge, Sir Thomas Gray and Sir Walter Lucy. But when he set out from Hamble in the Hook, he turned a different way: he went to see Henry at Porchester Castle. There he betrayed the conspirators who would have fought to make him king, telling Henry everything he knew. (Ibid., 306)

Mortimer's revelation preempted Scroop's/Scrope's, who was left in the embarrassing position of being knowledgeable of treason, but without a convincing rationale for not having revealed it in a timely manner.

24. *The Prince*, chap. 3, para. 4. As the choral Epilogue informs us, Henry V was blessed by fortune in conquering France, though not in his successors holding it. And it is worth recalling that while Welsh soldiers marched under Henry's banner, yet he knew from his experiences while yet Prince of Wales that the Welsh were ready to revolt against English rule more than a century after Edward I had subjugated their country and supposedly welded it to his throne.

25. Leggatt notes 'Like Tamburlaine, he conquers not just with his sword but with his language' (*Shakespeare's Political Drama*, 126–27). I suspect Shakespeare would be amused by how many scholars and critics hold it against his Henry that he can so graphically *threaten* brutality—almost as if he were as guilty for having so threatened as they would judge him to be for having caused such threats to be carried out. They seem to believe that the very capacity to conceive and utter such threats is evidence of a brutish nature, perhaps forgetting that it is Shakespeare who has done the conceiving and uttering. And mesmerized by the awful image his words arouse, they fail to appreciate what he shows the King thereby *accomplishing* by rhetoric, rather than by the sword.

26. In accordance with his claim to be the rightful ruler of France, the historical Henry 'had made it clear from the outset that he regarded the defenders of Harfleur as rebels against his authority, rather than loyal subjects of another country resisting a foreign invasion' (Barker, *Agincourt*, 201).

27. *Leviathan*, chap. 14, para. 3.

28. Thucydides, 5.84–111.

29. According to Barker, 'more [of Henry's soldiers] died from disease at Harfleur than from the fighting throughout the campaign' (*Agincourt*, 215). Indeed, 'the king lost between a quarter and a third of his men to dysentery as a result of the siege' (216).

30. Thus, the dogged resolve with which Britain, virtually alone, withstood the German assault in the early stages of the Second World War persuaded the American leadership that all was not lost, and that consequently providing material assistance would not necessarily be wasted.

31. However, according to Holinshed, 'the towne [itself was] sacked, to the great gaine of the Englishmen' (Bullough, 388). Shakespeare chose to leave this an

unstated likelihood, much as he suppressed entirely Henry's brutal reprisal against the besieged citizenry of Caen for choosing, unlike those of Harfleur, to resist to the bitter end.

32. As he did, again according to Holinshed (ibid.): 'the king ordained capteine to the towne his uncle the Duke of Exeter, who established his lieutenant there, one sir John Fastolfe'.

33. Describing the incident of the stolen pyx (the 'pax' of Shakespeare's play) and Henry's prompt punishment of the offender, Holinshed makes this utilitarian dimension explicit: 'The people of the countries thereabout, hearing of such zeale in him, to the maintenance of justice, ministred to his armie victuals, and other necessaries, although by open proclamation [i.e., of French authorities] so to doo they were prohibited' (ibid., 389). This is not to minimize the historical Henry's comparable 'zeale' for strict discipline irrespective of whether it affected anyone other than the soldiers of his own army. Holinshed includes a striking instance of this: 'Now as it chanced, the king in going about the campe, to surveie and view the warders, he espied two soldiers that were walking abroad without the limits assigned, whom he caused straightwaies to be apprehended and hanged upon a tree of great height, for a terror to others, that none should be so hardie to breake such orders as he commanded them to observe' (ibid., 401). There is no comparable evidence of the King as a ruthless disciplinarian in *Henry V*. To the contrary, he professes a willingness to 'wink at little faults', thus his theatrical pardoning of 'the man ... that railed against [his] person' (2.2.40–41, 54–55). Is Shakespeare's Henry, then, 'softer' than the historical figure he found in Holinshed? Perhaps, though one must bear in mind that the soldier who stole the pyx remains anonymous in Holinshed's *Chronicles*, but becomes one of the King's former boon companions in Shakespeare's play—which surely 'intensifies' whatever might be the moral significance of Henry's attitude. And what is that attitude? One of callousness? Or is it an insistence that justice be impartially administered? Of course, there is also his controversial 'kill the prisoners' edict, still to be examined.

Commenting on these matters, Traversi seems to me dead on:

> These soldiers will steal, moreover, not in the spirit of the earlier Falstaff defying 'the rusty curb of old father antic the law', but to keep body and soul together or in simple obedience to their innate cupidity; and, in the intervals of stealing, there will be abundant opportunity for the throat-cutting that plays so great a part in the military vocation. As Macmorris reminds his fellows, 'there's throats to be cut and work to be done', so that Henry's coming treatment of his prisoners in the hour of battle, far from being an isolated incident, simply answers to the common reality of war.
>
> The presence of these elements in his army imposes on the king certain necessities in the fulfilment of his responsibilities. Cupidity is balanced by an uncompromising rigour in the maintenance of elementary moral law. Besides being ready to inflict suffering upon his enemies, Henry has to enforce good conduct upon his own men. In so doing, the claims of morality and those of political calculation are intertwined in a way highly typical of this play. When Bardolph, adding sacrilege to theft, steals a pax from a French church on the march to Picardy, Henry has no hesitation in ordering him to be hanged

[actually, he merely registers approval after the fact]; for discipline, as the faithful Fluellen observes, 'ought to be used', and the offender should die, even if 'he were my brother'. In thus imposing discipline Henry makes the sacrifice called for by his office. Once more, justice requires authority to be ready, when necessary, to cut across human feelings; and we shall not be responding fully to the spirit of the most individual parts of the play unless we are continually ready to balance hard necessity against humanity. (*Shakespeare from 'Richard II' to 'Henry V'*, 184–85)

34. Or rather, according to one of Machiavelli's dialogical characters (Fabrizio): 'By having payment made for the wood he had used to make the palisade around his army in France, Caesar gained for himself such a name for justice that he made the acquisition of that province easy' (*Art of War*, 139).

35. Though I regard Graham Bradshaw's analysis of the play in *Misinterpretations: Shakespeare and the Materialists* as unnecessarily convoluted mainly because it is too respectful of the defamers of Henry, his observations about the King's courtship of Kate makes a point frequently overlooked: 'the power politics that deny Katherine any choice about when and whom she marries also constrain Henry himself—and once the human swag has been carried back to England, these two must live together. Seen in this way, those very jokes that acknowledge the brutal realities of a 'power' that admits no 'dissembling' figure in an appeal *to Katherine* to move *beyond* helpless acquiescence' (120).

36. I basically agree with Cantor's observation in 'Shakespeare's *Henry V*': 'As always, Henry seeks to cover over a stark political reality with a false front. His marriage to Katherine will be as political as a marriage could be.... But Henry knows that the marriage cannot work, even in political terms, if its political character is too evident. Hence he must play a part, the role of Katherine's ardent suitor, and not her military conqueror'. However, Constance C. T. Hunt, in 'The Origins of National Identity in Shakespeare's *Henry V*', argues against the view that the French princess is a mere pawn, much less (symbolically) a rape victim, as some feminist critics assert. She contends, 'To the contrary, the language lesson and the courtship scene show that Kate is neither a pawn nor a victim and that Henry does not treat her as such' (135). Moreover, 'The contrast between these scenes and the battle scenes highlights the role of love throughout the play and its importance as a key to understanding Shakespeare's presentation of Henry V's character'. The 'Kate scenes' provide vital evidence regarding Henry's success as a political leader 'in uniting the ethnically disparate, ragtag troops he leads into a national army' (136–37). That is, 'The loyalty that Henry V requires can only be achieved by a monarch who both acknowledges the place of erotic longing in political life and successfully inspires such love in others. He must possess both the insight of a lover and the attractiveness of a beloved' (137).

37. The risqué banter vis-à-vis the French princess with which Burgundy later teases Henry (5.2.278–312) would also suggest that they have previously established a relationship of familiarity.

38. Machiavelli teaches that historically all princedoms have been governed in one of 'two diverse modes: either by one prince, and all others servants who as ministers help govern the kingdom by his favor and appointment; or by a prince

252 NOTES TO PP. 156–159

and by barons who hold that rank not by favor of the lord but by antiquity of blood line'. Kingdoms of the former kind are hard to conquer, but once conquered are easy to hold; whereas the reverse tends to be the case with latter kind, because one can usually find some disaffected baron who is willing to facilitate gaining access to it. He explicitly cites France as an example of a state governed in the latter mode: 'the king of France is placed in the midst of an ancient multitude of lords, acknowledged in that state by their subjects and loved by them: they have their privileges, and the king cannot take them away without danger to himself'. Accordingly, 'you can easily enter there, having won over to yourself some baron of the kingdom; for malcontents and those who desire to innovate are always to be found [who] can open the way for you into the state and facilitate victory for you' (*The Prince*, chap. 4, paras. 1–2, 4).

39. Burgundy's elaborate description of the effects of the war on the French countryside and its people (5.2.34–62) partially anticipates Hobbes's description of what results when universal civil war returns a polity to 'a state of mere nature' (*Leviathan*, chap. 13, para. 9).

40. According to Keen, 'Before Henry's return from France in 1421 [at the conclusion of his second campaign] the commons were becoming patently fretful about the inconveniences arising from his prolonged absence. On the whole, however, there seems to have been agreement that in spite of all the strains the country was better governed than it had been, or would be, for many a long year' (*England in the Later Middle Ages*, 345).

41. *The Prince*, chap. 3, paras. 9–10.

42. Allmand, *Henry V*, 82. The French recovered Harfleur in 1450.

43. Thus, Spiekerman asks, 'Is the war against France just, and if not, does King Henry know as much? . . . In calling the war unjust, I mean nothing fancier than this: it is unjust to take what doesn't belong to you, and France doesn't belong to Henry V. Theft on a grand scale is still theft' (*Shakespeare's Political Realism*, 131). True enough, but does not the play invite us to *question* who this ambiguous thing called 'France' *does* rightfully 'belong to'? The corrupt French elite? Why are *they* the *naturally* 'legitimate' rulers of France? Moreover, Henry claims that it *does* belong to him by virtue of the long-established 'laws' of inheritance.

44. A partial explication of the parallels between Henry and Alexander is in note 12 of chapter 2.

45. As Hobbes observes in his 'A Review and Conclusion' of *Leviathan*, 'Therefore I put down for one of the most effectuall seeds of the Death of any State, that the Conquerors require not onely a Submission of mens action to them for the future, but also an Approbation of all their actions past; when there is scarce a Common-wealth in the world, whose beginnings can in conscience be justified' (end of para. 8); cf. chap. 20. I provide a detailed analysis of this matter in chapter 19 of *The Platonian Leviathan*.

46. Spiekerman seems simply to assume so in arguing, 'Shakespeare [poses] the question of whether France belongs to England. . . . Only if a country with a native tongue, established borders, and a distinctive national character belongs to its aggressive, ambitious neighbor. . . . Shakespeare clearly goes out of his way . . . to show that whatever motivates this war, it is being fought by two separate nations. . . . By continually reminding us that the French and the English are different peoples,

Shakespeare continually asks us to question why one country should belong to another' (*Shakespeare's Political Realism*, 135). But does not this reification of the contestants hopelessly confuse the 'justice' issue? It's not a matter of one *country* 'belonging' to another *country*. Henry claims to be the *rightful* king of *both* England and France, which would amount to a united kingdom (much as today are England, Scotland, Wales, and Northern Ireland). For that matter, 'France' at the time was composed of fluctuating parts, often at odds with each other; this is an important reason it was so much weaker than its size and resources would suggest. For example, Burgundy didn't join the effort against Henry. Were Henry's conquest successful, the everyday life of ordinary Frenchmen, including their property rights, need not change at all—or perhaps change for the better! We tend to forget that virtually all present nations are composed of once separate parts that have been unified by conquest.

47. As Derek Traversi observes, in *Shakespeare from 'Richard II' to 'Henry V'*, '[Hal's] conduct is marked from the first by a sense that the traditional sanctions of monarchy are no longer immediately valid, that the implications of the royal office need to be reconsidered in a new world of uncertainties. This reconsideration, presented through the successive stages of the action, is the principal theme of the *Henry IV* plays' (3).

48. Leggatt, in *Shakespeare's Political Drama*, notes the irony of Henry's prayer:

> This man who keeps shifting responsibility to others is himself haunted by the guilt of a crime he did not commit. . . . On the eve of his great victory his mind goes back to the past, and he reveals that the problem created in *Richard II* has not been solved and may be insoluble. It seems to bother no one else in the play; but it bothers him. Why does Henry connect his inherited guilt and his war with France? He does not say explicitly, but we may make the connection ourselves. Kingship can never again be the sacred office it was for Richard; the best it can be is a vehicle for worldly achievement, and on those limited but real terms Henry is determined to restore it, to undo the damage his father did. (135)

49. For instance, Tim Spiekerman, in *Shakespeare's Political Realism*, clearly does not regard the term 'Machiavellian' as complimentary: 'Beneath his new moral exterior, skeptics may well see something else in Henry V, namely, a battle-hardened, sly Machiavellian prince who is only pretending to be a Christian hero-king fighting a just war—all in order to establish a patriotic basis for his illegitimate rule' (125). Whereas, Marjorie Garber, in *Shakespeare After All*, seems 'crafty' neutral: 'And although [Hal] studies statecraft and policy with the crafty zeal of a born Machiavellian, we could say that in *I Henry IV* the chief study for the rising Prince is the study of language' (332). Allan Bloom, seems to impart more of a negative spin to the term:

> Hal becomes a real Machiavellian king, which means . . . that he is reputed to be just, even while fighting unjust but successful wars. Above all, like the Machiavellian king, he appears to be very religious and manipulates the prejudice in favor of religion by using the prelates. But he is also

> Machiavellian in the sense that he gives up all the sub- or suprapolitical pleasures that he experienced with Falstaff. He proves the usefulness of Falstaff, but his political ambition allows him to suppress the charms of Falstaff. What is interesting and sinister about Hal is the degree to which politics consumes him even though he is the beneficiary of a powerful critique of it'. (*Love and Friendship*, 409)

As I argued in the preceding chapter, I regard this supposed 'critique' to be mainly a contribution of Bloom's own political understanding, imaginatively invested in the fat bounder.

50. W. H. Auden seems fairly sure: 'By the time the curtain falls on *Henry V*, ... he is recognized by all to be the Ideal Ruler. Like his father in his youth, he is brave and personable. In addition, he is a much cleverer politician. While his father was an improviser, he is a master of the art of timing. His first soliloquy reveals him as a person who always sees several steps ahead and has the patience to wait ... ; he will never, if he can help it, leave anything to chance. Last but not least, he is blessed by luck' (*Dyer's Hand and Other Essays*, 189).

51. Cf. Plato, *Republic*, 537c.

52. Of course, the very next scene provides reason to doubt that there are *none* 'so mean and base' as to lack such 'noble lustre', since Bardolph, Pistol, and Nym—far from 'straining at the leash'—must be literally driven 'to the breech' by Fluellen's blows (3.2.21–27).

53. *The Prince*, chap. 9, para. 2, 39.

54. Ibid., para. 5, 41.

55. Ibid., chap. 14, paras. 3–4, 59–60. According to McFarlane, regarding the historical Henry: 'In 1421 a London Scrivener received £12. 8s. 0d for making copies of twelve books on hunting. A year later, at his death, the king had failed to return two chronicles of the Crusades which he had borrowed from his able aunt the Countess of Westmorland. ... When the poet Lydgate describes him as given to the study of ancient histories, it was not pure flattery' (*Lancastrian Kings and Lollard Knights*, 117).

56. In considering the radical difference between ordinary people's attitude towards heroic conquerors and that typical of a certain class of scholar-critic, one is reminded of Hegel's comments about such conquerors in his lectures on history (published posthumously as *The Philosophy of History*):

> Great men have formed purposes to satisfy themselves, not others. Whatever prudent designs and counsels they might have learned from others, would be the more limited and inconsistent features in their career; for it was they who best understood affairs; from whom others learned, and approved, or at least acquiesced in. ... Their fellows, therefore, follow these soul-leaders; for they feel the irresistible power of their own inner Spirit thus embodied. ...
>
> ... They are *great* men, because they willed and accomplished something great; not a mere fancy, a mere intention, but that which met the case and fell in with the needs of the age. This mode of considering them also excludes the so-called 'psychological' view, which—serving the needs of envy most effectually—contrives so to refer all actions to the heart—to bring them

under such a subjective aspect—as that their authors appear to have done everything under the impulse of some passion, mean or grand—some *morbid craving*—and on account of these passions and cravings to have been not moral men.... What pedagogue has not demonstrated of Alexander the Great—of Julius Caesar—that they were instigated by such passions and were consequently immoral men?—whence the conclusion immediately follows that he, the pedagogue, is a better man than they, because he has not such passions; a proof of which lies in the fact that he does not conquer Asia—vanquish Darius and Porus—but while he enjoys life himself, lets others enjoy it too. (30–32)

57. Thus, for example, Michael Drayton's fifteen-stanza 'Agincourt', written nearly two centuries after the battle it celebrates, which concludes:

Upon Saint Crispin's Day
Fought was this noble fray,
Which fame did not delay
To England to carry.
O when shall English men
With such acts fill a pen?
Or England breed again
Such a King Harry?

58. That the scene which immediately follows shows Henry doing something quite different (i.e., first, conversing incognito with Pistol, then eavesdropping unnoticed on Gower and Fluellen, then arguing his case with three common soldiers) needn't confute the claims of the Chorus, as all of this may be subsequent to his making the rounds according to the choral description. Just prior to his meeting the three soldiers, one of them observes the first glimmerings of the autumnal morning (4.1.90).

59. Campbell's *Shakespeare's Histories: Mirrors of Elizabethan Policy* remains a valuable text for the historical background it provides about military thinking (and disputes) in Shakespeare's day; some of the information she provides is practically essential for making sense of certain details in the play. With respect to Henry's catechism here, for example, she shows that his position is pretty much the orthodox doctrine of the day: 'King Henry replies [to Williams] by making clear the distinction between the private and the military crimes of his soldiers' (277). 'The soldier is thus responsible to the king as a soldier, but as a man he is responsible to God. Conversely, the king is responsible for the cause in which he orders his soldiers to fight, but he is not responsible for their sins as private persons' (279). Speaking more generally:

Henry V's army in France was governed by articles of war which Shakespeare probably knew. But because soldiers are much the same in every generation and the 'evil inclined' commit the same wicked deeds, the soldiers of Henry V were like Elizabethan soldiers, and the articles of war are very like Elizabethan articles of war....

The articles of war generally give first consideration to the spiritual welfare of the soldier and to the preservation of churches and other religious institutions. The first of Henry's laws for his army was unusually specific, however, decreeing that anyone removing without the permission of the constable of the army any church goods was to be hanged, and the stolen goods returned to the church. A special provision was added: 'We moreover ordain, that no one, under pain of death, shall dare irreverently to touch the sacrament of the Eucharist, nor the pyx or box in which the said sacrament is contained'. (293–94)

Without mentioning his name, Campbell contradicts E. M. W. Tillyard's criticisms of the play in *Shakespeare's History Plays*. For example, Tillyard had argued, 'A third sign of weak construction is the casualness of the comic scenes. Whereas in *Henry IV* these were linked in all sorts of ways with the serious action, in *Henry V* they are mainly detached scenes introduced for mere variety' (317). Campbell argues precisely the opposite: 'This weaving of the comic episodes into the texture of the play by making them all contribute to the development of the theme of war makes *Henry V* a much more unified play than *Henry IV*. Discussing the philosophy of war, picturing the accepted procedures of war, building comic scenes about the violations of the articles of war and the current Elizabethan dispute over the preferred "school of war", it is a great war play' (*Shakespeare's Histories*, 305).

60. A useful analysis of the disguised King's dialogue with the three soldiers, relating Henry's argument to the 'double effect' doctrine of the Just War theory of the day, is that of John M. Parrish, in 'Shakespeare's *Henry V* and Responsibility for War'. As Parrish states it, 'According to this doctrine . . . harmful actions that would otherwise be wrong in themselves can be justified if the wrong is a side effect (or 'double effect') of the actor's intention, rather than its true aim. As educated listeners would have known, however, the argument's original purpose had been to justify the unavoidable deaths of innocent casualties of *civilians* in war' (141)—*not*, that is to say, of soldiers who fall in battle.

61. Cf. Plato, *Republic*, 342e, 346e–347b.

62. Thus Holinshed:

This Henrie was a king, of life without spot, a prince whome all men loved, and of none disdained, a capteine against whome fortune never frowned, nor mischance once spurned, whose people him so severe a justicer both loved and obeied (and so humane withall) that he left no offense unpunished, nor freendship unrewarded; a terrour to rebels, and suppressour of sedition, his vertues notable, his qualities most praise-worthie.

In strength and nimbleness of bodie from his youth few to him comparable, for in wrestling, leaping, and running, no man well able to compare. . . . Never shrinking at cold, nor slothful for heat; . . . verie valiantlie abiding at needs both hunger and thirst; so manfull of mind as never seene to quinch at a wound, or to smart at the paine; . . . no man more moderate in eating and drinking, with diet not delicate, but rather more meet for men of warre, than for princes or tender stomachs. . . . He slept verie little, but that verie soundlie . . . ; of courage invincible, of purpose immutable, so wisehardie alwaies, as fear was banisht from him. . . .

... Wantonnesse of life and thirst in avarice had he quite quenched in him; vertues in deed in such an estate of sovereigntie, youth, and power, as verie rare, so right commendable in the highest degree. So staid of mind and countenance beside, that never jolie or triumphant for victorie, nor sad or damped for losse or misfortune. For bountifulnesse and liberalitie, no man more free, gentle, or franke, in bestowing rewards to all persons, according to their deserts: for his saieng was, that he never desired monie to keepe, but to give and spend. (Bullough, 406–7)

63. As Richmond observes, 'In some ways, Henry is thus as guilty of "stealing the pax" as Bardolph—in that he has "broken the peace" for his own advantage. That Shakespeare consciously sought the punning analogy may appear from his substitution of "pax" (a plate stamped with Christ's picture) for Holinshed's "pyx" (the vessel containing the consecrated wafer)' (*Shakespeare's Political Plays*, 184).

64. Vickie Sullivan, in 'Princes to Act: Henry V as the Machiavellian Prince of Appearance', argues (as her title suggests) that 'the being of Hal and Henry V is all seeming—all appearance', but nonetheless prefers to take him at his word here, and so concludes that he is oblivious 'to any pursuit higher than honor' (144). Whereas, I regard Henry's claim as simply rhetoric aimed at solidifying a bond between him and his men, to whom he can offer little but the honour of serving with him.

65. Apparently there is an historical basis for something like the wishful speech for ten thousand more men that Shakespeare gives to Westmorland, and Henry's negating reply (4.3.16–22), though the various sources attribute the wish to Sir Walter Hungerford. Ian Mortimer (*1415*) quotes a couple of versions of the colloquy, but—ever disdainful of 'the post-Shakespearean "great man" view of Henry' (447)—he registers a guarded skepticism as to whether such a conversation ever took place (424).

66. This list of English casualties is taken directly from Holinshed, 'as some doo report'. However, he continues, 'but other writers of greater credit affirme, that there were slaine above five or six hundred persons' (Bullough, 400). Shakespeare has opted for the report that magnifies the near-miraculous nature of the English victory. The reality is reflected in the fate of the Duke of York and his contingent, which were stationed on the right of the English line. According to Barker, 'The manner of the duke's death is not recorded by contemporaries, but it is suggestive that there was a remarkably high casualty rate among his own retinue. . . . his entire company at the battle consisted of only 370 men. The records of those who reshipped home from Calais reveal that only 283 of them survived the battle' (*Agincourt*, 317–18)

67. Here one might recall Helena asking, 'Which is the Frenchman?' and Diana answering, 'He—that with the plume' (*All's Well That Ends Well*, 3.5.77–78).

68. He is more emphatic on the latter occasion, perhaps because when conversing incognito the previous night with the three soldiers, his claim that he 'heard the King say he would not be ransomed' was met with a skeptical response: 'Ay, he said so to make us fight cheerfully; but when our throats are cut he may be ransomed and we ne'er the wiser' (4.1.189–200).

69. *The Prince*, chap. 12, para. 3; chap. 14, para. 1.

70. Holinshed reports that Henry had proven himself such a master of war 'that the Frenchmen had constant opinion he could never be vanquished in battell' (Bullough, 407). But the French were more cunning in matters of love: 'The said ladie Katharine was brought by hir mother, onelie to the intent that the king of England beholding hir excellent beautie, should be so inflamed and rapt in hir love, that he to obteine hir to his wife, should the sooner agree to a gentle peace and a loving concord'. The strategy was not immediately effective, but eventually it was inasmuch as 'a certaine sparke of burning love was kindled in the kings heart by the sight of the ladie Katharine' (ibid., 403–4).

71. *The Prince*, chap. 13, para. 3.

72. Since this is unhistorical (Henry's army in this first French campaign had no Irish or Scottish component), we should presume that there is some purpose served by Shakespeare's introducing this fiction. And he would have read in Holinshed that the composition of the army was otherwise in Henry's subsequent campaign—that, for example, Irish soldiers did good service at the siege of Rouen, so 'that no men were more praised, nor did more damage to their enemies than they did' (Bullough, 401).

73. Both the numbers arrayed for battle on each side and the numbers of each side's casualties in this historic battle have always been difficult to establish with any confidence, and have recently become even more controversial as reflections of pro and con views about Henry. With respect to numbers engaged, Shakespeare simply followed Holinshed's account. Thus, he has Westmorland observe, 'Of fighting men they have full threescore thousand', to which Exeter rejoins, 'There's five to one; besides, they all are fresh'. Salisbury drives home the point: "Tis a fearful odds'. Barker writes, 'Unlike the English army, where contemporary administrative records support the chroniclers' assessment of its size as being in the region of six thousand fighting men, no evidence exists for the French' (*Agincourt*, 274). Of the various possibilities, she thinks 'most likely' the 36,000 claimed by 'Jehan Waurin, a Burgundian in the French army', though other accounts claim 50,000 to 60,000. It must have been a huge gathering, for despite a few prestigious absentees, 'the list of nobility in the French army . . . reads like a roll-call of the chivalry of France' (274–75). Ian Mortimer's revisionist account, *1415*, claims, 'the most extreme imbalance which is credible is fifteen thousand French troops against 8,100 English: a ratio of about two-to-one' (566). Mortimer's efforts to explain away so much evidence to the contrary are more ingenious than persuasive.

74. Traversi tacitly implicates Shakespeare himself in Henry's handling of this matter:

> It is a necessary part of Henry's triumph. Justified as it no doubt is in terms of military tactics, it is also related to the tougher strain of disillusioned realism that emerges from the play. The self-control that we have learned to associate with the victorious king is, as we have repeatedly had occasion to see, not without a suggestion of harshness and inhumanity. His righteousness is of the kind that does not prevent him from inflicting merciless reprisals on his enemies. . . . This is once more the Henry who can contemplate suffering from which his normal, peaceful humanity would recoil, but which he

feels himself, in war, not to be the cause.... By such excellence, Shakespeare would seem to say, must wars be won. (*Shakespeare*, 194–95)

If one agrees with this judgment, even Gower's endorsement of the throat-cutting order ('O 'tis a gallant king!') is not necessarily either outrageous or ironic.

75. As others have noted, it is curious that in his treatment of the battle, Shakespeare makes no mention of the crucial contribution of the English longbow and the special class of professional archers who wielded this powerful weapon ('in whome the force of his armie consisted': Holinshed). Nor, for that matter, does he indicate anything else as to the tactical disposition of either the English or the French forces, or of the material circumstances in which they fought (e.g., the previous night's heavy rain which turned to gumbo the meadow through which the heavily armoured but dismounted French knights slogged to the attack). Whereas, his source (Holinshed) gives a detailed account of these matters (Bullough, 395–99).

By way of explaining this curiosity, Pamela Jensen, in an insightful essay to which I am particularly indebted, suggests:

Shakespeare may want to show that the cause of the English victory is not discernible in weapons or combat tactics at all, but is, on the contrary, entirely a matter of hearts and minds. As Henry himself insists: 'All things are ready, if our minds be so' (IV.iii.71). On the English side, the cause of victory is manifest therefore in Henry's speeches to his men before battle. From these speeches we can conclude that Agincourt does indeed represent a departure from tradition; not because of the new preponderance of the common man's weapons, but because of the new preponderance of the common man's heart. This is not to say that King Henry is a democrat in disguise. From Henry's actions we can, however, infer his recognition of the common humanity underlying all social and political distinctions. ('Famous Victories of William Shakespeare', 248)

Jensen's interpretation seems valid to me, though I would add for the sake of clarity that this 'recognition of the common humanity' does not preclude Henry's awareness of natural differences in strength of mind and spirit.

76. Holinshed more than once reminds his reader of this normal means of communicating on the battlefield. 'Thus the Frenchmen being ordered under their standards and banners, made a great shew: for suerlie they were esteemed in number six times as manie or more, than was the whole companie of Englishmen, with wagoners, pages, and all. They rested themselves, waiting for the bloudie blast of the terrible trumpet' (Bullough, 392). And, 'When the messenger had come backe to the French host, the men of warre put on their helmets, and caused their trumpets to blow to the battell' (ibid., 395).

77. About this belated effort to salvage French honour, Barker writes, 'It was doomed to failure.... The nobility and self-sacrifice they had shown earned them nothing but contempt from their compatriots, who laid the blame for Henry's order to kill the prisoners squarely at the door of "this cursed company of Frenchmen"' (*Agincourt*, 307).

78. However, Mortimer contends, 'there are good reasons to believe it was a planned attack on the English, directed by a French commander.... The fact that men-at-arms were involved suggests that this was not meant to be a self-seeking raiding party, even if it turned into one. Nor was it without organization—an attack on the English baggage had been envisaged in the first battle plan' (*1415*, 444).

79. Keegan, *Face of Battle*, 108–9. However, Keegan continues: 'Comprehensible in harsh tactical logic; in human, ethical, and practical terms much more difficult to understand. Henry, a Christian king, was also an experienced soldier and versed in the elaborate code of international law governing relations between a prisoner and his captor. Its most important provision was that which guaranteed the prisoner his life.... If Henry could give the order and, as he did, subsequently escape the reproval of his peers, of the Church and of the chroniclers, we must presume it was because the battlefield itself was still regarded as a sort of moral no-man's-land and the hour of battle as a legal *dies non*' (109). I must say, I see no need for this speculative explanation, nor is Henry's decision 'difficult to understand' on any terms whatsoever. The lack of criticism from contemporary quarters was in all likelihood simply a recognition of the obvious: that Henry was, both tactically and morally, *obliged* to do whatever was most apt to further the survival of the men he led into battle.

80. McFarlane, *Lancastrian Kings and Lollard Knights*, 129–30.

81. Meron, *Bloody Constraint*, 193. Desmond Seward, in his determinedly iconoclastic biography of the King, *Henry V: The Scourge of God*, challenges this claim: 'This massacre of prisoners in 1415 is Henry V's one generally acknowledged peccadillo. Almost every one of his English biographers and historians [!] tries to absolve him of guilt, referring to the lack of condemnation by contemporary English chroniclers, or to 'the standards of the time'. In reality, by fifteenth-century standards ... [it] was a peculiarly nasty crime' (81). The only evidence Seward provides for his view is a quote from one French chronicler who observed that the deed was done 'in cold blood'.

Speaking of 'in cold blood', a vignette from a few decades previous provides some additional context in which to view Henry's order:

> Of Du Guesclin [created constable of France in 1370], whom St-Palaye calls the flower of chivalry, two stories are told that throw a different but curious light on the manners of those times. Having on one occasion defeated the English and taken many of them prisoners, Du Guesclin tried to observe the rules of distributive justice in the partition of the captives, but failing of success and unable to discover to whom the prisoners really belonged, he and Clisson (who were brothers in arms) in order to terminate the differences which the victorious French had with one another on the subject, conceived that the only fair solution was to have them all massacred, and accordingly more than 500 Englishmen were put to death in cold blood outside the gates of Bressière. So, on a second occasion, such a quantity of English were taken that 'there was not, down to the commonest soldier, anyone who had not some prisoner of whom he counted to win a good ransom; but as there was a dispute between the French to know to whom each prisoner belonged, Du Guesclin, to put them all on a level, ordered them to put all to the sword, and

only the English chiefs were spared. This ferocious warrior [was] the product and pride of his time, the favourite hero of French chivalry. (James Farrar, *Military Manners and Customs* [London, 1885], as quoted in Hastings, *Oxford Book of Military Anecdotes*, 85)

With such glorious deeds to their historical credit, perhaps it is no wonder that the French chroniclers were loath to criticize what Henry ordered in the midst of a desperate battle.

82. Allmand, *Henry V*, 94. The bearer of this sacred banner, seigneur de Bacqueville, was killed and the banner never recovered, presumably buried in the mud.
83. Jacob, *Fifteenth Century*, 156.
84. Allmand, *Henry V*, 95.
85. Keegan, *Face of Battle*, 111.
86. Mortimer, *1415*, 451.
87. Churchill, *Birth of Britain*, 404, 408, 410.
88. In that case, *Henry V* would *not* be 'the centerpiece of the two tetralogies'— as Chris Barker rightly characterizes it, in 'Freedom in Shakespeare's English History Plays'—for there would have been no historical basis for the first tetralogy.

An Alternative Epilogue

1. *The Prince* (chap. 5, conclusion).
2. 'England', 'English', and their various cognates are mentioned a total of one hundred times. The very fact that the French elite do many times refer to the English as such—e.g., in the wee hours before the battle (3.7.81, 84, 91, 135, 151), and when the two sides meet to conclude peace (5.2.22, 361)—simply throws into relief those early occasions when they make a point of referring to the invaders as 'bastard Normans, Norman bastards'.
3. As noted in a previous chapter, McFarlane reports, 'Henry is the first king of England whose state papers, written in his own hand, have been preserved for us' (*Lancastrian Kings and Lollard Knights*, 116–17). Moreover, as previously noted, these papers are always in English: 'Though he could read, write, and speak Latin and French—and that for pleasure—Henry was the first king of England who preferred to conduct business in the vernacular and to encourage its use by others' (119). By the end of his reign, English had been established as the official language of the realm; hence parliamentary records were kept in English, wills and other legal transactions could be done in English, etc. So, rather than attempt to establish a bilingual polity—a recipe for chronic friction—Henry might, like the Normans, have chosen to stick with the language spoken in his reliable power base.
4. Recall, Machiavelli advises, 'a prudent man should always enter upon the paths beaten by great men, and imitate those who have been most excellent' (*The Prince*, chap. 6, para. 1). Moreover, we know that Henry was a reader of ancient histories and chronicles.
5. The irony of his assassination by a clique of senators—who had then to flee for their lives lest they be torn to pieces by plebian mobs—is that it effectively

elevated Caesar and his accomplishments to a status beyond criticism. Similarly, Henry's early death insulated him from blame for the setbacks his successors experienced in trying to carry out his French project.

6. Cf. Hobbes, *Leviathan*, chap. 20, para. 11.
7. Hobbes has this to say about the policy of the Romans:

> Strangers (that is, men not used to live under the same government, nor speaking the same language) do commonly undervalue one another... which is indeed a great inconvenience: but it proceedeth not necessarily from the subjection to a strangers government, but from the unskilfulnesse of the Governours, ignorant of the true rules of Politiques. And therefore the Romans when they had subdued many Nations, to make their Government digestible, were wont to take away that grievance, as much as they thought necessary, by giving sometimes to whole Nations, and sometimes to Principall men of every Nation they conquered, not onely the Privileges, but also the Name of Romans; and took many of them into the Senate, and Offices of charge, in the Roman City. (*Leviathan*, chap. 19, para. 23)

Paul Cantor begins his '"Christian Kings" and "English Mercuries": *Henry V* and the Classical Tradition of Manliness' with several observations pertinent to this 'alternative epilogue':

> At the core of the Renaissance lay the hope of reviving the political forms of classical antiquity and perhaps of rivaling the martial greatness of ancient Rome as an imperial power. Exploring in *Henry V* the political and military career of England's greatest foreign conqueror to date, Shakespeare seems to be raising the question of how England might follow in the footsteps of Rome as an imperial power.... Shakespeare's history plays helped provide the English with a vision of national greatness, and that vision was largely based on Roman models....
>
> What distinguishes Henry V as a king in Shakespeare's portrayal is precisely his ability to create a mixed regime on a Roman model. As the act V chorus suggests, Henry won the allegiance of his nobles and his people by giving both ranks an active role in his rule and his military campaigns. Above all, Henry's common touch makes him an effective leader of his largely citizen army and gives his rule the force and effectiveness that comes from incorporating a significant popular element. (74)

8. Mortimer, *1415*, provides an especially vivid account, day by day, of what a struggle securing finance was in regard to the first invasion.
9. That this same 'merit' principle has an underside is apparent in the dark irony with which Henry toys with the conspirators: 'And we shall forget the office of our hand / Sooner than quittance of desert and merit / According to their weight and worthiness' (2.2.33–35).
10. The foundation of the English army that was to prove so formidable under Edward III and his successors in the Hundred Years' War was laid nearly a half century earlier by his grandfather, Edward I, in order to subjugate Wales and Scotland.

See Morris, *Welsh Wars of Edward I*, esp. chap. 2, 'An Edwardian Army' (35–109). Morris writes that, prior to Edward I's reforms and innovations, 'There was very little real military training', and 'that without an able commander-in-chief the cavalry at the close of the thirteenth century were disorganized, personal bravery never compensating for lack of organized skill. Pride was the great fault of the period. . . . The more deeply lying fault was want of discipline due to want of proper subordination of commands' (66). Moreover:

> From the facts of Edward's wars, it would be difficult to believe that pugnacity was the inherent virtue of the Anglo-Saxon. The downright love of fighting and adventure for their own sake was the characteristic of the Norman, and the knight of this reign [i.e., of Edward I] may have been rash and impatient of discipline, but he loved to fight and charge. The Anglo-Saxon had to be taught to fight, and those counties first became warlike which were nearest to the theatre of war, the borders of Wales. These men may have had a considerable strain of Welsh blood in them; at any rate, they coalesced with the friendlies of the marches. Otherwise, . . . only the Sherwood foresters had a taste for fighting. But Edward was evidently hoping to create the taste in other counties by virtue of the 'view of arms' ordained by the Statute of Winchester. In 1295 he ordered to Winchelsea 25,000 foot of the counties from Dorset to Norfolk, bowmen and crossbowmen. This was the first time that so great a levy was ordered, and if he imagined that the whole body would come to the muster organized and skilled in the use of weapons, he must have been indeed sanguine. Most probably he ordered so many thousands in the hope that the few good men among them would form an efficient force. In 1294 and 1295 he was driven to the expedient of taking criminals into his ranks for the expeditions to Gascony. . . .
>
> Edward III had the greatest difficult in sweeping men into the ranks in 1333; Falstaffs and Shallows abounded in real life, and convicted criminals and poachers had to be impressed. Yet this army, collected with such difficulty, won a striking victory at Halidon Hill. Here, I take it, is the turning point. (97–98)

Morris notes that the radical organizational reforms which Edward I began in 1277 'he could not complete because the baronial pride was too strong even for him' (68). Hence, they were not brought to complete fruition until the reign of Edward III. Still, it was not until his victory at Crecy [1346] that Europeans learned how greatly things had changed in England since the days of Edward I, and that as a result of replacing feudal forms with paid military service the English had become a military power to reckon with. Had Henry V lived to complete his conquest and absorption of France, his personal power would have been virtually irresistible relative to the baronial class, and he could have carried through whatever political transformations he saw fit, regardless of any lingering 'baronial pride'.

11. One could regard this as the flaw in the democratic conception of legitimacy: its deriving 'consent of the governed' (expressed periodically in free elections) from people's assessments of the actual, or promised, performance of their governors. Although this has worked to provide long-term stability (so far) in

several modern polities that have successfully adopted representative democracy as their form of government, the fact remains that the gap between legitimate rule and good rule still exists, and—as I opined before—steadily widens, and may yet lead to a dangerous crisis in one or more of these regimes. The root of this problem is the extremely limited ability of the vast majority of people to understand political reality, and thereby to judge when it is being well dealt with. For as the wise Hobbes warned, there are those who 'think there needs no method in the study of Politiques, (as there does in the study of Geometry,) but onely to be lookers on; which is not so. For Politiques is the harder study of the two' (*Leviathan*, chap. 30, para. 25).

12. As Hobbes observes, 'Geometry ... is the Mother of all Naturall Science' (ibid., chap. 46, para. 11), not least because it is the paradigm of deductive reasoning. And, 'The skill of making, and maintaining Common-wealths, consisteth in certain Rules, as doth Arithmetique and Geometry; not (as Tennis-play) on Practise onely; which Rules, neither poor men have the leisure, nor men that have had the leisure, have hitherto had the curiosity, or the method to find out' (ibid., chap. 20, para. 19).

13. Ibid., chap. 38, para. 1.

Bibliography

Classic works of political philosophy and literature (e.g., Plato's *Republic*, Hobbes's *Leviathan*, Melville's *Moby-Dick*, Shakespeare's plays) are not included unless a specific edition is cited.

Ackroyd, Peter. *Shakespeare: The Biography*. New York: Nan A. Talese, 2005.
Allmand, Christopher. *Henry V*. Berkeley: University of California Press, 1992.
Alvis, John E. 'Spectacle Supplanting Ceremony: Shakespeare's Henry of Monmouth'. In Alvis and West, *Shakespeare as Political Thinker*.
Alvis, John E., and Thomas G. West, eds. *Shakespeare as Political Thinker*. Wilmington, DE: ISI Books, 2000.
Auden, W. H. *The Dyer's Hand and Other Essays*. New York: Vintage, 1989.
———. *Lectures on Shakespeare*. Edited by Arthur Kirsch. Princeton, NJ: Princeton University Press, 2000.
Barker, Chris. 'Freedom in Shakespeare's English History Plays'. *Interpretation* 40, no. 2 (2013).
Barker, Juliet. *Agincourt: The King, the Campaign, the Battle*. London: Abacus, 2006.
Bate, Jonathan. *The Romantics on Shakespeare*. London: Penguin, 1992.
Baxter, John. *Shakespeare's Poetic Styles: Verse into Drama*. London: Routledge & Kegan Paul, 1980.
Bloom, Allan. *Love and Friendship*. New York: Simon & Schuster, 1993.
———. '*Richard II*'. In Alvis and West, *Shakespeare as Political Thinker*.
Bloom, Harold. *Shakespeare: The Invention of the Human*. New York: Riverhead Books, 1998.
Bradley, A. C. *Oxford Lectures on Poetry*. Bloomington: University of Indiana Press, 1961.
Bradshaw, Graham. *Misinterpretations: Shakespeare and the Materialists*. Ithaca, NY: Cornell University Press, 1993.
Brennan, Anthony. *Twayne's New Critical Introductions to Shakespeare: Henry V*. New York: Twayne, 1992.
Bruce, Marie Louise. *The Usurper King: Henry of Bolingbroke 1366–99*. 1986. Reprint, London: Rubicon Press, 1998.
Bullough, Geoffrey. *Narrative and Dramatic Sources of Shakespeare*. Vols. 3 and 4. London: Routledge & Kegan Paul, 1960, 1962.
Campbell, Lily B. *Shakespeare's Histories: Mirrors of Elizabethan Policy*. London: Methuen, 1964.
Cantor, Paul. '"Christian Kings" and "English Mercuries"': *Henry V* and the Classical Tradition of Manliness'. In *Educating the Prince: Essays in Honor of Harvey Mansfield*, edited by Mark Blitz and William Kristol. Lanham, MD: Rowman and Littlefield, 2000.

———. 'Shakespeare's *Henry V*: From the Medieval to the Modern World'. In *Perspectives on Politics in Shakespeare*, edited by John Murley and Sean Sutton. Lanham, MD: Rowman and Littlefield, 2006.

Churchill, Sir Winston. *The Birth of Britain*. Vol. 1 of *A History of the English-Speaking Peoples*. New York: Dodd, Mead & Company, 1964.

Cowan, Louise. 'God Will Save the King'. In Alvis and West, *Shakespeare as Political Thinker*.

Coyle, Martin. *Critical Guide to Richard II*. Cambridge: Icon, 1998.

Craig, Leon Harold. *Of Philosophers and Kings: Political Philosophy in Shakespeare's 'Macbeth' and 'King Lear'*. Toronto: University of Toronto Press, 2001.

———. *Philosophy and the Puzzles of 'Hamlet'*. New York: Bloomsbury, 2014.

———. *The Platonian Leviathan*. Toronto: University of Toronto Press, 2010.

———. *The War Lover: A Study of Plato's 'Republic'*. Toronto: University of Toronto Press, 1994.

Craik, T. W., ed. *King Henry V*. 3rd Arden ed. London: Routledge, 1995.

Dobski, Bernard J. 'Friendship and Love of Honor: The Education of Henry V'. In *Souls with Longing*, edited by Bernard J. Dobski and Dustin A. Gish. Lanham, MD: Lexington Books.

Empson, William. *Essays on Shakespeare*. Cambridge: Cambridge University Press, 1986.

Forker, Charles R., ed. *King Richard II*. 3rd Arden ed. London: Thomson Learning, 2002.

Garber, Marjorie. *Shakespeare After All*. New York: Pantheon, 2004.

Greenblatt, Stephen. *Will in the World: How Shakespeare Became Shakespeare*. New York: W. W. Norton, 2004.

Hastings, Max, ed. *The Oxford Book of Military Anecdotes*. Oxford: Oxford University Press, 1985.

Hegel, G. W. F. *The Philosophy of History*. Translated by J. Sibree. New York: Dover, 1956.

Holderness, Graham. *Critical Studies: Richard II*. London: Penguin, 1989.

Hume, David. *History of England*. Vol. 2. Indianapolis: LibertyClassics, 1983.

Humphreys, A. R. *The Second Part of King Henry IV*. 2nd Arden ed. London: Methuen, 1966.

Hunt, Constance C. T. 'The Origins of National Identity in Shakespeare's *Henry V*'. In *Perspectives on Political Science* 36, no. 3 (2007).

Jacob, E. F. *The Fifteenth Century: 1399–1485*. Vol. 6 of *The Oxford History of England*. Oxford: Oxford University Press, 1961.

Jensen, Pamela K. 'Beggars and Kings: Cowardice and Courage in Shakespeare's *Richard II*'. In *Interpretation* 18, no. 1 (Fall 1990).

———. 'The Famous Victories of William Shakespeare'. In *Princes, Poets and Private Citizens*, edited by Joseph M. Knippenberg and Peter Lawler. Lanham, MD: Rowman and Littlefield, 1996.

Kastan, David Scott, ed. *King Henry IV, Part One*. 3rd Arden ed. London: Thomson Learning, 2002.

Keegan, John. *The Face of Battle*. New York: Viking, 1976.

Keen, M. H. *England in the Later Middle Ages*. London: Methuen, 1973.

Kernan, Alvin. 'The Henriad: Shakespeare's Major History Plays'. *Yale Review* 59 (1969).

Leggatt, Alexander. *Shakespeare's Political Drama: The History Plays and the Roman Plays*. London: Routledge, 1988.
Lewis, Wyndham. *The Lion and the Fox: The Rôle of the Hero in the Plays of Shakespeare*. 1927. Reprint, London: Methuen, 1951.
Machiavelli, Niccolò. *The Prince*. Edited and translated by Harvey Mansfield. Chicago: University of Chicago Press, 1985.
Marriot, J. A. R. *English History in Shakspeare*. 1917. Reprint, New York: Haskell House, 1971.
Maus, Katharine Eisaman. Preface to *Richard II*. In *The Norton Shakespeare: Histories*. Edited by Stephen Greenblatt. New York: W. W. Norton, 1997.
McFarlane, K. B. *Lancastrian Kings and Lollard Knights*. Oxford: Oxford University Press, 1972.
Meron, Theodor. *Bloody Constraint: War and Chivalry in Shakespeare*. Oxford: Oxford University Press, 1998.
Morris, John E. *The Welsh Wars of Edward I*. 1901. Reprint, New York: Haskell House, 1969.
Mortimer, Ian. *1415: Henry V's Year of Glory*. London: Vintage, 2010.
Neale, J. E. *Queen Elizabeth*. London: Jonathan Cape, 1934.
Norwich, John Julius. *Shakespeare's Kings*. London: Viking, 1999.
Nuttall, A. D. *Shakespeare the Thinker*. New Haven, CT: Yale University Press, 2007.
Parrish, John M. 'Shakespeare's *Henry V* and Responsibility for War'. In *Shakespeare and Politics*, edited by Bruce E. Altschuler and Michael A. Genovese. Boulder, CO: Paradigm, 2014.
Pater, Walter. *Appreciations: With an Essay on Style*. London: Macmillan, 1910.
Pierce, Robert B. *Shakespeare's History Plays: The Family and the State*. Columbus: Ohio State University Press, 1971.
Rabkin, Norman. *Shakespeare and the Common Understanding*. New York: Free Press, 1967.
Richmond, H. M. *Shakespeare's Political Plays*. Gloucester, MA: Peter Smith, 1977.
Roberts, Josephine A. *Richard II: An Annotated Bibliography*. New York: Garland, 1988.
Saccio, Peter. *Shakespeare's English Kings: History, Chronicle, and Drama*. New York: Oxford University Press, 1977.
Sandler, Robert, ed. *Northrop Frye on Shakespeare*. New Haven, CT: Yale University Press, 1986.
Seward, Desmond. *Henry V: The Scourge of God*. New York: Viking, 1987.
Spiekerman, Tim. 'The Making of a Politician: Shakespeare's Prince Hal at Work and Play'. In *Perspectives on Political Science* 41, no. 4 (2012).
———. *Shakespeare's Political Realism: The English History Plays*. Albany: SUNY Press, 2001.
Steel, Anthony. *Richard II*. Cambridge: Cambridge University Press, 1962.
Sullivan, Vickie. 'Princes to Act: Henry V as the Machiavellian Prince of Appearance'. In *Shakespeare's Political Pageant*, edited by Joseph Aulis and Vickie Sullivan. Lanham, MD: Rowman and Littlefield, 1996.
Tillyard, E. M. W. *Shakespeare's History Plays*. London: Chatto & Windus, 1944.
Traversi, Derek. *Shakespeare from 'Richard II' to 'Henry V'*. London: Hollis and Carter, 1957.

Ure, Peter, ed. *King Richard II.* 2nd Arden ed. Cambridge, MA: Harvard University Press, 1956.

Waith, Eugene M., ed. *Shakespeare: The Histories.* Englewood Cliffs, NJ: Prentice-Hall, 1965.

Wilson, J. Dover. *The Fortunes of Falstaff.* Cambridge: Cambridge University Press, 1943.

Index of Names

This index lists persons named in the text (as distinct from dramatic characters), excepting Shakespeare and all but the four citations of Bullough that figure substantially in the text (the others being redundant with Holinshed). Those named are listed alphabetically as they first or generally appear in the text.

Abel, 198n3
Achilles, 72, 91, 166
Ackroyd, Peter, 225n40
Agincourt, Isambard d', 177
Alexander the Great, xv, 49, 159, 166, 172, 219–20n12, 252n44, 255n56
Alkibiades, 239–40n25
Allmand, Christopher, 218n2, 219n5, 219n11, 221n16, 221nn21–22, 234–45n12, 248n23, 252n42, 261n82, 261n84
Alvis, John E., 195–96n4, 229n54, 243n2
Anne of Bohemia, 206n24
Aristotle, 212n51, 212n53
Arundel, Thomas, Archbishop of Canterbury, 51, 52
Asklepius, 239n25
Aubrey, John, 196n4
Auden, W. H., 232–33n3, 235n16, 236–37n20, 240n27, 254n50

Bacon, Francis, 215n67
Bacqueville, Guillaummme Martel, seigneur de, 261n82
Bagot, Sir John, 198–99n5, 209nn38–39
Bardolf, Thomas, Earl of Nottingham, 50
Barker, Chris, 261n88
Barker, Juliet, 219n7, 220n14, 221n22, 222n26, 223n30, 234n10, 234–35n12, 241n31, 249n26, 249n29, 257n66, 258n73, 259n77
Bate, Jonathan, 195n2, 195n3, 218n1

Baxter, John, 198n4
Beauchamp, Anne, 106
Beauchamp, Richard, Earl of Warwick, 49, 51, 106, 234n12
Beaufort, Thomas, Duke of Exeter, 52, 250n32
Becket, Thomas, 204n20
Bergson, Henri, 242n33
Blanche (younger daughter of Henry IV), 47
Bloom, Allan, 198n3, 201n13, 213–14n59, 230–31n57, 237n20, 239n25, 253–54n50
Bloom, Harold, 229–30n55
Bohun, Eleanor, Duchess of Gloucester (widow of Thomas of Woodstock), 218n3
Bohun, Humphrey de, Earl of Hereford and Essex, 218n3
Bohun, Joan, Countess of Hereford (Henry V's maternal Grandmother), 47
Bohun, Mary (Bolingbroke's first wife, mother of Henry V), 47, 218n3
Borgia, Cesare, 94, 235n17
Brabant, Antoine, Duke of, 176
Bradley, A. C., 226n42, 232n65, 237–38n21, 240–41n30
Bradmore, John, 220n14
Bradshaw, Graham, 251n35
Brennan, Anthony, 197n6
Bruce, Marie Louise, 199n8, 200n10, 202n14, 218n3, 222n25, 223n31, 224n35

Buckton, Piers, 209n38
Bullough, Geoffrey, 210n40, 224–25nn36–38

Caesar, Julius, 154, 164, 166, 167, 172, 183, 187, 193, 251n34, 255n56, 261–62n5
Cain, 198n3
Cambridge, Richard of Conisborough, Earl of, 146, 246n16, 246–47n18, 247n23
Campbell, Lily B., 197n2, 198n3, 204–5n20, 232n1, 255–56n59
Canterbury, Henry Chichele, Archbishop of, 244n9, 244n11
Cantor, Paul, 213n56, 251n36, 262n7
Carew, Lord Thomas, 51
Carlyle, Thomas, 195n2
Cecil, William, Lord Burghley, 205n20
Chambers, E. K., 217n77
Charlemagne, 136, 244n9
Charles VI, King of France, 52, 235n12, 247–48n18
Chastellain, Georges, 241n31
Chaucer, Geoffrey, 218n4
Churchill, Sir Winston, 179, 261n87
Cicero, 183, 218n4
Clifford, Maud, 146
Clifford, Richard, Lord, 247n23
Clisson, Oliver de, 260n81
Coleridge, Samuel Taylor, 198n4
Cowan, Louise, 198n3, 206n26, 207n27
Coyle, Martin, 204n20, 217n77
Cromwell, Oliver, 221n14
Cyrus, 166

Darius, 255n56
Despenser, Hugh de, 49
Dobski, Bernard J., 244n7
Douglas, Archibald, Earl of, 227n48
Drayton, Michael, 255n57
Du Guesclin, Bertrand, Constable of France, 260–61n81

Edward I, King of England, 47, 72, 74, 189, 249n24, 262–63n10

Edward III (the Great), King of England, 2, 72, 135, 136, 137, 138, 158, 159, 160, 180, 182, 205n21, 244n8, 246n17, 262–63n10
Edward IV, King of England, 215n67
Edward VI, King of England, 37
Edward the Confessor, King of England, 182
Elizabeth I, Queen of England, 197n2, 204n20
Empson, William, 231n63
Erpingham, Sir Thomas, 49
Essex, Robert Devereux, Earl of, 204–5n20

Fabyan, 219n9
Farrar, James, 260–61n81
Fastolf, Sir John, 250n32
Fauquembergheu, Count of, 176
Fevre, Jean de, 179
Fitzalan, Thomas, Earl of Arundel, 221n22, 234n12
Forker, Charles R., 197n3, 198n4, 206n24, 209n39
Frye, Northrop, 229n54, 237n20

Galeazzo, Duke Gian of Milan, 200n10
Garber, Marjorie, 253–54n49
Gascoigne, William, 224n35
Chastellain, Georges, 241n31
Glendower, Gruffydd (son of Owen) 50
Glendower, Owen (*Owain Glyn Dŵr*), 47, 49, 50, 51, 221n20, 225n38, 247–49n23
Glendower, Tudor (brother of Owen) 50
Goddard, Harold C., 198n3
Godwineson, Harold, King of England, 182
Gower, Lord Russell, 240n29
Grafton, Richard, 196n4
Greenblatt, Stephen, 238–39n23
Greene, Robert, 238–39n23
Grey ('Graie'), Sir Thomas, 246–47n18

Hall, Edward, 196n4, 197n2, 225n39
Hastings, Max, 261n81

Index

Hayward, Sir John, 197n2, 205n20
Hazlitt, William, 195n3, 218n1
Hector of Troy, 72, 91
Hegel, G. W. F., 254–55n56
Henry II, King of England, 204n20
Henry IV (Henry Bolingbroke, Duke of Hereford), King of England, 2, 21, 47–53, 146, 182, 189, 197n2, 199–201nn7–11, 201n13, 202n14, 205n20, 209–10nn38–39, 210n43, 218n3, 219n10, 221n17, 222n24, 223nn29–30, 223n34, 226n45, 227n48, 227–28n50, 234n10, 234–5n12, 243nn1–2, 243–44n5, 246nn15–17, 246n17 247n23
Henry V (Henry Monmouth, Crown Prince 'Hal'), King of England, 21, 37, 46, 47–54, 58, 106, 146, 157, 158, 176–82, 185, 188, 190, 195n3, 204n17, 218n2, 218n4, 219n5, 219nn8–10, 219–20n12, 221n15, 221n22, 222n23, 222nn27–28, 223n30, 223nn33–34, 225n38, 226n45, 228n50, 234n10, 234n12, 241n31, 243n1, 243–44n5, 246–47nn15–18, 247–49nn23–24, 249n26, 249n29, 249–50n31–33, 252n40, 252n44, 254n55, 255n57, 255–56n59, 256–57n62, 257n64, 258n70, 258n74, 260n79, 260–61n81, 261–62nn3–5, 262n7, 262–63n10
Henry VI, King of England, 37, 38, 46, 106, 180, 218n2, 246n16
Henry VII (Henry Tudor), King of England, 206n26, 215n67
Henry VIII, King of England, 37, 192, 243n1, 243nn1–2
Hobbes, Thomas, vi, xi, 1, 41, 46, 95, 123, 129, 153, 159, 181, 186, 191, 192, 196n4, 201n12, 204n18, 211n46, 212n52, 212n54, 213n58, 214–15n62, 215n64, 215n67, 216n69, 216n71, 216n73, 227n46, 230n56, 231nn58–59, 240n28, 247n21, 252n39, 252n45, 262nn6–7, 263–64nn11–13

Hoccleve, Thomas, 225n38
Holderness, Graham, 198n3, 202–3n16
Holinshed, Raphael, xvi, 17, 53, 146, 147, 151, 163, 171, 196n4, 199n7, 198–99n5, 199n9, 200n10, 201n13, 202n15, 203n16, 205n21, 207n28, 207n30, 209n38, 209–10n39, 210n40, 210n43, 215n65, 219n5, 219n9, 221n15, 221n18, 223n34, 225n39, 243n3, 243–44n5, 244n9, 244n11, 245n12, 246n17, 246–47n18, 247n19, 247n20, 247n22, 247–49n23, 249–50n31, 250n32, 250–51n33, 256–57nn62–63, 257n66, 258n71, 258nn73–74, 259nn75–77
Howell, Davy, 247n23
Hume, David, 202n14, 224n35
Humphrey, Duke of Gloucester (fourth son of Henry IV), 47, 48, 196n4, 219n5, 224n35
Humphreys, A. R. 232n2
Hungerford, Sir Walter, 257n65
Hunt, Constance C. T., 251n36

Isabella, Queen (daughter of Philip IV of France, mother of Edward III), 158, 160, 182, 244n8

Jacob, E. F., 222n23, 223n28, 227–28n50, 261n83
Jensen, Pamela K., 196n5, 198n3, 211n44, 217n74, 259n75
Jesus, 198n3, 207n27
John XXIII, Pope, 246n17
John of Gaunt, Duke of Lancaster (fourth son of Edward III, and father of Henry IV), 47, 48, 52, 136, 159, 180, 199n7, 215n67, 218n3, 222n25
John of Lancaster, Duke of Bedford (third son of Henry IV), 47, 48, 50
John the Fearless, Duke of Burgundy, 52
Johnson, Samuel, 229–30n55

Kantorowicz, Ernst H., 198n3

Kastan, David Scott, 225n40
Katherine, Princess, daughter of King Charles VI (marries Henry V), 258n70
Keegan, John, 260n79, 261n8
Keen, M. H., 210n43, 219n10, 221n17, 221n20, 222n24, 223n29, 227n48, 252n40
Kernan, Alvin, 204n17
Krito, 239n25

Lambarde, William, 205n20
Leggatt, Alexander, 201n13, 206n26, 208n34, 216n72, 226n43, 235n18, 241–42n33, 249n25, 253n48
Lewis, Wyndham, 208n32
Lincoln, Abraham, 177
Lionel, Duke of Clarence, third son of Edward III, 136, 205n21, 246n16
Livio, Tito (Titus Livius), 219n5, 224n36
Louis, Dauphin ('Lewis Dolphin'), French Crown Prince, 245n12, 247n22
Lucy, Sir Walter, 249n23
Lydgate, John, 218n4, 254n55
Lykurgus, 194

Machiavelli, Niccolo ('machiavellian'), xvi, 28, 29, 30, 58, 94, 113, 140, 143, 154, 156, 157, 161, 164, 165, 166, 173, 181, 203n16, 208n32, 210n43, 212–13n56, 215n66, 235nn17–18, 245–46nn13–14, 245–46n14, 247n21, 251n34, 251–52n38, 253–54n49, 257n64, 261n4
Malatesta, Pandolfo, 235n12
Marriot, J. A. R., 195n2, 198n3, 226n42, 235n18, 236n20
Mary Queen of Scots, 204n20
Masle, count of, 176
Maus, Katharine Eisaman, 206n23
McFarlane, K. B., 218–19n4, 219nn8–9, 224n35, 224n36, 254n55, 260n80, 261n3
Melville, Herman, 235n14
Meron, Theodor, 260–61n81

More, Sir Thomas, 196n4, 225n39
Morris, John E., 262–63n10
Mortimer, Anne. (sister of Edmund fifth Earl of March) 146
Mortimer, Edmund (uncle of fifth Earl of March), 227n47
Mortimer, Edmund, fifth Earl of March, 136, 146, 147, 159, 205n21, 227n47, 246n15, 246–47n18, 247–49n23
Mortimer, Ian, 248–49n23, 257n65, 258n73, 260n78, 261n86, 262n8
Mortimer, Roger, fourth Earl of March, 48, 146, 205n21
Mowbray, Thomas, Jr., Earl Marshall, 50
Mowbray, Thomas, Sr., Duke of Norfolk, 48, 197n2, 198–99n5, 199n8, 200n10, 201n13

Neale, J. E., 204n20, 238n22
Neville, Richard, Earl of Warwick, 106, 234n11
Nietzsche, Friedrich, 217n75
Norwich, John Julius, 198n3
Nuttall, A. D., 236n19

Oldcastle, Sir John, 49, 51
Orco, Remirro de, 94, 235n17
Orleans, Duke of, 52
Ormonde, fourth Earl of, 224n36

Parrish, John M., 256n60
Pater, Walter, 206n25
Paul, St., 123
Percy, Henry, Jr. ('Hotspur'), 49, 50, 225n38, 227n48, 227–28n50
Percy, Henry, Sr., Earl of Northumberland, 49, 50, 51
Percy, Henry, III (Hotspur's son), 247n23
Percy, Thomas, Earl of Worcester, 49, 165, 227n48, 227–28n50
Pharamond, King of France, 135, 244n9
Philip of Macedon, 49, 220n12
Philip IV, King of France, 160, 244n8
Philippa (daughter and heir of Lionel, Duke of Clarence), 136, 146, 205n21, 246n16

Philippa (elder daughter of Henry IV), 47
Pierce, Robert B., 198n3, 204n19, 206n26, 208–9n34
Plato (including references to *Republic*), 28, 44, 45, 211nn49–50, 212nn52–53, 216n73, 217–18n77, 226n44, 239–40n25, 241n32, 243n4, 254n51, 256n61
Pompey ('the Great'/'Major'), 183
Porus, 255n56
Powys, Lord, 49

Rabelais, Francois, 238n23
Rabkin, Norman, 206–7n26, 211n48
Richard I (Lion-heart), King of England, 201n13
Richard I, Count of Normandy, 182
Richard II, Count of Normandy, 182
Richard II, King of England, 1, 17, 37, 48, 49, 50, 146, 147, 182, 186, 192, 197nn1–2, 198n3, 199n5, 199n7, 200n10, 201–2nn13–15, 204n17, 204n20, 205n21, 206n24, 206n26, 207n28, 209n38, 218n3, 219nn8–9, 221n17, 224n35, 234n12, 246n15
Richard III, King of England, 38, 197n2, 215n67, 225n39
Richmond, H. M., 199n7, 257n63
Roberts, Josephine A., 197n3

Saccio, Peter, 198n3, 223n33
Saint Paule, Earl of, 200n10
Salisbury, John Montague, Earl of, 207n30
Sandler, Robert, 229n54, 237n20
Schlegel, August Wilhelm, 195n2, 218n1
Scipio Africanus the Elder, 166
Scroop, Lord Thomas of Masham, 246–47nn17–18
Scroop, Richard, Archbishop of York, 50, 51, 221n18, 247n23
Scroop, William, Earl of Wiltshire, 50, 247n23
Seneca, 218n4

Seward, Desmond, 219n6, 220n13, 221n17, 221n19, 224n35, 234–35n12, 246n15, 247n23, 260n81
Smart, Roger, 209n38
Sokrates, 28, 44, 217n75, 217n77, 239–40n25
Solomon, 213n58
Spiekerman, Tim, 198n3, 213n58, 229n54, 252n43, 252–53n46, 253–54n49
Stafford, Anne, 246n17
Steel, Anthony, 197n1, 209n39
St. Palaye, 260–61n82
Stow, John, 224n36
Sullivan, Vickie, 257n64
Swynford, Katherine, 52, 222n35

Talbot, Lord Gilbert, 50, 51
Tamburlaine, 249n25
Thomas, Duke of Clarence (second son of Henry IV), 47, 48, 52, 223n30, 224n35, 226–27n45, 234n10
Thomas of Woodstock, Duke of Gloucester, 48, 198n5, 202n14, 205n20, 218n3
Thrasymachus, 216n73
Thucydides, 196n4, 217n77, 249n28
Tillyard, E. M., 198n3, 256n59
Traversi, Derek, 198n3, 236n19, 236–37n19, 250–51n33, 253n47, 258–59n74
Trevelyan, G. M., 1

Ure, Peter, 210n40

Verdi, Giuseppe, 233n3

Waith, Eugene M., 229n54
Walsingham, Thomas, 224n36
Waurin, Jehan, 179, 258n73
William (the Conqueror, the Bastard), 40, 182, 194
Wilson, J. Dover, 229n54, 240–41n30
Westmorland, Countess of (aunt of Henry V), 254n55
Westmorland, Ralph Neville, Earl of, 50

York, Edward, Duke of (Duke of Aumerle), 210n39, 246n16, 257n66
York, Edmund of Langley, Duke of, 51, 246n16
York, Joan Holland, Duchess of, 210n39
York, Richard, Duke of, 146, 147, 246n16, 247n18

www.ingramcontent.com/pod-product-compliance
Lightning Source LLC
Chambersburg PA
CBHW031708230426
43668CB00006B/146